THE LAW AND ECONOMICS OF CYBERSECURITY

Cybersecurity is a leading national problem for which the market may fail to produce a solution. The ultimate source of the problem is that computer owners lack adequate incentives to invest in security because they bear fully the costs of their security precautions but share the benefits with their network partners. In a world of positive transaction costs, individuals often select less than optimal security levels. The problem is compounded because the insecure networks extend far beyond the regulatory jurisdiction of any one nation or even coalition of nations. This book brings together the views of leading law and economics scholars on the nature of the cybersecurity problem and possible solutions to it. Many of these solutions are market based, but they need some help, either from government or industry groups, or both. Indeed, the cybersecurity problem prefigures a host of 21st-century problems created by information technology and the globalization of markets.

Mark F. Grady is Professor of Law and Director of the Center for Law and Economics at the University of California at Los Angeles School of Law. He specializes in law and economics, torts, antitrust, and intellectual property. He received his A.B. degree summa cum laude in economics and his J.D. from UCLA. Before beginning his academic career, Grady worked for the Federal Trade Commission, the U.S. Senate Judiciary Committee, and American Management Systems.

Francesco Parisi is Professor of Law and Director of the Law and Economics Program at George Mason University School of Law and Distinguished Professor of Law at the University of Milan.

THE LAW AND ECONOMICS OF CYBERSECURITY

Edited by

Mark F. Grady
UCLA School of Law

Francesco Parisi
George Mason University School of Law

CAMBRIDGE
UNIVERSITY PRESS

CAMBRIDGE UNIVERSITY PRESS
Cambridge, New York, Melbourne, Madrid, Cape Town,
Singapore, São Paulo, Delhi, Tokyo, Mexico City

Cambridge University Press
The Edinburgh Building, Cambridge CB2 8RU, UK

Published in the United States of America by Cambridge University Press, New York

www.cambridge.org
Information on this title: www.cambridge.org/9780521855273

First published 2006

A catalogue record for this publication is available from the British Library

Library of Congress Cataloguing in Publication Data

The law and economics of cybersecurity / edited by Mark F. Grady, Francesco Parisi.
p.   cm.
Includes bibliographical references and index.
ISBN-13: 978-0-521-85527-3 (hardback)
ISBN-10: 0-521-85527-6 (hardback)
1. Computer security – Law and legislation.   2. Computer security – Law and legislation – Economic
aspects.   I. Grady, Mark F.   II. Parisi, Francesco, 1962–   III. Title.
K564.C6L376   2005
345′.0268 – dc22   2005012433

ISBN 978-0-521-85527-3 Hardback

CONTENTS

ACKNOWLEDGMENTS

The editors of this volume owe a debt of gratitude to many friends and colleagues who have contributed to this project at different stages of its development. Most notably, we would like to thank Emily Frey, Amitai Aviram, and Fred Wintrich for encouraging and helping coordinate the planning of this project. The Critical Infrastructure Protection Project and the George Mason University Tech Center provided generous funding for the Conference on the Law and Economics of Cyber Security, which was held at George Mason University on June 11, 2004. At this conference, several of the papers contained in this volume were originally presented. David Lord scrupulously assisted the editors in the preparation of the manuscript for publication and in the drafting of the introduction. Without his help, this project would not have been possible. Finally we would like to thank University of Chicago Press for granting the permission to publish the paper by Doug Lichtman and Eric Posner, which will appear in Volume 14 of the *Supreme Court Economic Review* (2006).

CONTRIBUTORS

Amitai Aviram Assistant Professor of Law, Florida Sate University College of Law

Yochai Benkler Professor of Law, Yale Law School

Mark Grady Professor of Law, University of California at Los Angeles, School of Law

Neal K. Katyal John Carroll Research Professor, Georgetown University Law Center

Bruce K. Kobayashi Professor of Law and Associate Dean for Academic Affairs, George Mason University School of Law

Doug Lichtman Professor of Law, University of Chicago Law School

Francesco Parisi Professor of Law and Director, Law and Economics Program, George Mason University School of Law

Randal C. Picker Paul and Theo Leffmann Professor of Commercial Law, University of Chicago Law School; Senior Fellow, The Computational Institute of the University of Chicago and Argonne National Laboratory

Eric P. Posner Kirkland and Ellis Professor of Law, University of Chicago Law School

Peter P. Swire Professor of Law and John Glenn Research Scholar in Public Policy Research, Ohio State University, Moritz College of Law

Joel P. Trachtman Professor of International Law, Fletcher School of Law and Diplomacy, Tufts University

THE LAW AND ECONOMICS OF CYBERSECURITY:
AN INTRODUCTION

Mark Grady and Francesco Parisi

Cybercrime imposes a large cost on our economy and is highly resistant to the usual methods of prevention and deterrence. Businesses spent about $8.75 billion to exterminate the infamous Love Bug. Perhaps far more important are the hidden costs of self-protection and losses from service interruption.

Unlike traditional crime, which terrorizes all but has far fewer direct victims, cybercrime impacts the lives of virtually all citizens and almost every company. The Computer Security Institute and the FBI recently released the results of a study of 538 companies, government agencies, and financial institutions. Eighty-five percent of the respondents reported having security breaches, and 64% experienced financial loss as a result (Hatcher 2001). Because this problem is growing on a daily basis, it is imperative that society identify the most economically efficient way of fighting cybercrime. In this volume, the authors present a cross section of views that attempt to identify the true problems of cybersecurity and present solutions that will help resolve these challenges. In the first section, two authors outline some of the major problems of cybersecurity and explain how the provision of cybersecurity differs from traditional security models.

Bruce Kobayashi examines the optimal level of cybersecurity as compared with traditional security. For example, while it might be more efficient to deter robbery in general, individuals may find it easier to simply put a lock on their door, thus diverting the criminal to a neighbor's house. Although in the general criminal context, the government can act to discourage *ex ante* by implementing a sufficient level of punishment to deter the crime from occurring in the first place, this is not so easily achieved in the world of cybercrime. Because the likelihood of detecting cybercrime is so low, the penalty inflicted would have to be of enormous magnitude to deter it.

In this context, companies can either produce private security goods that will protect their sites by diverting the hacker to someone else or they can produce

1

a public security good that will deter cybercrime in general. The former route will lead to an overproduction of private security, which is economically inefficient because each company takes individual measures that only protect itself as opposed to acting collectively to stop the cyberattacks in the first place. If collective action is used to produce public security, however, an underproduction will occur because companies will have an incentive to free-ride on the general security produced by others.

Kobayashi suggests using a concept of property rights whereby the security collective can exclude free-riders to eliminate this problem. Since security expenditures are not sufficiently novel or nonobvious to merit protection under patent or copyright law, Kobayashi suggests collective security action supported by contractual restrictions on members.

Peter Swire follows on Kobayahi's basic idea of collective action by introducing the notion of cooperation through disclosure. Swire attempts to answer the question of when disclosure may actually improve security. In probing this question, Swire develops a model for examining the choice between the open source paradigm, which favors disclosure, and the military paradigm, which advocates secrecy. The open source paradigm is based on three presumptions: attackers will learn little or nothing from disclosure, disclosure will prompt designers to improve the design of defenses, and disclosure will prompt other defenders to take action. The military paradigm is based on contrary presumptions: attackers will learn much from the disclosure of vulnerabilities, disclosure will not teach the designers anything significant about improving defenses, and disclosure will not prompt improvements in defense by others. Starting with these two paradigms, Swire offers two further concepts that take a middle ground. The first, the Information Sharing Paradigm, reasons that although attackers will learn a lot from disclosure, the disclosure will prompt more defensive actions by others and will teach designers how to design better systems. For example, the FBI's disclosure of a terrorist "watch list" may enable people to be more attuned to who is a terrorist, but it does so at the cost of alerting terrorists to the fact that they are being scrutinized. Opposed to the information sharing paradigm is the theory of public domain, which holds that although attackers will learn little to nothing from disclosure, disclosure will also not teach designers much and will not prompt many additional security steps by others.

Swire reasons that different scenarios warrant adherence to different security paradigms. Factors such as the number of attacks, the extent to which an attacker learns from previous attacks, and the extent of communication between attackers about their knowledge will influence which model should be followed. In general, secrecy is always more likely to be effective against the first attack. While this might favor the military paradigm in the realm of physical security because of a low number of attacks and relative lack of communication between attackers, the same assumptions do not necessarily hold true in the realm of cybersecurity. Because cyberattacks can be launched repetitively and at minor expense, secrets will soon be learned and companies will expend inordinate amounts of money vainly attempting to retain their secrecy. Further, as is true in traditional physical security, disclosure can often improve security by diverting an attack, presuming that the level of security is perceived as high.

Swire also argues that there are two specific areas in which the presumptions of the open source paradigm do not hold true. First, private keys, combinations, and passwords should never be disclosed because disclosing them does little to promote security or enhance security design, yet it obviously provides valuable information to attackers. Additionally, Swire argues that surveillance techniques should not be disclosed because an attacker is unlikely to discover them during an attack, and thus in the short run not disclosing them will provide the defender with an additional source of security.

In the second section of Part I, Yochai Benkler argues that cybersecurity is best addressed by making system survivability the primary objective of security measures rather than attempting to create impregnable cyberfortresses. By mobilizing excess capacity that users have on their personal devices, a network-wide, self-healing device could be created. The already existing system of music sharing offers a model for achieving this type of security.

While the sharing of music files is admittedly controversial, the systems that have been put in place to make music sharing a reality offer lessons for how broader cybersecurity can be achieved. Professor Benkler's proposal is based on three characteristics: redundant capacity, geographic and topological diversity, and the capacity for self-organization and self-healing based on a fully distributed system that in nowise depends on a single point that can become the focus of failure. The music-sharing industry has been hit by attacks a number of times, and Napster even had its main center of data search and location shut down. Nonetheless, the data survived because of the above characteristics. File-sharing systems have allowed data and capacity to be transferred to where they are most needed, permitting these systems to survive even after repeated attacks. In many file-sharing systems, because the physical components are owned by end users, there is no network to shut down when it is attacked by cyberterrorism.

This same degree of survivability can also be seen in distributed computing, where it easier for a task to be shared by several computers than to build a single, very fast computer. Benkler concludes his article by looking at different economic models that suggest when and how the lessons of file sharing can be implemented practically in order to achieve long-term survivability.

The article by Randy Picker examines whether and how security can best be achieved in an industry dominated by one company. Many people have come to believe that market dominance by Microsoft compromises cybersecurity by creating a monoculture, a scenario in which common computer codes help spread viruses easily, software facilities are too integrated and thus lead to security lapses, and software is shipped too soon and thus is not adequately developed to address security needs. In this article, Picker attempts to address these criticisms, believing that they are misdirected and will lead to inefficient results.

Those who believe that the monoculture of Microsoft threatens security often liken the situation to the boll weevil epidemic in the early 1900s. Because farmers in the South cultivated only cotton, when an insect arrived that attacked this crop, their fields and means of livelihood were both devastated. Opponents of monoculture believe that diversification helps insure against loss, whether in agriculture or the world of cybersecurity. Picker points out, however, that one of the primary problems with this logic is that it attempts to deal with the problem from the perspective of supply rather than crafting demand-based solutions. Sure, a farmer can protect against total devastation by diversifying and adding corn as a crop, for example, but if there is no demand for corn, the diversification is futile because consumers will not avail themselves of the corn.

Picker's second criticism of the monoculture theorists is that they argue heterogeneity is the best way to address the massive collapse that can result when a virus invades an interconnected world. However, ensuring that different sectors use different operating systems and computers will not mean that all are protected. When an attack hits, it will still shut down one sector. The only way to provide universal protection would be to have all work done on multiple systems, an inefficient solution to the problem. Picker advocates a security model that is very different from the increased interconnection supported by Benkler. Picker instead advocates autarky, or purposefully severing some of the connections that cause the massive shutdown in the first place. Picker argues that we need to accept the fact that interconnection is not always good. Which is economically more efficient, to have ten connected computers run ten different operating systems or to have ten isolated computers each running Windows?

Picker concludes his article by suggesting that security concerns can be remedied through the use of liability rules. Imposing liability through tort law would, however, create headaches because it would be hard to sort out questions of fault and intervening cause among the developer, the cyberterrorist who unleashed the virus, and the end user who clicked when he should not have done so. Likewise, requiring the purchase of mandatory insurance would be economically counterproductive. Rather, in Picker's view, partial insurance that focuses on the first wave of consumers who face greater risks (from the less developed product) is the economically most viable solution.

Part II of this volume offers regulatory solutions that address the major problems of cybersecurity. The authors highlight the debate between public and private security by presenting highly divergent positions. Amitai Aviram discusses private ordering achieved through private legal systems (PLSs), institutions that aim to enforce norms when the law fails (i.e., neglects or chooses not to regulate behavior). Aviram's article gives a broad perspective on how PLSs are formed and then suggests practical applications for the field of cybersecurity. Aviram reasons that PLSs cannot spontaneously form because new PLSs often cannot enforce cooperation. This gap occurs because the effectiveness of the enforcement mechanism depends on the provision of benefits by the PLS to its members, a factor that is nonexistent in new PLSs. Thus, new PLSs tend to use existing institutions and regulate norms that are not costly to enforce, ensuring gradual evolution rather than spontaneous formation. PLSs have widely existed throughout history. Literature about PLSs, however, has largely focused on how these organizations develop norms rather than how these organizations come into existence in the first place.

In examining this question, Aviram starts with a basic paradox of PLS formation: in order to secure benefits to its members, a PLS must be able to achieve cooperation, but to achieve cooperation, a PLS must be able to give benefits to its members. This creates a chicken-and-egg situation. While this problem could be resolved through bonding members in a new PLS, bonding is often too expensive. Accordingly, PLSs tend to simply develop and evolve from existing institutions rather than develope spontaneously and independently.

To determine when, how, and by whom a norm can be regulated, it is necessary to understand the cost of enforcing the norm. To understand this, it is necessary to fully comprehend the utility of the norm to the network's members, understand the market structure of the members, and understand what game type and payoffs have been set up by the norm for the network's members. Aviram introduces a variety of gametypes based on the expected payoffs to members. Some of the gametypes have higher enforcement costs, others have lower costs. It is the gametypes that have low enforcement costs that become the building blocks of PLSs, while those with high enforcement costs evolve gradually.

Aviram applies this concept to cybersecurity by looking at networks that aim to facilitate communication and information sharing among private firms.

Unfortunately, these networks have been plagued by the traditional problems of the prisoner's dilemma: members fear cooperation and the divulging of information because of worries about increased liability due to disclosure, the risk of antitrust violations, and the loss of proprietary information. Aviram thinks that part of the reason for the failure of these networks is that they are attempting to regulate norms with high enforcement costs without the background needed to achieve this. Aviram suggests restricting the membership of these networks so that they are not as broadly based as they presently are. This would allow norms to be developed among actors with preexisting business connections that would facilitate enforcement (as opposed to the broad networks that currently exist and cannot enforce disclosure).

The article by Neal Katyal takes a completely divergent position, reasoning that private ordering is insufficient and in many ways undesirable. Katyal argues that we must begin to think of crime not as merely harming an individual and harming the community. If crime is viewed in this light, solutions that favor private ordering seem less beneficial, and public enforcement appears to have more advantages. Katyal maintains that the primary harm to the community from cyberattacks does not necessarily result from the impact on individuals. Indeed, hackers often act only out of curiosity, and some of their attacks do not directly affect the businesses' assets or profits. Rather, these attacks undermine the formation and development of networks. Katyal contends that society can therefore punish computer crimes "even when there is no harm to an individual victim because of the harm in trust to the network. Vigorous enforcement of computer crime prohibitions can help ensure that the network's potential is realized."

Public enforcement is also defended because without governmental action to deter cybercrime only wealthy companies will be able to afford to take the necessary measures to protect themselves. Katyal compares the use of private ordering as the solution for cybercrime to the government's telling individuals that it will no longer prosecute car theft. Indeed, if the government adopted this policy, car theft might decrease because fewer people would drive and those that did drive would take the precautions necessary to protect themselves from theft. While this might seem logical (and has even been used to a large extent in the cyberworld), it fails to take into account exogenous costs. For example, less driving may equal less utility, while the use of private security measures raises distributional concerns (e.g., can only the wealthy afford the security measures necessary to drive?).

Finally, Katyal suggests that to some extent private security measures may increase crime. Imagine a community in which the residents put gates around their homes and bars over their windows. Such measures may deter crime for each individual, but "it suggests that norms of reciprocity have broken down and that one cannot trust one's neighbor." One result might be that law-abiding citizens would leave the neighborhood, resulting in a higher crime rate. One of the primary reasons for public law enforcement is to put measures into place that are needed to protect the citizens while averting sloppy and ineffective private measures.

Katyal concludes by arguing that not all cybercrimes can be punished and not all should be punished the same way. If the police were to go after every person who committed a cybercrime, it would lead to public panic and further erode the community of trust. Additionally, some crimes, like unleashing a worm in a network, are more serious than a minor cybertrespass.

The article by Lichtman and Posner attempts to move beyond the debate of public versus private enforcement by creating a solution that relies on private measures enforced and promoted by publicly imposed liability. The authors acknowledge that vast security measures have been taken both publicly and privately to address the problem of cybersecurity. However, these measures have not sufficiently addressed the harm caused by cybercrime because the perpetrators are often hard to identify, and even when they are identified, they often lack the resources to compensate their victims. Accordingly, the authors advocate adopting a system that imposes liability on Internet service providers (ISPs) for harm caused by their subscribers. The authors argue that this liability regime is similar to much of tort law, which holds third parties accountable when they can control the actions of judgment-proof tortfeasors. While this idea may run parallel to the common law, the authors acknowledge that it appears to run counter to modern legislation, which aims to shield ISPs from liability. However, even in these laws, the roots of vicarious liability can be seen in the fact that immunity is often tied to an ISP's taking voluntary steps to control the actions of its subscribers.

One of the objections that the authors see to their proposal is related to the problem of private enforcement that Katyal discusses in the previous article. Shielding ISPs from liability, like failing to publicly enforce cybersecurity, will give end users an incentive to develop and implement their own security devices. Lichtman and Posner counter that this argument does not suggest that ISPs should not face liability but that their liability should be tailored to encourage them "to adopt the precautions that they can provide most efficiently, while leaving any remaining precautions to other market actors." Indeed, just as auto drivers are not given immunity from suit based on the argument that pedestrians could avoid accidents by staying at home, the same should hold true in the cyberworld.

The second criticism to this proposal is that it might cause ISPs to overreact by unnecessarily excluding too many innocent but risky subscribers in the name of security. Increased security may indeed drive up costs and drive away marginal users, but likewise users may be driven away by insecurity in the cyberarena. Posner and Lichtman also believe that the danger of increased cost to ISPs can be alleviated by offering tax breaks to ISPs based on their subscriber base, prohibiting state taxation of Internet transactions, or subsidizing the delivery of Internet access to underserved populations. The problem of viruses traveling across several ISPs can be resolved through joint and several liability, while the fear that no one individual will be harmed enough by cybercrime to bring suit can be resolved through class action lawsuits or suits initiated by a state's attorney general.

The main concern regarding the use of ISP liability is that it would be ineffective because of the global reach of the Internet, for a cybercriminal could simply reroute his or her attack through a country with less stringent security laws. Posner and Lichtman address this concern by arguing that global regimes can be adopted to exclude Internet packets from countries with weak laws. As countries like the United States adopted ISP liability, it would spread to other nations.

Trachtman picks up on this final concern, which is common to many Internet security problems and proposals: the global reach of the Internet and accompanying issues of jurisdiction and international organization. This concern has become even more acute with the development of organized cyberterrorism, as evidenced by the cyberterrorism training camps run by Al Qaeda when the Taliban controlled Afghanistan. Throughout his article, Trachtman examines the same question seen in the articles by Aviram, Katyal, and Posner and Lichtman: to what extent is government regulation necessary to achieve cybersecurity? Trachtman acknowledges that private action suffers to some extent from the inability to exclude free-riders and other collective action problems. Trachtman suggests that private action may be sufficient to resolve some forms of cybercrime, but it clearly will not work to eliminate all cyberterrorism. There are areas that warrant international cooperation, including (1) the limitation of terrorist access to networks, (2) *ex ante* surveillance of networks in order to interdict or repair injury, (3) *ex post* identification and punishment of attackers, and (4) the establishment of more robust networks that can survive attack.

Once it has been decided whether private or public action should be favored, there remains the issue of whether local action is sufficient. Cybercrime proposes unique jurisdictional questions because actions in one country may have effects in another. If the host country will not enforce laws against the cybercriminals, how can the victim country stop the attack? Ambiguous jurisdiction is one of the main problems faced by modern international law in this area. The solution would seem to require international cooperation. Trachtman suggests creating an umbrella organization that has jurisdiction over these matters and can act transnationally. Trachtman concludes by offering a variety of game theory presentations that exhibit when and how international cooperation can best occur in the realm of cybersecurity.

The authors of the articles in this volume have attempted to provide a resource for better understanding the dilemmas and debates regarding the provision of cybersecurity. Whether cybersecurity is provided through private legal systems or public enforcement or a combination of the two, the development and implementation of new and more efficient tools for fighting cybercrime is high on the list of social priorities.

REFERENCE

Hatcher, Thurston. 2001. Survey: Costs of Computer Security Breaches Soar. *CNN.com.* http://www.cnn.com/2001/TECH/internet/03/12/csi.fbi.hacking.report/.

PART ONE

PROBLEMS

Cybersecurity and Its Problems

ONE

PRIVATE VERSUS SOCIAL INCENTIVES IN CYBERSECURITY: LAW AND ECONOMICS

Bruce H. Kobayashi*

I. INTRODUCTION

Individuals and firms make significant investments in private security. These expenditures cover everything from simple door locks on private homes to elaborate security systems and private security guards. They are in addition to and often complement public law enforcement expenditures. They also differ from public law enforcement expenditures in that they are aimed at the direct prevention or reduction of loss and not necessarily at deterring crime through *ex post* sanctions.[1]

A growing and important subset of private security expenditures are those related to cybersecurity (see Introduction and Chapter 5). Private security expenditures are important given the decentralized nature of the Internet and the difficulties in applying traditional law enforcement techniques to crime and other wealth-transferring activities that take place in cyberspace. These include difficulties in identifying those responsible for cybercrimes, difficulties arising from the large volume and inchoate nature of many of the crimes,[2] and difficulties associated with punishing judgment-proof individuals who are eventually identified as responsible for cyberattacks. As a consequence, those responsible

---

[1] This analysis does not consider the use of public sanctions and enforcement resources. The level of public enforcement will generally affect the level of private expenditures. For example, public enforcement and sanctions may serve to "crowd out" private expenditures. For analyses of private law enforcement systems, see Becker and Stigler (1974); Landes and Posner (1975); Friedman (1979 and 1984). See also Chapter 7, which discusses the use of vicarious liability as a way to increase security and law enforcement.

[2] For an analysis of punishment for attempts, see Shavell (1990) and Friedman (1991).

*Associate Dean for Academic Affairs and Professor of Law, George Mason University, School of Law. This paper presents, in nonmathematical form, the results presented in Kobayashi (forthcoming). The author would like to thank the Critical Infrastructure Protection Project at George Mason University Law School for funding.

for cyberattacks may perceive both that the probability of punishment is low and that the size of the sanction (when punishment occurs) is small; the final result will be a low expectation of penalty and inadequate deterrence (Becker 1968).

Although individuals and businesses have made significant private investments in cybersecurity, there is a concern that leaving the problem of cybersecurity to the private sector may result in an inadequate level of protection for individuals, firms, and critical networks.[3] Further, private efforts to identify and pursue those responsible for cyberattacks often will redound to the benefit of others, leading to free-riding and inadequate incentives to invest in cybersecurity.[4] This concern has led to calls for government intervention to remedy the perceived underinvestment in cybersecurity.[5]

The purpose of this paper is to examine the basic economics of private cybersecurity expenditures, to examine the potential sources of underinvestment, and to evaluate potential market interventions by the government. This paper begins by reviewing the existing literature on private security expenditures. This literature has concentrated on the provision of private goods such as locks and safes. Such goods are characterized as private goods because, for example, a physical lock or safe protecting a particular asset cannot generally be used by others to protect their assets. In contrast to the perceived underinvestment in cybersecurity, the existing literature does not predict an underinvestment in private security goods. Indeed, the models described in the literature show that, among other things, private security goods may serve to divert crime from protected to unprotected assets and that as a result equilibrium expenditures may exceed socially optimal levels. Further, attempts by firms to reduce wealth

---

[3] For a discussion of these issues, see Frye (2002). Katyal (Chapter 6) notes the existence of network and community harms caused by crimes that are not internalized by the direct victim of the crime. But see Chapter 5, which notes the benefits of network effects as a mechanism to enforce private norms.

[4] In some cases, firms able to internalize network benefits associated with their products may also be able to internalize the benefits of security expenditures. For example, Microsoft Corporation, in a November 5, 2003, press release, announced the initial $5 million funding of the Anti-Virus Reward Program, which pays bounties for information that leads to the arrest and conviction of those responsible for launching malicious viruses and worms on the Internet. For a discussion of bounties generally, see Becker and Stigler (1974). Microsoft, owing to its large market share, can internalize more of the benefits of private enforcement expenditures. However, its large market share and its de facto status as a standard setter serve to lower the costs of conducting a widespread cyberattack and have resulted in a many attacks directed at computers using Microsoft products. For an analysis of the trade-offs involved with de facto standards in the cybersecurity context, see Chapter 4, which describes the use of decentralized, distributed, and redundant infrastructures as a way to increase system survivability.

[5] Krim (2003) reports that Bush administration officials warn that regulation looms if private companies do not increase private efforts at providing cybersecurity. See also Chapter 6.

transfers that do not represent social costs may also cause private security expenditures to exceed socially optimal levels.

The paper next explores differences between the expenditures on private security goods and expenditures on cybersecurity. It focuses on two primary differences between cybersecurity and the type of security discussed in the existing literature: the public good nature of cybersecurity expenditures and the fact that the social harm caused by a cybercrime greatly exceeds any transfer to the criminal. The paper shows how each of these differences affects the incentives of individuals to invest in cybersecurity. Indeed, both differences serve to reduce any overincentive to invest in private security goods relative to the standard private goods case and suggest an underlying reason why cybersecurity expenditures may be too low. The paper concludes by examining several proposals for government intervention the private market for cybersecurity and how such proposals will address these underlying factors.

II. PRIVATE SECURITY EXPENDITURES

The existing literature on the private provision of security expenditures has focused on cases in which individuals or firms spend resources on private security goods (Shavell 1991).[6] According to the basic model, private individuals invest in goods private security such as locks or safes in order to prevent socially costless transfers. Security goods such as locks and safes are private goods because they cannot be used in a nonrivalrous manner. That is, a lock or safe protecting a particular asset cannot generally be used by others to protect their assets.

In the basic model, criminals expend resources in an attempt to transfer wealth by attacking the sites of potential victims. These potential victims invest in private security to reduce the impact of crime and other wealth-transferring activity. An increase in the level of private security expenditures, *ceteris paribus*, has several primary effects. Additional security expenditures decrease the magnitude of the expected transfer given an intrusion. As a result of this reduction in the expected net gain to the criminal, the equilibrium rate of intrusions will decrease, and the probability of an attack on the assets protected by the security goods will fall.

Under the assumption that the activity addressed by private security expenditures consists of costless wealth transfers, the social objective is to minimize the total resources used by criminals attempting to achieve these transfers and

---

[6] For an explicit mathematical treatment of this issue, see Kobayashi (forthcoming).

by potential victims attempting to prevent them. The existing literature has identified several reasons that private and social incentives to invest in private security diverge. The first is the existence of uninternalized spillovers or externalities (Shavell 1991; Clotfelter 1978). There are both positive and negative spillovers from private expenditures on security. Positive spillovers include the provision of a general deterrence effect: the expenditures by one individual decrease the net expected gain from wealth-transferring activity, which in turn reduces the general level of criminal activity and thus creates a positive spillover effect for all potential victims. That is, individual expenditures that increase the perceived level of expenditures will protect all sites, including those belonging to individuals who choose to provide no security. This effect will be strongest when criminals know the overall level of private security expenditures but cannot observe individual expenditures until after they have made an effort to engage in a wealth transfer. More generally, even observable private security goods, through their tendency to reduce the overall level of criminal activity, can generate a positive spillover effect that protects all sites. If such spillover effects are not internalized, and other effects are absent, there will be an underincentive for individuals to invest in security.

However, private security goods that are observable to a criminal at the time of a criminal act can simultaneously generate negative spillovers. Specifically, such observable goods can create a diversion effect; that is, they shift the costs of criminal activity to other less protected targets but do not serve as an overall deterrent to criminal and other wealth-transferring activity (Hui-Wen and Png 1994). Thus, the marginal reduction in the probability of an attack faced by a site protected as a result of a marginal increase in security expenditures is not a gross social gain, as it will be partially offset by an increase in the probability, *ceteris paribus*, that other sites will be attacked. One consequence of this diversion effect is that there can be an equilibrium over incentive to invest in observable private security goods.

Moreover, even if the between-site (victim) spillovers mentioned in the preceding paragraph are internalized, private security expenditures can be socially excessive. As noted, when private security expenditures address socially costless transfers, the social objective is to minimize the total resources spent on attempting to achieve such transfers and on preventing such transfers. However, the objective of victims is to minimize the total amount of wealth transferred from them and to minimize the expenditures aimed at preventing such transfers. And the objective of the criminal is to maximize the amount of transfers net of the resources used to achieve the transfers. Because expenditures aimed at reducing the size of the transfers are not socially beneficial, the fact that both the potential criminal and the potential victim take into account the size of the

Table 1.1. *A comparison of observable equilibrium security expenditure levels: private goods case with costless transfers*

	Socially optimal level (x^{**})	Individual level (x^*)	Cooperative level (x_0)
Socially optimal level (x^{**})		$x_0 > (<) x^{**}$ Ranking between individual and social levels ambiguous	$x^* > x^{**}$ Cooperatives overinvest
Individual level (x^*)			$x_0 > (<) x^*$ Ranking between individual and cooperative levels ambiguous
Cooperative level (x_0)			

transfers in making their individual resource allocations creates a divergence between the social and private incentives to invest in security.

One situation in which the between-site spillovers are internalized is where potential victims agree to collectively set the level of security expenditures. In this situation, the between-site spillovers will be internalized through the agreement setting the collective security level. Thus, to the extent that the individuals' incentives to divert crime to other sites would result in excessively high security expenditures, the collective agreement functions to suppress the individuals' incentives to engage in this type of socially inefficient "arms race." However, the cooperative will take into account the effect that security expenditures will have on the size of the transfers. In contrast, the social calculus ignores this effect on the size of the transfer. As a result, the cooperative will have a greater marginal incentive to invest in security than is socially optimal, and will set a level of expenditures that is above the socially optimal level.

Table 1.1 summarizes the primary results in the case where the criminal activity results in a socially costless transfer, the security goods are observable, and the only social costs are the resources spent by criminals attempting to achieve such transfers and by potential victims attempting to prevent them. In this case, the marginal social benefit from an incremental increase in security expenditures equals the marginal reduction in the resources used by criminals, which equals the decrease in the frequency of an attack times the incremental cost of an attack (Kobayashi forthcoming). If potential victims set security levels cooperatively, the marginal private benefit will contain this same deterrence effect. A cooperative will also take into account the marginal reduction in the expected magnitude of the transfer, which is a private but not a social benefit. This additional private benefit will cause the cooperative to overinvest in security.

Individuals setting the levels of security noncooperatively may either under- or overinvest in security. The individual's marginal benefit calculation will also take into account, as a private but not a social benefit, the same marginal reduction in the expected magnitude of the transfer taken into account by the cooperative. The individual also takes into account how an incremental expenditure will alter the frequency with which he or she will be attacked. However, this effect is distinct from the reduction in the overall frequency of attacks that yields the marginal social benefit and is part of the cooperative's calculus. Rather, the individual will take into account the reduction in the frequency of attack that results from criminals being diverted from his or her site to others' sites, whether or not any significant overall reduction in the frequency of attacks results. This individual incentive may be larger or smaller than the social deterrent effect. If it is larger, then individuals will set an equilibrium level of security expenditures that will exceed the cooperatively set level and thus the social level. If it is smaller, then individuals will have smaller incentives than cooperatives and may either under- or overspend the social level.

To illustrate the incentives facing agents considering investments in security and to provide a baseline for the discussion in the next section, Figure 1.1 shows the results of a simulation of the individual, social, and cooperative equilibrium levels of security.[7] The model used to generate Figure 1.1 assumes that security expenditures totaling x were produced under constant returns to scale and that the marginal cost of a unit of security equals 1. These security expenditures affect the activity level of criminals by decreasing the gain from criminal wealth-transferring activity. From a social standpoint, the marginal gain in the pure transfer case equals the marginal reduction in the costs of the criminals' efforts. The socially optimal equilibrium level of security x^{**} is reached when the decrease in the marginal cost of the criminals' efforts equals the marginal cost of the additional unit of security incurred by each potential victim. This occurs at the intersection of the social marginal benefit curve and the horizontal line that intersects the vertical axis at 1.

Figure 1.1 also illustrates the cooperative's incentive to overinvest in security. At any level of x, the marginal private benefit to the members of a security

---

[7] The underlying assumptions used to generate the simulations are described in Kobayashi (forthcoming).

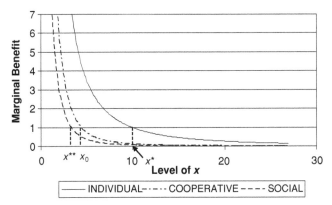

Figure 1.1. Equilibrium security expenditure levels: private goods case with costless transfers.

cooperative equals the social marginal benefit that results from a reduction in the criminals' level of activity plus the private (but not social) benefit associated with the reduction in the size of the transfer. As a result, the cooperative marginal benefit curve lies above the social marginal benefit curve for all levels of x, and thus the cooperative level of security x_0 will be greater than the social level x^{**}.

Figure 1.1 also illustrates a case where the diversion effect results in the individual, noncoordinated level of security (x^*) exceeding both the social (x^{**}) and the cooperative (x_0) levels of security.[8] In order to generate an equilibrium diversion effect, the model assumes that criminals perceive each individual's true level of security x_i with error[9] and will choose to attack the site with the lowest perceived level of protection (Kobayashi forthcoming). Under these conditions, potential victims have a marginal incentive to increase their individual level of security x_i in order to decrease the probability their site will be attacked. As illustrated in Figure 1.1, the incentive to divert criminals to other sites results in an equilibrium level of uncoordinated expenditures that is over three times the socially optimal level of security (Kobayashi forthcoming).

The relative importance of this diversion effect will be dependent upon the technology used to secure individual assets and the ability of criminals to perceive differences in individual security levels. For example, if individual security levels are observed with error, then the importance of the diversion effect

---

[8] Under the assumptions of the simulation model depicted in Figure 1.1, the social level of security (x^{**}) equals 3.2 units per site, the cooperative level (x_0) equals 4.3 units per site, and the individual, uncoordinated level (x^*) equals 9.9 units per site. For a detailed description of these simulations, see Kobayashi (forthcoming).

[9] Specifically, the criminal observes a proxy variable z_i that equals the actual security level x_i plus a random error term e_i. See Kobayashi (forthcoming).

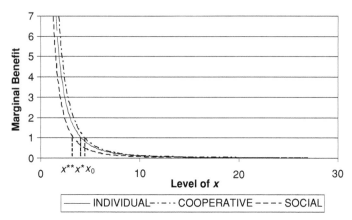

Figure 1.2. Equilibrium security expenditure levels: private goods case with costless transfers and low signal-to-noise ratio.

will depend upon the signal-to-noise ratio of such diversionary expenditures (Kobayashi forthcoming).[10] If the noise level is relatively high, then the diversion effect will be relatively unimportant. However, a relatively low noise level may elevate the magnitude of the diversion effect and create a large individual overincentive to invest in security.

Figure 1.2 shows the result of the simulation when the signal-to-noise ratio is diminished.[11] As shown in the figure, individuals' incentives to expend resources in order to divert attacks to other sites are diminished relative to the case depicted in Figure 1.1. While the simulation depicted in Figure 1.2 results in the individual level of security expenditures (x^*) exceeding the social level (x^{**}), the individual level is below the cooperative level (x_0).[12]

III. PUBLIC AND PRIVATE GOODS

The previous section examined the provision of private security goods such as door locks and security guards. In the cybersecurity context, expenditures on security are likely to be investments in information about the nature and

---

[10] For a similar analysis of the effect of uncertain legal standards on deterrence, see Craswell and Calfee (1986).

[11] This effect is achieved by assuming that the standard deviation of the random error term e_i is increased by a factor of 10. All other parameters are identical to those used in the simulation that generated Figure 1.1.

[12] Under the assumptions of the simulation model depicted in Figure 1.2, the social level of security (x^{**}) and the cooperative level (x_0) are unchanged. The individual, uncoordinated level (x^*) falls from 9.9 units per site to 4.0 units.

frequency of past attacks, about pending attacks, and about the existence of vulnerabilities to and potential defenses against attacks. Such information is a classic public good that, once produced, can be consumed by multiple sites in a nonrivalrous fashion.[13] Rather than having each site produce its own level of security, efficiency would dictate that these investments in information not be duplicated.[14]

The fact that cybersecurity-related information is a public good alters the analysis in several ways. First, the production of such information is subject to the familiar trade-off between social incentives to allow the free use of already produced information and the incentive to restrict such use to provide incentives for the creation of the information in the first place. Because information produced by one site can be used in a nonrivalrous fashion by other sites, it is not efficient for each site to separately produce its own information. Uncoordinated individual provision of security would likely result in inefficient duplication of effort.

On the other hand, this information cannot be a collective good freely available to all once produced. If security goods are collective goods, then individuals or firms that invest in information and other public security goods will not be able to exclude others from using them, resulting in an incentive to free-ride. An incentive to free-ride acts as a powerful disincentive to produce security, resulting in individual incentives for private security that will be below social levels. Further, the individual incentives to invest in security in order to divert attacks to other sites that cause the overproduction in the private security goods case will not exist in the collective goods case, as other sites would be protected by any collective goods that were produced.

---

[13] Aviram and Tor (2004) note the nonrivalrous nature of information. In Chapter 8, Tractman notes the public good nature of cybersecurity and the existence of collective action problems.

[14] This does not imply that security goods should be centralized. The analysis and detection of cyberattacks often require an examination of information distributed in a decentralized fashion among many different sites. Thus, a given level of security expenditures distributed over h different sites will reduce cybercrime more than the same level restricted to a single site. In other words, the provision of cybersecurity will exhibit network effects (see Chapter 5). Similarly, observations collected from numerous diverse sources may be more valuable than the same number of observations collected from a few firms (Hayek 1945). This analysis suggests that firms have a great incentive to share information in a cybersecurity setting. Similar incentives for sharing of information between competitive firms have raised antitrust concerns. For example, the McCarran Ferguson Act (U.S. Code Title 15, Chapter 20) makes the cooperative gathering of data for the purpose of rate making exempt from the federal antitrust statutes when undertaken by state-regulated insurance companies. For an analysis of information sharing and antitrust issues in the cybersecurity context, see Aviram and Tor (2004). For economic analyses of information sharing between competing firms, see Armantier and Richard (2003), Eisenberg (1981), and Gal-Or (1986).

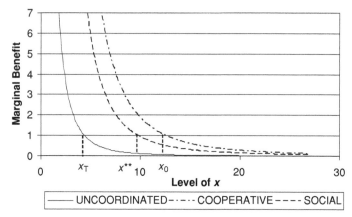

Figure 1.3. Equilibrium security expenditure levels: public goods case with costless transfers.

Figure 1.3 depicts the incentive to invest in security goods that are public in nature. As was the case in the simulations used to generate Figures 1.1 and 1.2, it is assumed that security expenditures totaling x were produced under constant returns to scale and that the marginal cost of a unit of security equals 1. Further, the functional forms for the criminals' cost of effort and gain functions, as well as the number of potential victims and criminals, are identical to those used to generate Figures 1.1 and 1.2.

However, in the simulations used to generate Figure 1.3, each unit of security x can be simultaneously applied to all potential victims. Because each unit of x is not separately incurred by each potential victim, the total level of protection applied to each site at the social optimum is greater than in the private goods case, but the total spending is less. In the private goods case depicted in Figure 1.1, each of sixteen sites spends 3.2 units on security at the social optimum. Thus, the socially optimal total level of security expenditures in the private goods case equals 51.2 units.[15] In the public goods case depicted in Figure 1.3, the socially optimal total level of security expenditures equals 9.7 units, which is applied to all sixteen sites.

In contrast to the private goods case, the uncoordinated level of security expenditures x_T is far below the socially optimal level. As depicted in Figure 1.3, the uncoordinated level of security would equal 4.3 units, compared to the social level of 9.3 units. This level does not equal the per-site expenditure. Rather, it represents an individual site's preference for the total level of expenditures on x by all potential victims. Moreover, while this level of total expenditures satisfies an individual site's first-order conditions, it does not define a unique

---

[15] See Figure 1.1 and the discussion of this figure in the text.

allocation of the security expenditures among the sites. Thus, suppose there are h sites that are potential targets of a cyberattack. While individual expenditures of x^*/h by all h sites produce an equilibrium, there are also multiple equilibria in which $h - k$ sites spend zero and k sites spend x^*/k. Any individual site would prefer an equilibrium where it was one of the sites spending zero. Indeed, this result is the familiar free-riding problem that arises in the presence of nonappropriable public goods.

The existence of multiple equilibria and the potential for free-riding suggest that some mechanism to mitigate the free-riding problem and/or solve the coordination problem is required. One way in which the free-riding and coordination problems can be addressed is through cooperative security arrangements to provide public security measures. Examples of such institutions include information sharing and assessment centers (ISACs) in the financial services, energy, transportation, vital human services, and communication information services sectors, as well as partnerships for critical infrastructure security (PCISs), which coordinate the activities of the industry-based ISACs. A primary function of these cooperative security institutions would be to set a level of security expenditure that would internalize the positive spillover effect generated by the individual production of public security goods.

While cooperatives in the public goods setting may help address the underproduction problem, the level of public security goods expenditures chosen by a cooperative will be higher than the social level. As was the case in the private security goods case, the incentive to overproduce security is due to the cooperative's incentive to reduce the size of socially costless transfers that do not represent social losses. Thus, in the pure transfer case, cooperatives investing in public security goods will still be expected to produce a socially excessive amount of security. This effect is also depicted in Figure 1.3, as the cooperative level of security expenditures (x_0) in the public goods case exceeds the socially optimal level (x^{**}).[16]

Some cyberattacks may be appropriately be characterized as involving few direct social costs. For example, consider a directed denial-of-service attack on one of many Internet vendors in a competitive industry. While the attacked site may lose a significant number of sales during the attack, such losses do not represent social losses if Internet shoppers can switch to other sites. Thus, the prior analysis suggests that cybersecurity cooperatives will overinvest resources under these circumstances.

---

[16] Under the conditions depicted in Figure 1.3, the cooperative level of expenditures (x_0) equals 12.5 units, compared with the social level (x^{**}) of 9.7 units.

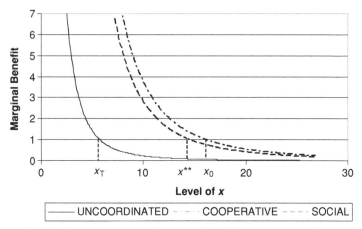

Figure 1.4. Equilibrium security expenditure levels: public goods case with socially costly cybercrime.

However, a significant number of cybercrimes may not involve socially cost-less transfers. For example, the social harm caused by a destructive worm or virus may greatly exceed the gain to the criminal that released it. If the gain-to-harm ratio is low, then the overinvestment inefficiency associated with cooperatives will also be small. To see this, consider the release of a destructive worm that yields negligible gain to its creator. An incremental increase in the level of security spending by the cooperative will reduce both the activity level of cybercriminals and the magnitude of the losses suffered by victims when cyberattacks occur. In the pure transfer case, the reduction in the losses suffered by victims is a private but not a social benefit. However, when the harm to a site represents a harm not offset elsewhere by a corresponding gain, the reduction in the loss is both a private and social benefit. Thus expenditures aimed at reducing the magnitude of such losses will yield social as well as private benefits, and the divergence between the cooperative and social levels of security will diminsh.[17]

Figure 1.4 shows depicts the equilibrium investment levels in public security goods when there are social costs that result from the cybercrime. The simulations hold the gain to the criminals constant but double the losses to the victim of an attack, *ceteris paribus*. As depicted in the figure, all levels of equilibrium security expenditures increase in response to the existence of social losses. The uncoordinated level increases from 4.3 units to 5.7 units, the social

[17] One possibility is that prevention of both types of cyberattacks would occur. This would mitigate the overproduction problem in the case of cyberattacks that have a high gain-to-harm ratio.

level increases from 9.7 to 14.5 units, and the cooperative level increases from 12.5 units to 16 units. More importantly, while the gap between the uncoordinated and socially optimal levels of security increases in both absolute and relative terms, the opposite is true for the gap between the cooperative and social levels.

A critical issue to be addressed by a cooperative formed to make investments in public security goods is ensuring that nonpayers can be excluded. A mechanism to exclude nonpayers will prevent a firm that refuses to join the cooperative from free-riding on the goods purchased by the cooperative. Further, given that the level of protection possessed by a firm that does not join the collective will be below that possessed by members of the cooperative, nonmembers will suffer more frequent attacks.[18] If nonpayers are not excluded, then firms will refuse to join the cooperative and attempt to free-ride on the information provided by the cooperative (Kobayashi forthcoming).[19]

As is the case with any idea or informational public good, the private production of public goods can be induced through intellectual property protection. For example, security research firms use proprietary technology to collect and analyze data about cyberattacks.[20] Although security goods that involve the collection and analysis of information may not be protected under the federal copyright laws or rise to the level of novelty or nonobviousness required for protection under the federal patent laws (Kobayashi forthcoming), the computer programs used to track and analyze such data may be. Further, patent protection may be available for novel and nonobvious computer programs and business methods.

Thus, clearly defining intellectual property rights as well as members' responsibility for preventing the further dissemination of sensitive information should be a central issue when an information-sharing or security cooperative is formed. Even if the use of statutory intellectual property right protection, such as copyright or patents, is not be feasible, a security collective can use secrecy, supported by contractual restrictions on its members, to prevent widespread free-riding (Kobayashi and Ribstein 2002b). In this context, secrecy means that the existence and content of a specific security level is not disclosed *ex ante* to other sites or to potential hackers. This form of secrecy has two offsetting effects.

---

[18] Aviram and Tor (2004) note that the potential loss of network benefits may serve as an effective self-enforcing mechanism for private cybersecurity cooperatives and other private legal systems.

[19] In Chapter 8, Trachtman analyzes collective action and free-riding problems in the provision of cybersecurity.

[20] Walker (2003) describes the use of proprietary software and systems to monitor and analyze the nature and frequency of cyberattacks. The information and analyses are subsequently sold to subscriber networks.

First, it allows a site to appropriate the gains from its private expenditures by precluding other sites from appropriating information it possesses.[21] To the extent secrecy prevents free-riding, its use can encourage private expenditures on public security goods. On the other hand, the use of secrecy may not allow for the diverting effect generated by expenditures that are publicly disclosed, and it may encourage free-riding if criminals cannot perceive *ex ante* which sites are protected. Thus, it may suppress the incentive for individuals to expend private resources on public security goods.

IV. CONCLUSION

The foregoing analysis has examined the incentive to produce private security goods. While prior analyses have examined the provision of security goods that have the characteristics of private goods, this chapter has examined security goods, such as information, that have the characteristics of public goods. In contrast to the private goods case, where uncoordinated individual security expenditures can lead to an overproduction of security, the public goods case is subject to an underproduction of security goods and incentives to free-ride.

It has been suggested, for example, that the government mandate minimum security standards or require private firms to disclose the nature and frequency of cyberattacks aimed at their sites and networks (Frye 2002).[22] However, government mandates can generate their own inefficiencies. For example, the government may choose a standard that is inferior to the standard that would have been chosen by the market (Liebowitz and Margolis 1999). Further, the government's standard may stifle experimentation and innovation and thus lead to dynamic inefficiency (Kobayashi and Ribstein 2002a). Mandatory disclosure can be overinclusive, requiring the disclosure of information with a marginal value less than the marginal cost of collection and disclosure.[23] Further, mandatory disclosure can induce firms to engage in less information collection and

---

[21] Note that such protection is not perfect. For example, Landes and Posner (2003, 354–71) discuss the economics of trade secret law. However, in the context of some cybersecurity settings, a timing advantage can be used to appropriate the returns from expenditures on information. For example, timely notice of IP addresses being used to launch distributed denial-of-service attacks or other types of cyberattacks allows the targets to block incoming mail from these addresses before large-scale damage is incurred. Small delays in the transmission of this information can delay such preventative measures and will increase the amount of loss from such attacks.

[22] In Chapter 2, Swire analyzes conditions under which disclosure promotes and reduces security.

[23] Easterbrook and Fischel (1984) discuss mandatory disclosure rules contained in the securities laws. In Chapter 2, Swire discusses this issue in the cybersecurity context.

can exaggerate rather than mitigate the free-riding problems that can cause a underinvestment in information.[24]

One alternative to government standards or mandated disclosure would be for the government to encourage firms to collectively produce information by facilitating the development of security cooperatives.[25] The protection of information produced by the cooperatives should be a central feature of these organizations, and the government can facilitate the protection of such information through the creation and enforcement of property rights to information (Demsetz 1970). While security cooperatives that successfully protect their information may have a tendency to overproduce security, this tendency will be mitigated in the case of serious crimes (i.e., where the intruder's gain is low relative to the social losses).

REFERENCES

Armantier, Olivier, and Oliver Richard. 2003. Exchanges of Cost Information in the Airline Industry. *RAND Journal of Economics* 34:461.

Aviram, Amitai, and Avishalom Tor. 2004. Overcoming Impediments to Information Sharing. *Alabama Law Review* 55:231.

Becker, Gary. 1968. Crime and Punishment: An Economic Approach. *Journal of Political Economy* 76:169.

Becker, Gary, and George Stigler. 1974. Law Enforcement, Malfeasance, and Compensation of Enforcers. *Journal of Legal Studies* 3:1.

Clotfelter, Charles T. 1978. Private Security and the Public Safety. *Journal of Urban Economics* 5:388.

Craswell, Richard, and John E. Calfee. 1986. Deterrence and Uncertain Legal Standards. *Journal of Law, Economics, and Organization* 2:279.

Demsetz, Harold. 1970. The Private Production of Public Goods. *Journal of Law and Economics* 13:293.

Easterbrook, Frank H., and Daniel R. Fischel. 1984. Mandatory Disclosure and the Protection of Investors. *Virginia Law Review* 70:669.

Eisenberg, Barry S. 1981. Information Exchange among Competitors: The Issue of Relative Value Scales for Physicians' Services. *Journal of Law and Economics* 23:461.

Friedman, David. 1979. Private Creation and Enforcement of Law: A Historical Case. *Journal of Legal Studies* 8:399.

————. 1984. Efficient Institutions for the Private Enforcement of Law. *Journal of Legal Studies* 13: 379.

---

[24] Johnsen (2003) discusses SEC disclosure rules and their suppression of information production.

[25] This would include policies that facilitate the sharing of information and an antitrust policy that explicitly recognizes the importance of information sharing among firms. For a discussion of these issues, see Aviram and Tor (2004).

————. 1991. Impossibility, Subjective Probability, and Punishment for Attempts. *Journal of Legal Studies* 20:179.

Frye, Emily. 2002. The Tragedy of the Cybercommons: Overcoming Fundamental Vulnerabilities to Critical Infrastructure in a Networked World. *Business Law* 58:349.

Gal-Or, Esther. 1986. Information Transmission: Cournot and Bertrand Equilibria. *Review of Economic Studies* 53:85.

Hayek, F. 1945. The Use of Knowledge in Society. *American Economic Review* 35:519.

Hui-Wen, Koo, and I. P. L. Png. 1994. Private Security: Deterrent or Diversion. *International Review of Law and Economics* 14:87.

Johnsen, D. Bruce. 2003. The Limits of Mandatory Disclosure: Regulatory Taking under the Investment Company Act. Mimeo, George Mason University.

Kobayashi, Bruce H. Forthcoming. An Economic Analysis of the Private and Social Costs of the Provision of Cybersecurity and Other Public Security Goods. *Supreme Court Economic Review*.

Kobayashi, Bruce H., and Larry E. Ribstein. 2002a. State Regulation of Electronic Commerce. *Emory Law Journal* 51:1.

————. 2002b. Privacy and Firms. *Denver University Law Review* 79:526.

Krim, Jonathan. 2003. Help Fix Cybersecurity or Else, U.S. Tells Industry. *Washington Post*, December 4, p. E02.

Landes, William M., and Richard A. Posner . 1975. The Private Enforcement of Law. *Journal of Legal Studies* 4:1.

————. 2003. *The Economic Structure of Intellectual Property Law*. Cambridge, MA: Belknap Press.

Liebowitz, Stan J., and Stephen E. Margolis. 1999. *Winners, Losers, and Microsoft: Competition and Antitrust in High Technology*. Oakland, CA: Independent Institute.

Shavell, Steven. 1990. Deterrence and the Punishment of Attempts. *Journal of Legal Studies* 19:435.

————. 1991. Individual Precautions to Prevent Theft: Private versus Socially Optimal Behavior. *International Review of Law and Economics* 11:123.

Walker, Leslie. 2003. The View from Symatec's Security Central. *Washington Post*, January 9, p. E01.

TWO

A MODEL FOR WHEN DISCLOSURE HELPS SECURITY: WHAT IS DIFFERENT ABOUT COMPUTER AND NETWORK SECURITY?

Peter P. Swire*

This article asks the question, When does disclosure actually help security? The issue of optimal openness has become newly important as the Internet and related technologies have made it seem inevitable that information will leak out. Sun Microsystems CEO Scott McNealy received considerable press attention a few years ago when he said, "You have zero privacy. Get over it" (Froomkin 2000). An equivalent statement for security would be, "You have zero secrecy. Get over it." Although there is a germ of truth in both statements, neither privacy nor secrecy is or should be dead. Instead, this article seeks to provide a more thorough theoretical basis for assessing how disclosure of information will affect security. In particular, it seeks to understand the differences between traditional security practices in the physical world, on the one hand, and best practices for computer and network security, on the other.

The discussion begins with a paradox. Most experts in computer and network security are familiar with the slogan that "there is no security through

*Professor of Law and John Glenn Research Scholar in Public Policy Research, Moritz College of Law of the Ohio State University. Many people from diverse disciplines have contributed to my thinking on the topic of this paper. An earlier version, entitled "What Should Be Hidden and Open in Computer Security: Lessons from Deception, the Art of War, Law, and Economic Theory," was presented in 2001 at the Telecommunications Policy Research Conference, the Brookings Institution, and the George Washington University Law School; it is available at www.peterswire.net. I am also grateful for comments from participants more recently when this topic was presented at the Stanford Law School, the University of North Carolina Law School, and the Silicon Flatirons Conference at the University of Colorado School of Law. Earlier phases of the research were supported by the Moritz College of Law and the George Washington University Law School. Current research is funded by an award from the John Glenn Institute for Public Service and Public Policy.

obscurity."[1] For proponents of Open Source software,[2] revealing the details of
the system will actually tend to improve security, notably due to peer review.
On this view, trying to hide the details of the system will tend to harm security because attackers will learn about vulnerabilities but defenders will not
know where to patch the vulnerabilities. In sharp contrast, a famous World
War II slogan has it that "loose lips sink ships."[3] Most experts in the military and intelligence areas believe that secrecy is a critical tool for maintaining
security.

Section I provides a basic model for deciding when the open source and
military/intelligence viewpoints are likely to be correct. Insights come from a
2×2 matrix. The first variable is the extent to which disclosure is likely to help
the attackers, by tipping them off to a vulnerability they would otherwise not
have seen. The second variable is the extent to which the disclosure is likely to
improve the defense. Disclosure might help the defenders, notably, by teaching
them how to fix a vulnerability and by alerting more defenders to the problem.
The 2×2 matrix shows the interplay of the help-the-attacker effect and help-
the-defender effect, and it identifies four basic paradigms for the effects of
disclosure on security: the open source paradigm, the military/intelligence
paradigm, the information-sharing paradigm, and the public domain.

---

[1] A search on Google for "security" and "obscurity" discovered 665,000 websites with those
terms. Reading through the websites shows that a great many of them discuss some version
of "no security through obscurity."

[2] Wikipedia, an online encyclopedia that uses open source approaches, defines "open source"
as "a work methodology that fits the *open source Definition*, and generally is any *computer
software* whose *source code* is either in the *public domain* or, more commonly, is *copyrighted*
by one or more persons/entities and distributed under an *open-source license* such as the
GNU General Public License (GPL). Such a license may require that the source code be distributed along with the software, and that the source code be freely modifiable, with at most
minor restrictions." http://en.wikipedia.org/wiki/Open_source (last visited July 16, 2004).
    Wikipedia states, "Source code (commonly just **source** or **code**) refers to any series of
statements written in some *human-readable* computer *programming language*. In modern
programming languages, the source code which constitutes a software program is usually
in several *text files*, but the same source code may be printed in a book or recorded on
tape (usually without a filesystem). The term is typically used in the context of a particular
piece of *computer software*. A computer program's *source code* is the collection of files that
can be converted from human-readable form to an equivalent computer-executable form.
The source code is either converted into *executable* by an *software development tool* for a
particular computer *architecture*, or executed from the human readable form with the aid of
an *interpreter*." http://en.wikipedia.org/wiki/Source_code.

[3] For images of World War II posters on the subject, see http://www.state.nh.us/ww2/loose.html.
The posters tell vivid stories. One poster has a picture of a woman and the words "Wanted
for Murder: Her Careless Talk Costs Lives." Another shows a sailor carrying his kit, with the
words "If You Tell Where He's Going . . . He May Never Get There."

Section II explains why many computer and network security issues are different from military and other traditional security problems that arise in the physical world. The discussion focuses on the nature of the "first-time attack" or the degree of what the paper calls "uniqueness" in the defense. Many defensive tricks, including secrecy, are more effective the first time there is an attack on a physical base or computer system. Secrecy is far less effective, however, if the attackers can probe the defenses repeatedly and learn from their probes. It turns out that many of the key areas of computer security involve circumstances where there can be repeated low-cost attacks. For instance, firewalls, mass-market software, and encryption algorithms all can be attacked repeatedly by hackers. In such circumstances, a strategy of secrecy – of "security through obscurity" – is less likely to be effective than in the military case.

Even recognizing the lower effectiveness of secrecy in many computer and network applications, there will still often be advantages to secrecy in practice. Section III relaxes the assumptions of the model presented in Section I. The open source approach makes three assumptions: (1) disclosure will offer little or no help to attackers; (2) disclosure will tend to upgrade the design of defenses; and (3) disclosure will spread effective defenses to third parties. In practice, secrecy will often be of greater use than the open source advocates have stated, because one or more of the three assumptions will not hold. Section III explains some of the major categories of situations where secrecy is likely to be more or less effective at promoting security.

The chief intellectual task of this article is to help us think about when disclosure will help or harm security. There are other major considerations that go into an informed judgment about whether to disclose information about a security vulnerability. For instance, it may promote accountability and the long-run health of the system to err on the side of disclosure. This instinct underlies the Freedom of Information Act[4] and many other laws and practices encouraging disclosure. As another example, disclosure can compromise personal privacy in some circumstances. Accountability and privacy are vital goals that need to be taken into account in the overall analysis of when to disclose information. Discussion of those goals figures prominently in my larger research project on openness and security. In this article, however, the focus is on when disclosure will help the specific goal of system security: when will disclosure protect against an attacker's gaining control of a physical installation or computer system.

---

[4] See 5 U.S.C. § 552, as amended by Pub. L. No. 104-231, 110 Stat. 3048 (1996).

When does disclosure help security? The intuition of many experts in the military and intelligence realms is that secrecy (lack of disclosure) is an essential tool for enhancing security. Military bases and weapon systems are cloaked in secrecy. Intelligence agencies tell little about their capabilities, sources, and methods. The slogan for this position is the World War II motto that "loose lips sink ships." The graphic image is that too much disclosure ("loose lips") will tip off the enemy where to send its submarines ("sink ships").[5] In such instances, disclosure can be tantamount to treason.

A. Case A: The Open Source Paradigm

In contrast to the World War II motto, a pervasive theme of many computer security discussions is that "there is no security through obscurity."[6] For people outside of the computer security realm, it may initially be difficult to understand how that slogan has become a truism. Research and discussions with computer security researchers suggest that there are three assumptions, often implicit, that undergird the slogan. In considering whether to disclose a vulnerability, supporters of openness seem to assume the following:

(A1) Attackers will learn little or nothing from disclosure.
(A2) Disclosure will prompt the designers to improve the design of defenses.
(A3) Disclosure will prompt other defenders to take action.

The discussion in Sections II and III develops in more detail the intuitions that underlie these three assumptions. It also critically examines each assumption. For the present, however, we can view assumption A1 as resting on the idea that software and network vulnerabilities, once discovered by any attacker, will often quickly become known to other attackers. For instance "warez" sites and other mechanisms exist to teach hackers about new attacks.[7] Public disclosure of a vulnerability will thus not significantly help attackers exploit the vulnerability.

---

[5] *See supra* note 2.

[6] *See supra* note 1. The origin of the slogan "no security through obscurity" is obscure. I would welcome information on who coined it. It was certainly used by the early 1990s. Rop Gonggrijp (1992) refers to "security through obscurity" as a policy used by Novell.

[7] For example, http://easywarez.com and http://ICEWAREZ.net (these are "warez" sites that provide downloads of software illegally, including software that can be used for hacking purposes).

The basic idea underlying assumption A2 is a deeply held tenet in the open source movement. The idea is that software will improve quickly if a wide array of programmers can see the code, find flaws in it, and fix those flaws. In the words of researchers Randy Bush and Steven Bellovin (2002), "Hiding security vulnerabilities in algorithms, software, and/or hardware decreases the likelihood they will be repaired."

The basic idea underlying assumption A3 is that many people may be affected by a vulnerability other than the software or system designers. For instance, assumption A2 focuses on the group of programmers who may write new code to improve a software program, yet there are likely many system owners who use the software program but are not involved in writing it. Assumption A3 focuses on how disclosure of a vulnerability can improve the security of these system owners. A system owner who learns of the vulnerability can install a patch or upgrade once it is available. If a patch[8] is not yet available, the system owner can decide to take other measures, such as taking the system offline or disabling the software until a defense does become available.

Implications of assumptions A1, A2, and A3: In the open source paradigm, the costs of the disclosure of a vulnerability are low because attackers learn little or nothing from the disclosure. The benefits of the disclosure are high because of improved system design and actions taken by nondesigners to protect their systems.

B. Case B: The Military Paradigm

The assumptions in the military setting are directly contrary to those of the open source paradigm:

(B1) Attackers will learn a lot from disclosure of a vulnerability.

(B2) Disclosure will teach the designers little or nothing about how to improve the defenses.

(B3) Disclosure will prompt little or no improvement in defenses by other defenders.

The intuition behind assumption B1 is that it is difficult in a military setting for the attackers to learn about a vulnerability. Consider a hill that is being defended by mines or camouflaged machine guns. Should the defenders publish

---

[8] See Webopedia, available at http://webopedia.internet.com/TERM/p/patch.html. Webopedia defines "patch" as follows: "Also called a service patch, a fix to a program bug. A patch is an actual piece of object code that is inserted into (patched into) an executable program. Patches typically are available as downloads over the Internet." See also Microsoft (2003).

the location of the defenses on the Internet? The answer clearly is no. It will be difficult and costly for the attackers to learn those locations and to determine the least-defended path up the hill. Metaphorically and literally, the attackers will have to "pay in blood" to learn the weak points of the defense. Disclosure in this setting would help the attackers considerably.

The intuition behind assumption B2 is a bit less clear-cut. It certainly is possible that public disclosure of a design will lead clever persons outside of the military to suggest improvements in design. More likely, however, the improvements from this source will be modest at best. For specialized military topics, there is likely no pool of helpful outside experts comparable to open source programmers. Instead of depending on outsiders, the military will often hire or train the best available experts in specialized military equipment (tanks or fighter planes) or applications (battlefield communications). Public disclosure of the defenses will then do little to improve the design of the defenses.

Under assumption B3, the military will often be the only organization affected directly by a vulnerability. There may be countermeasures for land mines (magnetic detectors) or for camouflaged machine guns (infrared detectors). If so, the military generally has confidential channels for telling its own people what to do in response. There are few or no third parties who would benefit from disclosure of the vulnerability or what to do about the vulnerability. (At least there would be no third parties on "our side" that we would want to tell.)

Turning briefly to the submarine situation during World War II, disclosure of the sailing time of a convoy helped attackers by revealing a vulnerability. Disclosure did little or nothing to help the Navy (the system designer for the defense) protect the ships. Disclosure also did little to help other parties defend themselves.[9] In this setting, "loose lips" did indeed "sink ships" – the costs of disclosure outweighed the benefits.

> Implications of assumptions B1, B2, and B3: In the military paradigm, the costs of disclosure of a vulnerability are high because attackers otherwise pay a high cost to learn of the vulnerability. The benefits of disclosure are low because outside designers are unlikely to improve the defenses and there are few or no third parties that the defenders wish to help through disclosure.

---

[9] It is possible to imagine some assistance to third parties from disclosure. For instance, other ships might venture to sea if it becomes known that there is a convoy in another area that will draw the submarines' attacks. This benefit from disclosure, however, is likely to be outweighed by the harm to the convoy that becomes the target of the attack.

Table 2.1. *The effects of disclosure under the two paradigms*

		Help-the-attackers effect	
		Low	High
Help-the-defenders effect	High	A: Open source	
	Low		B: Military

Note: Greater disclosure up and to the left, greater secrecy down and to the right.

Taking the open source and military cases together, we can create a 2 × 2 matrix that visually shows the different effects of disclosure under the two paradigms (Table 2.1). Under the open source assumptions, disclosure tends to improve the defense without helping the attackers. There are thus net benefits from disclosure. Under the military assumptions, the effects are reversed, and there are net costs from disclosure.

C. Case C: The Information-Sharing Paradigm

The matrix also sheds light on when greater "information sharing" will improve security (consider, for example, the numerous information-sharing provisions in the USA Patriot Act[10] or the proposals for the CIA and the FBI to share more of their data). Perhaps the easiest case to understand concerns the sharing of "watch lists" of suspected terrorists with defenders such as airport screeners, visa officers, and officials in other countries. Will greater disclosure of watch lists improve or harm security? The assumptions are as follows:

(C1) Attackers may learn a lot from disclosure.
(C2) Disclosure may teach defenders how to design better systems.
(C3) Disclosure will allow more defenders to take protective actions.

The intuition behind assumption C1 is that broader dissemination of a watch list may tip off attackers who are on the list. The attackers may learn of their inclusion either from a mole (a rogue employee) or because the list was kept in an insecure place and got leaked to the attackers. Persons on the list will then be on notice to avoid enforcement officials or to mask their identity. Persons not on the list will learn not to associate publicly with any colleagues on the list. Persons not on the list will also learn that they are "safe" and thus can fly on airplanes or otherwise get through screening processes. They will also then be able to infiltrate defenses more effectively to spy or launch an attack.

---

[10] See Swire (2004a) and USA Patriot Act of 2001, Pub. L. No. 107-56, 115 Stat. 272, §§ 203, 326.

The intuition behind assumption C2 is that broader use of watch lists may provide useful feedback regarding what sorts of watch lists are effective. The intuition behind assumption C3 is probably stronger: putting watch lists into the hands of more defenders increases the likelihood of spotting and capturing attackers. For instance, putting the picture of a "most wanted" criminal on television makes it harder for the criminal to escape. Especially when the criminal already knows that he or she is being chased, disclosure will help the defenders more than the criminal.

In practice, how the costs and benefits of disclosure compare will be an empirical question. Defenders will seek to create systems that allow defenders to learn information effectively but prevent attackers from doing so. As the number of defenders grows, however, it is less likely that every one of the defenders is trustworthy and every system containing pertinent information is secure.[11] Information sharing is likely to have both costs and benefits, which will vary with the circumstances.

> **Implications of assumptions C1, C2, and C3: In the information-sharing paradigm, there are significant costs and significant benefits from disclosure. The costs of disclosure may be high if attackers learn about the nature of the defense. The benefits of disclosure may be high if defenders can take additional effective measures against the attackers.**

D. Case D: The Public Domain

Another possibility is that disclosure of a vulnerability will have low costs and low benefits. In some instances, a vulnerability is so minor that attackers will not be inclined to exploit it. More broadly, in many settings the information is already in the public domain – the relevant information is already available to interested attackers and defenders. In such settings, the assumptions are as follow:

(D1) Attackers will learn little or nothing from the disclosure.
(D2) System designers will learn little or nothing from the disclosure.
(D3) Other defenders may learn little or a significant amount from the disclosure.

An example of information in the public domain is a street map of Manhattan or Washington, D.C. Having a detailed and accurate street map is a great advantage for an attacker. In wartime, attackers crave good maps as they move

---

[11] In some instances, technological measures may help deliver benefits of disclosure while minimizing the costs. The technological and institutional issues involved in such cases are beyond the scope of this paper. The most intense recent public debate has been about the CAPPS II system for screening airline passengers (Center for Democracy and Technology 2003).

into enemy territory. Good maps allow precise planning, facilitate coordinated attacks, and reduce the risk of hidden features that can booby-trap the assault. In response, defenders who know the terrain may remove street signs or take other measures to prevent the attackers from learning the area.

As part of the war on terrorism, it might thus be tempting for the United States to try to prevent terrorists from getting accurate street maps of potential targets such as Manhattan or Washington, D.C. The problem, however, is obvious. Detailed and accurate street maps of those cities are in the public domain, with innumerable copies in print and on the Internet. It would be very expensive even to try to hide the maps, and such efforts would almost certainly be futile. In addition to the costs of trying to hide the maps, there would be substantial costs incurred by all the legitimate users of the maps.

Tailored to this example, assumption D1 is that attackers would learn little or nothing new from a "disclosure" such as the publishing of an additional street map. Assumption D2 is that the designers of the defense would learn little or nothing when a new street map is published. Assumption D3 is that a new street map may in fact be of some use to other "defenders" – legitimate users of the information, including tourists, urban planners, and all others who rely on street maps.

Looked at from the other direction, efforts to hide or "reclassify" information will often be expensive and not very effective in an era of the Internet, online search engines, and archiving of information once it has been on the Internet.[12] The benefits of trying to hide the information will often be small because determined attackers will still acquire the information. The costs of trying to hide the information may be considerable, both in terms of the effort needed to find and destroy copies that already exist and in terms of the effects on legitimate users of the information.[13] Once a secret is exposed, it is often costly or impossible to put the genie back in the bottle.

Implications of assumptions D1, D2, and D3: For information in the public domain, there are few or no costs from additional disclosure. There may be benefits from additional disclosure if it gets the information into the hands of additional legitimate users (defenders). There are likely high costs from trying to hide information once it is in the public domain.

---

[12] For an informative discussion of the wealth of information available through the Google service, see Granneman (2004).

[13] The discussion here focuses only on the extent to which disclosure will help or hinder the attackers. Efforts to censor information in the public domain also can obviously raise serious First Amendment and other issues. Eugene Volokh (2004) has written an excellent analysis of these issues using an approach that is congruent in a number of respects with the analysis in this paper.

Table 2.2. *The effects of disclosure under four paradigms*

		Help-the-attackers effect	
		Low	High
Help-the-defenders effect	High	A: Open source	C. Information sharing
	Low	D. Public domain	B: Military

Note: Greater disclosure up and to the left, greater secrecy down and to the right.

E. The 2 × 2 Matrix for When Disclosure Improves Security

With the addition of case C (information sharing) and case D (the public domain), each cell of the 2 × 2 matrix has been filled in. Table 2.2 shows the result.

At this stage, a few comments will help to emphasize what is and is not accomplished by Table 2.2. First, a chief goal of the table is to organize current thinking about the dueling approaches of disclosure ("no security through obscurity") and secrecy ("loose lips sink ships"). By clarifying the assumptions underlying those two scenarios, the table also reveals the assumptions underlying two other common scenarios – information sharing and the public domain. Second, the table simplifies reality by showing a binary split between strong and weak effects of helping the attackers and improving the defense. In reality, there is a continuum between strong and weak effects. Real-world examples will range along the two dimensions. Third, the table is based on *assumptions* about the effects of disclosure on attackers and defenders. Conclusions about the desirability of disclosure will depend on how valid the assumptions are in a given setting.

II. THE KEY REASONS COMPUTER AND NETWORK SECURITY MAY VARY FROM OTHER TYPES OF SECURITY

In the legal academy, there has been a lively debate about the extent to which cyberspace and the law of cyberspace differ from the physical world and the law of the physical world. For instance, writers such as David Post and David Johnson (see Goldsmith 1998) have stressed the uniqueness of the Internet, whereas writers such as Frank Easterbrook (1996) and Jack Goldsmith (1998) have stressed that legal issues related to the Internet are fundamentally similar to previous legal issues. The purpose of this section is to examine the extent and nature of the differences between computer and network security, on the one hand, and military and other traditional types of security, on the other.

The conclusion reached is that there are no *logical* or *necessary* difference between cybersecurity and physical security. One can generate examples in which the nature of the security challenge and the optimal degree of disclosure are the same regardless of what is being protected. Nonetheless, important differences between cybersecurity and physical security *commonly* exist. These differences, I believe, go far toward explaining why so many cybersecurity experts intuitively believe the slogan "no security through obscurity" while so many military and other physical security experts intuitively believe that "loose lips sink ships."

A. Hiddenness and the First-Time Attack

Here is an organizing concept for understanding when hiddenness helps security: a hidden feature is more likely to be effective against the first attack but less likely to be effective against repeated attacks. Consider an example from the physical world. A fort is protected by a simple security device that relies on hiddenness. On the path up to the fort there is a pit covered by leaves, with a sharpened stick at the bottom. The first time an attacker comes up the path, the attacker might fall into the pit. Even if hiddenness works against the first attacker, however, later attackers will likely not "fall" for the same trick. The later attackers may know where the pit is or may come equipped with sticks to probe the path and discover any pits. In this simple example, obscurity may work against the first attacker but is unlikely to work once the attackers learn to watch for hidden pits.

The concept of the first-time attack can be generalized. Consider a "hidden" defensive feature as one that is not known initially to any attacker. The effectiveness of hiddenness will be a function of five variables:

1. The effectiveness of the defensive feature at stopping the first attack ("E" for effectiveness).
2. The number of attacks ("N" for number of attacks).
3. The extent to which an attacker learns from previous attacks ("L" for the learning that occurs).
4. The extent to which the attacker communicates this learning to other attackers ("C" for communication).
5. The extent to which the defenders can effectively alter the defensive feature before the next attack ("A" for alteration of the defense). Note that the alteration may come from the system designer/defender (A-D). The proposed alteration may also come from a third party who learns how to fix the vulnerability (A-T), such as when an open source programmer designs a patch.

The effectiveness of hiddenness will vary directly with the initial effectiveness (E) and the ability of the designer to alter the defense (A-D). It will vary inversely with the number of attacks (N), the degree of learning by attackers (L), the ability of attackers to communicate (C), and the ability of third parties to alter the defense (A-T). When N, L, and C grow very large, hiding the defensive feature will be of no use. All attackers will then know everything about the "hidden" feature.[14]

The military and open source examples described earlier illustrate how the effectiveness of hiddenness can vary depending on the five variables. Start with the example of camouflaged machine guns guarding a hill, where the effect of hiddenness is the difference between announcing the location of the machine guns and keeping them hidden. Initially, the attackers do not know where the machine guns are hidden. E, the effectiveness of the defense, will likely be high against infantry attackers because the hidden guns will make it hard for attackers to find a safe path up the hill.[15] N, the number of attacks, will be low, as each attack is a major event that is costly in terms of casualties. L, or learning, will vary depending on the ability of an individual attacker to get back safely from the first attack or go around the machine gun nest. If all the attackers are killed in the attack, then L will be zero. C, or the ability to communicate, will vary depending on the ability of any individual attacker to tell the rest of the troops about the location of the hidden guns. If the attackers have radios, then C will be a high because an attacker can tell their comrades what locations to avoid. If the attackers have to rely on word of mouth, then C will be low, and the defense may have time to move the machine guns to a new location for the second attack.

Pulling these observations together, each attack on the hidden machine guns is very expensive for the attackers. Hiddenness benefits the defenders in the first attack. The number of attacks will be small (would there be even three charges up a well-defended hill?). Attackers may not learn quickly about the hidden defenses, may find it difficult to communicate their knowledge to the other attackers, and may face a changed defense by the time they

---

[14] The discussion here does not present a detailed mathematical model of how hiddenness contributes to security. Identification of the five variables, however, should enable those who are mathematically more skilled than I am to build such a model. As suggested in conversation by Rena Mears, the approach here implicitly assumes a calculus function where the effectiveness of hiddenness goes to zero as the number of attacks approaches infinity (assuming a positive value for L and C (and also assuming the effect of L and C in helping attackers outweighs the effect of alterations in helping defenders).

[15] The example involves foot soldiers charging up a hill against machine guns. If the attack is made by heavy tanks, then ordinary machine guns will not stop the attack. For the tank attack, the value of E, the initial effectiveness, would be low.

launch their next attack. For all of these reasons, hiddenness will benefit the defense.

Under the assumptions used thus far for open source software, hiddenness will be much less effective. It is possible that the initial effectiveness of a defensive trick (E) will be substantial. The number of attacks (N) will quite possibly be high. Malicious hackers can probe for weaknesses in a software product over and over again. The attackers learn (L) from the attacks, such as by seeing whether they can gain control over the software. Attackers can communicate (C) about flaws, such as by posting their exploits to websites to let other attackers know about the flaws.

Under these assumptions, each attack on a software program is very cheap – attackers can probe the program over and over again from the comfort of their own homes or computer labs. They learn about flaws and tell others about flaws. Very quickly, under these assumptions, the hidden defense is exposed to the world. Thus, there is "no security through obscurity."

Altering the defense also works differently than for the physical attack against machine guns. In the machine gun setting, the defenders may be able to move the guns between each attack. If that is true, then the second ambush may be as effective as the first, and hiddenness once more favors the defenders. Under the open source assumptions, disclosure of the vulnerability actually increases A, the likelihood of effective alteration of the defense. The idea is that other open source programmers will come forward to write a patch for the vulnerability. In terms improving protection against the next attack, hiddenness works in opposite ways in the machine gun and open source examples.

B. Uniqueness of the Defense

How should we refer to the effect of the five variables? "First attack" has the advantage of being ordinary English and communicating the idea that a hidden trick may work against the first attack but fail against the 1,000th attack. Use of this term, however, makes it difficult to generalize the effect to "second attack" (hiddenness may still work very well), "twentieth attack" (hard to know how well hiddenness will work), and "nth attack" (the hidden features will quite possibly have been discovered).

This paper uses the word "uniqueness" to refer to the usefulness of hiddenness for the defense. Despite possible complaints from English teachers,[16] this

---

[16] One web page lists "errors" in English usage and says, "'Unique' singles out one of a kind. That 'un' at the beginning is a form of 'one.' A thing is unique (the only one of its kind) or it is not. Something may be almost unique (there are very few like it), but nothing is 'very unique.'" http://www.wsu.edu:8080/~brians/errors/unique.html.

paper discusses uniqueness as a function that varies from "unique" or "entirely unique" through "somewhat unique" to "not unique at all."[17] The function for uniqueness (U), or the usefulness of hiddenness for the defense, is as follows:

$$U = f(E, N, L, C, A)$$

"High uniqueness" refers to situations where hiddenness is effective because of a combination of high values for initial effectiveness (E) and ability to alter the defense (A) and low values for the number of attacks (N), learning from previous attacks (L), and communication among attackers (C). "Low uniqueness" refers to situations where the values are reversed.

C. Why Low Uniqueness May Be Typical of Computer and Network Security

Important areas of computer and network security include perimeter defenses such as firewalls; mass-market software, including video games; and encryption. In each of these areas, there is often a low degree of uniqueness, so secrecy is unlikely to be very effective.

1. **Firewalls.** A plausible case can be made that firewalls are subject to a large number of attacks (N), considerable learning by attackers (L), and effective communications among attackers (C). Using the Internet, attackers can probe a firewall from anywhere on the planet. They can attack again and again at low cost, trying various combinations of attacks until they find one that works. They can then tell other attackers about the vulnerability, such as by posting a script of the attack to a website or e-mail list. Even unskilled "script kiddies"[18] may then be able to use the attack to pierce that firewall or other firewalls using the same defenses.

Comparison with an attack on a walled city illuminates the way that computer and physical attacks are both similar and different. The similarities between a computer firewall and a medieval city wall are easy to see. A strong barrier is designed to allow friends to enter but keep foes out. Either sort of

---

[17] When I gave this paper at a conference at the Stanford Law School, Bruce Schneier and Matt Blaze both suggested the term "instance" to refer to what I am here calling "uniqueness." I have chosen the latter term for two main reasons. First, "instance" has so many uses in English that it may be confusing to readers for it to have a more technical definition. Second, my sense is that readers will intuitively understand the idea of different degrees of uniqueness.

[18] "Script kiddies" are unskilled programmers who merely follow a script rather than understanding how to write code themselves. See, for example, the definition of "script kiddies" in *The Jargon Dictionary*, http://info.astrian.net/jargon/terms/s/script_kiddies.html: "the lowest form of cracker; script kiddies do mischief with scripts and programs written by others, often without understanding the exploit."

defense can be set to various levels of security. In times of peace, a city gate may allow anyone to enter, with guards on hand to handle anyone suspicious. At a higher level of alert, guards might check the credentials of each person before he or she is allowed to enter the city. During a siege, the gates might be closed completely, barring all entry. Additional security might exist within the city wall. For instance, the armory (containing weapons), the mint (containing treasure), and the castle keep (containing the ruler) all would have additional protections against entry.

A company's firewall is similar. For nonessential systems, most messages will be allowed entry. For secure systems, a password or other credential is required. Under severe conditions, such as a distributed denial-of-service attack, all messages may be blocked from entering the company's system. Additional security will exist for priority functions, such as the system security (the armory), the corporate treasury (the mint), and the root directory (the ruler's residence).

Along with these similarities, it is logically possible for attacks against a physical wall to have high N, L, and C. For a long and badly defended wall, for instance, intruders might repeatedly probe for weak spots, learn about weak spots, and tell fellow attackers where to enter.[19]

Many attacks against a city wall, however, do not fit that pattern. In medieval warfare, an attack against a walled city was a major event in which many people might die. Any hidden trick by the defenders might cost attackers' lives or save defenders' lives before the attackers learned how to counter the trick. The number of attacks was low, attackers might not survive to tell about weak spots, and communication back to the attacking generals was rudimentary. Similarly, any hidden weaknesses might not be revealed in time to help the attack. In short, N, L, and C would all be low.

In sum, low N, L, and C values likely meant that medieval city walls had high uniqueness – secrecy was likely to be a useful tool. Firewalls using standard software likely have low uniqueness due to the high N, L, and C values.[20]

---

[19] An example of a physical barrier with high N, L, and C might be the border between the United States and Mexico. There are many persons who seek to cross the border, there are professionals who learn the soft spots in the defenses, and others who wish to cross the border learn from earlier successes.

[20] Despite the intuition that firewalls have low uniqueness, I have talked with some computer security experts who build higher uniqueness into their own firewalls. Even some experts who support the idea of "no security through obscurity" believe that putting some hidden tricks into a defensive system such as a firewall can be helpful. The hidden or subtle changes notably can stop attacks by script kiddies and others who are not able to modify their attacks in the face of a new defense.

2. Mass-Market Software and Computer Games. A second modern computer security issue is how to protect standardized software against hackers. Popular products may be on thousands or millions of desktops. Designers of standardized software might try to use hiddenness to stop the hackers. For instance, the designer might have a program freeze up permanently if a user hacked into inappropriate portions of the software. This kind of defense would be similar to falling into the pit covered with leaves – the attacker who goes into the wrong place never comes out again.

This hiddenness will often not work well, however, for mass-market software. Suppose, for instance, that there are a dozen paths for hacking a piece of code to do something forbidden, such as send a virus or make illegal copies. Suppose the designer puts traps on eleven of the twelve, to freeze up the program permanently if a hacker trespasses into the wrong part of the code. Suppose further that the designer leaves the twelfth path free so that he or she can get back in to rewrite the code.

This sort of defense would work reasonably well against a one-time attack. In the physical world, an attacker would face a grave risk (an 11 in 12 chance) of falling into the pit and getting injured. Similarly, in the computer world, a hacker who can get only one copy of the program and needs that program to keep functioning will find it too risky to fool around with the program and likely have it freeze into uselessness. By contrast, a hacker who can buy (or illegally copy) many copies of the program will not mind much if a few copies freeze up. This hacker can systematically try one possible attack after another until something works (N and L are both high). Meanwhile, other hackers around the world can also try their favorite attacks, and the hackers can communicate among themselves when they find a vulnerability (C is high.)

The combination of high N, L, and C also exists for computer and video games today when players try to "beat the game."[21] Beating the game is a (presumably) innocent version of hacking a software system – users ultimately reach their goal of gaining control over the software. An old-fashioned (although perhaps satisfying) way to beat the game is to keep trying by yourself until you overcome all the obstacles. As an alternative, video game players today can also enlist a global network of fellow aficionados. Websites appear almost instantly after release of a game. The sites offer "secrets" (press the third brick on the left to get a magic sword), "walk throughs" (on level 13 here are the seven things you have to do before you attack the dragon), and even "cheats" (if you enter this code, your player will become invulnerable to all attacks and as strong as Superman). Translated back into the language of

---

[21] This paragraph is based on insights from my sons Nathan and Jesse Swire, now 15 and 13.

computer security, there are a high number of attacks (N) – just ask the parents. Users learn from experience and communicate the knowledge gained (L and C are high). A hidden measure by the game designers will not stay hidden for long.

> In summary, where there are high N, L, and C values for attacks on mass-market software, there will tend to be low uniqueness and little "security through obscurity."

3. Encryption. Encryption is a third major area of modern computer security, along with system defense (firewalls) and defending software. The word "encryption" comes from the Greek word for "hidden," so it might seem exceedingly odd to say that being hidden does not work well for encryption.[22] Yet, as "encryption" is used in this chapter, that is precisely the claim. The question, for our purposes, is whether hiddenness paired with encryption that suffers from vulnerabilities will succeed or whether security can be provided only by strong encryption – that is, encryption that is successful even when the attacker knows the method used to encrypt the message.

Modern cryptographers are likely the most avid believers that there is no security through obscurity. Cryptographic authority Bruce Schneier (2002, 2003a) stated,

> A basic rule of cryptography is to use published, public, algorithms and protocols. This principle was first stated in 1883 by Auguste Kerckhoffs: in a well-designed cryptographic system, only the key needs to be secret; there should be no secrecy in the algorithm. Modern cryptographers have embraced this principle, calling anything else "security by obscurity." Any system that tries to keep its algorithms secret for security reasons is quickly dismissed by the community, and referred to as "snake oil" or even worse.[23]

The Schneier quotation, with its mention of "snake oil," highlights the risk that a vendor will dupe purchasers of an allegedly secure system. Once the system is exposed to attack, it may have only weak defenses, and all of the communications of the purchaser may be exposed to view. Having "published, public, algorithms and protocols" is thus an important consumer protection against the vendor who tries to hide the vulnerabilities of a weak system.

A second reason for the cryptographers' belief in openness is that a secret is unlikely to remain secret when known to a large number of people.

---

[22] For excellent historical introductions to encryption, see Kahn (1996) and Singh (1999).

[23] These writings are extremely insightful and the most detailed I have found on the issues that appear in this paper and in the draft version posted to the Internet in 2001.

Cryptography today is used by an enormous number of users on the Internet. In earlier times, by contrast, encryption was used by far fewer people, most prominently by diplomats and the military. Encryption became more widespread when people wished to send a lot of important messages through a channel where other people could see or hear the message. In times when the post was not secure, letter writers used encryption. In the days of the telegraph, many businesses used encryption to keep their commercial secrets away from the eyes of the telegraph operators. For radio communications, anyone with a receiver could hear the message. Most famously, German submarines in World War II used the Enigma system when radioing back to headquarters. Allied cryptographers learned to break the system after enormous effort, helping to win the war and more or less inventing the computer as a by-product.

The need for encryption is thus not new with the Internet. But the Internet has been accompanied by an enormous increase in the need for and use of encryption by ordinary people and businesses. The Internet is a famously "open" system (Winn 1998). A message from Alice to Bob is typically routed through many computers on its way through the Internet. A hacker might be in control of any of those computers. The hacker might make a copy of all the messages coming through the system and then comb through the messages looking for any that have commercial, diplomatic, or military value. Consequently, Alice and Bob need to encrypt their important messages, those containing credit card numbers, trade secrets, large transfers of currency, and anything else they do not want a hacker to read and copy.

The Internet does more than increase the number of messages that use encryption. The Internet has also accelerated the demand for public-key encryption approaches that permit anyone to send an encrypted message to anyone else. The basic idea of a public-key system is that a user, Alice, can send a message to a recipient, Bob, whom she has never met before.[24] She uses Bob's public key to encrypt her message. Bob can then decrypt it using his private key. The public key can be posted on the Internet or otherwise revealed to the world. The private key is kept secret by Bob and not made known to attackers. The combination of many messages sent through insecure channels (the Internet) and many users who wish to communicate securely with each other (as in e-commerce) has meant that an unprecedented number of individuals rely on cryptosystems.[25]

---

[24] For further discussion, see, for example, Schneier (1996).

[25] Modern encryption draws a distinction between the "cryptosystem" and the "key." The cryptosystem is a mathematical technique that has a standard way of rearranging symbols ("put every second letter in front of the letter before it") and substituting one symbol for another ("change each letter A to the number 1"). The most widely used modern cryptosystems publish the algorithm for converting between plaintext (readable English)

Given the nature of today's networked encryption, we can better understand why modern cryptographers believe there is no security through obscurity. Because so many communications flow through the Internet and can be read by hackers, the number of attacks (N) is extremely high. If L and C are even slightly positive, then attackers will learn about the vulnerabilities in a method for encrypting messages and communicate about those vulnerabilities to others. The response by cryptographers is to use methods for encryption that do not rely on secrecy. Instead, cryptographers increase the length of the secret key to try to make brute force attacks prohibitively costly.

The combined effects of N, L, and C mean that the cost of disclosure of the cryptosystem – the help-the-attackers effect – is low. The benefit of disclosure to defenders is also likely to be high. For one thing, use of a public-key algorithm means that myriad users can easily send encrypted messages to each other. In addition, there is likely a high value for A, the ability of defenders to improve the defensive system. The rise of the Internet and the spread of public-key encryption means that the number of encryption experts has grown rapidly in recent years. The likelihood of improved defenses is thus substantial: "The long history of cryptography and cryptanalysis has shown time and time again that open discussion and analysis of algorithms exposes weaknesses not thought of by the original authors, and thereby leads to better and more secure algorithms" (Bush and Bellovin 2002).

Before leaving the topic of encryption, it might be useful to see how this conclusion – that an open cryptosystem has advantages – would have been less true in Roman or Medieval times. In those periods there likely would have been

---

and ciphertext (the message as transmitted in its encrypted form). A well-known example is the RSA algorithm developed in 1978 by mathematicians Ronald Rivest, Avi Shamir, and Leonard Adleman. The security of the RSA cryptosystem depends on a mathematical algorithm that is easy to calculate in one direction (when one encrypts the message) but extremely difficult to calculate in the other direction (when an unauthorized person tries to decrypt the message.) For the mathematical basis of the RSA algorithm, see "What is the RSA Cryptosystem?" http://www.rsasecurity.com/rsalabs/node.asp?id=2214.

The security of the RSA cryptosystem also depends on each user having a secret key to turn ciphertext back into plaintext. The idea of a key is simple enough. Suppose that the cryptosystem turns each letter into a number, such as A = 1, B = 2, C = 3, and so on. There are 26 possible starting points, such as A = 25, B = 26, C = 1, and so on. In this simplified example, the cryptosystem is a regular pattern for turning letters into numbers. The key indicates how to begin the calculation by indicating which number corresponds to the letter A. In actual cryptosystems, the key is a long chain of randomized numbers. Attackers who do not have the key then need to try every possible combination of numbers until a key fits the lock (decrypts this plaintext). Trying each of the combinations, which can easily number in the billions, trillions, and up, is called a "brute force attack." An attacker who can try every single possible key will eventually be able to read the code. The response by those who build cryptosystems is to try to make the number of combinations so large that no available computer can try all the combinations.

lower values for N, L, C, and A. The number of encrypted messages subject to interception would have been far lower than on the Internet. The sophistication of those intercepting the messages would have been lower. Slow communications would have meant that other attackers would have learned very slowly, if they learned anything at all, from the breakthrough by one attacker. In addition, the chances of "outside cryptographic experts" improving the system would have been low. All of these variables would therefore have pointed toward the usefulness of a hidden cryptosystem, in contrast to conditions today.[26]

In summary, secrecy in modern cryptosystems is unlikely to be useful due to high N, L, C, and A values. Modern encryption relies, however, on strict secrecy for private keys.

III. RELAXING THE OPEN SOURCE ASSUMPTIONS: COMPUTER AND NETWORK SECURITY IN THE REAL WORLD

Section II sought to explain why computer security experts so often believe there is no security through obscurity. Firewalls, mass-market software, and encryption are major areas of computer and network security. In each, there are typically high values for number of attacks (N), learning by attackers (L), and communication among attackers (C). Secrecy is of relatively little use in settings with high N, L, and C values – attackers will soon learn about the hidden tricks. By contrast, many physical-world security settings have lower values for N, L, and C. In these settings of persistent and higher uniqueness, secrecy is of greater value to the defense.

Section II thus solidified the assumptions of the open source paradigm, that (1) disclosure will offer little or no help to attackers, (2) disclosure will tend to upgrade the design of defenses, and (3) disclosure will spread effective defenses to third parties. High N, L, and C values strengthen the first assumption, because attackers will quickly learn about secrets. Alterations (A) from outside

---

[26] In comments on an earlier draft, cryptographer Susan Landau disagreed with the discussion of the role of hiddenness in earlier times. She mentioned a fourteenth-century Arabic encyclopedia, the Subh al-a 'sha, that contained sophisticated mathematical techniques for breaking ciphers. My response is that secrecy is more likely to have net benefits in situations with lower N, L, C, and A. Where attackers such as users of that encyclopedia have sophisticated techniques, they will have higher L, reducing the effectiveness of secrecy. My claim is that in earlier periods attacks generally had far lower N, L, and C than would attacks today on a widely used cryptosystem on the Internet. Modern attackers will thus be more efficient at overcoming hidden defenses (because of today's higher learning) and modern defenders will be more likely to get suggestions for useful alterations (because of today's larger group of potentially helpful cryptographic experts). There will thus be higher expected benefits today of disclosure of the cryptosystem.

experts, in cryptosystems and elsewhere, fit with the second assumption. Finally, under the third assumption, high A and C values mean that other defenders will be alerted to vulnerabilities.

Section III tests these assumptions against the real world. In practice, secrecy will often be of greater use than suggested by the assumptions of the open source paradigm.

A. The Assumption That Disclosure Will Not Help the Attackers

The first assumption of the open source paradigm is that disclosure will provide little or no help to the attackers. The assumption is based on the notion that there are many capable persons who are willing and able to launch attacks against firewalls, mass-market software, and cryptosystems.

To scrutinize this assumption, it is important first to develop the intuition that the public domain of information is expanding in a world of search engines such as Google. The next step is to establish that disclosure can sometimes help defenders by detering attacks. The third step is to show that the case for disclosure of private keys, such as cryptographic keys, is especially weak. The fourth step is to show that the area of surveillance is subject to a different analysis. The investigation of this assumption ends with a more specific discussion of the extent to which attackers already know about how to launch effective attacks against firewalls, mass-market software, and cryptosystems.

1. The Enlargement of the Public Domain in a World of Search Engines. Do attackers know specific facts about defenders? The answer today, in a world of the Internet and search engines, is that the cost of doing searches has gone way down. Many facts that were impossible or costly to find in the past are easy to find today.

All readers of this paper know this to some extent, but it is helpful to flesh out some of the reasons that so much more information is currently in the public domain. The Internet itself has only recently expanded beyond the domain of DARPA[27] and the academic community. Indeed, it was not until 1992 that the terms of service for the Internet changed to permit commercial activity on the Internet.[28] The growth in commercial activity coincided with the incredible

---

[27] DARPA is the Defense Advanced Research Projects Agency, which played a key role in fostering the early stages of the Internet (Hauben 2004).

[28] The Scientific and Advanced Technology Act of 1992, signed into law on October 23, 1992, "subtly modified [the National Science Foundation's] authority to support computer networks that are not limited to research and education" (National Science Foundation 1993). This change was one important legal step toward development of commercial activity over what is now called the Internet.

expansion of Internet use, so that ordinary people all over the world could find information, at no cost, about a huge range of topics. Search engines have made it trivially easy to search through the many websites to find specific information. Google was launched in 1998 and indexed 30 million items at that time. Today, it indexes over 6 billion items (Weisman 2004).

The ubiquity of search engines (and the other research tools of the Information Age) increases the amount and range of information available to attackers. Further, attackers can correlate information from diverse sources to infer facts that are themselves not explicitly made public. Attackers can communicate with other attackers through blogs,[29] websites, and global, free e-mail. Search engines are extremely useful. For instance, an attacker can pick the mass-market software or firewall he or she wishes to attack and search on Google for the name of the product and "bugs" or "vulnerabilities." The search may reveal a known bug and a patch that has been announced for that bug. In launching an actual attack, the attacker is likely to discover that a large portion of the product's users have not installed the patch.

The increase of information in the public domain increases the set of instances where the open source paradigm is a better approximation than the military paradigm. More often than before, disclosure of a security flaw will add little or nothing to attackers' knowledge. It will be harder to keep many things secret, because attackers will be able to infer the truth from other available information. At the very least, the ubiquity of search engines increases the costs of trying to keep information out of the hands of attackers.[30]

In summary, the growth of the Internet and of search engines means that the optimal solution often shifts toward openness. In many instances, the help-the-attacker effect is likely to be low, while the costs to defenders of trying to keep secrets will have risen.

---

[29] For an early discussion of the legal implications of weblogs, or "blogs," see Malik (2003).

[30] There is a growing literature that laments the shrinking of the public domain (Boyle 2003; Lessig 2002). This literature emphasizes, for instance, the ways in which copyright and other intellectual property rules have expanded. Even though copyright law itself does not apply to facts, some actual and proposed legal developments could reduce the set of facts available to the public. For instance, the anticircumvention provisions of the Digital Millennium Copyright Act, 42 U.S.C. § 1201, can make it illegal to access facts that are in a format protected by anticircumvention measures. In addition, there have been repeated legislative attempts in the United States to enact *sui generis* database protection, which would create new limits on the ability of users to reproduce facts in certain databases (Band 2003).

   Notwithstanding these concerns, the argument here is that the development of the Internet and of search engines has made available an increased range of factual information at lower cost than previously. Especially in the wake of the attacks of September 11, the U.S. government has instituted some measures to reduce the information available to the public (Lee 2003). Despite these changes, vastly more security information is available today to a teenage hacker or a foreign terrorist than before the rise of the Internet.

2. Deterrence as a Result of Disclosure. Up until this point, the focus has been on how disclosure may reveal vulnerabilities and thus help the attackers. More generally, the analysis should include the full range of ways that attackers might respond to disclosure about the defense. One principal way that disclosure can help the defense is through deterrence – the tendency of disclosure to *reduce* the likelihood of attack.

The distinction between a "strong" defense and a "weak" defense is likely the main axis for when disclosure will lead to deterrence. Attackers who perceive a defense as strong will be less likely to attack. Attackers who perceive a defense as weak will be more likely to believe that they can overcome the defense. The deterrent effect of perceived strength does not always prevail – a "strong" defense, for instance, might be a clue to an attacker that something valuable is contained inside.[31] Nonetheless, the appearance of strength is generally a good predictor of the magnitude of deterrence.[32]

Deterrence can exist because the defense is strong in an absolute sense. In such circumstances, the defender will perceive that the costs of the attack are greater than the benefits. An example in the physical world is a high fence topped with razor wire and spotted with surveillance cameras in clear sight. A potential trespasser who sees this defense may estimate that it will be difficult to climb the fence, dangerous to get over the razor wire, and risky in terms of being detected and caught.

Deterrence can also exist in a relative sense. There is the old story about the two hikers in the woods who see a dangerous bear rushing toward them. One of the hikers turns around and starts running. The other hiker asks why he is running when everyone knows that bears can run faster than people. The first hiker responds, "I don't have to run faster than the bear. I just have to run faster than you." In terms of deterrence, a house with bars on the windows and large locks on the front door may simply be more trouble to attack than a neighboring house that lacks these features. The visible defense measures, in such circumstances, may shift the risk of attack to the neighboring house.

An essential element of successful deterrence is the attackers' knowledge of the strong defense. This element was memorably missing in the movie

---

[31] As another example where deterrence would not succeed, some attackers might be attracted to a strongly defended target simply because it is strongly defended. Just as medieval knights sought glory by attacking famous champions, modern-day hackers sometimes seek "hacker glory" by attacking systems that are thought to be highly secure.

[32] The strong/weak distinction was first suggested to me by Jim Steinberg, who served as deputy national security advisor under President Clinton. The fact that the suggestion came from a person steeped in national security issues suggests that military and national security experts may take the deterrence effect into account when determining whether disclosure will help security.

"Dr. Strangelove," where the Soviet Union had failed to tell the rest of the world about the existence of a doomsday device that would be triggered by any nuclear attack. When one nuclear bomb was accidentally used, the entire world was destroyed. The complete failure of communication in that instance drives home the point – it is the perception of the defense by the attackers that is the key to deterrence.

> In summary, the effects of disclosure on security include the deterrent effect (a help-the-defense effect) as well as the help-the-attackers effect discussed previously. The chief predictor of deterrence is the extent to which attackers perceive the defense as strong.

3. **Do Not Disclose Private Keys, Passwords, or Combinations to a Safe.** The earlier discussion of encryption drew a sharp distinction between the cryptosystem and the private key. Modern cryptographers generally support "no security through obscurity" and favor disclosure of the cryptosystem. They also support secrecy for the private key or password. Modern cryptographic systems feature a high initial effectiveness for the cryptosystem (E). They also are resistant to a high number of attacks (N). The private keys are long enough to require brute force attacks that are too lengthy for attackers to undertake.

A similar analysis applies to physical protections such as a combination safe. The initial effectiveness (E) is high because attackers cannot easily get through the metal skin of the safe. The combination needed to open the safe is then complicated enough to make a brute force attack difficult (and is thus resistant against a high N). A complex combination can be very effective – bank robbers typically do not wish to stay in the bank vault long enough to try every possible combination to open the safe.

For passwords, the main objective is to make it difficult for attackers to guess them. Programs to guess passwords are easily available on the Internet.[33] Consequently, a good practice is to require each password to include symbols and numbers in addition to letters. This practice increases the initial effectiveness (E) by forcing users not to use the defaults that come with software or common terms such as "password." Use of different characters in the password increases the number of attacks (N) needed to guess the password. In addition, altering the password periodically (A) reduces the likelihood that attackers can continue to take advantage of one successful attack.

For all three defenses – the private key, the safe combination, and the password – there is a large help-the-attacker effect from disclosure of the secret

---

[33] For the person interested in testing this, simply use a search engine with terms such as "password hacker."

information. All three defenses are designed to frustrate a brute force attack by having too many possible combinations. If there is disclosure of the secret key, then the entire defensive strategy falls apart.

Is there a help-the-defender effect from disclosure? Almost always the answer is no. In these examples, the defenders are relying on fundamentally sound defenses, such as a strong cryptosystem or a heavy metal safe. These defenses will not be designed better just because the user's key or the safe combination is revealed.

> In summary, there is a large help-the-attacker effect from disclosure of a private key, safe combination, or password. There is usually no help-the-defender effect. Even supporters of "no security through obscurity" accept that this sort of information should stay secret.[34]

4. Why Secret Surveillance May Improve Security. The next question is whether revealing the surveillance techniques used by defenders improves security. Under the open source paradigm, one might believe that disclosure will help the defenders because outside experts will suggest how to improve the surveillance system. In addition, the open source paradigm suggests that attackers already know or will readily learn about the defenses of a system and that disclosure thus will not help the attackers. The intuitions of intelligence experts are precisely the opposite. These experts believe that it is imperative to keep secret the sources and methods used for intelligence gathering.

The model for uniqueness shows why keeping surveillance secret is usually better for achieving security. The key factual point is that attackers usually learn little or nothing about surveillance (low L) from their attacks. As the level of L approaches zero, attackers do not learn about vulnerabilities even after a high number of attacks. Where L is so low, the effectiveness of hidden surveillance persists.

To see the difference between surveillance and most physical security measures, consider once more the example of the machine guns or the hidden pit covered by leaves. In each case, the attackers learn a lot from an attack (L is high) – they learn about the location of the machine guns or of the existence of the hidden pit. By contrast, suppose that there are well-hidden observers or

---

[34] One can imagine situations where disclosure of the private key may be justified. For example, suppose the defender does not deserve to win because he or she is a criminal. Or suppose the defender will not change a compromised password or private key even after being told about the vulnerability. Telling the defender that the entire world will learn the password might be the drastic step needed to prompt the change. These examples, however, do not take away from the general point – it almost always helps the attackers more than the defenders to disclose the private key.

surveillance cameras that watch the attack. Even an attack that succeeds quite possibly would not lead to the capture of the observers or uncover the hidden cameras.

The same pattern exists for wiretaps or bugs on networked systems such as telephones or the Internet. A person using a tapped telephone is not supposed to be able to tell if the line is tapped. Even a hacker who gets past a firewall may trigger alarms that he or she cannot perceive. Once again, surveillance defenses are associated with a low L.

Those involved in surveillance have long understood the importance of preventing the opposition from knowing the nature of their surveillance. For instance, Neal Stephenson (2002) organizes his masterful novel *Cryptonomicon* around precisely this theme. The novel retells the story of the Allies' decryption of the German Enigma encryption system during World War II. The strategic question for the Allies is how much to act on the secret messages they have decoded. For instance, if a convoy is crossing the Atlantic and the U-boats are poised to attack, should the convoy shift course? If the convoy does, then the Germans might deduce that the Enigma system had been broken, undermining the Allies' long-term ability to win the war. If it does not, then many people and boats will be lost. The novel describes elaborate efforts by the Allies to create cover stories for how they got useful intelligence. They seek to reduce the learning (L) by the attackers who are subject to surveillance.

The importance of retaining a hidden surveillance capability was also crucial to the entry of the United States into World War I.[35] At a time when Germany and the United States were officially neutral, the Germans sent the famous "Zimmerman telegram" to the government of Mexico. The telegram offered enticements to Mexico to persuade it to ally with Germany against the United States, including a promise to return to Mexico territories that it held prior to the 1848 war. British intelligence decrypted the communication, but the intelligence agency was extremely loath to reveal to anyone else that it had the capability of breaking German codes. British intelligence then went through an elaborate (and successful) effort to make the leak appear to come from within the Mexican government. The Zimmerman telegram became public, speeding the entry of the United States into the war while allowing the British to continue conducting hidden surveillance of German communications.

These examples highlight the reasons that intelligence experts believe that sources and methods of surveillance should remain secret. They believe that disclosure of sources and methods will increase L and thus significantly help

---

[35] The account here follows Singh (1999).

attackers. Even in many computer security settings, there is often a low L, and surveillance measures can stay hidden. If these factual assertions are correct, as I believe they are, then disclosure of surveillance sources and methods will typically have a large help-the-attacker effect. Persons subject to wiretaps will stop talking on the phone, persons who know that some radio frequencies are being monitored will shift to other frequencies, and so on.

It is vital to underscore the nature of the claim here. The claim is that secrecy regarding surveillance sources and methods will often improve security. Hidden surveillance will improve the ability of defenders to protect their systems from the attackers. The claim is not, however, that hidden surveillance is therefore desirable (or lawful) in any particular setting. The assessment of overall desirability involves judgments about multiple and often conflicting goals. The employment of wiretaps and other means of surveillance, for instance, intrudes on personal privacy. Fear of surveillance may chill desirable uses of communications networks, with negative effects on the economy and free speech. Public disclosure and debate about surveillance techniques are also crucial to holding government accountable. My article "The System of Foreign Intelligence Surveillance Law" examines these issues of security, privacy, and accountability in great detail (Swire 2004b). The claim here is about the effectiveness of keeping surveillance hidden. Disclosure about sources and methods will rarely make surveillance more effective at stopping attacks.

In summary, hidden surveillance techniques mean that there is a low level of learning (L) from attacks. Disclosure of the sources and methods of hidden surveillance is likely to reduce security, at least in the short term. Any overall judgment about the desirability of surveillance depends, in addition, on important other values such as the protection of privacy and the accountability of those conducting the surveillance.

5. **When Do Attackers Already Know of the Vulnerability?** We now can return to the first assumption of the open source paradigm: that attackers will learn little or nothing from disclosure. The discussion here has identified one setting in which attackers learn from disclosure but in ways that benefit the defenders – attackers will sometimes be deterred when they learn about the defense. The discussion has also identified two important categories where the assumption seems incorrect. First, private keys and the safe combinations should stay secret, because the defense is based on the strategy of hiding that information from attackers. Second, surveillance measures will often not be observable by attackers, so in many case an assumption that attackers already know about such measures will be wrong.

a. Discovering and Exploiting Vulnerabilities. The main debate regarding software and network security, however, concerns scenarios that do not primarily involve deterrence, private keys, or hidden surveillance. These scenarios involve the following question – do hackers already know about, or will they promptly know about, the vulnerabilities in a firewall, a mass-market software program, or a cryptosystem?

In answering this question, an important variable to consider is the difficulty outsiders would have in discovering a vulnerability. If it is generally easy to spot a vulnerability and exploit it, then the open source assumption will be correct – additional disclosure will not help the attackers much. Based on my discussions with computer security experts, however, there are at least three reasons to believe that spotting a new vulnerability in a mass-market software program is often quite difficult. First, modern software programs often are incredibly complex, involving millions of lines of code (Fisher 2002). Spotting any individual vulnerability requires considerable searching. There is thus often a lower number of attacks (N) on any piece of code than might otherwise be assumed. Second, the greater emphasis on computer security in recent years possibly has reduced the number of bugs per line of code. Third, my discussions with professional "bug hunters" suggest that finding a single vulnerability often takes considerable work by a highly skilled person. In the case of a cryptosystem rather than a mass-market software program, the task is even harder – it will take a skilled person a considerable amount of work to find a vulnerability (if there is one).

If a vulnerability is discovered, the next question is how difficult is it to write the exploit code to take advantage of the vulnerability. If it is hard to write the exploit code, then discovery of the vulnerability will not lead to rapid attacks on the vulnerability. Writing such code, however, may actually be easier for experts to do than might be suspected. My interviews with computer security experts indicate that for large software programs an announcement at a high level of generality about a flaw often quickly translates into exploit code. The progression from description of the vulnerability to successful attack happens rapidly because of quick learning about what attacks work (high L) and extensive communication with other potential attackers (high C). Even a fairly general description of a vulnerability can focus skilled attackers on a subset of the millions of lines of code, speeding discovery of the exploit code.

Experts' ability to exploit a vulnerability rapidly may or may not translate into nonexperts' ability to do the same. At issue are attacks by "script kiddies," the often young hackers who find a step-by-step script on the Internet for performing an attack. Script kiddies can effectively attack a system that is configured in a standard way and has not installed a patch for a known vulnerability. On the other hand, defenders can often defeat script kiddies by altering the system in some way. In terms of the model developed in this chapter, uniqueness (U) aids the defense. Having a unique and hidden defense quite possibly will defeat attackers who are simply following a script.

b. The Analogy between Exploiting Vulnerabilities and the Efficient Capital Markets Hypothesis. There is a useful analogy between exploiting software vulnerabilities and the efficient capital market hypothesis (ECMH) in economics.[36] Efficiency as defined in the ECMH means that the current price of a stock or other security accurately includes all the relevant information. Efficiency as defined in the open source paradigm also means that all the relevant information is already known to outsiders – disclosure of a vulnerability does not help the attackers.

The claim here is that the open source paradigm has implicitly assumed what is called the "strong" form of the ECMH, that "current security prices fully reflect all currently existing information, whether publicly available or not" (Cunningham 1994, 560). The efficiency of capital markets, in this theory, depends on the actions of a large number of traders who follow the market extremely closely and exploit any opportunity to make a profit. The traders who analyze new information more quickly and accurately than other traders can gain a temporary advantage. The combined effect of all these traders' actions is to push the market very quickly to the point where the price reflects all available information.[37]

The open source paradigm makes assumptions similar to those of the ECMH – attackers learn little or nothing from disclosure because they have already efficiently figured out the vulnerabilities. It is possible to identify some important differences, however. First, the number of traders in the capital markets is very high, with numerous experts and traders for even the lesser-known stocks. By contrast, there is not necessarily a supply of expert hackers for each aspect of a large computer program or for each lesser-known computer

---

[36] Credit for the ECMH is often given to Eugene Fama (1965). For a detailed explanation of the ECMH in historical perspective, together with critiques of it, see Cunningham (1994).

[37] The strong version of the ECMH assumes that the market price of the security reflects publicly available information as well as information known only to the company itself. Under the semistrong view, insiders might know additional information that would shift the price of the security if publicly revealed. This "insider information" can thus be valuable to insiders because they can predict the price better than public traders. Section 10(b) of the Securities Act of 1934 prohibits insider trading [15 U.S.C. § 78j(b)].

The semistrong view of the open source paradigm, by analogy, holds that insiders might know of vulnerabilities that are unknown to the outside attackers. The efficiency of the market would be determined by how well the outsiders could detect and exploit the vulnerabilities that do not depend on having such insider information.

program. Second, the structure of the incentives to create "efficiency" is quite different. In the stock market, it is lawful trading that pushes the stock market to efficiency. The successful analyst buys stock and makes money immediately and in large quantities. By contrast, there is seldom a big cash reward for discovering a vulnerability (although the "bug finder" may develop a good reputation and gain consulting contracts). Exploiting the vulnerability also has different incentives – there are criminal penalties for attacking computers, so the incentive to use the knowledge is presumably lower than for lawful stock trading.

These differences would predict that the market for finding computer vulnerabilities is less efficient than the market for finding wrongly priced securities. The likely inefficiency in finding vulnerabilities undermines the open source assumption that attackers already know about vulnerabilities or will promptly discover them. The likely inefficiency is even greater, moreover, if the criticisms made against the ECMH in recent years are correct. There has been a significant and growing literature showing ways in which capital markets are not as efficient as the ECMH's proponents had previously thought (Allen 2003; Stout 2003).

Additional research might fruitfully further develop the analogy between the ECMH and the efficiency of finding vulnerabilities in computer systems. For instance, researchers might explore each of the criticisms of the ECMH in order to examine the possible sources of inefficiency in the exploitation of vulnerabilities. By analyzing the possible sources of inefficiency, computer security researchers can identify areas where vulnerabilities are less likely to be known to attackers and where disclosure is thus more likely to provide substantial assistance to attackers.

On the other hand, there are scenarios where attackers have very strong incentives to discover vulnerabilities. In future military conflicts, for instance, attackers will be highly motivated to discover any vulnerability in the computer or network systems used by their enemy. Where there are determined and well-financed adversaries, the attackers may be very effective in discovering vulnerabilities. One can therefore imagine the following counterintuitive situation. Civilian attackers may be inefficient, so disclosure has a large help-the-attacker effect. Military attackers, by contrast, may be efficient in exploiting vulnerabilities that can be perceived from the outside. For those vulnerabilities, greater disclosure might actually be rational. The disclosure will do little or nothing to help the attackers, but there may be help-the-defender effects for system designers or for other defenders who rely on the system.

In summary, there is likely greater inefficiency today in the discovery of computer and network vulnerabilities than assumed in the open source paradigm. The analogy to the efficient capital markets hypothesis shows that the degree of efficiency depends on the incentives and institutional arrangements that attackers have to discover and communicate about vulnerabilities.

B. The Assumption That Disclosure Will Tend to Improve the Design of Defenses

The next assumption is the one most strongly held by open source proponents – disclosure of code and vulnerabilities will improve security because it will result in improved design of defenses. As firewall experts Chapman and Zwicky (1995) have written,

> Some people feel uncomfortable using software that's freely available on the Internet, particularly for security-critical applications. We feel that the advantages outweigh the disadvantages. You may not have the "guarantees" offered by vendors, but you have the ability to inspect the source code and to share information with the large community that helps to maintain the software. In practice, vendors come and go, but the community endures (p. 23).

In this paper, I do not take a position on the almost theological issue of whether Open Source software provides better security than proprietary software.[38] Instead, I seek to identify some of the variables that would tilt the outcome in one direction or the other. The previous discussion showed how mass-market software and firewalls are subject to more efficient attacks due to the high number of attacks (N), learning from attacks (L), and communication among attackers (C). The focus here is on how defenders can alter the defense (A) in ways that improve it over time. After looking at variables that affect when open source or proprietary software may provide better security, the discussion turns to how openness has particular value in promoting security and accountability in the long run.

1. Variables That Affect When Open Source or Proprietary Software May Provide Better Security. Consistent with the goals of this paper, the objective here is to identify situations where openness is more or less likely to improve security. In this discussion, it is helpful to distinguish between two meanings of "open." As used in this paper, "open" means "not hidden." In particular,

---

[38] In the interests of full disclosure, I note that I am a member of Microsoft's Trustworthy Computing Academic Advisory Committee, which is a group of nineteen academics who have been asked to provide advice on security and privacy issues to Microsoft. I have also discussed the issues in this chapter at great length with many open source advocates. The views expressed herein are entirely my own.

outsiders can generally see the source code for open source software but not the source code for proprietary software. This paper does not address the extent to which software should be "open" in the sense of "not owned" under copyright or other laws.

a. Expertise of Inside and Outside Programmers. The security of proprietary software relies substantially on the expertise of "inside" programmers. These individuals are employees or contractors of the company that owns the mass-market software or the organization that operates the firewall.[39] By contrast, the open source paradigm relies on "outside" programmers – individuals who usually are not employed by or under contract to whomever initially designed the software.

The effectiveness of either the open source or the proprietary approaches will depend on the relative quantity and expertise of inside and outside programmers. Chapman and Zwicky (1995) emphasized the advantage of outside programmers when they referred to "the large community that maintains the software" (p. 23). In other settings, an organization might be able to bring more and better programmers (i.e., programmers with the relevant expertise) to the inside. For example, consider the software for specialized military uses such as the launching of rockets. For such software, there may not be a "large [outside] community that maintains the software" (Chapman and Zwicky 1995, p. 23). The more effective approach, in the absence of an outside community, quite likely would be to rely on inside programmers – persons who are hired or trained by the military. In such instances, disclosure of the software does not enlist a community of outside programmers, although it may help the attackers find vulnerabilities.

b. The Incentives to Improve the Defense. One of the chief arguments of supporters of the proprietary approach is that the owner of the software or the system has strong incentives to provide security. The reputation of the software manufacturer or system owner is on the line, and bad security can lead to a direct loss of revenue. In the open source model, the incentives are less clearly defined. The outside programmers might gain a good reputation by designing a patch. A good reputation might translate into consulting contracts or other remunerative work, although the time spent working on a patch seems less directly profitable for the open source programmer than it is for a company that increases sales due to better security. Open source programmers may also

---

[39] Proprietary organizations may also get tips about problems and solutions from users of the software and other outsiders, but the emphasis is likely to be on inside programmers.

improve software from a combination of other motives, including membership in a community of programmers and the feeling of satisfaction from helping solve problems facing others.

The extent to which one approach – proprietary or open source – will provide greater incentives to improve the defense is essentially a question of sociology and organizational behavior. Over time the sociological context might shift. A vibrant open source community in one period might descend into a "what's in it for me?" approach in a later period. Alternatively, a vibrant open source community might become broader and deeper in its skills over time compared with the inside programmers engaged in proprietary efforts.

c. Persistence of the Expertise. Chapman and Zwicky (1995) point out the risk that any single company can disappear: "In practice, vendors come and go, but the community endures" (p. 143). Users of a proprietary product thus risk the chance that the company will go bankrupt or otherwise stop supporting the product. On the other hand, there are scenarios where the proprietary approach would likely lead to greater persistence of expertise. The owner of a software program or a firewall might invest in having specialized expertise.[40] For instance, the owner of a software program might find it worthwhile to keep on staff a person who is expert in one complex piece of a software program. Similarly, the military might decide to keep on staff persons who are experts in software that only the military uses. In these instances, the proprietary model may well lead to greater persistence of expertise than an open source approach.

d. The Institutional Context for Patching. The usual open source belief has been that patching – the release of improved code that addresses a vulnerability – works better if the open source community can probe for vulnerabilities and then fix them. The accompanying belief has been that many proprietary companies have been reluctant to admit to vulnerabilities or to invest the resources to issue good patches.

My interviews with computer security experts suggest that these conclusions have possibly become less true over time. First, proprietary companies have shifted to a norm of issuing patches as part of the overall effort to improve cybersecurity. Second, proprietary companies have in some instances created substantial institutional structures to create and disseminate patches. These institutional structures can respond to vulnerabilities in a coordinated way. A

---

[40] The economist Oliver Williamson (1998) calls this sort of investment "transaction specific capital" and considers it an important predictor of where firms make investments.

coordinated approach, if carried out effectively, may lead to faster and more consistent responses to problems across different platforms.

The point here is not to announce that one approach or the other is necessarily the winner when it comes to effective patching. To do so would be to neglect the fact that the speed and quality of patching are likely to vary over time depending on the institutions that create and disseminate patches.

e. Interoperability and Openness. Having open source code can facilitate interoperability. System owners will have the ability to see what they are including in their system and how to integrate it with existing programs. For this reason, greater disclosure can improve security to the extent it permits system owners to know their systems and avoid vulnerabilities.

On the proprietary side, there is the usual market incentive to provide effective solutions for clients. Software companies want their products to work well for a large range of users. They often design their products to interoperate with other products, and they work with system integrators to create overall systems that work.[41] As with other factors discussed in this section, the extent to which the possible advantages of openness outweigh the possible advantages of vendors directly seeking to satisfy the market by increasing sales is an empirical question.

2. The Role of Disclosure in Creating Long-Run Security and Ensuring Accountability. Much of this paper's comparison of the Open Source and proprietary approaches has implicitly concerned short- and medium-term security (e.g., which approach would typically create a better patch for a newly discovered vulnerability). An additional issue regarding disclosure of information is the improvement of *long-run* security. Bruce Schneier (2003b), for instance, writes that "public scrutiny is the only reliable way to improve security – be it of the nation's roads, bridges and ports or of our critically important computer networks" (p. D5). The belief is that organizations that rely on secrets are unlikely in the long run to update their security effectively. On this view, testing by outsiders is crucial to overcoming inertia within each organization. Even if secrecy masks vulnerabilities in the short run, the secretive organization is laying the groundwork for a larger-scale problem in the long run.

It is difficult to provide empirical tests for when secrecy leads to long-run failure to adapt and modernize. One can try to compensate for secrecy by creating institutions that inspect and challenge the status quo without disclosing

---

[41] For a discussion of the incentives for software and other manufacturers to promote interoperability, see Farrell and Weiser (2003).

secrets to the world. Organizations can hire "Tiger Teams"[42] and other sorts of outside experts to probe for weaknesses. Organizations can hire independent auditors and create oversight boards to watch for areas of weakness. The usefulness of these institutional responses will vary widely, but they are unlikely to be effective unless they can probe into possible areas of vulnerability and then have institutional support when they recommend changes.

Over the long run, the usefulness of openness for promoting security overlaps with the usefulness of openness for ensuring accountability more generally. The Freedom of Information Act[43] and other openness mechanisms are useful in part because they allow vulnerabilities to be discovered and security to be improved. These mechanisms are also useful, however, for exposing corruption, abuse of power, and the other evils that can flourish in secret. One purpose of my continuing research is to shed light on situations where openness is most important to accountability and long-run improvements in security. In this chapter, however, my goal is more modest. Once an analysis has been done on the extent to which disclosure helps security, there is reason to place a thumb (and perhaps an entire palm) on the scale on the side of disclosure. That tilt is due to the recognition that secrecy decreases security and accountability in the long run. The longer that information is designed to stay secret, the greater the risk to system security and general accountability.

> This paper does not take a position on the contentious issue of which approach – open source or proprietary – provides better overall security. Significant variables include the relevant expertise of inside and outside programmers, the incentives to improve the defense, the persistence of relevant expertise, the institutional context for patching, and the means of ensuring interoperability. Disclosure is often additionally useful for promoting long-run security and ensuring accountability.

C. The Assumption That Disclosure Will Spread Effective Defenses to Others

The third assumption of the open source paradigm is that disclosure will spread effective defenses to third parties. The corresponding assumption of the military paradigm is that disclosure will prompt little or no improvement in defense by other defenders. The discussion here seeks to explain when each assumption is more likely to be true and thus when disclosure is likely to help other defenders.

---

[42] Lee et al. (1999) define a "Tiger team" as computer security experts who are hired by the owner of a computer system to simulate hostile break-ins.

[43] 5 U.S.C. § 552.

The military assumption is more convincing in settings where mechanisms exist to restrict disclosure to trusted defenders. In the military setting, there are strongly authenticated fellow defenders, such as the others that share the same uniform. When changes should be made in the defenses, the military has a hierarchical command structure. Orders can be given to the appropriate units to implement the change in defense. In settings characterized by strong authentication and an established hierarchy, disclosure to the entire world has low or zero benefits (it does not generally help other defenders improve their defenses) and potentially significant costs (it can have a strong help-the-attacker effect).[44]

The situation changes for mass-market software. There is no strong authentication for "authorized security specialists" for widely used software. Suppose that a large software company tried to send security information to every "authorized security specialist" while trying to keep the information secret from all potential hackers. That sort of mass notification, with no leakage, is highly unlikely to succeed. In the absence of strong authentication separating "good guys" from "bad guys," any information that is disclosed will generally be available to both. The military option of selective disclosure is much less likely to be a realistic option.

The mass-market software programmer also has less hierarchical control over defenses than does a military commander. For mass-market software, many users lack expertise. Many defenders also may not pay much attention to the programmer's plea to install patches or otherwise upgrade the defense. Given the lack of hierarchical control, those seeking to spread a new defensive measure may have to rely on widespread publicity to alert third-party defenders about the threat.

In short, disclosure is more likely to help attackers where there is a unified defense (one organization with hierarchical controls). Disclosure is more likely to help defenders where there are numerous third parties that risk harm from a vulnerability. The latter situation is more likely to occur in the area of computer and network security. For firewalls and mass-market software, there are many ordinary users who might have the vulnerability. For encryption, the messages of many users are subject to attack if the cryptosystem is broken. Because there are so many third parties, disclosure becomes more important in order to alert defenders about whether a product is secure or whether a patch is needed.

---

[44] In the real life of the military, of course, strong authentication and effective hierarchy do not always exist. Spies might learn about information that was supposed to go only to members of the military. Orders might not be followed. Nonetheless, the ability to get information to selected fellow defenders is likely much greater in a well-run military organization than it is for mass-market software companies.

Interestingly, the needs of the U.S. military seem to have played a role in prompting mass-market software companies to disclose more about vulnerabilities. Over time, the military has followed the dictates of Congress and bought a great deal of COTS (commercial off-the-shelf) software. My interviews with security experts[45] indicate that the military became aware over time of software vulnerabilities that had not been disclosed either to the military or to the general public. The military found it unacceptable to be vulnerable to attacks that were known to attackers and to the software company but not to the military. The military thus put pressure on software providers to increase the disclosure of vulnerabilities so that users such as the military would be in a better position to know about vulnerabilities and develop a response.

In summary, disclosure will tend to help the attackers but not the defenders in a military setting, where there is strong authentication of defenders and an established hierarchy to implement improvements in defense. Disclosure provides greater benefits to defenders when there are numerous third-party users, no effective way to communicate only to friendly defenders, and no hierarchical way to ensure that defense improvements are put into place.

IV. CONCLUSION: SECURITY, PRIVACY, AND ACCOUNTABILITY

This paper has addressed when disclosure of information will improve security. "Security," for its purposes, is defined as preventing an attacker from gaining control of a physical installation or computer system.[46]

There are clearly other compelling goals to consider in deciding when to disclose information. Accountability usually increases with greater disclosure. Disclosure of information can produce economic winners and losers. Free speech and other First Amendment issues are implicated by disclosure policy. Personal privacy, the subject of much of my previous academic and government

---

[45] The information about this history was provided to me by persons in both the public and private sector.

[46] A more expansive definition of "information security" is given in the Federal Information Security Management Act of 2002, Pub. L. 107–347, 116 Stat. 2946, § 301:

(1) The term "information security" means protecting information and information systems from unauthorized access, use, disclosure, disruption, modification, or destruction in order to provide –
(A) integrity, which means guarding against improper information modification or destruction, and includes ensuring information nonrepudiation and authenticity;
(B) confidentiality, which means preserving authorized restrictions on access and disclosure, including means for protecting personal privacy and proprietary information; and
(C) availability, which means ensuring timely and reliable access to and use of information.

work, can also be compromised when information is disclosed.[47] Compelling goals such as accountability, economic growth, free speech, and privacy should be taken into account in any overall decision about whether to disclose information.

An essential part of the analysis, however, is to understand when disclosure helps security. Understanding this is important in its own right, as an intellectual topic that has not received sufficient attention to date. It is also crucial in the debates about how to create cybersecurity and physical security in the age of the Internet and of terrorist threats.

This paper seeks to correct two common misunderstandings about when disclosure improves security. Secrecy helps much more often than is suggested by the slogan "No security through obscurity." When presented earlier versions of this chapter, the most sophisticated technologists understood this fact. They know that keys and passwords should remain secret and that a good firewall can benefit from idiosyncratic features that defeat the script kiddies. This paper draws on the literature on the Efficient Capital Markets Hypothesis, however, to suggest that the efficiency of attackers in discovering vulnerabilities will often be less than open source proponents have presumed. More broadly, my discussions with security experts have uncovered no models or systematic ways to analyze the limits of what I have called the open source paradigm for security through openness.

This paper also teaches that disclosure improves security much more often than is suggested by the slogan "Loose lips sink ships." First, military systems often rely on commercially available software, and the security of those systems thus depends on military system owners learning about vulnerabilities. Second, military actions are subject to the growth of the public domain, where information gets communicated quickly and effectively among potential attackers.[48] Third, and most broadly, the model presented herein suggests that

---

[47] From 1999 until early 2001, I served as the Clinton administration's Chief Counselor for Privacy, in the U.S. Office of Management and Budget. This research project arises from my perception at that time that some of the hardest and least understood issues concerned how privacy and security should intersect. My work on the topic began in the summer of 1999, when the Federal Intrusion Detection Network (FIDNet) became a topic of controversy. In the wake of criticism of FIDNet (see Markoff 1999), I was asked to work with Richard Clarke's cybersecurity team to ensure that federal computer security was consistent with privacy and civil liberties. The next year, I served as chair of a White House working group on how to update electronic surveillance laws for the Internet Age, another topic where privacy and security concerns intersected. Since my return to academic life, many of my writings have addressed the intersection of security, privacy, and surveillance issues. My privacy and other publications are available at www.peterswire.net.

[48] The growth of the Internet, with its lack of national boundaries, has lowered the cost and increased the effectiveness of research about other countries. Military commanders expect

openness may be the best general strategy in situations with low uniqueness – that is, where there are high values for number of attacks (N), learning from an individual attack (L), and communication among attackers (C).

In terms of methodology, this paper offers an economic analysis for determining when "there is no security through obscurity" and when "loose lips sink ships." The first step is to assess the costs and benefits of disclosure with respect to potential attackers. In some instances, for strong positions, disclosure will deter attacks and is thus beneficial. In other instances, disclosure tends to spread information about vulnerabilities. Even then, where the facts fit the open source and public domain paradigms, disclosure will offer little or no aid to attackers. Thus, disclosure can go forward if there are benefits to the defenders or if other values favor disclosure. When the facts fit the information-sharing and military paradigms, disclosure is more likely to help the attackers. Nonetheless, disclosure is likely to have net benefits in cybersettings and other modern settings where attackers can mount numerous attacks (high N), gather information cheaply (high L), and communicate efficiently about vulnerabilities (high C).

Another important theme of this paper is that there are often third-party defenders who benefit from disclosure about vulnerabilities. The military paradigm implicitly assumes that defenders act in a unified way, with strong authentication (which allows allied soldiers to be recognized) and hierarchical control (which allows fixes for vulnerabilities to be ordered). When these assumptions no longer hold, such as for mass-market software and networks operated by diverse actors, then disclosure is much more likely to have net benefits for defenders.

By defining the factors that contribute to high uniqueness, this paper identifies the variables that determine when secrecy will improve the defense: the effectiveness of the defensive feature against the initial attack (E), the number of attacks (N), the degree of learning by the attacker (L), the degree of communication with other potential attackers (C), and the extent to which defenders can effectively alter the feature before the next attack (both alteration by the system designer [A-D] and alteration by third parties such as open source programmers [A-T].

Identification of these variables provides the answer to the question asked in the paper's title: What is different about computer and network security? For key computer and network topics such as firewalls, mass-market software,

to use new technologies to "see the battlespace" and have "integrated sight" of the enemy's capabilities. Admiral Bill Owens (2000) describes the increase in information gathering and processing as central to the "revolution in military affairs." Opposing forces will similarly pursue strategies of high N, L, and C to "lift the fog of war."

and encryption, the effect of variables such as N, L, C, and $A\text{-}T$ shows why the benefits of disclosure of vulnerabilities often outweigh the benefits of secrecy. Disclosure is not necessarily or logically more desirable for computer and network security than for physical security, but the crucial variables much more often result in net benefits from disclosure. Examination of the variables also illuminates important special cases, such as why disclosure of passwords and private keys will almost always be harmful and why surveillance generally benefits from secrecy concerning sources and methods.

The intellectual structure of this paper provides a systematic way to identify the costs and benefits of disclosure for security. Further research can assess the empirical levels of the relevant variables in different security contexts. It can also enrich the theoretical structure for assessing the effects of disclosure on security, such as by drawing more on the Efficient Capital Markets Hypothesis literature to identify where vulnerabilities are most likely to be discovered by attackers. Finally, it can aid in explaining how security goals should be integrated with other compelling goals such as accountability, economic growth, free speech, and privacy.

REFERENCES

Allen, William T. 2003. Securities Markets as Social Products. The Pretty Efficient Capital Market Hypothesis. *Journal of Corporate Law* 28:551.

Band, Jonathan. 2003. New Theories of Database Protection. *Managing Intellectual Property*, March. https://www.firstmonday.org/issues/issue5_10/adar/index.html.

Boyle, James. 2003. The Second Enclosure Movement and the Construction of the Public Domain. *Law and Contemporary Problems* 66:33.

Bush, Randy, and Steven M. Bellovin. 2002. Security through Obscurity Dangerous. Working draft for Internet Engineering Task Force. https://rip.psg.com/~randy/draft-ymbk-obscurity-01.html.

Center for Democracy and Technology. 2002. TSA Issues Second Privacy Act Notice Expanding and Narrowing CAPPS II, July 31, 2003. http://www.cdt.org/wiretap.

Chapman, D. Brent, and Elizabeth D. Zwicky. 1995. *Building Internet Firewalls*. Sebastopol, CA: O'Reilly & Associates.

Cunningham, Lawrence A. 1994. From Random Walks to Chaotic Crashes: The Linear Genealogy of the Efficient Capital Market Hypothesis. *George Washington Law Review* 62:546.

Easterbrook, Frank H. 1996. Cyberspace and the Law of the Horse. *University of Chicago Law Forum* 1996:207.

Fama, Eugene. 1965. The Behavior of Stock Market Prices. *Journal of Business* 38:34.

Farrell, Joseph, and Philip Weiser. 2003. Modularity, Vertical Integration, and Open Access Policies: Towards a Convergence of Antitrust and Regulation in the Internet Age. *Harvard Journal of Law and Technology* 17:85.

Fisher, Dennis. 2002. Microsoft Puts Meat behind Security Push. *EWeek*, September 30. http://www.landfield.com/isn/mail-archive/2002/Oct)0004.html.

Froomkin, A. Michael. 2000. The Death of Privacy. *Stanford Law Review* 52:1461.

Goldsmith, Jack L. 1998. Against Cyberanarchy. *University of Chicago Law Review* 65: 1199.

Gonggrijp, Rop. 1992. Netware Users React to Security Threat. *Internet Week*, October 5, p. 2.

Granneman, Scott. 2004. The Perils of Googling. *The Register*, March 10. http://www.theregister.co.uk/content/55/36142.html.

Hauben, Michael. 2004. History of ARPANET: Behind the Net – The Untold History of the APRANET: Or The "Open" History of ARPANET/Internet. http://www.dei.isep.ipp.pt.docs/arpa.html.

Kahn, David. 1996. *The Codebreakers: The Story of Secret Writing*. New York: Penguin/New American Library.

Lee, Edward. 2003. The Public's Domain: The Evolution of Legal Restraints on the Government's Power to Control Public Access through Secrecy or Intellectual Property. *Hastings Law Journal* 55:91.

Lee, Michael, et al. 1999. Electronic Commerce, Hackers, and the Search for Legitimacy: A Regulatory Proposal. *Berkeley Technology Law Journal* 14:839.

Lessig, Lawrence. 2002. *The Future of Ideas: The Fate of the Commons in a Connected World*. New York: Random House.

Malik, Attiya. 2003. Are You Content with the Content? Intellectual Property Implications of Weblog Publishing. *John Marshall Journal of Computer and Information Law* 21:349.

Markoff, John. 1999. U.S. Drawing Plan That Will Monitor Computer Systems. *New York Times*, July 28, p. A1.

Microsoft. 2003. Understanding Patch and Update Management: Microsoft's Software Update Strategy. White paper.

National Science Foundation. 1993. Review of NSFNET. Arlington, VA: National Science Foundation, Office of Inspector General, March 23.

Owens, Bill. 2000. *Lifting the Fog of War*. Baltimore: John Hopkins University Press.

Schneier, Bruce. 1996. *Applied Cryptography*. 2d ed. Hoboken, NJ: Wiley.

———. 2002. Secrecy, Security, and Obscurity. *Cryptogram Newsletter*, May 15. http://www.schneier.com/crypto-gram-0205.html.

———. 2003a. *Beyond Fear: Thinking Sensibly about Security in an Uncertain World*. New York: Copernicus Books.

———. 2003b. Internet Shield: Secrecy and Security. *San Francisco Chronicle*, March 2.

Singh, Simon. 1999. *The Code Book: The Evolution of Secrecy from Mary Queen of Scots to Quantum Cryptography*. New York: Doubleday, p. D5.

Stephenson, Neal. 2002. *Cryptonomicon*. New York: Avon.

Stout, Lynn A. 2003. The Mechanisms of Market Efficiency: An Introduction to the New Finance. *Journal of Corporate Law* 28:635.

Swire, Peter P. 2004a. Information Sharing, the Patriot Act, and Privacy. Presentation made February 28. www.peterswire.net.

———. 2004b. The System of Foreign Intelligence Surveillance Law. *George Washington Law Review*.

Volokh, Eugene. 2004. Crime-Facilitating Speech. Unpublished draft.

Weisman, Robert. 2004. Investors Monitoring Climate for Google IPO. Miami-Herald.com, March 21. http://www.miam.com/mld/miamiherald/business/national/8243019.htm.

Williamson, Oliver E. 1998. *The Economic Institutions of Capitalism.* New York: The Free Press.

Winn, Jane Kaufman. 1998. Open Systems, Free Markets, and Regulation of Internet Commerce. *Tulane Law Review* 72:1177.

Intervention Strategies: Redundancy, Diversity, and Autarchy

THREE

PEER PRODUCTION OF SURVIVABLE CRITICAL INFRASTRUCTURES

Yochai Benkler*

I. INTRODUCTION

Imagine a data storage and retrieval system that stores millions of discrete files in such a way that they can be accessed, searched, and retrieved by millions of users who can access the system wherever they are connected to the Internet. Imagine that this system is under a multipronged attack. Its enemies have used a variety of techniques, ranging from shutting down the main search server under the threat of armed seizure, to inserting malicious files to corrupt the system, to capturing and threatening the operators of storage devices. Imagine that even through all these assaults, the system continues to operate and to provide high-quality storage, search, and retrieval functionality to millions of users worldwide. That would be a system worth studying as a model for cybersecurity, would it not?

That system has in fact been in existence for five years. It has indeed been under the kinds of attacks described over this entire period. It is the peer-to-peer music file–sharing system. It is the epitome of a survivable system. Its primary design characteristic is radically distributed redundant capacity. The primary economic puzzles in understanding whether it is a model that can be harnessed to design survivable systems more generally are these: Why there is so much excess capacity for its core components – storage, processing, and communications capacity, in the hands of many widely distributed users? And how one might replicate it for uses that are somewhat less controversial than sharing music files.

Peer-to-peer file-sharing networks are but one highly visible example of a much broader phenomenon in present computation and communications systems. Shareable goods – goods that have excess capacity and are

*Professor of Law, Yale Law School.

widely distributed throughout the economy in the hands of many users –
are widespread in the digitally networked environment. Personal computers
and handhelds, wireless transceivers, DVRs, microwave ovens, and many other
devices have excess capacity of one or more of the following basic functionalities – computation, storage, and communications capacity. These goods are
widely distributed and diversely located both geographically and in network
topology. Their excess capacity and topological diversity can, with the right network design, be made available as redundant capacity that is highly survivable
in case of attacks in either physical or network space.

This paper begins with a very brief definition of survivability and how it
differs from hardening or impregnability as an approach to security. I then
consider three areas of focus in which we already see sharing networks that provision the three primary functionalities of communications and computation
infrastructures – computation, communications, and storage – on a radically
distributed peer-production model. All these systems share three characteristics
that make them highly attractive from a survivability perspective. They all have
(1) redundant capacity that is (2) geographically and topologically diverse, and
they are (3) capable of self-organization and self-healing on a fully distributed
model without need for reference to any single point of organization that can,
in turn, become a single point of failure. How do these networks of redundant
capacity arise? Why is the excess capacity provisioned in the first place, and how
is it then harnessed? The answer described in Section III is that the case studies
represent specific instantiations of a general category of economic production
(social sharing and exchange) that harnesses the excess capacity of a particular
type of goods (shareable goods). The characteristics of shareable goods make
them widely distributed in the population (at least of relatively wealthy nations)
and hence available for the creation of survivable systems. The characteristics of
shareable goods are generally possessed by most, if not all, communication and
computation devices presently deployed and planned. In other words, the universe of end user computation and communication equipment systematically
includes the excess capacity necessary to produce the kinds of survivable systems
that the case studies suggest. These can be harnessed in a variety of ways, ranging from managerially mandated sharing of excess capacity in large-scale enterprises or networks for pooling redundant capacity among smaller enterprises,
through secondary markets, all the way to sharing models such as peer-to-
peer file-sharing networks and ad hoc mesh wireless networks. But for reasons
to do with transactions costs and the diversity of motivations of the owners
of the resources, social sharing and exchange has distinct advantages over secondary markets for pooling resources not already owned by a single enterprise.

It is the opportunity for social sharing that offers the most interesting policy
implications. If indeed we live under technical-market conditions that lead

to the possession by many individuals of large quantities of excess capacity of all three core functionalities in communication and information systems, what can policy do to facilitate these individuals' joining sharing networks that could eventually provide a valuable source of survivability to the digitally networked environment? One approach whose effects would mostly be felt in wireless carriage and storage and retrieval systems is to adjust the laws – for example, spectrum regulations – that have been hampering the growth and adoption of sharing-capable systems. Another approach may be a *quid pro quo* whereby the sharing networks receive some form of regulatory relief in exchange for making their capacity available for an emergency system. This might include, for example, permitting use of frequencies normally allocated to public use for unlicensed wireless devices that use ad hoc mesh architectures in exchange for utilizing protocols that would recognize public use, on a "sirens and lights" model, and hand over their excess capacity to aid public safety in an emergency. It might take the form of a more explicit safe harbor for peer-to-peer sharing networks if their design makes them available to use incrementally for survivable data storage and retrieval systems. The last part of the chapter explores these options.

The basic point of the paper is simple. We live in a technological context in which a tremendous amount of excess capacity of the basic building blocks of our information and communications infrastructure is widely deployed. The widely distributed and topologically diverse deployment of these resources makes them ideally suited for building redundant, survivable backup systems for our basic information and communications infrastructure. Harnessing this excess capacity to create such a survivable infrastructure will likely be done most effectively, not through improving the ability to price these resources, but through improving the conditions for social sharing and exchange of the excess capacity users own. If we invest our policy efforts in hardening our systems to attack instead of rendering them survivable, if we ignore in our institutional design choices the effects of policy choices on social sharing and exchange, focusing solely on their effect on price-based markets and enterprise organization, we will lose a significant opportunity to improve the survivability of our information systems at relatively low cost and with minimal bureaucratic intervention.

II. SURVIVABLE SYSTEMS VERSUS IMPREGNABLE ARTIFACTS

In AD 69, facing a siege by the Roman legions led by Vespesian, two groups of Jews in Jerusalem took two radically different approaches toward defending Jewish life and praxis. The zealots, headed by Shimon Bar Giora and Yochanan of Gush Chalav, fortified the citadel and the temple. Rabban Yochanan

Ben-Zakai, on the other hand, appealed to Vespesian to allow him, along with other rabbis who wanted to join him, safe passage to Yavneh – an unfortified area of no strategic or spiritual consequence – to set up a center for rabbinic study. Vespesian agreed, hoping, no doubt, to win "hearts and minds." The results of these choices are well known. The zealots burned with their temple and citadel, bringing an end to ten centuries of temple-centric Jewish life. Ben-Zakai began the rabbinic tradition that allowed Jewish belief and praxis to evolve and adapt to changing conditions in the face of repeated destruction of one major center after another – from Babylon to Alexandria, from Spain to Poland and Lithuania.

The story encapsulates two basic models of attaining security. One model is the survivable system model. The other is the hardened or impregnable artifact model. System survivability as a concept for communications infrastructures has been around at least since Paul Baran's (1964) germinal memorandum *On Distributed Communications*. Its core parameters already were understood to be distributed redundant capacity that can learn about system condition and adapt in real time to changing requirements and available resources. It presaged the core characteristics of the Internet as a survivable system. What it means for a system to be "survivable" is that it is capable of fulfilling its mission in a timely manner in the presence of attacks, failures, or accidents (Ellison et al. 1997). The emphasis is not on repelling or preventing any attack or failure; instead, the goal is to prevent such events from causing the system to fail to perform its mission. What it means for an asset or artifact to be impregnable, on the other hand, is that it is hard enough to break that it will not be broken or compromised for as long as it is relevant that it not be broken.

Redundancy, adaptability, and recombination are the core properties of survivability defined in terms of a system. These are how cultures store knowledge. Durability, imperviousness, and retrieval are the core properties of an impregnable artifact. They are how buried time capsules preserve knowledge. Since survivability is in the system, not in any given artifact, it uses redundancy instead of durability to ensure that any given functionality that an artifact could have is available from any artifact or relationship of artifacts usable for the functionality. It uses adaptability to respond to environmental changes and challenges to minimize stress on, or loss of, the system rather than building imperviousness into artifacts to ensure that they are not compromised by changes. And it uses recombination of capacities from the system, rather than the retrieval of a unique durable and impervious artifact, to provide a particular functionality.

Whether a given asset requires survivability or impregnability depends on the user and the use that makes the asset valuable. If the asset is valuable because of the use functionality it makes possible for its owner, then survivability is more important than impregnability. What is valuable to the user is that the asset continue to be usable by the user, even under attack, not that it be untouched by another. If the asset is valuable because it is unavailable for use by another, impregnability rather than survivability is genuinely necessary. Many assets have aspects of both, and the relative importance of survivability and impregnability will depend on their relative value. Further, determining their relative importance would only be useful if one had to make trade-offs between what survivability required and what impregnability required.

Consider a customer database in the hands of three different types of companies. Company A is a customer-oriented company. Its market position is widely understood as stemming from its responsiveness to customers – a responsiveness that results from its maintenance of excellent data on past purchases and its heavy emphasis on the personal responsibility of each customer care agent for the entire pre- and postpurchase customer experience. Company B is a transactional data collection and sales company. Its business is built around an algorithm that, based on past purchase decisions, allows it to predict within 75 microseconds of a user's browser identifying itself to the website what products, out of a lineup of products any given web-based merchant offers, will likely capture the attention and money of that particular customer and then to display those items to that user. Company C sells mailing lists to bulk mail advertisers. Clearly Company C needs strictly to exclude competitors from its customer database, because if they extracted the information, they could simply directly replicate its product. The same cannot be said about either Company A or B. Each of these two companies has another major input into the mix that gives it a market advantage: if competitors got the contents of its customer information database, its operations would be little affected, and its competitiveness would also likely be little affected, unless the competitor successfully replicated either the customer care staff or the algorithm, respectively. For each, on the other hand, denial of access to or loss of, say, 30% of the data in the database would be entirely disruptive, because it would disable the leveraging of the human or algorithm advantage in 30% of cases, undermining the reputation of the firm. Companies A and B are, then, much more reliant upon the survivability of their database than upon its impregnability, while the inverse is true of Company C. Company B, in turn, is more dependant on the impregnability of its algorithm, because that, if taken by another, can lead to matched competition, whereas Company A's core advantage is outside any of its information system's exclusive features. As long as the system is up and running timely, that firm's advantage – human connection relying on the information flow from the system – is unaffected.

While the Internet as a whole functions on a distributed, redundant, self-configuring, and self-healing model that results in enormous survivability, not all points or functionalities in the digital environment are similarly designed. Most processing that is directly relevant to users of any type occurs in discrete processors – personal computers, servers, and so on. Most storage happens in discrete storage media – hard drives, CDs, tapes, and so on. Most last/first mile physical links are single nonredundant or at least low-redundancy links, such as a single cable into a home or small office and the one or two major cables that in some cases service an entire corporate campus. While a redundant survivable system approach is used to preserve the flow of packets once in the Internet cloud, computation, storage, and even physical links from the user into that cloud are not designed in the same way. They are, instead, usually designed on an impregnable artifact model – typified by the firewall, the password, and the locked office door. These are all artifact-oriented hardening strategies. They are not survivability strategies. Given enough time, and given interconnected, unbounded networks whose very purpose is to reach across organizational domains and entity boundaries – individual or corporate – hardening to the point of perfect success is quite possibly unattainable. Given that survivability is the primary value to at least some substantial subset of users of computation and communications networks, the remainder of this paper asks whether there are approaches to replicating the redundant, distributed, self-healing architecture of the Internet for functionalities other than long-distance packet forwarding – specifically, for physical link capacity in the first mile, for data storage and retrieval systems, and for raw computation.

III. EXAMPLES OF PEER-PRODUCED
CAPACITY-GENERATING SYSTEMS

A. Ad Hoc Mesh Wireless Networks

In the days following September 11, 2001, a group of volunteers delivered broadband connectivity to downtown Manhattan by setting up three WiFi hotspots (Myers 2001). The group, NYC Wireless, had been engaged in a number of experiments throughout the city involving the placement of open WiFi gateways to allow users to connect freely to the Internet. When major infrastructure-based systems were down, connectivity was rapidly deployed, using unlicensed spectrum, not public safety spectrum, and off-the-shelf commercial equipment, not dedicated public safety equipment. The story suggest there is good reason to look at other, more sophisticated systems that would not similarly require volunteers to come and set up connectivity. Two elements of currently developed systems would produce a similar WiFi-based alternative connectivity system but would do so automatically, without human intervention. These two elements are (1) mesh architecture and (2) ad hoc configurability.

WiFi systems as currently familiar to American users are deployed in a terminal-based station architecture, similar to a mobile phone system. We largely use WiFi devices to connect to a fixed gateway to the Internet. This is neither the only way nor necessarily the most efficient way to deploy an unlicensed wireless system. A number of companies, beginning at least with Rooftop Community Networks in the mid-1990s, have developed an approach called *wireless mesh network architecture* (developed most extensively in DARPA projects). In a mesh, every node, every device represents both a user node and a component of the infrastructure. The purpose of mesh architecture is to create multiple possible paths between any two points in the network such that for any given required end-to-end link there are multiple possible paths at any given moment. As a result, if any one, node in the system goes down because it lost power, or because its owner is a mobile unit that went out of range, or because a tree has fallen and blocked a transmission path given the propagation characteristics of the carrier frequency, nodes still active in the network can identify and compute new paths from any point to any other point in the network. A mesh network has no single point of failure. Redundancy of possible links replaces any single base station as a critical node of transmission and replaces any efforts at making that single base station durable and impregnable to achieve a survivable communications system. Mesh networks can combine repeater networks (i.e., each node helps the transmitting node to forward messages to the intended recipient, thereby reducing the power necessary to achieve effective communication and making the signal less subject to interference) and multiuser detection (which allows the receiver to cooperate with its neighbors' antennae better to filter out interference and correctly to decode a message from a transmitter).

An independent characteristic of these mesh networks is that many of them are also ad hoc networks. An ad hoc network is one that has no fixed infrastructure. Each node is an end user of the network as well as a component of the network infrastructure. As a node is turned on, it searches for neighbors and announces itself to neighboring systems. It provides its own information and in return receives information about its next neighbors and the network topology, or at least the near network topology. Nodes continue to inform each other at intervals about their presence and availability, roughly in the way that Internet routers do. Ad hoc architecture adds immense survivability to the network through its capacity to self-heal. Because each node can serve as infrastructure, and because the network is designed to be self-configuring as each node joins and leaves the network, without requiring any dedicated infrastructure prior to the existence of usable nodes, an ad hoc network can deal with failures automatically and as part of the same process by which the network is formed in the normal course of its use.

In combination, ad hoc mesh networks are highly survivable in the event of an attack or other substantial disruption. Because of their mesh architecture, they are designed to create numerous redundant optional physical paths from any point in the network to any other point. Because of their ad hoc nature, they can adapt to radical changes in the environment and recombine the components that survive an attack into a communication system using the very same built-in characteristics that allow them to form in the first place, when each node is first deployed.

Although none of these technologies is already a major market presence, none is futuristic. The properties of repeater networks and multiuser detection in mesh networks and ad hoc architectures have become the focus of bur-geoning research.[1] A number of practical implementations and businesses are being developed and deployed, including Mesh Networks and Packethop (both civilian commercializations of DARPA-funded projects aimed at providing the military with robust ad hoc mobile data networks) and Tropos. The first gen-eration of companies offering ad hoc wireless mesh technologies, like Rooftop Networks (later Nokia Rooftop), preceded the explosion of WiFi and therefore had to build the devices, the radio link protocols, and the network. This cre-ated a high entry barrier for adoption, because unless an entire neighborhood could be persuaded to join the network, one or two devices would provide little benefit to their users until a certain threshold adoption was in place, and a lack of economies of scale in production made the equipment unnecessarily expen-sive. The new generation of businesses focusing on ad hoc mesh networking can now rely on existing deployed wireless devices that are adopted by their users for mobile access "tethered" to an access point or cell site. What this new generation of products does is provide a software implementation that allows these already existing devices – most ubiquitously WiFi-enabled devices – to form ad hoc mesh networks.

Usefully for this paper, the first market into which these firms are selling is the public safety market. During the first quarter of 2004, a number of field deploy-ments for public safety high-speed mobile data networks have been undertaken. Garland, Texas, and Medford, Oregon, are deploying ad hoc mesh networks based on the Mesh Networks technology for use by their first responders. San Mateo, California, and North Miami Beach, Florida, have also begun to deploy

---

[1] For a brief bibliography and description of the research, see Benkler (2002b).

an ad hoc wireless mesh network for first-responder high-speed data access, from Tropos. Both of these solutions rely on providing some fixed backbone access points, on the cellular style instead of on a purely ad hoc infrastructure, but each device can operate as a network node that is adaptable ad hoc to achieve survivability. The backbone is necessary only because of the relatively small number of nodes involved. If nodes were universally distributed throughout the relevant environment, there would be no need to seed the environment with fixed nodes. San Francisco, Marin County, and California State participants in the Golden Gate Safety Network ran a successful informal trial of PacketHop's solution, based on a purely ad hoc mobile network with no preexisting backbone, in February 2004. The test reportedly enabled three different systems whose traditional radio systems are not interoperable to form an ad hoc wireless local network on both sides of the bridge and in the water and to link this ad hoc network to a command center, allowing voice, text, and video to be exchanged among a number of fixed and mobile stations participating in the exercise.

While the technologies are reasonably well understood, their implications as a model of peer production of connectivity and survivability of networks are less emphasized. They are still packaged as either last-mile solutions that competitive access providers could offer to compete with cable or DSL – this was the pitch of the first generation – or as a way for a single entity, usually a municipality, to meet its own needs using its own network of devices and users as both the network and the users. This is so largely because mesh networks require some threshold density, derived from the power constraint regulations imposed on unlicensed devices, to achieve the state where any given individual could purchase a single unit and be reasonably assured that when he or she turns that unit on it will have neighbors with whom to form a metropolitan or wide area network. Last-mile carriers or single entities can invest in strategically located fixed backbone nodes to ensure connectivity under most conditions. Although achieving threshold density is a genuine transition problem, as a matter of business rationale, a carrier or a fixed backbone is not necessary for the survivability of the architecture itself once a sufficient number of individual users have joined the network to create the redundancy. Indeed, a carrier is more a potential source of failure, because if configuration is dependent on a carrier rather than attainable locally by each node and its neighbors, then carrier-operated nodes or base stations become potential points of failure.

Once mesh networking becomes a software overlay on top of WiFi devices, the path to a municipal-level mesh network made of end-user devices is fairly straightforward to map – even if it is not without some bumps. You start with the frustration felt by any given household because there may be dead spots in the house or in the yard. You add at least two WiFi-enabled devices per household. A utility that allows a user to place the desktop or laptop in such a location vis-à-vis the access point so that it bridges to the dead spots and also allows visiting friends to check their e-mail from their PDA in the yard becomes an obvious extension for off-the-shelf WiFi devices. Individual consumers, seeking to fulfill their own needs for wireless networking in the home or their place of business will provision devices that can cooperate to form a highly redundant, self-configuring, and self-healing wireless network. Which leaves genuine policy questions regarding, for example, how to make sure that people share their wireless capacity with each other to provide municipal coverage or how to coax people into giving priority to public safety or mission critical data, at least in emergencies. These become the subject of the kind of policy interventions outlined in Section V.

For now, all that is necessary to realize is that we are already seeing the emergence of device-based wireless connectivity built on top of an already widely adopted infrastructure of devices – WiFi equipment. What is unusual about this connectivity infrastructure is that it requires no carrier, no fixed backbone, and no centralized source of investment. It could be built spontaneously, out of cooperative protocols implemented using of equipment capitalized and owned by end users. If this were done, the metropolitan-level networks that could form would provide a distinct benefit to the owners of the equipment that participated in creating them. It would give them a last mile that they were all privileged to access and would therefore enable tremendous competition in broadband Internet access by circumventing the only major bottleneck to competition in that area, the last mile of physical connectivity to the Net. These networks would have highly redundant physical links and large amounts of excess wireless transport capacity because of the reuse of spectrum and because each device would contribute resources to the network whenever it was not actively transmitting or receiving information – which, in an Internet model of communications, is much of the time. This system of user-owned, cooperatively created wireless transport networks would then be available, with the right regulatory system or incentives, as a source of survivable carriage capacity in the face of an emergency, whether its source was intentional attack, system failure, or some external random event, like a hurricane that brings down major connection links. Understanding how a user-based network of sharing could emerge and the motivations and information characteristics of such a network will provide the basis for recommendations for optimizing the adoption of connectivity-producing cooperation and coaxing its users-owners into making their connectivity available as a survivable backup system for mission critical communications.

In the ideal scenario, during an emergency or in the event of a major disruption, such as an attack on a major wired switching point, public safety officials would be able to rely on the widespread availability of wireless nodes to provide them with survivable communications at the basic connectivity layer. If every apartment or house in a metropolitan area, or every other apartment or house, had a wireless node connected in a mesh with nodes at the homes of some set of neighbors, it would be practically impossible to bring down communications in that area except by annihilating a very large portion of the homes. It is likely that, for congestion avoidance purposes, nodes that are already highly attached would be treated as less attractive than nodes that were less linked. This would tend to avoid the emergence of a network topology that would be vulnerable to even a well-informed attack on the network itself. That vulnerability is characteristic of redundant networks whose degree distribution follows a power law. While *ad hoc* networks grow, congestion avoidance would require that they resist preferential attachment. In any given geographic locale a super node that would create some vulnerability could emerge, but there is reason to think that this will not characterize *ad hoc* mesh wireless networks as a class. The more the device manufacturers are permitted to build their equipment with dynamic power management so as to increase or decrease power as hop distance requires, the more survivable the network would be everywhere, because the lower the threshold density required for connectivity. Survivability and ubiquity of connectivity are achieved in such a system, not through providing a particular impervious access point, but by seeding a network of devices installed by individuals throughout the area for their own personal needs and available to provide backup connectivity everywhere and anywhere in a way that is highly robust to attack because redundant, adaptive, and self-healing (that is, capable of recombining itself through dynamic reconfiguration).

One common objection might be that wireless communications are less secure than wired communications. In considering this objection, it is necessary to recognize that there are two issues involved. First, are the data secure? Are the data capable of being read by an enemy? The answer is the same for all Internet communications. Communications are as safe as the encryption they use. No more and no less. A well-encrypted bitstream will take a lot of time and money to decrypt. Its content is secure even if the whole bitstream is acquired by an enemy. Moreover, because of the packetized, multipath nature of communications in a mesh network, acquiring the entire bitstream is not a trivial task. Second, can an enemy disrupt the link between the *a* and *b* who are users of the system? That question is one instance of the question of survivability in general. If the most that an enemy can do is cause the desired communications to lose packets, the system is survivable. The defense of the communication from a to b is in the survivability of the system, not in the imperviousness of the energy received on a single link. To conclude, then, a wireless mesh network deployed and owned by many users and manufactured by device manufacturers, in contrast to a network created by service providers who "own spectrum," is highly survivable. Data that it carries are no less secure than any Internet communication, wired or wireless – its security depends on the strength of data encryption, not any supposed imperviousness of the physical link channel.

B. Distributed Data Storage and Retrieval

The second piece of the puzzle for provisioning a survivable computation and communications infrastructure is data storage and retrieval. As mentioned at the beginning of this paper, we have an extraordinarily robust example of such a system already in operation. It utilizes the storage capacity of millions of end-user computers to store data in redundant storage. It uses their distributed processing power to search for it. And it uses their excess bandwidth to retrieve it on a global scale. I am speaking, of course, of the peer-to-peer file-sharing networks that have been used so successfully as a survivable, adaptive, self-healing system of data storage and retrieval. Despite a series of attacks on major points of failure, and in the case of Napster a successful shutdown of the main point of data search and location, the data survived in user-owned storage media, new systems of search and retrieval were created, and these in turn proved substantially more distributed and highly resistant to attack from a persistent enemy – to wit, the recording industry backed by the force of the United States and other sympathetic governments. While one may argue whether the particular use to which this system has been put is desirable or not, that is not the point. The point is that Napster introduced and Gnutella, Kazaa, Grokster, Aimster, and the many other systems that followed it developed a highly survivable system for data storage and retrieval that has tremendous redundancy, capacity to migrate data across the system to where they are most needed, and resilience to geographically or topologically focused attacks and to diffuse injections of malicious data into the system.

The first major peer-to-peer file-sharing network, Napster, relied on decentralized storage and retrieval, with one major deviation – a centralized server that stored information about which peer had what music. Although peers communicated directly with each other and downloaded music one from the other's computer from one end of the network to another, no peer could communicate directly with another without first identifying the other by reference to a central listing. This made the communications protocol simple to design and execute, it made the system highly scalable, but it also made the system vulnerable to attack and failure. The particular attack on that server was legal, and the failure was a court-ordered closure. But the weakness was architectural – there was a single point of attack that could bring the system down. The response of technology developers was to treat the legal attack like any other failure and to design a system that did not offer a single target. The result was Gnutella and a class of approaches to peer-to-peer network design that avoided creating a center that would be vulnerable to attack. Each node in the network would tell some number of its neighbors what it had on its hard drive. Each node looking for a song would query its neighbors for the song. If information about what everyone had and what everyone wanted propagated in this way throughout the network, then anyone who wanted anything that anyone else had could find it. The problem with this approach was that it required a lot of overhead, and the overhead increased as more users joined. This required some trade-off between comprehensiveness of availability of material and the cost of information needed to recognize what people have and what people want.

Gnutella worked reasonably well up to a point, but it was not perfect. Fast-Track, with its best-known clients Kazaa and Morpheus, was an improvement. It added structure to the network of peers, but structure that was not sufficiently centralized, stable, or single-point dependent to make it vulnerable to the kind of failure suffered by Napster. FastTrack introduced Supernodes – a dynamically determined class of nodes in the network that offer the functionality of the Napster server on an ad hoc, dynamically reconfigurable basis. Based on the users' material characteristics – underutilized processing power and the bandwidth of their connection – the software assigns to some users "Supernode" status. Instead of every node telling every other node everything it had and everything it wanted, as in the Gnutella model, every node sends a list of its available files and requests to its nearest Supernode. Supernodes tell each other who has what and who wants what, keeping network traffic and information overhead low while retaining redundancy, flexibility in the distribution of the location of information, load balancing among nodes with more or less free capacity, and flexible rerouting around points of failure (self-healing). The result is a system that is even more widely used than Napster was at its height yet offers no single point of failure for attack. Like Napster, Kazaa was sued. Unlike Napster, Kazaa won in the Dutch courts. But even if Kazaa had lost, the FastTrack network architecture would not have been eliminated. If it had been shut down by litigation, there are other clients that could have taken its place effortlessly, or new network architectures on the same principles that could have been written. The physical components of the network are individually owned by users. The connections among these individually owned nodes are software-implemented network relations running on top of the Internet protocol. There is no "network" to shut down. There are only algorithms that tell user computers how to organize themselves into a network on an ad hoc, dynamically updated basis. As long as people have files on their hard drives that can be run on any generic computer, and as long as they want to share these, there is nothing that can be done to prevent them from using these architectural principles to do so. This is why the present attacks by the recording industry are aimed at hardware regulation – forcing the computer and consumer electronics industries to build equipment that will not run generic files but will only run permission-controlled files[2] – and at raising the costs of sharing to users by suing users civilly and by pushing criminal enforcement authorities to prosecute users criminally.[3]

From Napster to Kazaa, file-sharing systems relied on complete redundant copies existing around the network. Other systems, however, have begun to increase both survivability and secrecy by breaking down individual documents and storing pieces of data on different computers, encrypted so that no user who has a piece of a file on his or her hard drive can compromise the document, and they allow data "retrieval" to occur as a recombination of bits of files, rather than as retrieval of whole files, from many different points in the network, accompanied by what are essentially assembly instructions for recombining a replica of the document at the point of retrieval. These approaches include, at the simplest level, BitTorrent, which accelerates downloads of large files (it was developed for large software distributions) and distributes bandwidth costs of replicating portions of files and allowing a user to download segments of a file from different peers, load balancing for bandwidth and availability across nodes.

An earlier and more complete implementation of this approach, as well as a more readily recognizable system of data storage and retrieval that is even more resilient in its characteristics, is Ian Clark's Freenet (Clark et al. 2000). Freenet was designed for censorship-resistant publication, not for easy music downloading. It trades off easy availability of files for music usage for a series of security measures that prevent the owners of the hard drives on which the data reside from knowing what is on their hard drives or controlling what is stored on their hard drives. This step is crucial in shifting from distributed storage and retrieval systems that are intended to give the owners

---

[2] 107 S. 2048, Consumer Broadband and Digital Television Promotion Act (March 21, 2002).
[3] Landler (2004), for example, describes transnational efforts, including criminal prosecutions in Italy.

of the contributed hardware access to the information stored toward a more generally applicable facility for storing data in a survivable form by harnessing widely distributed excess storage capacity on the Net. If banks, hospitals, or national security bodies are to harness distributed storage approaches, either on individually owned unaffiliated computers or even only on employee computers harnessed for this purpose, then the function of providing data storage capacity must be separated from the capacity to read the data stored from the computer providing the storage capacity. This is precisely what Freenet does: segmenting documents among drives so that no single drive has the whole of the document and preventing any single drive from becoming a significant point of failure or compromise. In order to improve access, the system automatically migrates the topological location of data based on demand patterns so that, for example, documents critical of a repressive government that are often accessed by residents of that country will topologically migrate toward network locations that would increase the speed and availability of document retrieval.

A similar but perhaps even more ambitious project, though not yet a deployed system, is OceanStore. OceanStore is a concept developed by John Kubiatowicz at UC Berkeley for what he describes as a global, self-repairing, secure, and persistent storage system. It is built precisely on the concept of ubiquitous computing, which provides ubiquitous storage in units small and large (desktops to handhelds, and automobiles and microwave ovens to walls and shoes in the not-too-distant future). The particulars of the system are fascinating (Rhea et al. 2001). The overarching principle, however, is all that we need here. Storage exists almost wherever computation exists. And computation exists almost everywhere. Connectivity is also being brought in anywhere, mostly for purposes of controlling mechanical systems – Zensys, for example, is selling ad hoc mesh network–enabled WiFi radios implemented in a five-dollar chip in anything from air conditioning units to refrigerators. When connectivity does in fact become ubiquitous, we will have a global medium of storage as long as we solve a series of questions involving security, privacy, and authentication, all of which are done with encryption irrespective of whether the physical network is diversely owned or under single entity control; resilience over time, which Kubiatowicz proposes to achieve by migrating replicated data from older servers to newer ones automatically, so as to avoid sensitivity to units going off line and losing data; and adaptability to failure and attack. Survivability is addressed by wide fragmentation and distribution of redundant file fragments. Kubiatowicz's Tapestry retrieval (or rather recombination) system weaves the files out of fragments distributed across many computers, none of which is readable by the owner of the storage medium on which it resides. Like mesh networks, peer-to-peer file-sharing systems, and FreeNet, Kubiatowicz's system relies on a peer-based model; it uses the large amount of redundant storage/caching capacity owned by individuals distributed throughout the world and the network but assumes that nodes are only mostly, not always, available or connected and that they are at best partially reliable – because of possible technical problems or agent untrustworthiness. The system as a whole uses redundancy of the basic desired capacity – storage – coupled with adaptive algorithms to achieve survivability through adaptation and recombination and to manage load balancing and usability despite the unreliability of any given node. These same everyday design components that allow the system to operate efficiently under normal operating conditions are also germane to ensuring the survivability of the storage and retrieval system as a whole.

It is important to note here that the diversity of the nodes – their topological and geographic dispersion, the diversity of users and primary uses – immensely increases the complexity of the network they form and the difficulty of ensuring a steady flow of functionality from a network formed from such nodes. You cannot store a unique copy of a document that is needed on average every thirty minutes on a laptop that sometimes goes on a plane and is unavailable for six or twelve hours. But this same characteristic also adds to the survivability of the system as a whole. The fact that not all nodes are always connected increases the survivability of the system because any node not connected to the network during an attack is safer from the attack. It can later become available as a source of backup storage to recreate the data if all nodes connected to the network at the time of the attack are affected. Having a storage and retrieval system resident on many devices owned and used by many different users in many locations, with more or less stable network locations and availability and with highly diverse usage patterns, makes for a complex but highly survivable system.

C. Distributed Computing

Distributed computing is a particular implementation of the broader phenomenon of parallel computing. Parallel computing is driven by the economic fact that it is cheaper to lash together large numbers of commodity processors and divide a task among them than it is to build a single fast computer capable of running the same number of operations in a given time frame on a single processor. Imagine that a computation requires 100 operations to run in a time unit t. If the cost of a processor that runs 50 operations per second is c, the cost of a processor that runs 100 operations per second is $4c$, and the task of coordinating among more than one processor imposes a 30-percent loss of computation efficiency, then at a price of $3c$ a computer designer could build a processor capable of running 105 operations a second ($3 \times 50 \times 0.7 = 105$). This would be more efficient than investing fabricating in the more expensive ($4c$) single-processor system, which would perform only 100 operations per second. This simple example makes clear why parallel computing came to dominate more exotic materials–based approaches in supercomputing over the course of the 1990s. Parallelization became over that period a major area in computer engineering, with a focus on how to design problems so that they were amenable to computation in many discrete computations that could be run in parallel without relying too heavily on each other for inputs.

Distributed computing involves the same calculus, but instead of lashing together thousands of processors that are contained in a single box and connected very closely to minimize the time needed for communication among the processors and from them to the system memory, a distributed computing system is built around tens to hundreds of thousands (and in one case millions) of processors donated by Internet users during their downtime (Shirts and Pande 2000). Problems designed for such systems are parallelized on the assumption that vast computation is available, vastly more than in a single proprietary supercomputer, but that no single processor is reliably available, and communications among processors and to system memory are orders of magnitude slower than those in a supercomputer. Using this approach, SETI@Home has become the fastest supercomputer in the world, performing, as of the end of 2003, calculations at a speed 60% faster than the IBM GeneBlue and the NEC Earth Simulator, the two that are formally considered the supercomputers fastest in the world; and four times faster than the next fastest supercomputers.[4] SETI@Home harnesses idle processor cycles of about 4,500,000 users around the world. The users download a small screensaver. When a user is

---

[4] SETI@Home statistics showed a speed of over 54 Teraflops per second. The more traditional supercomputers, where a single firm or organization builds on computation cluster from processors under its ownership or control, achieved 35.8 Teraflops for the NEC Earth simulator, 13.9 Teraflops for the HP ASCI-Q at Los Alamos National Laboratories, the Linux Network with 7.6 Teraflops, and the IBM ASCI White mentioned in the preceding note, both at Lawrence Livermore Laboratories. See Top 500 Supercomputer Sites, at http://www.top500.org/list/2003/06/. These numbers and relationships offer, of necessity, a snapshot. When looked at again five months later, the numbers for the mainstream supercomputers remained similar, but the number for SETI@Home had increased to over 64 Teraflops.

not using his or her computer, the screensaver starts up, downloads problems for calculation – in the case of SETI@Home, radio astronomy signals to be analyzed for regularities as part of the search for extraterrestrial intelligence – and solves the problem it has downloaded. When a solution is calculated, the program automatically sends it to the main site. The cycle will continue for as long as, and every time that, the computer is idle from its user's perspective and the screensaver is activated. I have elsewhere described SETI@Home and other distributed computing projects on the Internet in more detail (Benkler 2004).

Distributed computing provides a readily available model for producing a system of survivable computation capacity, when combined with the insights one gets from the model of ad hoc mesh networks and distributed storage systems. While the focus in distributed computing today is on its cost/performance characteristics, another critical feature of distributed computing is its topological diversity. No attack or failure in a particular geographic location or a particular portion of the network will disable the entire array of processors participating in a distributed computing exercise. Because it relies on parallelization that explicitly assumes nodes that are highly variable and unreliable in terms of availability, and have extremely high delays in communication among processes and from processors to memory, distributed computing can tolerate many more points of failure and radical shifts in availability of processors due to attack. Like a mesh network, a distributed computing system need not have any single point of failure, may run redundant processes, may reassign discrete pieces of computation to available nodes when nodes otherwise tasked with running a process do not deliver, and can load-balance among the available processors according to their particular conditions of availability of processing and communications capacity. In other words, such systems have the required characteristics of redundancy, adaptability, and capacity for recombination as basic design features of their normal operation. These make distributed computing system highly survivable.

Distributed computing also introduces us to another potential advantage, which is less readily available for connectivity (though still possible) but is shared with distributed storage: not only can it be implemented by relying on the participation of individual users or equipment owners, but it can be implemented within a single enterprise or by a coalition of enterprises. Any enterprise that places into the hands of its employees thousands or tens of thousands of desktops, laptops, and handhelds, owned either by the firm or by its employees as work tools, or any alliance of enterprises with similar characteristics, can self-provision a substantial backup emergency computation system solely from enterprise or alliance resources.

IV. ECONOMICS OF SHAREABLE GOODS

A. What Are Shareable Goods?

The systems described in Section III have the following characteristics in common:

1. They rely on widely distributed physical goods.
2. These goods have excess capacity of some desideratum (e.g., transmission, storage, or processing).
3. They are privately owned by many distinct users.
4. The users pool their excess capacity without relying on either prices or managerial commands to motivate and coordinate the pooling.

The wide distribution of physical capital goods capable of provisioning some level of capacity of the desideratum – be it storage, processing, or communications carriage capacity – is a direct requirement of survivability. It is the wide distribution and diversity of types of nodes and their geographic and topological diversity that make the systems they combine to form survivable. This design requirement – that the system integrate the capacity of widely distributed, diverse physical goods – raises an unremarkable economic question: Who will invest in these goods and why will they pool their capacity?

The second, third, and fourth characteristics shared by the systems described offer an unorthodox answer to this fairly straightforward economic question. The system is provisioned by many different users who are not otherwise affiliated and who coordinate their behavior without reference to a price mechanism or a managerial hierarchy. These users pool their privately owned, standard economic goods – the CPUs, hard drives, and wireless transceivers are all privately owned rival goods, they are not public goods, and at least the CPUs (for processing) and hard drives do not have network externalities or demand side economies of scale. The owners of units that participate in these practices appear to do so for a variety of motivations, ranging from some that look like altruism (in the case of distributed computing) to others that look like a willingness to engage in in-kind exchange that is not quite barter (because there is no accounting of the values given or received and the owners seem to tolerate high variability and lack of correlation among contributions to and calls on the system) to free-riding, if you will (as in the case of file-sharing). My object in this section is to (1) provide a set of sufficiency conditions for this kind of non-market-based (in the sense of lacking an explicit price mechanism), non-firm-based social provisioning of a good or service that depends on material inputs and (2) provide a transactions costs–based and motivation-based explanation of why agents might choose to act through a social-relations transactional framework rather than through a price-based or firm-based transactional framework. I have provided a more complete statement of the argument elsewhere (Benkler 2004) and here will only restate the central elements of the argument.

There is a class of goods that have the following two characteristics. First, they are lumpy, or indivisible – at a given technological state, they cannot be produced in quantities that precisely match the demand for them. The minimum size of a CPU available in markets today, for example, exceeds the processing needs of many home users; CPU capacities, hard drive capacities, and wireless transmission capabilities increase in coarsely grained intervals, such that the probability that any population of users would be able to find a distribution of technically available units that precisely matches their demand for the capacity of these units is low. Second, the package size or granularity of the indivisible good is relatively small – unlike an airplane or a steam engine – and their cost, relative to the degree and distribution of wealth in a society, is sufficiently low that a substantial portion of the population could justify putting them into service to satisfy their own individual or household needs. I called these "midgrained" goods because they are neither so coarse grained that putting them into service necessarily requires pooling the demand of many users – through a market, a firm, or a club, for example – nor so fine grained that an individual could purchase precisely the amount of capacity the individual requires and no more.

Where these two conditions hold, we will see a distribution in the society of capacity-generating goods that are widely owned by many users for their own personal use but have excess capacity relative to the needs of their owners. The current distribution of CPUs, storage media, and wireless transmission devices fits this model. So does the distribution of automobiles in the United States today, and it is this distribution that underlies the phenomenon of carpooling, which accounts for roughly 17% of work-related commuting trips – four times more than all forms of public transit combined (Pucher and Renne 2003; Benkler 2004). One day, depending on the costs of home solar power electricity generators, on the one hand, and the costs of fossil fuels, on the other hand, electricity generation could fit this model as well.

I call goods with these characteristics "shareable goods," because when goods have these characteristics, the individual owners can, if they choose, share their excess capacity in social sharing or exchange networks – relying on social and psychological cues and motivations, rather than on money or commands, to inform and motivate behavior. The conditions are not necessary for sharing to occur – people share goods that have no excess capacity in acts of pure altruism (in fact sacrificing something for the benefit of another) or exchange them in complex instrumental gift and social exchange systems. Conversely, people sometimes sell the excess capacity of their shareable goods, as I define them here. They may, for example, sell a used book in a second-hand book market rather than lend it to a friend – indeed there are two online distributed computation projects to which people can sell their computer cycles. My claim is much narrower. These conditions make social relations–based clearance of the excess capacity feasible. Whether it is desirable or not – which may depend on whether conditions exist that would make it more efficient to share or exchange socially than to sell – is a separate consideration. Whether social sharing or exchange will or will not occur, even if feasible, will also depend on cultural conditions. Most importantly, are these shareable goods deployed in a society with a well-developed or poorly developed social transaction framework or market transactional framework?

So, the characteristics of shareable goods define conditions that, if present, are sufficient to make feasible the clearance of a set of physical capital goods through a social sharing or exchange system. The question we turn to now is, What are possible reasons for the excess capacity of these goods to be cleared through a social transactional framework as opposed to a market (price-based) transactional framework?

B. Differences in Information Costs

Social transactional frameworks and market transactional frameworks have substantial and different setup costs. Markets require the definition of property rights and contracting arrangements, legal enforcement systems, often physical exchange locations and information flow mechanisms, and so on. Social arrangements require norms to be developed, social networks formed, cultural values of cooperation inculcated, and so on. Assuming, however, that a society has invested in both types of transactional frameworks, individual marginal transactions within each system also have a marginal cost. We have long understood that these marginal transaction costs can lead resources to be allocated through a managerial firm–based transactional framework rather than through a price-based transactional framework. What I add here is that a similar calculus could lead resources to be most efficiently cleared through a social sharing and exchange system rather than through the price system.

For goods that meet the focused definition of shareable goods, there are two discrete differences between the information characteristics of market transactions and social transactions, the first more important than the second. A market transaction, in order to be efficient by its own measures, must be clearly demarcated as to what it includes so that it can be priced efficiently. That price must then be paid in equally crisply delineated currency. Even if initially a transaction may be declared to involve sale of "an amount reasonably required to produce the required output," for a price "ranging from x to y," at some point what was provided and what is owed must be crystallized and fixed for a formal exchange. The crispness, or completeness of the information regarding all aspects of the transaction, is a functional requirement of the price system and derives from the precision and formality of the medium of exchange – currency – and the ambition to provide refined representations of the comparative value of marginal decisions through denomination in the exchange medium that represents these incremental value differences. Social exchange, on the other hand, does not require the same degree of crispness. As Maurice Godelier (1997) put it, "The mark of the gift between close friends and relatives . . . is not the absence of obligations, it is the absence of 'calculation'" (p. 5). The point is that social exchange does not require one to say, for example, "I will lend you my car and help you move these five boxes on Monday, and in exchange you will feed my fish next July," unlike a statement used to fix a formal exchange, such as "I will move five boxes on Tuesday for $100, six boxes for $120," etc. Instead, actions enter into a cloud of good will or membership, out of which each agent can understand him- or herself as being entitled to a certain flow of dependencies or benefits in exchange for continued cooperative behavior. The basis may be an ongoing relationship between two people, joint membership in a small group like a family or circle of friends, or the general level of generosity among strangers that makes for a decent society.

Because the difference in cost is at the margin per transaction, it increases linearly with the number of discrete transactions necessary to obtain a sufficient quantum of capacity to achieve the goals of a person relying on flows of capacity from the owners of the capital goods that provide the capacity. Imagine that in order to run a single computation, the excess capacity of only one computer is needed, and the difference in transaction costs between using market-based clearance and social exchange is x. If, instead, in order to run a single computation, the person seeking to use excess capacity of others needs to pool the excess processing power of two idle computers, then the cost difference is $2x$ *per computation*, and so forth. This pattern indicates that when slack capacity is located in small amounts distributed among many owners, it becomes increasingly more costly to harness that excess capacity through markets than through social exchange systems. Given that the interest of each individual owner to buy as little excess capacity as technically feasible places a downward pressure on the expected amount of each unit's excess capacity, shareable goods are likely to have this characteristic – widespread distribution of excess capacity in smallish dollops. This is precisely the domain in which share-able goods become very interesting as objects of social sharing and exchange rather than market exchange and in which distributed computing, file sharing, and ad hoc mesh wireless networks can be helpfully described as shareable goods.

The second information difference is that markets sacrifice texture for computability and comparability. In order to allow the comparison of different courses of action in a clearly computable form, market systems must abstract from the particulars of any given sought transaction to a limited set of standardized data – price, quantity, more or less standardized quality measures. Social systems, on the other hand, tend to use more "analog" or textured modalities of information rendering, which make decisions less clearly computable but likely provide more richly textured information about the relevant transaction. The answer to an agent's question, "Should I sell my excess processor cycles at all, and if so should I sell them to a or b?" is informed in a different way when the relevant information is that "a will pay me 0.2 cents per processing hour, and b will pay me 0.25 cents per processing hour" rather than that "a is dedicated to finding extraterrestrial life, b is dedicated to finding promising compounds for AIDS drugs, and I was so close to John who died in the early days of the pandemic. . . . "

The trade-off between formal clarity and computability, on the one hand, and texture, on the other hand, suggests that social systems will be relatively weaker in organizing actions for which there are clear, computable, but fine differences between alternative courses of action. Conversely, such systems will be particularly valuable as information-processing systems where the context, the precise nature of the alternative possible actions, and the range of possible outcomes are persistently vague or difficult to specify formally. To the extent that information about production opportunities, cooperative actions, and motivational inputs can be represented effectively through social communications systems, it would represent a more complete statement of the factors relevant to an agent's decisions than could information available in systems – like the price system – that require formalization of the data so that they can be represented adequately for the particular process of computation defined as necessary to a decision in those systems. This is particularly important where uncertainty cannot be eliminated at an acceptable cost.

C. Differences in Motivation Structures

Markets and social production systems appeal to different motivations. Actual behavior is diversely motivated in either type of transactional setting, and agents may act for composite motivations in either setting. But the basic motivation in market transactions is to improve material welfare. The motivations in social settings are more varied. They include material instrumental motivations (e.g., *a* helps take care of *b*'s child today, expecting to be able to call on *b* some time in the future when *a* needs help with his children), intrinsic psychological motivations (e.g., acting in a way that makes one understand oneself to be a self-respecting, well-adjusted member of society), social relations building (e.g., spending time with friends), and pure altruism (e.g., donating blood to an unknown recipient). This diversity of motivations and the differences between market and social relations in harnessing them would not matter if we thought that (1) all agents were identical in their motivational structure and (2) the two types of motivation were purely cumulative. In that case, working through the market or through social relations would motivate all agents identically, and the number and mix of agents would depend purely on the magnitude of the reward, not on its form (material welfare, social-psychological). It also would not matter whether the total value of the reward was purely monetary, purely social-psychological, or some mix – adding more of one or the other would always increase the level of activity.

But agents are diverse in their motivational preferences, and money and social-psychological rewards are not cumulative. The former is not a highly controversial claim; the latter more so. The *locus classicus* of this latter issue is the Titmuss-Arrow debate. In his classic critique of the U.S. blood system, which was market based at the time, Richard Titmuss found that the United Kingdom, which had an all-volunteer system, had lower rates of hepatitis-infected blood (Titmuss et al. 1971). He claimed that when money was offered for blood, donors were driven away from donating blood, leaving money-seeking blood sellers who did not care about the unobservable quality of what they were selling (at that time there was no relevant test for hepatitis). Kenneth Arrow criticized Titmuss's interpretation, though not his basic finding of the differences in infection rates. Arrow's (1971) claim was that eliminating the market in blood supply could in fact remove the incentives of the "bad blood" suppliers to give blood, thereby improving the overall quality of the blood supply. In other words, Arrow claimed that people are in fact diversely motivated and that some people who will be moved for money will not similarly be moved for social reasons. What he rejected, however, was the claim that by introducing a market in blood, by commodifying blood, we would crowd out the volunteer donors. He saw the two systems as independent of each others – those moved to donate would donate, those moved to sell would sell. Adding money would therefore likely increase the activity, because it would bring sellers into the cycle of blood suppliers without crowding out volunteer donors.

Even this minimal divergence from the assumption that all agents are similarly motivated suggests that a system that is seeking to harness resources from widely divergent individuals needs to know something about this population. Imagine that there are two types of agents, Bs, who are driven to do good in society, and Cs, who are driven to make money. Imagine that putting a motivation scheme in place is costly. The designer of a project that wishes to tap the resources under the control of these agents would want to choose the higher-yield strategy and must study whether the population has more Bs or Cs: if the former, then the project organizer should invest in social-psychological motivations, and vice versa. Of course, if Arrow was right in his second critique of Titmuss, and if investing in motivation was costless, then the ideal strategy would be to include both motivations.

Subsequent theoretical and empirical literature has substantially bolstered Titumss's claim that introducing markets for an activity crowds out volunteer efforts.[5] There are now quite extensive studies that show that adding money to an activity may decrease the level of activity from levels previously attained when the activity was carried on purely for social and psychological motivations (Frey and Jege 2001; Frey 1997, 2001; Bewley 1995; Osterloh and Frey 2000; Frey and Oberholzer-Gee 1997; Kunreuther and Easterling 1990; Gneezy and Rustichini 2000). One theoretical framework – put forward in economics mostly by Bruno Frey – for explaining these findings is based on social psychology and focuses on the introduction of monetary interventions understood by agents as impairing their sense of self-determination and self-respect.[6] An alternative causal explanation is formalized by Benabou and Tirole, who claim that the person receiving the monetary incentives infers that the person offering the compensation does not trust the offeree to do the right thing, or to do it well of his or her own accord, and the offeree's self-confidence and intrinsic motivation to succeed are reduced to the extent that the offeree believes that the offeror – a manager or parent, for example – is better situated to judge the offeree's abilities (Benabou and Tirole 2000). These causal explanations may well be an important part of the story, but they tend to underplay the instrumental importance of social interactions to their participants, which has been so central to the claims of the social capital literature.[7] For social capital

---

[5] For a more complete statement, see Benkler (2004).

[6] Frey (1997) relies on the line of psychology literature that he follows back to Deci (1971).

[7] Lin (2001) makes the claim that "there are two ultimate (or primitive) rewards for human beings in a social structure: economic standing and social standing" (pp. 150–1), and elaborates a thesis according to which both represent relational standing, in terms of capacity to mobilize resources, some that can be mobilized by money, others those that can be mobilized by social relations. Coleman (1988) similarly is focused on the functional characteristics of social networks. See also Granovetter (1973, 1974) and Ben-Porath (1980).

to be not perfectly fungible with financial capital, as social capital is usually described, actions within a social framework must be nonfungible with actions in a market – otherwise market-based behavior could accumulate social capital seamlessly. It is fairly plausible to assume that ready availability of any given action or service from a market would debase the currency of that action as a mode of building social networks of reciprocity and social exchange. The personal sacrifice and connection between the actor and reciprocator loses its value if the agent's action is perfectly fungible with the actions of total strangers in the market. This instrumental, social capital–based hypothesis for crowding out would then explain the empirical literature that shows that the introduction of money decreases reciprocating cooperation.[8]

The most likely implication of the empirical findings and the theoretical interpretations is that people are indeed diversely motivated. They seek material welfare. They seek psychological coherence. They seek social relations of affirmation and companionship as well as relations of reciprocity and instrumental advantage. The relationship between these various social-psychological motivations and the presence of money in the relationship is at least ambiguous. It may be cumulative, with one adding to the value of the other. It may, however, be negative – in particular, where the presence of money could undermine the quality of the social-psychological relationship. Paying a friend at the end of a dinner party or paying one's sexual partner are ready examples of stark cases where money would completely crowd out the social-psychological rewards from the activity (Benkler 2002a). But the relationship of money to social-psychological rewards is not fixed or uniform. At one time, being a "professional" paid athlete or performer detracted from the social respect one could earn in these fields. That has now changed drastically. In any given period, money can be culturally framed in ways that are congruent with esteem and social motivations rather than opposed to them. For example, an academic offered a million dollars to make a scientific claim would not gain any respect in academia, though he or she may well decide to forgo the respect for the money and write the paper nonetheless. The same academic who writes the paper in the pursuit of, and eventually receives, the Nobel Prize gains respect rather than losing it.

If the relationship between money and social-psychological motivations described here is correct, this has substantial implications for how to structure one's activities in attempting to harness human behavior – be it labor or the contribution of excess resources like processor cycles. Returning to the

---

[8] In particular, studies that focus on the crowding out of reciprocity are supportive of a social causal theory (Fehr and Gechter 2002).

problem of the project designer trying to harness efforts or resources offered by a population of Bs and Cs, for example, the designer needs to recognize the possibility of an even stronger loss of Bs from the introduction of money. In other words, use of a cumulative activity – offering both money and social relations – will not lead to an aggregation of Bs and Cs. It will affirmatively crowd out Bs, unless the person seeking to harness the agents finds a way of culturally framing the money so that it does not crowd out the socially driven contributors.

It is possible, indeed likely, that there are different people with systematically different preferences on social-psychological as opposed to monetary motivations. But it is equally plausible that any given individual has different preferences along these dimensions at different stages of the day, week, month, and lifetime. Once an agent has received enough money to maintain whatever material standard of living she aspires to in the relevant time frame (today, this week, at the time of her retirement), her monetary appetite is at least partially satiated. At that point, her relative appetite for companionship or psychological affirmation may increase, and she would divert her actions toward activities that would satisfy that appetite. Anyone who looks forward to going home at the end of a workday or workweek and spending time with family and friends rather than staying to work overtime is experiencing such a motivation model. In designing a system to harness contributions, then, one of the considerations must be how well the platform for harnessing the effort can be calibrated to allow people to participate only when they are at a moment of the day or week when their preference for money is relatively satiated. The opposite is true if one believes that money is likely to be the primary motivator for agents who are likely to participate in his project.

D. Information and Motivation: Cumulative Considerations

Anyone considering how to structure a transactional framework for harnessing resources – like CPUs, storage media, or wireless capacity – is faced, then, with a choice among three transactional frameworks. It is possible to try to structure the transaction through one of the two more widely used models – either through a market-based transactional framework or internally through an enterprise. But it is also possible to use a social sharing or exchange system. Such a system is likely to have lower marginal information costs, will provide its users more textured information, and will have a greater capacity to harness social-psychological motivations.

In the case of shareable goods whose excess capacity is very widely distributed in relatively small incremental quanta – that is, in precisely the case that could be most valuable for constructing survivable backup systems for communications and computation infrastructures – the costs of using a market-based systems may be high and the crowding out effect strong. This is because, in order to achieve a usable robust system, contributions from a very large number of discrete individuals, in many discrete instances, will have to be harnessed. As the number of transactions necessary to achieve a working system increases, the relative per-transaction cost advantage of a social sharing system will become more salient. Furthermore, if each contributor is likely to provide a relatively small incremental contribution to the overall system, the amount of money that can be paid per user or per transaction is quite small. Crowding-out theory predicts that where the negative effects of commodifying an activity are made to kick in by the introduction of payment for the activity but the positive effects of adding money are low because the compensation offered is small, the crowding-out effect is likely to dominate and the activity level decline. This does not necessarily mean that social sharing is the only feasible approach to harnessing the large quantities of excess capacity that users connected to the Internet have for purposes of building survivable infrastructures. But it does suggest that for those organizations or in those settings where a social transactional framework can be used, that framework will be more effective than a market-based approach.

V. SOME PRACTICAL PROPOSALS FOR ORGANIZATION AND POLICY

The object of the paper to this point has been to describe a particular class of survivable infrastructures for computation and communication – those that rely on widely distributed components that are also widely owned and shared by their owners cooperatively. I suggested that the cooperative practices that underlie these behaviors are varied and diverse and that they range from the directly instrumental, as in the case of peer-to-peer file-sharing systems, to the altruistic, like SETI@Home. In this last section I briefly outline the approaches that organizations and individuals seeking to harness excess capacity in the traditional modalities (of markets and firms) might take, and then I provide a more detailed analysis of what sort of policy interventions would be appropriate to foster the adoption of such cooperative practices for purposes of survivability more generally.

A. Pooling Resources through Firms

The simplest avenue for adopting some of the insights of the systems described in Section III is to reorganize the use of computation and communications systems within firms. The personal computer revolution got a great lift when firms shifted from mainframes to PC-based information systems. Their use of PCs has remained unabated. The consequence is that any large firm has employees using large numbers of computers, usually all or most networked for purposes of information exchange as well as linked to a centralized backup facility. Firms that have employees in more than one location or that furnish or subsidize at least some of their employees' home computers/laptops, handhelds, and so on, can solve the cooperation problem trivially, by fiat.

A storage system like OceanStore, a processing load-balancing utility like SETI@Home, or a campuswide high-speed data network (e.g., a mesh network) could be implemented by a single firm if it has a sufficient number of employees with a sufficient number of devices. The more diverse the locations of the users and the more diverse the devices on which the systems are implemented, the greater the internal survivability that the firm is able to achieve. A single firm implementing any such system need not face any of the motivation or coordination problems that may create difficulties for the other alternative means of pooling these resources because of its ability to manage its employees rather than motivate and inform action by independent agents.

One degree removed from within-firm cooperation are platforms for pooling firm resources. Here, again, instead of efforts aimed at pooling individually owned resources, midsized firms can decide to form alliances or networks of pooled resources. The transaction costs would, of course, be much higher than those of a single large firm, but the number of independent decision makers who must reach agreement is still smaller, per computer, than in the case of fully decentralized systems. One option for such a network to emerge would be through a market actor that would provide the technology and know-how to pool resources and would cut its own costs by using the physical facilities of the businesses it organizes. The advantages of a cross-enterprise effort would include the relative diversity of its constituent components, which would give a successful cross-enterprise implementation greater resistance to viruses and other system failures, in addition to intentional attacks, than obtainable by a single large firm.

B. Secondary Markets in Excess Capacity

In moving away from enterprise-owned resources toward attempting to harness the excess capacity of individually owned resources, economists' standard market-based response would take aim at pricing capacity. This approach, despite its higher transaction costs and the possibility of lower participation than sharing-based systems, may nonetheless be the only approach available to certain types of enterprises. For example, a motivational message that sounded roughly like "Contribute a little bit of hard drive capacity to help ensure that our bank records do not get deleted in the event of a terrorist attack on our main databanks" is not likely to have the same motivational effect as, say, "Contribute your unused CPU cycles to help fight AIDS." While there may be some degree of goodwill toward helping prepare for terrorism, it is still likely that pleas to help commercial entities will not easily harness social-psychological mechanisms. This does not mean, however, that it is impossible to achieve similar results through markets.

In the distributed computing world, Gomez Performance Networks and Capacity Calibration Networks are examples of enterprises that harness user capacity through a payment system. Gomez Performance Network specializes in analyzing the actual speed and availability of corporate websites for access by users in different locations and with different connection speeds. Gomez appears to use end user–installed clients, not for their aggregate computational capacity, but for their location in network topology and their connection speed. They harness end users to run a client by promising payment based on a rate schedule per computation, per minute on the Net, and per user referred. But the users cannot set how often they participate or where they will go. Rather, the client, running testing tasks downloaded from the company's site, checks the speed and availability of websites when accessed from the user's desktop. Payment is capped at forty-five dollars a month. What is interesting about the site is that, while it uses the term "peer to peer" often, it constantly reinforces the message of "making money while you sleep," a message particularly clear from the client interface, which constantly shows the user's session, monthly, and lifetime balance of returns from running the program. It is difficult to measure the efficacy of this network's use of money as compared with the efficacy of the science-oriented volunteer distributed computation projects, however, because Gomez is not really harnessing raw distributed computation power but rather the participants' topological diversity. It limits the number of users connected based on the information sought, not on raw processing capacity needed. Therefore, neither the processing cycles harnessed nor the number of users recruited can offer a quantitative measure of comparative efficiency. Capacity Calibration Network (CapCal), like Gomez, primarily harnesses the topological diversity and bandwidth of users rather than their processing power. It pays users $0.30 per hour that CapCal uses the client. The user has no control over when the client is used.

A number of regularities in these sites are useful to note. First, all these payment-based systems are sensitive to transaction costs and use PayPal – a system designed specifically to be a cheap payment mechanism for micropayments on the Internet – to pay their participants. Another characteristic shared by Gomez and CapCal is that they need topological diversity, and hence contributors are nonfungible to them. It is insufficient for the purpose of these projects simply to harness as many users as possible. They must harness only some users and reject others in order to create a good topological distribution of users. The specificity of the requirements, which generates the need to reject many putative contributors, likely adds to the difficulty of attracting volunteers. Who, after all, wants to volunteer for a project that rejects many of its applicants for no apparent reason other than that they happen to be instrumentally useless? Beyond this is the fact that the motivational call to "help organizations solve their business problems" does not sound quite as inspiring as "help fight AIDS." Money then steps in as a reasonably well understood motivational source for a project ill suited to mobilize contributors socially. Measuring the comparative efficiency of these projects to the nonmarket projects is difficult. On the one hand, none of these systems has grown to a size that seriously competes with the volunteer projects as mechanisms for mobilizing the vast untapped resources connected to the Internet. On the other hand, they have been in existence for a while and do seem to generate the resources they need by paying for users' excess capacity.

A central design requirement for expanding the use of price mechanisms will be structuring the flow of funds so as to minimize the "crowding out" phenomenon. One approach to solving this problem may be to build resource-harnessing strategies into preexisting consumer relations. For example, one could imagine banks harnessing consumers who use online banking services as components in a financial data backup system. One simple but relatively weak version would be to make a tamper-proof, time-stamped cached copy of each user's own account information that gets automatically updated whenever the user logs on. Another would be to make a more explicit trade, where customers are given some discount in exchange for agreeing to offer backup facilities. This would then require an architectural approach similar to that of FreeNet and OpenStore to make sure that no participating customer could tamper with any document. The general point, however, is a simple one. Organizations that have preexisting relations with consumers and can integrate the survivability-creating cooperation into their service may have opportunities to harness distributed capacity through various add-on or bonus features at rates that would not have drawn users into a pool of resources without a prior relationship. Such low rates will, of course, be crucial given the amount of resources needed in relatively fine grained quanta.

C. Social Production of Survivable Infrastructures

1. Instrumental Exchange and Noninstrumental Giving. Observation of social production systems suggests that they capture a wide range of phenomena that draw on a wide range of motivations. File-sharing systems, for example, are systems of instrumental reciprocity. Participants do not explicitly barter with one another directly ("I will give you these three popular songs in exchange for that rare live recording") but rather enter a vast transactional framework where they provide their own songs to some unspecified number of unidentified users in exchange for access to the songs stored on the hard drives of other anonymous or pseudonymous users. An application like Skype – the voice-over Internet application provided by the makers of Kazaa that offers fully end-to-end encrypted telephony service from PC to PC and requires no dedicated infrastructure but uses the FastTrack architecture – similarly seems most readily explained as an instrumental exchange system. Users who wish to have the benefits of using Skype and being available so that their friends can call them will keep their applications running. Whenever they are not themselves speaking, the computer on which they run the application ready to receive calls is also available to relay the calls of others or to provide Supernode functionality. Although there are no test reports on the quality of Skype, anecdotally the application delivers quite impressive quality of service despite its lack of dedicated infrastructure and its strict reliance on peer-to-peer provisioned excess bandwidth, processing, and storage.

Distributed computing systems, on the other hand, are not helpfully described as exchange systems. The users do not have either direct or possible downstream access to resources or products they need. The contribution must be explained in terms other than reciprocal instrumentalism. Observation of the practices and interfaces of these systems suggests that they mix and match a variety of assumptions about the nature of the social giving that they pool. Sites describe the scientific purpose of the models and the specific scientific output, including posting articles that have used the calculations and in some cases offering interfaces that allow – with greater or lesser degrees of legibility – contributors to see the scientific contribution their computation is making.[9] In these components, the project organizers seem to assume some degree of taste for generalized altruism and the pursuit of meaning in contributing to a common goal. They also implement a variety of mechanisms to reinforce the sense of purpose, so there are aggregate statistics about total computations

---

[9] Climateprediction.net in particular provides each user with a discrete run of a simulated world with certain assumptions about CO_2 levels; the run shows the user how his "world" is doing relative to a baseline run.

performed – again, indicating a sense that users want to belong to a project that is successful and larger than themselves. Alongside these more solidaristic practices, the sites run components that are much more indicative of the mainstream anthropology of gift literature interpretation of giving as agonistic, on a "Big Man" model, that is, as a form of expressing social position. Here, we see most sites not only allowing individuals to track their own contributions but also providing "user of the month" type rankings – displaying who contributed the most cycles and similar statistics. Nonetheless, in an informal survey that SETI@Home conducts among its own users, only a little more than 5 percent focused on answers that tended to suggest a search for fame or explicit recognition, like getting one's name on the site's top 100 list. The majority of users describe themselves as contributing "for the good of humanity" (58%) or simply to keep their computer productive (17%).[10] Another interesting feature of these sites, which pool capacity from a range of the most advanced economies around the globe, is the appeal to ready-made identities, encouraging users to compete not as individuals but as teams sharing national or ethnic bonds, (e.g., Overclockers Australia or Alliance Francophone), technical minority status (e.g., Linux or MacAddict4Life), or organizational affiliation (University of Tennessee or University of Alabama).

2. Policy and Design Issues for Harnessing Instrumental Exchange. These observations suggest that the organizers of distributed computing systems do not themselves have a clear model of why some or most of their contributors contribute. Nor do we have an empirical or a theoretical basis to state whether different modalities of motivating social sharing and exchange crowd each other out, so that implementing one approach (e.g., user of the month) would have a similar crowding-out effect of introducing money relative to other, less individually oriented or agonistic forms of social motivation, like "help find a cure for AIDS." The little we have to go on suggests that the most successful projects have indeed been using mixed strategies. The applicability of crowding out theory to different social motivational structures would seem to be a fruitful and important focus of future research.

As a practical matter, ad hoc mesh networks that provide survivable last/first-mile connectivity are readily obtainable on an instrumental exchange model and can most readily be achieved or seeded by specific policy moves. Adoption of WiFi for in-home or office wireless LANs and the emergence of WiFi-based protocols for making transceivers self-organize into ad hoc mesh networks that use autonomic formation and self-heal provide the building blocks of such a

---

[10] http://setiathome.ssl.berkeley.edu/polls.html.

system. The primary remaining obstacle to the simple market-based emergence of neighborhood-level and municipal last-mile redundant wireless transport networks is the timing of reaching a critical density of adoption of these devices and networking protocols in any given area. Once devices are deployed in geographic space with sufficient density, the advantages of buying a device and implementing a mesh networking protocol as a means of reaching a competitive broadband Internet point of presence that can circumvent the wired pipelines to the home or small office will be available to any individual making a decision about purchasing a device with a networking capability installed. Until that density of deployment is reached, however, the additional cost, whatever it may be, of adding mesh networking capability will do the individual no good because she cannot rely on there being a sufficient number of others to allow her to reach the neighbor she wants, the local public library on a municipal WAN, or, most importantly, the competitive broadband POP that could save her ten dollars a month on her broadband access fee. Because of the path of development of WiFi, this problem may eventually solve itself, since users are deploying WiFi networking devices for their own home networking needs. Nonetheless, the move to implement wider-range networking may be delayed, or even stalled, by a lack of sufficient adoption of networking capabilities.

There are two distinct types of intervention by different levels of government that would speed up adoption and solve the problem of threshold density. Each could work independently of the other, but they would be mutually reinforcing.

At the federal level, the FCC could orient its unlicensed devices spectrum use rules with an eye to making mesh networking simpler. One type of intervention would be to allow greater flexibility in the design of unlicensed devices. Currently, constraints on unlicensed devices are defined in terms of a maximum peak power spectral density permitted for each device. What that means, as a practical matter, is that whether a device is deployed in Manhattan or in a ranch in Montana, it may transmit only a certain level of energy in a given bandwidth – which in turn limits the distance that a signal can travel. In Manhattan, the limitation is plausibly related to preventing interference with other nearby devices, and given the density of neighbors, it may impose no functional constraint on the ability of one transceiver to reach the neighbors it needs to in order to form a mesh. In Montana, on the other hand, the device could be cranked up to much higher power without interfering with any neighbors, and if it is not cranked up, it will fail to reach the next-door neighbor in the mesh. While implementing a "fix" for this problem is far from trivial, the basic idea of *in situ* measurement proposed by the Federal Communications Commission's own Spectrum Taskforce report (2002) may provide the correct way of thinking about a more locally adaptable regulatory requirement. While the specific solution proposed in that report – the "interference temperature" model – may or may not work, the basic idea is promising, namely, that devices that are context aware and can measure whether they are in an energy-soaked or energy-sparse environment should be permitted to adjust their transmit power accordingly.

The second type of FCC intervention is more of a "carrot" than regulatory relief and was also suggested by the Spectrum Taskforce Report. Here the idea is that device manufacturers get the "carrot" of being permitted to operate their devices in public safety spectrum, as well as in the general unlicensed spectrum, in exchange for designing their devices to be aware of and compliant with the highly bursty pattern of public safety use. The basic model is a "lights and sirens" model, where the highway is used by all vehicles, rather than having a reserved fire lane or emergency vehicle lane, but all drivers know they must pull over when an ambulance, fire truck, or police car is flashing its lights and sounding its siren. Device manufacturers who build devices that will recognize a siren and shift the device from normal user mode to an "infrastructure only" mode available to help in public safety communications but not using those frequencies for the users' own communications will be able to take advantage of wider and lower frequencies most of the time – improving their performance relative to competitors who do not take advantage of the same framework.

At the state and even more so at the local level, government agencies can help to seed mesh networks by adopting the kinds of public safety systems described in Section III and, importantly, making those facilities available to non-public-safety users under nonemergency conditions. The idea parallels the public safety spectrum use described in the preceding paragraph but is implemented by using resources under the control of local and state governments (fixed infrastructure points on fire houses, police stations, public libraries, schools, or utility poles to provide threshold density). Local authorities cannot change the operating parameters of the equipment but they can locate a larger number of off-the-shelf devices that are mesh enabled throughout the community. This would increase the probability that any individual would be able to connect to a network if he bought a device, even without coordinating with anyone else. The sirens-and-lights effect would then have to be implemented in the network access protocol rather than in the end-user device, but since the mesh architecture is now becoming separate from the off-the-shelf device, and since the local government will be the primary purchaser of the mesh protocol, it would be possible to specify respect for sirens in that protocol instead of in the device itself.

Implementing a parallel policy intervention for distributed storage and retrieval systems will likely be much more controversial. As the opening paragraph of this chapter suggests, we already have a highly survivable storage and retrieval system in the shape of peer-to-peer file-sharing networks. We have working distributed storage systems like FreeNet and working models like OceanStore that are already available as models to achieve highly distributed, redundant, survivable storage and retrieval systems. Because of the powerful lobby of Hollywood and the recording industry, however, peer-to-peer systems are under tremendous pressure, and deploying such systems presents a substantial business risk. The *Grokster* case is still being deliberated as of this writing. But while some of the most recent decisions suggest that systems with diverse uses may enjoy the benefit of the *Sony* case's privilege for manufacturers of devices/systems that have noninfringing as well as infringing uses, the fate of Napster and Aimster must weigh heavily on any U.S. domestic firm that is a stable and reachable defendant and that intends to offer a distributed storage and retrieval system. As Larry Lessig (2004) put it so well in *Free Culture*, however, the theoretical availability of various defenses, like fair use, may be enough for lawyers to claim that a law is "balanced"; it does not, however, actually provide a comfort zone for businesses given the realities of liability insurance and litigation risk. In order to overcome this risk, one would need to amend the Digital Millennium Copyright Act to make explicit a safe harbor for distributed storage and retrieval systems that have noninfringing uses.

The primary question with respect to using approaches oriented toward instrumental social exchange in the context of storage and retrieval is the extent to which one could structure the network so that its benefits were globally reciprocal. Consider OceanStore. Its designers, concerned with designing the technical attributes of the system as opposed to its social design, simply assumed that the capacity would be harnessed and distributed through some price mechanism (Rhea et al. 2001). This assumption was not, however, necessary to the design. One could instead design the system such that it is available as a backup system for all of its contributors on a reciprocal basis. With that type of system, the reason I would contribute my hard drive would be that I could then use it for my own data backup. If I want to use the system, I must contribute some of my hard drive capacity. The potential problem of free-riding could be solved by tying the amount of resources that the system uses on a particular machine to the amount of storage that the machine's user requires of the system (the ratio of the resources contributed by the user to the resources the user uses would be greater than 1).

This problem of how to resolve free-riding in peer-to-peer file-sharing networks arose first in a critique of the Gnutella network. Adar and Huberman (2000) showed that the distribution of files shared was highly skew – that 70% of Gnutella users did not share their own files and that over 50% of the files shared came from the top 1% of nodes. There was one interesting theoretical response and one valuable set of practical responses to this concern. The theoretical response was Clay Shirky's (2000). Shirky focused on the nonrivalry of music files, the renewability of bandwidth, and the high costs of micropayment systems (e.g., Mojo Nation) that might replace social sharing. His basic point was that systems that share nonrival or perfectly renewable resources can withstand a large degree of free-riding because the free-riders, while not contributing to the quality of the enterprise, take relatively little from it. The practical reality is that (1) efforts like Mojo Nation, which attempted to formalize the barter system in file sharing by giving anyone who gave resources "Mojo" (system-specific money that could be used to "purchase" system resources), failed and (2) clients of the Gnutella system and later the FastTrack system, like Limewire, BearShare, and later Kazaa, implemented much coarser mechanisms to improve the performance of a user's system, depending on the extent to which the user contributed resources for the benefit of the system as a whole.

Kazaa, for example, has created a system that motivates its users to share more content and review the quality of the files shared so that they have both technical and content integrity.[11] The system assigns to each user a "participation level" that is coarsely defined as low, medium, or high. A user begins with a level of medium. A user who systematically downloads more megabytes than he or she allows others to download or whose files are often corrupt or incomplete will eventually be downgraded to "low." Users whose files are downloaded more often than they download other users' files and/or who ensure that the files they make available have high technical and content integrity are upgraded to "high." Participation level is translated into a somewhat improved search capacity. In order not to put new users at too great a disadvantage, the system does not use participation level to affect initial search results. But the system offers "deeper" searches under a "search more" function, and the availability of the "search more" function is coarsely rationed based on the user's participation level.

Without suggesting that Kazaa's solution is the only or best way of achieving ideal levels of participation in peer-based survivable storage and retrieval systems, it does offer the flavor of the design solution. If one is designing a system like OceanStore and is concerned about improving participation levels, one could (1) make the system available for its users to store and back up their own data (with the increase of unique files like digital photographs that users would want to store and view from anywhere and whose loss would be irretrievable, this function will become ever more valuable) and (2) tie the

---

[11] http://www.kazaa.com/us/help/glossary/participation_ratio.htm.

availability of system resources to the degree of contribution that each participant makes. Because of the relative transaction cost advantages of social exchange systems relative to market exchange systems, and also because of the potential crowding-out effect, it would be best not to provide too fine an accounting system, however. Relatively coarse measures of participation seem to comport more with the relatively informal ways in which social sharing and exchange systems often work, and they certainly have been the more successful approach in the peer-to-peer file-sharing arena.

3. Noninstrumental Sharing and Giving. The description of the motivational structure of distributed computing projects suggests that these represent the least studied and understood type of social production – that is, nonprice, nonenterprise/firm-based activities. They seem to be instances of cooperation that are not exchange systems but rather operate on a model of pure redistribution with no exchange expected (Woodburn 1998). At most, if they do involve exchange, they are not a form of coarsely accounted in-kind barter but are rather a form of producing social relations and social hierarchy or some other symbolic meaning. Gift giving as a mechanism of producing social meaning has been the dominant focus of the anthropology of gift literature.[12]

The practices of the distributed computing models outline the elements that would be available to either individuals or organizations seeking to harness excess capacity for computation, communications, and storage in ways that were not easily attainable through instrumental exchange systems. To generate the signaling effects associated with public giving, one would have to ensure that individuals can track their own contributions and that there would be a facility to identify and recognize high contributors. To provide the context for social connections, communications systems for participants (e.g., discussion boards) could be maintained to produce activity-based social interaction. One could also attempt to harness preexisting identity categories, such as nationality or university or other organizational identity, by fostering extramural competition, as SETI@Home and Folding@Home do in their reliance on national and other affiliation identities.

These are approaches familiar from the philanthropy world, and to a great extent this aspect of sharing systems is parallel to the phenomenon of in-kind giving. Systems like distributed computing have the advantage, however, of harnessing privately owned resources in ways that make it unusually "cheap"

---

[12] The anthropological literature on sharing and the gift has been vast, starting with Malinowski (1922) and Mauss (1925). A combination of a broad intellectual history and a major contemporary contribution to this literature is Godelier (1997). See also Carrier (1998) and Hann (1998).

for the donor to give. First, because things are less fungible than money, the opportunity cost of giving a thing is lower than the opportunity cost of giving money. Giving $600 in cash imposes a higher opportunity cost for the donor than donating an old computer worth $600, because the mechanisms for liquidating those $600 and reusing them for some other activity are more costly than using the retained cash. Second, as long as the systems are tailored to harness genuinely excess resources – like computation, bandwidth, or storage that is genuinely renewable or nonscarce – the "contribution" given by the individual is costless to the individual. The only "costs" are (1) the forgone market opportunity and (2) the transaction costs of participation in the social giving system. Because of the relative advantage of social production systems in terms of marginal transaction costs, secondary markets may not be a feasible alternative for widely distributed excess capacity. Because the resources at stake – electrons and photons in one form or another – flow easily over a network in ways that need not be transparent to the contributor, the decision and implementation costs are lower than, say, donating a physical computer to a school. A system that reduces participation costs sufficiently should be able to motivate participation as long as it provides any meaningful social-psychological rewards.

VI. CONCLUSION

In an open network whose value inheres in global connectivity, achieving security through impregnability is difficult. For large classes of system requirements, survivability is more important than impregnability. In particular, where the value of a system – what makes it a critical system – is its availability for reliable use by its intended users in the face of attack, failure, or accident, rather than its denial to an enemy or competitor, survivability, not impregnability, is the primary security desideratum.

Since the early 1960s, and consistent with the design of the Internet itself, survivability has been understood to require distributed resources and redundant capacity organized so that the system can learn of failures and self-heal by reconfiguring its redundant resources to provide the functionalities threatened by the attack or failure. The greater the degree of distribution or diversity in the location and types of sources of capacity, the greater the resilience of the system to an attack on any particular resource or class of resources.

In the past five to ten years, a series of developments in distributed computing, ad hoc mesh networking, and peer-to-peer file-sharing systems have outlined an approach to replicating the survivability characteristics of the Internet as a data transmission network with regard to the three central attributes of any computation and communication system: basic physical-layer local connectivity (through wireless), data storage and retrieval (p2p), and processing (distributed computing). These systems all rely on the pooling of individually owned private computation and communications resources (PCs and laptops) into networks that share the excess capacity (processing, storage, and bandwidth) productively. They provide us with a template for how we could deploy similar strategies to develop peer-based survivable infrastructures for the core requirements of a computation- and communications-dependent economy and society.

These systems are instances of the general category of social production, or sharing and exchange of shareable goods. These are goods whose technical characteristics make it highly likely that there will be a relatively large amount of excess capacity distributed in relatively small dollops owned by individuals. Under these conditions, the transaction costs associated with harnessing the excess capacity of these resources through a secondary market are likely high, and the crowding-out effect of trying to harness it through markets is likely to decrease, rather than increase, total activity, because the attempt will likely drive off more social contributors than it will lure in market vendors of excess capacity. Resources distributed in this particular pattern may instead be more amenable to being harnessed through social production systems rather than through price-based markets and firms. Further, as this chapter makes clear, there are a variety of specific policy and organizational actions that could be used to improve the degree to which we harness these excess resources and help provide our society with redundant, survivable backup communication and computation systems.

While my focus here has been on computation and communications, nothing in the analysis limits my observations to these resources alone. Any type of capital good or source of capacity that is sufficiently fine grained to be widely owned in society yet sufficiently coarse grained or lumpy to possess more capacity than its owner typically can use is a candidate for mobilization through such social production systems. Learning how to build sharing systems and facilitating the conditions of social sharing and exchange rather than focusing purely on ways to perfect price-based markets in capacity or other types of goods could yield great improvements in productivity and, in the case of goods that can be harnessed to provide survivable critical infrastructures, security.

REFERENCES

Adar, Eytan, and Bernard Huberman. 2000. Free Riding on Gnutella. *First Monday*, October. http://ww.firstmonday.org/issues/issue5_10/adar/index.html.
Arrow, Kenneth. 1971. Gifts and Exchanges. *Philosophy and Public Affairs* 1:343.

Baran, Paul. 1964. On Distributed Communications. RAND RM-3420. http://www.rand. org/publications/RM/RM3420.

Ben-Porath, Yoram. 1980. The F-Connection: Families, Friends and Firms and the Organization of Exchange. *Population and Development Review* 6:1.

Benabou, Roland, and Jean Tirole. 2000. Self-Confidence and Social Interactions. NBER Working Paper W7585.

Benkler, Yochai. 2002a. Coase's Penguin, or Linux and the Nature of the Firm. *Yale Law Journal* 112:369.

———. 2002b. Some Economics of Wireless Communications. *Harvard Journal of Law and Technology* 16:25.

———. 2004. On Shareable Goods and the Emergence of Sharing as a Modality of Economic Production. *Yale Law Journal* 114:273.

Bewley, T. F. 1995. A Depressed Labor Market as Explained by Participants. *American Economic Review* 85:250.

Carrier, James G. 1998. Property and Social Relations in Melanesian Anthropology. In *Property Relations, Reviewing the Anthropological Tradition*, ed. Christoper Hahn, 85. Cambridge: Cambridge University Press.

Clark, Ian, et al. 2000. Freenet: A Distributed, Anonymous Information Storage and Retrieval System. http://citeseer.ist.psu.edu/clarke00freenet.html.

Coleman, James S. 1988. Social Capital in the Creation of Human Capital. *American Journal of Sociology* (Suppl) 94:S95.

Deci, Edward L. 1971. Effects of Externally Mediated Rewards on Intrinsic Motivation. *Journal of Personality and Social Psychology* 18:105.

Ellison, R. J., et al. 1997. Survivable Network Systems: An Emerging Approach. CMU-SEI Technical Report CMU/SEI-97-TR-013. www.cert.org/research/97tr013.pdf.

Federal Communications Commission. 2002. Spectrum Policy Taskforce Report. (Federal Communications Commission Washington, DC)

Fehr, Ernst, and Simon Gechter. 2002. Do Incentive Contracts Undermine Voluntary Cooperation? IERE Zurich Working Paper No. 34.

Frey, Bruno S. 1997. *Not Just for Money*. Boston: Beacon Press.

———. 2001. *Inspiring Economics*. Cheltenham, England: Edward Elgar Publishing.

Frey, Bruno S., and Reto Jege. 2001. Motivation Crowding Theory: A Survey of Empirical Evidence. *Journal of Economic Surveys* 15:589.

Frey, Bruno S., and Felix Oberholzer-Gee. 1997. The Cost of Price Incentives: An Empirical Analysis of Motivation Crowding-Out. *American Economic Review* 87:746.

Gneezy, Uri, and Aldo Rustichini. 2000. A Fine Is a Price. *Journal of Legal Studies* 29:1.

Godelier, Maurice. 1997. *The Enigma of the Gift*. Chicago: University of Chicago Press.

Granovetter, Mark. 1973. The Strength of Weak Ties. *American Journal of Sociology* 78: 1360.

———. 1974. *Getting a Job*. Cambridge, MA: Harvard University Press.

Hann, C. M. 1998. Introduction. In *Property Relations: Renewing the Anthropological Tradition*, ed. Christoper Hann, 23. Cambridge: Cambridge University Press.

Kunreuther, H., and D. Easterling. 1990. Are Risk-Benefit Tradeoffs Possible in Sitting Hazardous Facilities? *American Economic Review* 80:252.

Lander, Mark. 2004. Fight against Illegal File-Sharing Is Moving Overseas. *New York Times*, March 31. Section W, p.1.

Lessig, Lawrence. 2004. *Free Culture*. East Rutherford, NJ: Penguin.

Lin, Nan. 2001. *Social Capital: A Theory of Social Structure and Action*. Cambridge: Cambridge University Press.

Malinowski, Bronislaw. 1922. *Argonauts of the Western Pacific*. Long Grove, IL: Waveland Press.

Mauss, Marcel. 1925. *The Gift: Forms and Functions of Exchange in Archaic Societies*. Trans. I. Cunnison. London: Cohen and West.

Myers, Peter. 2001. In Crisis Zone, a Wireless Patch. *New York Times*, October 4. Section G, Circuits, p. 8.

Osterloh, Margit, and Bruno S. Frey. 2000. Motivation, Knowledge Transfer, and Organizational Form. *Organization Science* 11:538.

Pucher, John, and John L. Renne. 2003. Socioeconomics of Urban Travel: Evidence from the 2001 NHTS. *Transportation Quarterly* 57:49.

Rhea, Sean, et al. 2001. Maintenance Free Global Data Storage. *IEEE Internet Computing* 5:40.

Shirky, Clay. 2000. In Praise of Free-Loading, *OReilly Open P2P*, December 1. http://www.openp2p.com/pub/a/p2p/2000/12/01/shirky_freeloading.html.

Shirts, Michael, and Vijay Pande. 2000. Screen Savers of the World Unite! *Science* 290:1903.

Titmuss, Richard M., et al. 1971. *The Gift Relationship: From Human Blood to Social Policy*. New York: New Press.

Woodburn, James. 1998. Sharing Is Not a Form of Exchange. In *Property Relations: Reviewing the Anthropological Tradition*, ed. Christoper Hahn, 48. Cambridge: Cambridge University Press.

FOUR

CYBERSECURITY: OF HETEROGENEITY AND AUTARKY

Randal C. Picker*

The Internet is an almost organic mix of actors and their machines, an eclectic scheme of government and private decision-making, of nonprofits and for-profits. As in any integrated system, my choices affect your life in a very direct way. So "Zombie PC Army Responsible for Big-Name Web Blackout" sounds like a headline from a bad Hollywood B movie when instead it means that computer users could not access the websites of Apple, Google, Microsoft and Yahoo because a Trojan horse program – which, by definition, had been placed surreptitiously on thousands of personal computers, turning those machines into zombie computers under the control of their cybermaster – launched a simultaneous attack on a key piece of the domain name system infrastructure (Lemos and Hu 2004). Here we have perhaps one bad actor, thousands of sloppy computer users, and externalities galore.

Taking down prominent websites is one way for a malicious computer pro-grammer to seek fame (perhaps infamy), but spam provides perhaps a more meaningful way in which the day-to-day computer experience is degraded by our shared network decisions. Some estimates suggest that 80% of spam arises from zombie machines (Sandvine Inc. 2004). Many of these are residential PCs with broadband hookups. Why? This is the dark side of Yochai Benkler's (2004) work on shareable goods. From the consumer's perspective, both the PC and the broadband connection are shareable goods. Given the lumpiness

*Copyright © 2004, Randal C. Picker. All Rights Reserved. Paul and Theo Leffmann Professor of Commercial Law, The University of Chicago Law School, and Senior Fellow, The Computation Institute of the University of Chicago and Argonne National Laboratory. This paper was given at the conference under the title "Raising Transaction Costs and Network Security: Of Heterogeneity and Autarky." I thank Ryan Foreman for able research assistance; Ira Rubinstein for comments; and the Paul Leffmann Fund, the Russell J. Parsons Faculty Research Fund, and the John M. Olin Program in Law and Economics at The University of Chicago Law School for their generous research support, and through the Olin Program, Microsoft Corporation and Verizon.

115

of processing power, the average PC user has power to spare. This makes it easy for users to contribute computing cycles to the search for extraterrestrial life and to other large-scale projects.[1] But at the same time, excess cycles can be stolen with little obvious consequence to the computer owner. The consumer may experience no real loss when the evil cybermaster enslaves the consumer's PC to devote a chunk of the cycles and broadband connection to spam or a denial-of-service attack (White House 2003).[2]

But this is driven by more than excess cycles. The spam externality also has arisen from important changes in the way in which the network is organized. We moved from centralized processing power accessed through distributed dumb terminals (the 1970s) to distributed processing power in freestanding PCs (the 1980s) to, with the rise of the Internet, highly interconnected PCs (the 1990s). Nineteen seventies centralized processing was coupled with centralized control, a Soviet-style computer architecture. Users were eager to control their own destinies, and the personal computer made that possible.

The freestanding PC world that supplanted centralized computing gave rise to few direct externalities, positive and negative. Viruses could be spread through shared floppy disks, but the transactions costs of this type of inter-computer communication were sufficiently high that viruses didn't pose a particularly large problem. Plus a zombie PC wasn't even possible: even if the hacker could figure out how to get malicious software – malware – onto a floppy and from there to a particular PC, there was no easy way to get information or cycles back out. The hacker would have needed physical access to future floppies to get content out, a cumbersome arrangement.[3]

The rise of the networked PC changed this completely. E-mail and the Web make the spread of viruses and bots easy, plus the hacker can initiate access to the infected machine at will. This has made the decentralized decisions of end users much more salient. My failure to manage my computer appropriately puts you at risk.

All of this has made cybersecurity increasingly important. The concept of cybersecurity is sufficiently new that we should draw some lines of demarcation to understand what is at stake. Consider three categories that might be

---

[1] Visit the SETI@home web page to donate cycles (http://setiathome.ssl.berkeley.edu/).

[2] "In recent years, with the spread of 'always on' connections for systems, such as cable modems, digital subscriber lines (DSL), and wireless and satellite systems, the security of home user and small business systems has become more important not only to the users themselves, but to others to which they are connected through the Internet" (White House 2003). CNET News.com ("Scotland Yard" 2004) describes the rental of zombie networks – botnets – created by teenage hackers.

[3] For lack of a generally accepted alternative, I use the term "hacker" to refer to a malicious computer programmer. I do realize that this use is a bone of contention in some parts of the computer community. For discussion, see Bradley (2004).

encompassed within the notion of cybersecurity: cybervandalism, cybercrime, and cyberterrorism. Offline vandals break windows and deface buildings; online vandals – cybervandals – take down websites through denial-of-service attacks or deface websites by having an alternative web page load. The Recording Industry Association of America (RIAA) is front and center in the record industry's effort to combat music downloading, and that has made the RIAA's website a popular target (McCullagh 2002). Microsoft is frequently targeted as well (Lyman 2003). Like its offline counterpart, cybervandalism can inflict real costs on its targets.

Cybercrime is just crime over the Internet. So "phishing" – the cybercriminal sends a fake e-mail that appears to be from the recipient's financial institution seeking "reconfirmation" of financial information – is big business, with a 5% to 20% response rate that would make most marketers drool (Stewart 2004).[4] Congress recently made life harder for phishers by passing the Identity Theft Penalty Enhancement Act.[5] Other approaches to illicitly obtaining financial data seek to induce users to download software that sits in the background and records keystrokes, enabling the criminal to extract credit card information, passwords, and the like (Delaney 2004). The Computer Crime and Intellectual Property Section (CCIPS) of the Criminal Division of the U.S. Department of Justice focuses on these issues, though other parts of the federal government exercise authority as well.[6]

We might distinguish cybervandalism and cybercrime from cyberterrorism, even though the boundary lines aren't particularly clear.[7] We should probably define terrorism before defining cyberterrorism. The legislation creating the Department of Homeland Security defines both "terrorism" and "act of terrorism." The "act of terrorism" definition focuses on any act that "uses or attempts to use instrumentalities, weapons or other methods designed or intended to cause mass destruction, injury or other loss to citizens of institutions of the United States."[8] A cyber version of that might overlap with notions of cybervandalism or cybercrime. In contrast, the "terrorism" definition looks to acts directed at human life, critical infrastructure, or key resources where the motive is political.[9] *The National Strategy to Secure Cyberspace*, issued by the White

---

[4] For background, see U.S. Department of Justice (2004).

[5] P.L. 108-275 (July 15, 2004).

[6] Go to www.cybercrime.gov for info; see also U.S. Secret Service (2003).

[7] And they might not even distinguish cybervandalism from cybercrime. See Chapter 6 of this volume.

[8] The Homeland Security Act of 2002, P.L. 107-296 (November 25, 2002), § 865; see also 6 CFR 25.9 (definition of "act of terrorism").

[9] Idem at § 2 ("appears to be intended – (i) to intimidate or coerce a civilian population; (ii) to influence the policy of a government by intimidation or coercion; or (iii) to affect the conduct of a government by mass destruction, assassination or kidnapping").

House in February 2003, focuses on "threat[s] of organized cyber attacks capable of causing debilitating disruption to our Nation's critical infrastructures, economy or national security" (White House 2003, viii).

Within the U.S. Department of Homeland Security (2003, 2004), the recently created National Cyber Security Division focuses on the ways in which cybersecurity implicates key infrastructure. In January 2004, the NCSD launched its National Cyber Alert System, which builds on the prior work of the CERT Coordination Center at Carnegie-Mellon.[10] I grabbed at random a cybersecurity bulletin: it opened with a twenty-five–page list of software vulnerabilities identified between May 12, 2004, and May 25, 2004 (US-CERT 2004). *Ten days, twenty-five pages.*

Who is on this list of infamy? To choose just a handful of prominent names: Apache, Apple, BEA Systems, Eudora, GNU, Hewlett Packard, KDE, the Linux kernel, Microsoft, Netscape, Novell, Opera, Sun, and Symantec. This list covers both commercial and open source software, companies with dominant and used-to-be-dominant market positions, PCs and microcomputers. And it isn't the sheer number of vulnerabilities alone that is problematic: the time between knowledge of the vulnerability and exploitation by a hacker is dropping, as hackers pursue the zero-day exploit (no gap between knowledge of the vulnerability and malware that exploits it) (Rink 2004).

We need to figure out how to deal with this systematic cyberinsecurity. The problem arises from the underlying architecture of the system as implemented in the joint decisions of hardware makers and software creators, from the malware creators themselves, and from the aggregate consequences of many individual decisions made by end users. We have a number of possible targets and instruments to work with.

The hackers themselves are the most natural target, and we clearly will pursue them, but they can be quite elusive. We might consider end users themselves. After all, their infected machines do much of the work of the system: take those machines off of the system and the hackers will be deprived of one of their most valuable resources. And end users repeatedly create problems by clicking on executable e-mail attachments. Think of end users as engaging in negligent computer setup or negligent computer use. In a parallel setting, the RIAA has sued consumers for copyright violations tied to uploading and downloading music. The RIAA switched to this approach after it was frustrated in its efforts to hold liable Kazaa and other creators of file-sharing software (Borland 2003).

Internet service providers are another natural target. As critical intermediaries in the network, they are operationally situated to intervene in the working

---

[10] See www.cert.org.

of the network. The institutional structure matters too. The always-on, one-price all-you-can-eat structure for consumer broadband means that end users pay no attention to how bandwidth is used. I have no reason to pay attention when a hacker turns my home broadband-enabled PC into a zombie.

I will not consider the position of end users or of Internet service providers.[11] Instead, I examine two topics related to our management of cyberinsecurity: (1) the monoculture argument, which favors forced heterogeneity in operating systems, and (2) the ways in which liability rules influence software.

First, the software adoption choices of individual users create a software infrastructure against which hackers operate. One prominent argument – dubbed the "monoculture" argument – suggests that the collective choice is flawed, even if the individual choices are perfectly sensible. These individual choices have led to a Microsoft Windows monopoly in personal computer operating systems. According to the claim, the Microsoft operating system monopoly creates a harmful monoculture – a common code base through which computer viruses spread easily, putting the computing network at risk (Geer et al. 2003; Pope 2004; Whittaker 2003).

I begin by looking at the monoculture argument's focus on forced heterogeneity as a means of creating redundancy in our integrated computer network. I believe that forced heterogeneity would be quite expensive and that we would be better off focusing on autarky, meaning here the conditions under which individual computers or internal systems within a firm should be isolated from the rest of the public network. That is already a standard cybersecurity practice, and one frequently associated with the management of critical assets. Heterogeneity and autarky are substitutes in pursuing redundancy, but I think that there is a decided advantage for autarky in protecting key assets.

Second, I consider the overall question of software quality, since the implicit (explicit?) premise of the monoculture argument is not merely that we have *a* software monoculture but that it is also a particularly bad one. I consider the way in which liability rules – understood generally to include as a family insurance (contractual liability), warranties (more contracts), and torts – might influence software quality. Full-blown liability would help solve a software adoption version of the prisoner's dilemma – each user wants other users to adopt early and get the bugs out of the system – but would also introduce standard adverse selection problems. Voluntary contractual liability – a warranty to some customers – would mitigate those problems while permitting a natural improvement of software over time.

---

[11] For views on the potential liability of the latter, see Chapter 7 of this volume.

Sometimes it seems almost impossible to pay too much attention to Microsoft. As perhaps the leading firm of the Information Age, Microsoft is everywhere, an unavoidable fact in the daily life of every computer user. Windows, Office, and Internet Explorer are ubiquitous, with market shares to die for (and many competing products have done just that). Yes, Linux chips away on the desktop, and cell phones grow more powerful each day, but for the foreseeable future – say, the next decade – there is every reason to think that Microsoft will continue to define the computing experience of most users.

Monopoly inevitably brings attention. Good students of U.S. antitrust law understand that Judge Learned Hand's famous statement on monopoly – "The successful competitor, having been urged to compete, must not be turned upon when he wins"[12] – is at best a half-truth. We will scrutinize winners to make absolutely sure that they dot their Sherman Act i's and cross their Clayton Act t's. I know less about European competition policy, but we all know that Microsoft has received the most exacting attention on both sides of the Atlantic for more than a decade.[13]

The governments have focused on the competition policy consequences of Microsoft's monopolies. These are the usual issues of antitrust: Are prices too high? Has competition on the merits been squelched? Has output been reduced? These inquiries have not focused on the security consequences of monopoly, but others have rushed in to fill the void. The most visible strain of this analysis is the monoculture argument, namely, the argument that the Microsoft

---

[12] *United States v. Aluminum Co. of America*, 148 F.2d 416, 430 (2nd Cir. 1945): "A single producer may be the survivor out of a group of active competitors, merely by virtue of his superior skill, foresight and industry. In such cases a strong argument can be made that, although the result may expose the public to the evils of monopoly, the Act does not mean to condemn the resultant of those very forces which it is its prime object to foster: finis opus coronat. The successful competitor, having been urged to compete, must not be turned upon when he wins."

[13] *United States v. Microsoft Corp.*, 56 F.3d 1448 (D.C. Cir. 1995) (ordering the federal district court to approve the July 15, 1994, settlement between the United States and Microsoft regarding licensing practices for Windows and DOS); *United States v. Microsoft Corp.*, 253 F.3d 34 (D.C. Cir. 2001) (en banc) (unanimously affirming the district court finding of illegal monopoly maintenance under Section 2 of the Sherman Act); *Commonwealth of Massachusetts v. Microsoft Corp.*, 373 F. 3d 1199 (D.C. Cir. 2004) (affirming district court approval of a settlement agreement among certain states, the United States, and Microsoft); Commission of the European Communities, Commission Decision of 24.03.2004 (COMP/C-3/37.792 Microsoft) (finding an abuse of a dominant position in refusing to disclose certain interoperability information for servers and in conditioning acquisition of Windows on simultaneous acquisition of the Windows Media Player). For my views on the most recent U.S. antitrust case against Microsoft, see Picker (2002a).

operating system monopoly creates a harmful monoculture – a common code base through which computer viruses spread easily, putting the computing network at risk (Geer et al. 2003). The National Science Foundation (2003) is pouring $750,000 into funding research on ways of creating cyberdiversity, one possible antidote to the monoculture.

A. Monocultures: Supply versus Demand

Consider one formulation of the monoculture argument:

> Most of the world's computers run Microsoft's operating systems, thus most of the world's computers are vulnerable to the same viruses and worms at the same time. The only way to stop this is to avoid monoculture in computer operating systems, and for reasons just as reasonable and obvious as avoiding monoculture in farming. Microsoft exacerbates this problem via a wide range of practices that lock users to its platform. The impact on security of this lock-in is real and endangers society. (Geer et al. 2003, 7)

This argument builds on other work that draws out the analogy between farming – in particular cotton growing – and computer software (Quarterman 2002). That work suggests that in the United States in the early twentieth century, a cotton "monoculture" had emerged – that only one strain of cotton was grown and that too much acreage was devoted to cotton, especially given the risks posed by the boll weevil. The presumptive solution to monoculture is diversification, presumably meaning here that farmers shift fields from cotton to other crops.

Now I must confess that my knowledge of cotton is limited to thread counts and the supposed virtues of Pima, Supima, and Egyptian cotton for sheets (definitely go with the Egyptian), so I am not particularly well situated to make claims about cotton growing in the United States in the 1920s to 1940s. But a brief incursion into the world of cotton suggests that the analysis is tricky. Consider the most direct suggestion about boll weevil devastation and diversification. The boll weevil spread throughout the U.S. cotton belt during thirty years, from roughly 1892 in the southern tip of Texas to 1922 in northeastern North Carolina (Brown and Ware 1958). Between 1866 and 1892, harvested cotton acreage rose from 7,666,000 acres to 18,896,000 acres (U.S. Department of Agriculture 2004). Between 1892 and 1922, while the boll weevil worked its way across the cotton belt, harvested cotton acreage rose to 31,361,000 acres. The number of bales produced rose as well, from 6.7 million bales in 1892 to 10.1 million in 1922. As a group, farmers weren't exiting cotton growing at all; quite the opposite.

We can also look at the data slightly differently. Between 1909 and 1933 in the United States, cotton's share of planted acres fluctuates, but there is barely any net movement between 1909 (10.57%) and 1933 (10.78%).[14] Cotton does decline relatively during the Depression and World War II, and I don't begin to understand why that is, but it seems hard to trace any of this to the boll weevil.[15] While the boll weevil was spreading, cotton acreage was increasing in absolute terms, and cotton held its own as measured against other crops until 1933. We dealt with the weevil by switching to early blooming cotton varieties (Christidis and Harrison 1955) and by moving production to less humid locations (Brown and Ware 1958).

Now one might say that this just makes the monoculture point, that switching varieties or growing on different land is an example of heterogeneity in action.[16] But I think that the point is slightly different. The real point is about the cost of generating variety and how quickly adaptations can be made. Think of the point this way: do we need to have an existing stock of varieties in place to be drawn upon at the point where the dominant variety has been found to be wanting or does it suffice to implement just-in-time variety, variety when and as we need it? This is a point about the speed of adaptation in the face of a threat.

But there is a more basic problem with the monoculture idea, at least in farming. For the individual farmer, growing multiple crops is a way of self-insuring against the failure of any one crop. Self-insurance may be sensible if more direct insurance markets are underdeveloped or aren't sustainable for any of the standard reasons that insurance markets are difficult to establish (adverse selection and moral hazard, for example). But fundamentally, the monoculture idea says nothing about how much cotton should be grown. While individual farmers might want to grow a mix of cotton and corn to self-insure against the boll weevil, they shouldn't grow corn if no consumer wants it.

---

[14] This is calculated using the data series for all planted crops and the comparable series for cotton (U.S. Department of Agriculture 2004).

[15] If the numbers are right – and they are sufficiently dramatic that they are difficult to believe – the change in U.S cotton industry in one year was startling. In 1932, roughly 36.5 million acres of cotton were planted and 35.9 million were harvested. In 1933, the corresponding figures were 40.2 million and only 29.3 million. And in 1934, the figures were 27.8 million and 26.8 million. In one season, the harvested numbers fell through the floor, and plantings tracked that going forward. And it is unlikely that the change in harvested cotton in 1933 was due to the boll weevil or disease: productivity per harvested acre actually rose from 173.5 pounds in 1932 to 212.7 pounds in 1933 (presumably in part as a result of only harvesting the most productive fields) (U.S. Department of Agriculture 2004).

[16] Neil Katyal made this point in his oral remarks on his paper at the conference (published as Chapter 6 of this volume).

The cotton-corn trade-off is a great example of the difference between supply-side and demand-side substitutes. Cotton and corn might be supply-side substitutes for the individual farmer – grow one, grow the other, grow both (but they also might not be, as we clearly just shifted cotton production across states). But for the consumer, cotton and corn are poor substitutes: we don't see magazines extolling the virtues of corn-silk sheets, and no one suggests that you serve cotton as a side dish at your next Fourth of July celebration. The monoculture notion completely ignores consumer demand: it is a supply-side production idea tailored to the individual farmer for use when insurance markets are incomplete.

B. Heterogeneity and Autarky

Those concerned about monoculture might respond to this by noting that individually rational decisions can be collectively foolish. In choosing a computer and an operating system, the individual may take into account some of the externalities associated with computers. So computer software is frequently discussed as having network externalities: for example, I benefit when other users have the same software, as it makes it easier for us to swap documents. Sheer number of users can give rise to less direct network externalities, as many users will support a greater variety of software.

Individual users probably pay little attention to whether they should seek to contribute to software diversity by using software that runs against the mainstream. Some individuals may value difference and choose accordingly, and that would have the same consequence for increasing diversity in the installed base of computers. In contrast, large-scale choosers might be more sensitive to diversity benefits. They might seek to minimize the chance of a correlated failure of their computer systems by sprinkling pockets of Linux and Macs in a Windows-dominant population.

This means, in an almost a double-negative fashion, that the disconnect between the monoculture argument and what consumers want shouldn't necessarily dispose of the monoculture argument. But there is another set of arguments to consider, in particular those organized around the ideas of interconnection and autarky. Interconnection is the great issue of modern network industries. We impose connection obligations on firms that control key bottleneck facilities and seek ways to simplify how those connections are made. So, to take quick examples:

- *Electricity.* As electricity generation ceased to be subject to substantial economies of scale, we moved to encourage merchant generation by imposing an open access regime on the electricity grid. Vertically integrated grid owner/generators wouldn't be able to advantage their own generation over competing outside generation.[17]

- *Telecommunications.* To switch from electricity to phones, under the Telecommunications Act of 1996, we imposed on telephone incumbents three key sharing obligations: they must interconnect with entrants, so that new customers of entrants can call the incumbent's customers; an entrant can buy telcom services from incumbents at wholesale prices for resale to the customers of the entrant; and, most onerous, entrants can mix and match pieces of the incumbent's network and other facilities at cost-based prices under the unbundled network elements regime.[18]

- *Windows.* Interconnection is not only the dominant issue in traditional physical network industries. How the Windows operating system interconnected with other software was one of the key issues in the antitrust actions brought by the United States and the European Union against Microsoft. The consensual final judgment between the United States and Microsoft requires Microsoft to make available to third parties certain communication protocols to facilitate communications between third-party software and Windows.[19] The European Union case focused on two issues: bundling of the Windows Media Player with Windows and server interoperability, meaning how well do computer servers communicate with Windows?

But as we should have guessed, there is a real downside to all of this connectivity: problems percolate quickly throughout an interconnected system, and problems that might have been just local disturbances end up everywhere. The August 14, 2003, power blackout in Canada and large chunks of the eastern United States, which affected nearly 50 million people, emphasized again how a local problem – here overgrown trees in northern Ohio – could spillover throughout the electricity grid.[20]

---

[17] Promoting Wholesale Competition through Open Access Non-Discriminatory Transmission Services by Public Utilities, 61 FR 21540, 21544 (1996), *substantially affirmed sub. nom.* Transmission Access Policy Study Group v. FERC, 225 F.3d 667 (D.C. Cir. 2000), *affirmed sub. nom.* New York v. FERC, 535 U.S. 1 (2002).

[18] 47 USC § 251(d)(2). For discussion, see Lichtman and Picker 2003).

[19] Final Judgment, ¶ III.E. http://www.usdoj.gov/atr/cases/f200400/200457.htm.

[20] "After 15:05 EDT, some of [FirstEnergy]'s 345-kV transmission lines began tripping out because the lines were contacting overgrown trees within the lines' right-of-way areas. . . . The loss of the Sammis-Star line triggered the cascade because it shut down the 345-kV path into northern Ohio from eastern Ohio. Although the area around Akron, Ohio, was already blacked out due to earlier events, most of northern Ohio remained interconnected and electricity demand was high. This meant that the loss of the heavily overloaded Sammis-Star line instantly created major and unsustainable burdens on lines in adjacent areas, and the cascade spread

The monoculture is another name for a homogenous, connected system. In the monoculture framework, heterogeneity is used as a barrier to the spread of a virus throughout a connected computer system. The antimonoculture idea also taps into our sense of necessary biodiversity. It is reasonably straightforward to articulate possible benefits of biodiversity and to simulate those in a simple environment (Picker 2002b). Systems without sufficient diversity can be very brittle, especially as conditions change. An adaptation poorly matched to one environment may become the dominant adaptation as the environment changes.

But heterogeneity isn't equivalent to redundancy: if the University of Chicago Law School used only Windows computers, whereas Yale Law School used only Macintoshes, a Windows-only virus would decimate Chicago, and although Yale could continue to produce scholarly articles, we know that the world would be a very different place without articles written at Chicago. As this example suggests, we can achieve redundancy through heterogeneity only if we have done a good job of matching the level of heterogeneity with the level of unique assets. So if Stanford Law School and Yale Law School are good substitutes, we could afford to have each school specialize in a computer operating system, so long as each specialized in a different operating system. In contrast, to ensure that we don't lose Chicago scholarship – a unique asset in my world! – my law school needs to create heterogeneity internally (most dramatically, my colleagues Richard Epstein and Cass Sunstein should each have at least one Windows machine, one Linux box, and a Macintosh to ensure that not a single moment of writing time is lost).

The last example suggests some of the complexities of using heterogeneity to achieve redundancy. How would we ensure that substitutes use different operating systems? Across-firm heterogeneity might arise spontaneously – if there were two substantial choices with a 60/40 market share, for example. But unless the differentiated inputs are an important part of production – can you really write better papers on a Macintosh? – we shouldn't expect substitutes at the firm level to necessarily choose different substitutes in inputs, here different operating systems.

But heterogeneity may be a particularly clumsy approach to redundancy. Take two steps back on our path: we went from monoculture as connected homogeneous computers to looking at a system of connected heterogeneous computers. Maybe we just need to sever the connection, to isolate computers and to head toward an autarkic computer network. Think Tom Cruise and

rapidly as lines and generating units automatically tripped by protective relay action to avoid physical damage" (U.S.-Canada Power System Outage Task Force 2004, 45).

the first *Mission Impossible* movie: Ving Rhames can't just hack into the CIA computer at Langley to get the NOC list because the computer isn't on the network, so Tom has to dive in and hang from the ceiling.

Embracing isolation – disconnection or autarky – breaks the modern pattern of network industries. But interconnection is not always good, and we need to focus on an optimal amount of interconnection. These are obviously not new points to professionals whose job is to engineer safety. So the Nuclear Regulatory Commission (2003) has regulations that address how safety-related computer systems need to be isolated or send-only. At the same time, the regulatory push toward electricity generator neutrality is precisely about making better information available to outsiders about the state of the transmission grid. If done poorly, however, requiring interconnections for competitive purposes may create security problems.[21]

The extent of autarky is a choice, and in some cases we have reduced the degree of autarky in critical systems by moving more communications onto the public Internet. In many critical infrastructure industries, equipment is operated and assessed through SCADA systems (supervisory control and data acquisition systems). The SCADA systems are the eyes and ears of these systems, and systems that once ran on closed, isolated networks – autarkic networks – are migrating to the Internet (White House 2003). Moving control systems back to separate communication networks – so-called out-of-band management – is one of the approaches being considered by government officials to enhance cybersecurity (White House 2003; Lemos 2004).

So here is the question: should we buy redundancy through heterogeneity or through autarky (isolated systems)? Heterogeneity and autarky are substitutes, but quite imperfect substitutes. At an abstract level, we would need to do a social cost-benefit analysis on the costs of redundancy versus our tolerance for downtime and then figure out the different ways in which we might implement the same level of redundancy.

Try this: we can have ten connected computers running different operating systems or ten isolated computers running Windows. We know that it is cheap to make the next computer, quite expensive to make the next operating system. Meaningful variety in connected computers is quite expensive if that means

---

[21] "Although not all utilities have an interface between the control center and the corporate information system, the distinct trend within the industry is to link the systems to access control center data necessary for business purposes. One utility interviewed considered the business value of access to the data within the control center worth the risk of open connections between the control center and the corporate network" (National Security Telecommunications Advisory Committee 2004).

creating different operating systems. This is expensive redundancy. Simply creating the operating systems would be quite expensive; adding the associated software ecosystems – the actual application programs that do something – would make the costs extraordinarily high. In contrast, we can isolate ten computers running the same operating system for next to nothing. And of course this overstates the cost of autarkic redundancy. Software and data have a zero marginal cost and computer infections don't affect monitors and CPUs. We are really talking about redundant hard disks, and even an infected hard disk can be wiped clean and reused.[22]

Autarky works best for critical infrastructure, where we can invest the resources required to have isolation and parallel independent communication paths. Autarky addresses cyberterrorism, but autarky makes little sense for dealing with cybercrime. We can't very well tell Amazon.com to take its servers off the network to "solve" its cybercrime problems. Amazon lives and dies on the state of the public network. But Amazon also is a good example of the distinction between critical and noncritical assets. I would find it disruptive if Amazon were offline for a month, but we have many good substitutes for Amazon (BN.com, physical bookstores, books that I already own, libraries). Take the electricity system offline for a month, and much of our current infrastructure – almost of all which runs off of electricity – starts to break down.

C. The Cost of Engineering Heterogeneity

We can now circle back to the core remedies suggested in the monoculture literature, namely, mandatory porting of Office and Internet Explorer to other platforms and a 50% cap on the market share of Windows. Consider two quotations from Geer et al. (2003):

> Instead, Microsoft should be required to support a long list of applications (Microsoft Office, Internet Explorer, plus their server applications and development tools) on a long list of platforms. Microsoft should either be forbidden to release Office for any one platform, like Windows, until it releases Linux and Mac OS X versions of the same tools that are widely considered to have feature parity, compatibility, and so forth. (p. 18)

> A requirement that no operating system be more than 50% of the installed base in a critical industry or in a government would moot monoculture risk. (p. 19)

---

[22] And, for better or worse, the telecommunications bubble has created much redundant infrastructure, making it much cheaper now to create separate, isolated communications networks, with some estimates suggesting that only 3% of the fiber in the ground is being used (Dreazen 2002).

Mandatory porting of Office to "a long list of platforms" is an almost certainly an extraordinarily expensive way to seek heterogeneity, and one with no assurance of achieving the end in mind. Microsoft would be required to invest resources in creating a Linux version of Windows independent of any possible consideration of the economic returns from doing so. This remedy was suggested in the remedial phase of the U.S. antitrust case and was squarely rejected by the government "as far beyond the violations found."[23] So we won't impose a mandatory porting obligation as an antitrust remedy. And, in *Trinko*, the Supreme Court recently narrowed the circumstances in which a dominant firm might have an independent antitrust duty to deal with a rival, so we won't get porting through antitrust.[24] This would require federal legislation, and that would raise other issues. The possible Taking Clause claims associated with the duty-to-deal obligations in telecommunications and electricity have never been fully litigated, and a porting obligation might be far more onerous than those obligations.

It also might not work, and this takes us back to the cotton-corn discussion. Consumers might continue to purchase Windows even with Office ported to Linux. After all, Office has been available on the Mac operating system for some time, and we don't see consumers heading in droves to the Mac. Office is just one piece – a key piece to be sure – of the Windows ecosystem.

But the point of the second remedy – limiting the market share of Windows to 50% in critical industries – is to make sure that other operating systems thrive when they would not otherwise. Assume that we can surmount the question of which industries are critical – though we have struggled with that question for as long as we have had regulated industries[25] – and turn to the merits of the proposal. Given the advantages of autarky over heterogeneity, we should be focusing on the marginal benefit that we would achieve in a more heterogeneous environment.

---

[23] See Response of the United States to Public Comments on The Revised Proposed Final Judgment ¶¶ 433–34 (February 27, 2002): "The Court of Appeals did not find that Microsoft's unlawful actions created the barrier to entry. The United States crafted the [Revised Proposed Final Judgment] to restore the competitive conditions in the market that were impeded by Microsoft's actions, allowing consumers, software developers, OEMs, and others to make decisions based on the competitive merit of their options. In this way, the market will determine whether particular products will erode the applications barrier to entry. The commentors' and Litigating States' proposal, however, goes far beyond the violations found by imposing on the market a porting requirement for Office that substitutes for competition on the merits and preordains the market outcome."

[24] *Verizon Communications Inc. v. Law Offices of Curtis V. Trinko, LLP*, 540 U.S. 398(2004).

[25] *New State Ice Co. v. Liebmann*, 285 U.S. 262 (1932) (considering whether an ice business in Oklahoma was a public business and therefore appropriately subject to state regulation).

How many operating systems would we need to mitigate the monoculture problem? If we were a biculture or a triculture, would that be sufficient? Unsurprisingly, Microsoft believes otherwise, having taken the position that a truly diverse operating system culture would require thousands of operating systems.[26] The 50% cap in the monoculture literature is just asserted, without any reason being offered to believe that the limit would actually be effective.

And to take the cybersecurity question seriously, we need to switch from sport hackers seeking an idiosyncratic version of fame, if not fortune, to cyberterrorists intent upon taking down key infrastructure. Sport hackers probably just seek attention and dislike Microsoft, so for them Windows is the natural target. As other operating systems grew in market share, they might become attractive targets as well (Whittaker 2003).

Dedicated cyberterrorists would take into account the organization of the network and the number of operating systems at work.[27] A cascading failure – a failure that starts with one node and propagates throughout the network as loads are redistributed – is most likely to occur if the loads are distributed unevenly across the network and the node that fails first has a relatively high load (Motter and Lai 2002). An attacker seeking to bring down the entire system – power grid or Internet, for example – might naturally concentrate her attack on key nodes, perhaps the root servers in the case of the Internet (Whittaker 2003). And a cyberattack that relied on congestion, as occurs in a typical denial-of-service attack (CERT 1998), would almost certainly seek to exploit any substantial operating system.

In sum, I see little reason to think that a strategy of forced heterogeneity in operating systems would yield meaningful returns at an acceptable cost. This really would be market engineering of a particular sort, and there would seem to be more traditional responses available that will do a better job of creating meaningful redundancy and cybersecurity. We have frequently isolated networks from other networks – a strategy of disconnection or autarky – and I see little reason to think that we should not continue that policy in preference to a strategy of forced heterogeneity.

---

[26] "[Scott] Charney [chief security strategist for Microsoft] says monoculture theory doesn't suggest any reasonable solutions; more use of the Linux-source operating system, a rival to Microsoft Windows, might create a 'duoculture,' but that would hardly deter sophisticated hackers. True diversity, Charney said, would require thousands of different operating systems, which would make integrating computer systems and networks nearly impossible. Without a Microsoft monoculture, he said, most of the recent progress in information technology could not have happened" (Associated Press 2004).

[27] Hackers already write malware that infects across multiple platforms. See, e.g., the description of the virus {Win32,Linux}/Simile.D at http://securityresponse.symantec.com/avcenter/venc/data/linux.simile.html.

II. UNDERSTANDING COMPUTER SOFTWARE PRODUCT QUALITY

If we are likely to continue to have a monoculture in operating systems – and not just in operating systems, as, for example, Cisco's market share of high-end routers has been running in the 65% to 70% range (Reardon 2004) – what, if anything, can the legal system do to improve software quality? Microsoft gets a lot of attention, but as the Department of Homeland Security's cybersecurity bulletins make clear, Microsoft isn't the only company that produces software with vulnerabilities – far from it, in fact. For me, at least, the more relevant question is what is the relationship between software quality and the liability rules that relate to it? And what should be the source of the liability rules: voluntary contract, default or mandatory warranties tied to contract, or perhaps tort?

We should start with a typical Microsoft End User License Agreement, the basic contract between Microsoft and those using its software. Microsoft disclaims all warranties to the maximum extent permitted by law, seeks to limit any possible damages, and seeks to limit any other possible remedies.[28] For Microsoft to be held liable for software defects, an end user would have to surmount these contractual barriers. Of course, producers have been disclaiming warranties for some time, but only with limited success in the face of judges willing to expand tort doctrines of product liability. In *Henningsen v. Bloomfield Motors, Inc.,*[29] the New Jersey Supreme Court ran right over a warranty disclaimer in, as my colleague Richard Epstein (1980) puts it, "inaugurat[ing] the modern age of products liability."[30]

Tort liability here would be especially tricky, as we will frequently have three parties to consider: Microsoft, as producer of the software; the hacker, who has created the virus or worm; and the harmed end user, who very well may have contributed to the harm by clicking when he shouldn't have done so. We would need to sort through complex tort doctrines relating to causality, the intervention of third parties, and basic questions regarding strict liability, negligence, and contributory negligence. These are not sure winners for Microsoft, as key infrastructure providers have been held liable even in the face of malicious acts by third parties who might naturally be understood to be the actual source of the harm. So the railroad was held liable in *Brauer* when its train struck a horse-drawn wagon and thieves made off with empty barrels and a keg of

---

[28] See End-User License Agreement for Microsoft Software § 8. http://www.gotdotnet.com/team/clr/samples/eula_clr_cryptosrc.aspx.

[29] *Henningsen v. Bloomfield Motors, Inc.,* 161 A.2d 69 (1960).

[30] To put it mildly, Epstein (1980) is skeptical of the path launched by *Henningsen:* "However popular the *Henningsen* approach might be today, it remains clearly flawed in all its essentials" (p. 53). For additional discussion in the context of software, see Alces (1999).

cider.[31] And Consolidated Edison was held liable for damages resulting from looting and vandalism when its gross negligence allowed the lights to go out in New York City in 1977.[32] But these issues, while critical for anyone seeking to impose liability on software providers, are not my target here, and I will instead consider how liability rules influence software quality and software adoption decisions.

A. Consumer Software Adoption with Full Liability

Start with a system of full liability: Microsoft would be liable for the harms that result from its products. With full liability, how would consumer behavior change? A key issue for consumers of software is what version of a product to purchase. Street "wisdom" has it that Microsoft doesn't get its products right until at least the third version, so a prudent user may wait before jumping in. When Microsoft issues a new version of Windows, you are frequently advised to wait until the first service pack is issued before embracing the new operating system. In each case, the consumer trades off the benefits of the new product against the costs of that product. Those costs include the actual purchase price, the hassle of making changes, and also the expected costs associated with buggy software. Buggy software costs include downtime from software that works poorly, the cost of installing frequent patches, and the possible costs of a hacker harming your computer system.

A consumer compares the benefits of the new software against these costs in making a purchase or installation decision. These benefits and costs are private information, known only to the individual consumer. Hacker insurance – actual insurance or de facto insurance imposed under the guise of product liability – could change that decision, as the consumer would no longer face the hacking costs. Such is the nature of insurance: the insured rationally ignores real social costs. As a society, for given software we want consumers to wait for a revised version or not install the software at all if the full social costs of the software exceed the benefits.

Mandatory full insurance – put differently, broad product liability – would result in overconsumption of the software. In a competitive market, mandatory insurance would result in a cross-subsidy from one set of consumers to another. Consider a simple example to make this point.

We have two types of consumers. C1 values the software in question at a benefit of $200 and has no hacking costs. C2 values the software at $20 and has

---

[31] *Brauer v. New York Cent. & H.R.R. Co.*, 103 A. 166 (N.J. Ct. Errors and Appeals, 1918).

[32] *Food Pagent, Inc. v. Consolidated Edison Co.*, 429 N. E.2d 738 (N.Y. 1981); *Koch v. Consolidated Edison Co. of New York, Inc.*, 468 N. E.2d 1 (N.Y. 1984).

hacking costs of $50. We have nine C1s and one C2. It costs $50 to make the software and nothing to make each copy. Let us use a zero profit condition to define a competitive outcome. Full costs if all ten consumers buy the software equal $100. The social benefit from the software is $9 \times \$200 + \$20$, or $1,820, against costs of $100, so we should build the software. If we sell ten copies, then a price of $10 per copy would cover the costs of the software. At that price, all ten consumers would buy, and the net gain from the software would be $1,720.

But without bundled mandatory insurance, we would do better. C2 wouldn't buy, and we would have costs of $50, benefits of $1,800 and net benefits of $1,750. The bundled "insurance" is worthless to the C1 consumers, and when it is required, we have overconsumption by C2 – a social loss – plus a cross-subsidy running from the C1s to C2 to boot.

B. Quality Investment and Full Liability

Mandatory insurance affects investment in product quality in a number of interesting ways. So, to continue the example, suppose that Microsoft could spend $10 to redesign Windows to eliminate all of the hacking costs. From a standpoint of overall social welfare, we would like this to happen: C2 values the software at $20 but faces hacking costs of $50. Microsoft could eliminate those costs by spending $10. Will Microsoft do so?

No, at least not if we assume that Microsoft is selling only one product and therefore must sell the same quality product to each consumer. Our C1 consumers don't value the higher-quality product: they don't face any hacking costs and would not want to pay a penny more for a better product that lowers hacking costs. If Microsoft spent $60 to make the software – the original $50 cost plus the additional $10 to eliminate hacking costs – then Microsoft would need to charge $6 a copy to cover its costs, assuming that all ten consumers bought a copy of Windows. C1s would end up with a net benefit of $194 ($200 – $6). An operating system entrant facing the same costs could build the $50 version of the product and cover its costs selling only to the nine C1s at a price of $5.55, making the C1s better off. (Obviously, if Microsoft could sell two versions of the product, it could separate the market and it would then make the $10 investment. So low-quality Windows would sell for $5, high-quality Windows for $15, C1s would buy the low-quality version, and C2 would buy the high-quality version.)

How would mandatory insurance change these decisions? Again, if Microsoft sells only one version of Windows, mandatory insurance "solves" the quality underinvestment problem. Recall how the prior example worked. With bundled insurance, Microsoft's total costs were $100, the $50 product cost and the $50 insurance payment for C2's hacking harms. Microsoft could lower those costs by spending the $10 to eliminate C2's hacking costs, in which case total costs would drop to $60. With mandatory insurance, Microsoft would do this.

So should we think that we have two countervailing effects of mandatory insurance, overconsumption by some consumers but better product design decisions by Microsoft? Not really. To bring the two examples together, from a social standpoint we would like Microsoft to spend up to $20 to eliminate C2's hacking costs, and no more. Remember that C2 puts a value of $20 on the product and faces hacking costs of $50. Microsoft is going to build the software for the C1s of the world, and there is no marginal cost to putting a copy in C2's hands. Microsoft gains C2's value if it can eliminate the hacking costs, so it should spend up to $20 to do that.

Mandatory insurance would get Microsoft to do that. Unfortunately, as set out in the first example, C2 will take the software period and won't internalize the costs of that decision. So with mandatory insurance, Microsoft will have an incentive to overspend on quality, to invest up to $50 to eliminate C2's hacking costs. What we would really like, socially, is for Microsoft to spend up to $20 to eliminate the hacking costs and for C2 to stop buying the software if it costs more than $20 to eliminate those hacking costs. That is the first-best outcome, but mandatory insurance doesn't get us there.

At least in this framework, unbundling the insurance and allowing Microsoft to offer insurance on a voluntary basis doesn't accomplish anything. No C1 would buy insurance, and Microsoft would not sell C2 insurance for less than $50. You can't pool risk without more types than we have in this example.

C. Timing of Software Release and Adoption

When should Microsoft release software? When should a consumer adopt new software? How do the liability and warranty rules matter for these decisions? To build on the prior example for just a bit, instead of imagining that Microsoft faces an initial design choice, think of Microsoft as learning about its software over time through use by consumers. So a sufficient amount of use during period 1 means that Microsoft can redesign the software for use in period 2. We know of course that this tracks actual practice: Microsoft releases service packs for Office and Windows.

In a basic sense, this is a question about the optimal time to release software, a product likely to have two distinctive characteristics (at least as compared to an exploding Coke bottle). First, we think that we will learn about the product through consumer use. We may learn a bit about Coke bottles in consumer hands, but we think that we will learn vastly more about a given piece of software as end users explore the full set of possibilities inherent in it. So we think that the scope of learning is much greater for software. Second, software can be modified after the fact at very little cost. Said again, software is continuous whereas physical products are lumpy and discrete. Once the Coke bottle is in my hands, Coca-Cola can alter it after the fact only at high cost. Think of the burdens associated with recalls of physical products for retrofitting. In contrast, software could be adjusted across the network while in place. The learning associated with software and its installed malleability should push toward earlier product release than for physical goods.[33]

To just focus on learning, suppose that Microsoft will learn from period 1 use how to eliminate C2's hacking costs and that by using the knowledge gained it can eliminate those costs at a cost of $1. Period 1 use saves Microsoft $9 in reduced design costs, assuming it would have cost $10 in period 1 to eliminate C2's hacking costs.

Now we can look at insurance a little differently. A no-insurance approach helps to segregate and sequence adoption by end users. Consumers who anticipate deriving substantial net benefits from the product adopt early, conferring a use externality on those who wait. These guinea pigs pay a higher price for the software – higher because they bear period 1 hacking costs, which will be eliminated for period 2 users. Absent the insurance, we end up with a form of price discrimination.

Indeed, the story gets even better. We don't see Microsoft selling two versions of Windows – one with bugs and one without – simultaneously. But this is close to what we see occurring over time (okay, perhaps one version with many bugs and one with fewer bugs). Selling different quality software at different times separates the market and makes it possible to make the socially sensible investment in reducing hacking costs that couldn't occur in the one-period version of the model above.

To see this, imagine this path for use and sales. Microsoft anticipates selling one version of the software today and a second, improved version tomorrow. Microsoft spends $50, builds Windows, announces a $5 per copy price, and sells without insurance. C1s buy today – an assumption for now and an important issue below – and get a benefit of $195. No entrant can offer them a better deal. C2 doesn't buy today, as the buggy software is a bad deal for him. The next period, Microsoft invests $1 in a service pack for the software. Microsoft raises the purchase price for Windows to $6, and C2 buys, with a net benefit to C2 of $14.

---

[33] A more formal analysis of these issues would look to the burgeoning literature on real options, which makes timing and the costs and benefits associated with delay central to its analysis (Dixit and Pindyck 1994). Product liability policy almost certainly needs to take into account these critical questions regarding the optimal time at which to release products.

Why didn't Microsoft just spend the $10 in the first period to eliminate the bugs? Two reasons. First, society saved $9 in quality improvement costs in using the software in the first period. Whether that makes sense depends on C2's discount rate, as C2 gets the software only in the second period. But second, and more importantly, we avoid the defecting-coalition problem that we saw above. Were Microsoft to spend the extra $10 on Windows in the first period and sell the bug-free version to all, it would charge $6 to everybody. An entrant could produce the buggy version for $50 and sell nine copies to the C1s for $5.55 a piece, and the C1s would defect.

By selling different quality software at different times, it is possible to support the incremental expenditure on quality. Once the C1s have purchased, they can't defect to a competitor. The purchases by the C1s create the learning that reduces the costs of improving the software. With mandatory insurance, C2 would have no incentive to internalize the costs of early adoption of the software.

We have relied on consumer heterogeneity – C2 differs from C1 – to get the results we have seen so far. If consumers are identical, then we may confront a waiting problem, where each consumer waits for another consumer to adopt first. Put differently, users may believe that there is a second-mover advantage to software adoption. Or, more jargon, we may have a prisoner's dilemma in software adoption, where each person wants the other guy to go first, and no one adopts the software. Insurance, voluntary or mandatory, would help to solve the second-mover problem.

How would this work? Suppose that consumers are identical. In choosing whether to adopt new software today or tomorrow, consumers should compare the net benefits today against the discounted benefits of adoption tomorrow. The key point here is that costs tomorrow depend on the number of adoptions today, where the greater the number of adopters, the lower the costs.

Insurance reduces the costs of adoption today. We could imagine a partial insurance scheme, as the learning that emerges from use may not require that all consumers use the software in the first period. We should want an insurance scheme that incurs just the cost required – and not a penny more – to learn enough to lower the costs of adoption tomorrow. Note that that won't happen with mandatory insurance. Partial insurance might be implemented by insuring only a fraction of the customers or by insuring only a fraction of the harms.

III. CONCLUSION

The wonder of the Internet is incredibly capable computers connected with each other under the control of individuals. Think that decentralization is a powerful force, we have applauded the ability of individual users to set up websites and make their ideas available to others. But there is a dark side as well. Always-on connections, extra computing cycles, and gigabytes of storage to burn mean that individual decisions can propagate throughout the network quickly. The small-worlds phenomenon that is the Internet means that my computer is only a handful of clicks away from a malicious computer programmer.

My decisions matter for your computing life. A malicious hacker can turn my computer into a zombie and use my broadband connection and my computer to shut down websites, to send millions of spam e-mails, or worse. The network is a sea of computing externalities, many extraordinarily positive but others that can range from everyday bothersome to enormously disruptive. Indeed, the more we embed critical infrastructure into the public network, the more we make it possible for a cyberterrorist to turn our computing resources against us and thereby harm critical infrastructure, such as the electricity grid or our communication networks.

Addressing cybersecurity is a mixed question of engineering – computing architecture – and legal rules. The zombie PC problem emerges with the rise of the Internet and decentralized control over PCs. The pricing structure of the Internet world – one-price, all-you-can-eat broadband and lumpy computing power in the form of powerful CPUs – kills off many of the natural incentives for an individual to ensure that her computing resources are not being used by others. This can be good, as it creates many opportunities for sharing, but the downside is that there is little reason for the individual computer user to police against zombification.

We need to look for mechanisms, architectural and legal, to boost cybersecurity. Obviously, we will always pursue cyberterrorists, but we want to take steps before cyberterror takes place. We could consider actions targeted at individuals, perhaps legal actions for negligent computer setup or computer operation, or more centralized approaches to kicking poorly configured machines off the network. We might enlist Internet service providers, original equipment manufacturers, or software producers in those efforts.

But I have not considered those issues here. Instead, I have looked at two topics in detail. The monoculture argument supports one approach to architecting the network. That argument suggests that we should focus on forcing heterogeneity in operating systems to enhance our cybersecurity. I think that is the wrong emphasis. On its own terms, the argument tells us little about the extent of diversity that would be required to achieve meaningful protection, especially if our concern is the cyberterrorist. The argument also ignores the more important question of adaptability, meaning how quickly can the current system adapt to new conditions. Instead, I argue in favor of the traditional approach of isolation – autarky – and recommend separating critical infrastructure from the public network.

Second, I consider the way in which liability rules that apply to software might influence the quality of software and software use decisions. Hackers can exploit defects in software to seize control of machines. Fewer defects to exploit and we might reduce the harms of hackers. This turns out to be tricky. Broad liability rules that would protect consumers from the harms of hacking will lead to the standard moral hazard problem that we see in insurance. Consumers who shouldn't be using computers or be on the network will jump on once they are protected from hacking losses.

These are standard product liability issues, but software has two particular features that suggest that we should not apply our standard approaches only to product liability. First, we learn about software through use. One piece of software is combined with other software in a way that a Coke bottle is rarely combined with anything else. Second, software can adapt and can be fixed in place after the fact. Both of these features should push toward earlier release of software, as buggy software can be fixed later.

REFERENCES

Alces, Peter A. 1999. W(h)ither Warranty: The B(l)oom of Products Liability Theory in Cases of Deficient Software Design. *California Law Review* 87:269.

Bank, David. 2004. Computer Worm Is Turning Faster. *Wall Street Journal*, May 27.

Benkler, Yochai. 2004. Sharing Nicely: On Shareable Goods and the Emergence of Sharing as a Modality of Economic Production. *Yale Law Journal.* 114:273.

Borland, John. 2003. RIAA Sues 261 File Swappers. *CNET News.com*, September 8. http://news.com.com/2102-1023_3-5072564.html.

Bradley, Tony. 2004. What Is in a Name? http://netsecurity.about.com/cs/generalsecurity/a/aa070303.htm.

Brown, Harry Bates, and Jacob Osborn Ware. 1958. *Cotton.* 3rd ed. New York: McGraw-Hill.

CERT. 1998. Smurf IP Denial-of-Service Attacks. CERT Advisory CA-1998–01.

Christidis, Basil G., and George J. Harrison. 1955. *Cotton Growing Problems.* New York: McGraw-Hill.

Delaney, Kevin J. 2004. Web-Data Hackers Thwarted, but PCs Are Still Vulnerable. *Wall Street Journal*, June 28.

Dixit, Avinash K., and Robert S. Pindyck.1994. *Investment under Uncertainty.* Princeton, NJ: Princeton University Press.

Dreazen, Yochi J. 2002. Behind the Fiber Glut. *Wall Street Journal*, September 26, Section B, p. 1.

Epstein, Richard A. 1980. *Modern Products Liability Law.* New York: Quorum Books.

Geer, D., et al. 2003. The Cost of Monopoly. http://ccianet.org/papers/cyberinsecurity.pdf.

Lemos, Robert. 2004. Sprint Touts Off-Net Networks. *CNET News.com*, July 22. http://news.com.com/2102-7355_3-5280148.html.

Lemos, Robert, and Jim Hu. 2004. Zombie PC Army Responsible for Big Name Web Blackout. *CNET News.com*. http://software.silicon.com/malware/0,3800003100,39121439,00.htm.

Lichtman, Douglas, and Randal C. Picker. 2003. Entry Policy in Local Telecommunications: Iowa Utilities and Verizon. *Supreme Court Review* 2002:41.

Lyman, Jay. 2003. Denial-of-Service Attack Brings Down Microsoft. *TechNews World*, August 4. http://www.technewsworld.com/story/31258.html.

McCullagh, Declan. 2002. Recording Industry Site Hit Again. *CNET News.com*, September 3. http://news.com.com/2102-1023_3-956398.htm.

Motter, Adilson E., and Ying-Cheung Lai. 2002. Cascade-Based Attacks on Complex Networks. *Physical Review* 66:E 065102(R).

National Science Foundation. 2003. Taking Cues from Mother Nature to Foil Cyber Attacks. http://www.nsf.gov/od/lps/news/03/pr03130.htm.

National Security Telecommunications Advisory Committee. 2004. Electric Power Risk Assessment. http://www.ncs.gov/n5_hp/Reports/EPRA/electric.html.

Nuclear Regulatory Commission. 2003. NRC Issues Information Notice on Potential of Nuclear Power Plant to Worm Infection. NRC Press Release No. 03-108.

Picker, Randal C. 2002a. Pursuing a Remedy in Microsoft: The Declining Need for Centralized Coordination in a Networked World. *Journal of Institutional and Theoretical Economics* 113:158.

————. 2002b. SimLaw. *University of Illinois Law Review* 2002:1019.

Pope, Justin. 2004. Biology Stirs Microsoft Mono-Culture Debate. http://concretewerk.com/blosxom/archives/monoculture.html.

Quarterman, John S. 2002. Monoculture Considered Harmful. *First Monday*, February. http://www.firstmonday.dk/issues/issue7_2/quarterman.

Reardon, Marquerie. 2004. Cisco Bets on New High-End Router. *CNET News.com*, May 24. http://news.com.com/2102-1033_3-5218356.html.

Rink, David. 2004. Computer Worm is Turning Faster. *Wall Street Journal*, May 27.

Sandvine, Inc. 2004. Trend Analysis: Spam Trojans and Their Impact on Broadband Service Providers. http://www.sandvine.com/soloutions/pdfs/spam_trojan_trend_analysis.pdf.

Scotland Yard and the Case of the Rent-A-Zombies. 2004. *CNET News.com*, July 7. http://news.com.com/2102-7349_3-5260154.html.

Stewart, Christopher S. 2004. Fighting Crime One Computer at a Time. *New York Times*, June 10, Section C, p. 5.

U.S.-Canada Power System Outage Task Force. 2004. Final Report on the August 14, 2003 Blackout in the United States and Canada: Causes and Recommendations.

US-CERT. 2004. Cyber Security Bulletin SB04-147. http://www.us-cert.gov/cas/body/bulletins/SB04-147.pdf.

U.S. Department of Agriculture. 2004. *Historical Track Records.* Washington, DC: U.S. Department of Agriculture, National Agricultural Statistical Service.

U.S. Department of Homeland Security. 2003. Ridge Creates New Division to Combat Cyber Threats. Press release, June 6. http://www.dhs.gov/dhspublic/display?theme=52&content=918.

————. 2004. U.S. Department of Homeland Security Improves America's Cyber Security Preparedness – Unveils National Cyber Alert System. http://www.us-cert.gov/press_room/cas-announced.html.

U.S. Department of Justice. 2004. Special Report on "Phishing." http://www.usdoj.gov/criminal/fraud/Phishing.pdf.

U.S. Secret Service. 2003. United States Secret Service and Romanian Police Work Together to Solve Major Computer Fraud Investigation. http://www.secretservice.gov/press/pub2503.pdf.

Warning: Microsoft "Monoculture." 2004. Associated Press. http://www.wired.com/news/privacy/0,1848,62307,00.html.

White House. 2003. The National Strategy to Secure Cyberspace. http://www.whitehouse.gov/pcipbcyberspace_strategy.pdf.

Whittaker, James A. 2003. No Clear Answers on Monoculture Issues. *Security and Privacy* 6:18.

PART TWO

SOLUTIONS

Private Ordering Solutions

FIVE

NETWORK RESPONSES TO NETWORK THREATS: THE EVOLUTION INTO PRIVATE CYBERSECURITY ASSOCIATIONS

Amitai Aviram*

The enforcement of certain norms on network participants – such as norms supporting information exchange and governing access to the network – is critical for ensuring the security of the network. While a public norm enforcer may be feasible in many situations, private norm enforcement may, and frequently does, complement or substitute for public enforcement. Private enforcement of cybersecurity is often subsidized, primarily in nonpecuniary manners (e.g., by exemption from antitrust laws). These subsidies may be necessary to capture the positive externalities of providing security to the network, but they also bias private parties' incentives and may result in the formation of inefficient security associations that are beneficial to their members only due to the subsidy. To mitigate this concern, subsidies should be awarded only to associations that are likely to be effective in enforcing norms on the network participants. This article offers a framework for assessing the likelihood that an association would become an effective norm enforcer.

Norms that are expensive to enforce are rarely enforced by newly formed private legal systems (PLSs) because the effectiveness of mechanisms used to secure compliance (e.g., the threat of exclusion) depends on the PLSs' ability to confer benefits on their members, and newly formed PLSs do not yet confer such benefits. Preexisting functionality inexpensively enhances a PLS's ability to enforce norms, and therefore most PLSs rely on preexisting institutions that

* Assistant Professor, Florida State University; LL.B., Tel-Aviv University, 1995; LL.M., University of Chicago, 2000; J.S.D., University of Chicago, 2003. This article is an expansion and application to the realm of network security of Aviram (2004). I am grateful to Baran Alpturk and R. Christian Walker for their research assistance, and to Robert Ahdieh, Daniel Cole, Saul Levmore, Richard Posner, Mario Rizzo, Amy Sweeney, Oliver Williamson, and the participants of the New York University Colloquium on Market Institutions and Economic Processes and of the Institutional Analysis Workshop at the Haas School of Business, University of California at Berkeley, for their invaluable comments. My gratitude also goes to the Critical Infrastructure Protection Project for generous financial support.

already benefit members, typically by regulating norms that are not very costly
to enforce. The threat of losing these benefits disciplines members to abide by
the PLS's rules, thus permitting the PLS to regulate behavior.

Network security norms are usually expensive to enforce, and thus a private
association enforcing them would be more successful and thus more deserving
of public subsidies if it relied on a suitable preexisting functionality. This article
suggests criteria for assessing the effectiveness of preexisting functionalities.

I. INTRODUCTION

As computer networks play an increasing role in our lives, threats to these
networks become a growing source of concern. Computer viruses seemed so
innocuous just two decades ago that the prestigious journal *Scientific American*
offered its readers technical details on how to create computer viruses (Malone
and Levary 1994). Earlier this year, a single computer virus called Sasser caused
an estimated $3.5 billion of damage to computer systems, and this figure earned
the virus only third place on the list of most-harmful computer viruses (Grow
2004). Harm from future attacks on information networks threatens to be
even greater as reliance on information networks increases and as the networks
become more attractive targets for organized attacks motivated by ideology
and politics.[1] The rising risk to information networks is driving increased
investment in, and greater public attention to, network security.[2]

Actions necessary to maintain a network's security can be categorized
into two abstract tasks: forming norms that mitigate threats to the network
and enforcing those norms.[3] There is lively discussion, especially among

---

[1] Ideologically and politically motivated cyberattacks are numerous but thus far have not caused
the same magnitude of harm as the worst nonideological malicious code attacks. For some
examples of ideologically motivated attacks, see "Islamic Hackers" (2002), "Israel under Hack
Attack" (2002), Gentile (2000), and Olsen (2001).

[2] This article refers to "network security" rather than cybersecurity, since the analysis applies
to all network industries, including but not limited to information networks.

[3] Scholars offer a variety of definitions of the term "norms." Cooter (1996) defines norms as
obligations. Eisenberg (1999) defines norms as "all rules and regularities concerning human
conduct, other than legal rules and organizational rules" (p. 1255). McAdams (1997) defines
norms as "informal social regularities that individuals feel obligated to follow because of an
internalized sense of duty, because of fear of external non-legal sanctions, or both" (p. 339).
E. A. Posner (1996) defines norms as rules that distinguish desirable and undesirable behaviors
while giving a third party the authority to punish those engaging in undesirable behaviors.
Strahilevitz (2003b) defines norms as "behavioral regularities that arise when humans are
interacting with each other, regardless of whether that interaction is face-to-face" (p. 363
n. 24) Sunstein (1996) uses a rough definition of norms as "social attitudes of approval and
disapproval, specifying what ought to be done and what ought not to be done" (p. 914).
Since the same "norm" may potentially be enforced by one of several regulators (i.e., norm

information technology specialists, on the appropriate norms: the technologies that should be implemented to mitigate risks to the network (e.g., antivirus software, firewalls, etc.), the appropriate precautions and safeguards to prevent unauthorized access to the network, the types of information that network members should exchange to improve their ability to defend the network, and so on.

The debate on the proper way to enforce network security norms is held primarily, though not exclusively, within legal academia. Significant attention was given to alternative forms of public enforcement – tort liability (Brooks 1998), criminal liability (Katyal 2001), international cooperation between governments (Goodman and Brenner 2002), and even securities laws.[4]

The debate on norm enforcement has not been restricted to public enforcers but has also extended to private ordering (Cunningham 2004) – enforcement of norms by nongovernment institutions called private legal systems (PLSs), which are intended to regulate the behavior of its members.[5] PLSs either replace or complement an extant public legal system ("the law"). They can take a multitude of forms. Some PLSs are as simple as a contract between two parties, assigning rights and duties differently from the default set by public law. Other

enforcers), including government as well as private actors, depending among other things on the relative efficiency of each regulator in enforcing the specific norm, it is not sensible for this article to use a definition that is based on the identity of the regulator (e.g., it is a norm if a private actor enforces it but not if a government actor does). Therefore, the article uses a very broad definition of the term "norm," taking it to encompass all rules and regularities concerning human conduct (including legal and organizational rules).

[4] The *Law Week* article "DHS, SEC Talking about Requirements to Disclose Information about Cybersecurity" (2003) discusses the possibility that the Securities Exchange Commission (SEC) would require public companies to disclose their activities for the purpose of maintaining cybersecurity. Though the SEC's proposal only requires disclosure of activities taken rather than mandates any activity, the disclosure requirement creates an incentive for firms to initiate some cybersecurity measures so as not to affirmatively report that they are not doing anything.

[5] Though usually discernable, the dichotomy between public and private legal systems is not always a clear one. Some PLSs have a significant public backing and are very similar to public legal systems. For example, the King of England enacted in 1353 the "Statute of the Staple," which prohibited Common Law courts from hearing disputes arising from contracts made on the staple markets (markets for important commodities, such as wool). Instead, the statute created Staple Courts and instructed them to apply the (privately formed) law to merchants. Thus, private law was given exclusive jurisdiction by public decree (Zywicki 2003).

Conversely, some public legal fora defer to private ordering fora (e.g., arbitration proceedings), and some public legal fora compete with other legal fora and thus act more like PLSs. For example, the common law developed in England from the rulings of judges of the Court of King's Bench. For centuries this court had competed with several other royal courts (notably the Court of the Exchequer and the Court of Common Pleas), the ecclesiastical courts, town and feudal courts, and merchant courts (Zywicki 2003). Though the courts had, in theory, limits to their jurisdictions, they each used legal fictions to expand their reach (Zywicki 2003). As Adam Smith (1776) noted, this led to improved quality and impartiality of judicial decisions.

PLSs are elaborate and rely on private courts. Lex Mercatoria, the PLS that governed a significant portion of long-distance trade in the Middle Ages, is an example of this type of PLS.[6] A PLS may be based on hierarchy, such as the internal rules of a company. Other PLSs do not have clear hierarchies. These include the system of social norms that leads most of us to stand in a queue, to be polite to strangers, to yield to an anonymous driver who is trying to switch lanes on a highway, and so on.

While the private ordering literature examines PLSs and tracks the evolution of norms that are created and enforced by these systems, it pays scant attention to how the institutions themselves evolved to become PLSs (Bernstein 1992; Clay 1997; Ellickson 1989, 1991; Greif 1993; Milhaupt and West 2000; Oedel 1993). In the context of network security, there is a dearth of discussion on what forms of private enforcement are effective, as compared with discussions on forms of public enforcement. On the surface, there may be at least two reasons why it is not necessary for scholars to identify which forms of private enforcement of network security are effective. Both reasons are seen to be weak when examined in greater depth.

The first reason is that PLSs that enforce network security should be disciplined by the invisible hand of the market. The members of a PLS are assumed to bear the full costs of its operation and thus are expected to have an incentive to design the institution efficiently. Failing that, the members have an incentive to identify more effective PLSs and imitate them, or leave the PLS and join a more effective one. Thus, over the long term PLSs are expected to either become efficient in enforcing network security or disappear. The fault in this argument lies in its factual basis – PLSs that enforce network security are subsidized by government. We will discuss these subsidies below.[7] These subsidies bias the incentives of the PLS members. They may continue operating a PLS after discovering that it is inefficient (or even form one knowing it is inefficient) in order to receive the public subsidies given to PLSs.[8]

The second reason stems from an expectation that efficient PLSs are the result of identifying efficient norms. Under this view, the main bottleneck to a successful PLS is finding a norm that is Pareto efficient[9] (or that through side

---

[6] On lex mercatoria, see, for example, Benson (1989).

[7] See Section II.C. These subsidies are mostly nonpecuniary and are typically a privilege (e.g., exemption from antitrust laws, preferential access to information, etc.).

[8] For an example of a form of private ordering that, despite being ineffective, is allegedly maintained to receive subsidies, see Krawiec (2005), who argues that corporate compliance programs are often "window dressing" maintained by companies to benefit from the preferential treatment given to these programs in the U.S. Sentencing Guidelines. Aviram (2005) argues that this "subsidy" is justified.

[9] A Pareto efficient (or Pareto superior) transaction "is one that makes at least one person better off and no one worse off" (R. A. Posner 1998a; p. 14).

payments can become Pareto efficient)[10] and persuading others that the norm is in fact efficient. Once participants realize that the norm is efficient, the PLS is expected to be efficient, because the participants realize that it is in their interest to ensure that they all follow the norm.

Some of the private ordering literature seems to endorse this view implicitly, and thus very little attention has been paid to the evolution of norm enforcement mechanisms (as opposed to the evolution of the norms they enforce), despite calls by some scholars to study this issue.[11] Perhaps drawing on the Coase theorem, as well as assuming negligible transaction costs[12] and perhaps expanding on Friedrich Hayek's (1978) theory of spontaneous order, much of the literature presupposes that PLSs emerge spontaneously in response to a governance need unfulfilled by government.[13] Even those works that explicitly recognize the high transaction costs borne by a PLS in enforcing norms focus (with rare exceptions) not on the effects of these costs on the evolution of institutions but on what institutions eventually evolved (Ellickson 1986; Ellickson and Thorland 1995).[14]

If this view was true, then discussion should focus, as it does, on identifying efficient norms for network security. Such research will not only identify the most effective norms but also explain to would-be participants why they are effective and persuade them of the norm's efficiency, thus paving the way for an efficient PLS to form spontaneously.

But this view is flawed, because it fails to note a pattern in the evolution of private ordering.[15] PLSs typically do not form spontaneously but build on existing institutional infrastructure – networks that originally facilitated low enforcement cost norms (i.e., norms that do not require coercion to effect compliance). PLSs that lack this preexisting functionality are likely to be ineffective

---

[10] For example, if having A and B comply with a norm makes A better off by eight dollars and B worse off by two dollars, and A is able to identify B, monitor B's compliance, and pay B three dollars if B complies, then the combination of norm and side payment is Pareto efficient, as A is better off by five dollars and B is better off by one dollar.

[11] "Let me identify two [problems] that seem most urgent and should provide the basis for future research. First, there is not yet a precise understanding of the way norms work and evolve . . ." (E. A. Posner 1996, 1743).

[12] On the Coase theorem and its relation to PLSs, see the discussion in Section III.B.

[13] The term "spontaneous formation" as applied to a PLS may be ambiguous. By "spontaneous formation" I mean the creation of a PLS without reliance on a preexisting foundation. In this chapter, I claim that such patterns of PLS formation are rare. Some of the literature uses the term "spontaneous formation" in regard to private ordering to mean that its evolution is decentralized or private (i.e., not dictated by a government) (Benson 1989). I do not dispute that PLSs may evolve in a decentralized process.

[14] Greif et al. (1994) discuss the evolution of a specific institution that became a PLS: the merchant guild.

[15] This pattern was first espoused in Aviram (2004). Portions of Section III were taken from this article.

in enforcing norms (except in rare situations where enforcing a norm requires very low enforcement costs) because of a "chicken and egg" paradox. This paradox, which I refer to as the paradox of spontaneous formation, runs as follows: To direct behavior efficiently, PLSs must ensure the cooperation of their members. But the effectiveness of the mechanisms used to secure this cooperation (e.g., the threat of exclusion) depends on PLSs' ability to confer benefits on their members – primarily the ability, not yet existing in a spontaneously formed PLS, to direct behavior efficiently.

This paradox could, in theory, be resolved if there was an efficient bonding mechanism that assured the members of a spontaneous PLS (i.e., a newly formed system not based on a preexisting network)[16] of members' mutual obedience to the rules. But bonding of this sort is very expensive, and its costs often outweigh the benefits conferred by the PLS.[17] At the very least, enforcing a norm with a spontaneously formed PLS that overcomes the paradox through bonding is much more costly than enforcing the same norm by relying on a preexisting network that already enforces another norm on its members. Thus, in most cases, bonding is not a practical solution to the paradox of spontaneous formation.

Rather, an effective and inexpensive enforcement mechanism relies on preexisting functionality. If a norm is to be enforced on a group of people and an existing PLS already enforces another norm on the same people, the PLS can impose the new norm and threaten members with exclusion from the group if they violate the new norm. Thus, the paradox of spontaneous formation is avoided because the sanction to a norm violator includes not only the loss of the future benefit from the new norm (the successful enforcement of which is uncertain) but also the certain loss of benefits from the norm that is already enforced. For example, the preexisting PLS could be a social network, and the new norm could be a prohibition on stealing from members of the social network. A group of strangers may steal from each other despite preferring a world in which no theft exists, because they may feel that if they do not seize the opportunity to steal from others, another person will steal from them. If this norm was enforced by a social network, however, theft would result in exclusion from the group and loss of one's friends. Not only could this be a

---

[16] The term "spontaneously formed" is used rather than "new" because an existing network that has hitherto regulated a low–enforcement cost norm (e.g., social interaction) and has now evolved to regulate another, higher–enforcement cost norm (e.g., restriction of warfare) would be a "new" PLS with respect to regulating the latter norm. However, the preexisting functionality is an important difference in the system's ability to regulate, and therefore a term is needed to distinguish between a completely new ("spontaneously formed") system and an existing system that begins to regulate a new norm.

[17] See Section III.B.

significant sanction, but knowing that other members will be excluded if they steal helps assure each member that others will not violate the norm, thus making the perceived benefit from being a member of this social circle greater (and the threat of exclusion from it more effective).

Of course, the preexisting norm has to form somehow, and it too may suffer from the paradox of spontaneous formation. How is it, then, that PLSs exist? The answer lies in an exception to the paradox: if the norm has negligible enforcement costs (i.e., no coercion is needed to cause members to comply with the norm), members will adhere to the norm even if they expect the PLS to be an ineffective enforcer. A social circle may again serve as a useful example. Most people enjoy the company of their friends and will attend social events of their group even if they expect some of the other members of the group not to attend. Thus, they will attend an event even if they think the social circle cannot punish them or others for failing to attend.

Once the PLS provides members with benefits of complying with the norm, it can also threaten to take those benefits away by exclusion, giving the PLS a preexisting functionality that can be used to enforce another norm with a higher enforcement cost. And after enforcing this new norm, the PLS has an even more powerful sanction (exclusion from the benefits of both the original and the new norms) and thus can attempt to enforce norms that are yet more costly to enforce.

By applying this theory to the context of network security, we may derive useful guidelines for the scope of public subsidies to private network security associations. Public subsidies of private network security efforts may be appropriate in some cases because of the significant positive externalities network security confers on people who are not network members (e.g., individual users of the power grid benefit from security measures implemented by the utility companies, which enhance the reliability of the supply of electricity). However, as stated earlier, such subsidies are harmful when they create an incentive for private parties to maintain inefficient PLSs. By understanding how effective PLSs evolve and what characteristics make them more likely to succeed in enforcing new norms, we may direct subsidies to those PLSs that have the greatest promise of success and away from others that are more likely to fail (unless artificially sustained by the subsidies).

The rest of this chapter discusses the theory of PLS evolution and its application to network security. Section II examines the private provision of security by networks, using an example from early medieval Europe before proceeding to a modern counterpart, the information sharing and analysis center (ISAC). A discussion of the types of public subsidies that are given or are proposed to be given to ISACs concludes this section.

Section III introduces a theory of how PLSs form and evolve. First it delineates the scope of private ordering this article claims to explain: the private enforcement of norms through networks rather than through hierarchies.[18] It then reveals the flaws in the extant literature's implied assumption that PLSs form spontaneously and explains why decentralized bonding cannot effectively enforce a norm without reducing the volume of transactions to which the norm applies below the efficient level.[19] This section then examines the role of existing functionality of a PLS in lowering the costs of enforcing a new norm and proposes criteria to determine which networks have the lowest enforcement costs (and are thus likely to undertake to enforce norms that are relatively more expensive to enforce).[20]

Section IV revisits network security PLSs, armed with an understanding of how PLSs form. It demonstrates that most network security norms are likely to have high enforcement costs, and thus a PLS enforcing them is unlikely to form without a preexisting basis. It then describes, through a case study of one ISAC, how private network security associations are likely to evolve. Finally, it suggests how public subsidies of ISACs should be allocated to increase their ability to foster effective ISACs. Section V concludes.

II. PRIVATE PROVISION OF SECURITY BY NETWORKS

A. Private Security Associations in the "[Very] Old Economy"

Life in Western Europe in the late tenth century was, for most of its inhabitants, dismal and unsafe. The decline of the Carolingian Empire created a political vacuum and intensified the decentralizing forces that had plagued the empire since its inception. Throughout the region, independent warlords consolidated power through private warfare, unhindered by the ineffective central government.[21] Peasants were among the main victims of this warfare, since it was far more difficult for the warlords to breach a fortified stronghold than to starve it out by destroying the surrounding fields.

Mutual destruction of farms was an unattractive result even to a heartless warlord, but destroying the farms of a rival warlord was the most rational action for each warlord to undertake. If one warlord expected his rival to show mercy

---

[18] See Section III.A.
[19] See Section III.B.
[20] See Sections III.C–E.
[21] On the Pax Dei movement and conditions in Western Europe at the time of the movement's birth, see Head and Landes (1992); see also *Peace of God: Pax Dei*, at http://www. mille.org/people/rlpages/paxdei.html.

to the warlord's peasants, then attacking the rival's peasants would bring a quick and decisive victory. And if a warlord expected his rival to show no mercy to the warlord's peasants, then the warlord's only chance was to preemptively strike the rival's peasants.

In some situations, this gloomy outcome could have been averted either through intervention by a third party capable of enforcing its will on the opposing parties or by a warlord's exercise of self-restraint in order to garner a reputation for fairness. Such a reputation could benefit the warlord in future encounters with the same rival and in encounters with others who had learned of the magnanimous party's reputation. But in West Frankland in the tenth century, central government was too weak to assume the role of third-party enforcer, and a reputation for benevolence was of little use. A warlord whose mercy was taken advantage of, even once, would likely die, precluding his receipt of any future benefit from possessing a benevolent reputation.

This bleak dynamic of mutual destruction was halted, however, by a unique institution that surfaced in response to the situation: Pax Dei (Latin for "Peace of God"), one of the world's first decentralized, popular peace movements. The movement created rules to regulate warfare, prohibiting a combatant from harming noncombatants, suspending warfare during the harvest season and during times of religious significance (e.g., Lent and the Sabbath), and so on.

These rules were not promulgated by a king or parliament. Rather, they were voluntarily undertaken by the warlords, who swore oaths before large crowds of commoners to abide by the rules. These crowds gathered around saints' relics, on which the warlords typically swore their commitments. The enthusiasm and religious fervor driving this movement were great.[22]

Though the warlords participated voluntarily in the movement, they did not necessarily desire to do so. Some, perhaps, were willing to refrain from destroying others' farms provided their rivals would likewise refrain from destroying theirs. Other, more ambitious warlords were driven to participate by fear of crossing both the large enthusiastic crowds and divine will. Unlike governmental decrees, which are typically backed by a strong centralized institution, the oaths were not enforced by a force stronger than the violating warlords. In this fragmented region, such a force did not exist. Rather, the oaths were enforced by the diffuse threat of social and religious ostracism.

---

[22] A chronicler of that time, Ralph Glaber (2004), describes one such gathering: "At this all were inflamed with such ardour that through the hands of their bishops they raised the pastoral staff to heaven, while themselves with outspread palms and with one voice cried to God: Peace, peace, peace! – that this might be a sign of perpetual covenant for that which they had promised between themselves and God."

B. Private Security Assiciations in the "New Economy": ISACs

The Pax Dei movement provides a colorful example of a PLS that enforces norms that provide security. Pax Dei enforced norms through use of network externalities rather than through use of hierarchy.[23] That it was an example of "network enforcement," however, does not mean that it provided "network security." Pax Dei used network enforcement to enhance security generally. This chapter focuses on "network solutions to network threats": the use of network enforcement to increase security within a network. Networks, and thus network vulnerabilities, existed since the dawn of time. The Bible reports the earliest recorded attack on a network, perpetrated by none other than God: confusing the languages of the people building the Tower of Babel.[24] Financial and trading networks were of great value in medieval commerce (Greif 1993). But the importance of and reliance on network industries increased significantly in recent times, and with it the cost of network vulnerability and the benefits of network security.

In 1998, following a report by the Presidential Commission on Critical Infrastructure Protection, President Clinton issued Presidential Decision Directive (PDD) 63, which identified the United States' reliance on certain critical infrastructures and cyber-based information systems[25] and took action to protect against the growing vulnerability from their disruption. Noting that in some sectors the majority of critical infrastructures were in private hands, PDD 63 sought to enhance the protection not only of government-owned or -controlled critical infrastructure but also of those facilities controlled or owned by the private sector (Lichtenbaum and Schneck 2002).

PDD 63 recognized a need for information sharing among private firms (in addition to information sharing between private firms and the government), in order to enhance both detection of attacks and coordination of defenses. It provided that, for each of the major sectors identified in it, the federal government would appoint an individual from a relevant agency to work with a representative of the private sector. In addition, the national coordinator was to communicate with owners and operators of the critical infrastructures within

---

[23] On the distinction between enforcement by network and by hierarchy see Section III.A.

[24] Gen 11:6–8 (New English Version). Language is characterized by network effects – the benefit derived from communicating in a language increases significantly as more people are familiar with it. Increased "membership" in this network (i.e., fluency in the language) allows communication and coordination among a larger number of people, which confers greater benefits on each of them. For a more contemporary analysis of the network effects of language, see Church and King (1993).

[25] "They include, but are not limited to, telecommunications, energy, banking and finance, transportation, water systems and emergency services, both governmental and private" (White House 1998).

the sector "to strongly encourage the creation of a private sector information sharing and analysis center" (Lichtenbaum and Schneck 2002, Annex A). Though it envisioned each ISAC as a "mechanism for gathering, analyzing, appropriately sanitizing and disseminating private sector information to both industry and [the government's National Infrastructure Protection Center]" (Annex A), PDD 63 explicitly left the design, functions, and membership of ISACs to the discretion of the private sector participants that create them.[26] However, the fifteen ISACs that have formed to date correspond to broad industry sectors similar to those defined in PDD 63: Chemical, Electricity, Emergency Fire Services, Emergency Law Enforcement, Energy, Financial Services, Food, Highway, Information Technology, Interstate, Real Estate, Research and Education Networking, Surface Transportation, Telecommunications, and Water.[27]

One example of an ISAC is the Energy ISAC. The Energy ISAC "provides a near-real-time threat and warning capability to the energy industry.... Members voluntarily report information to the database either anonymously or on an attributed basis. Input is analyzed by security specialists for potential solutions; depending upon the seriousness of the case, the Energy ISAC will distribute an alert to members" (ISAC 2004a).[28]

Membership in the Energy ISAC is voluntary, and open to "companies in the oil, natural gas, and electric power industries. . . . Relevant energy activities include exploration, production, processing, transmission, distribution, transportation, storage, trading, supervisory control and data acquisition (SCADA), and e-commerce of energy commodities" (ISAC 2004a, 2004b).

Though each of the ISACs was given birth by the same presidential initiative (PDD 63), they are far from identical. Membership size varies widely. The structures of the ISACs vary, along with their management. Some ISACs are predominantly composed of government entities (e.g., the Interstate and Emergency Law Enforcement ISACs), while others are completely private (e.g., the Financial Services and Energy ISACs).

Most importantly, it seems that certain ISACs have achieved some level of success and others have struggled (McCarthy 2003). This assessment must be

---

[26] "The actual design and functions of the center and its relation to the NIPC will be determined by the private sector, in consultation with and with assistance from the Federal Government" (Lichtenbaum and Schneck 2002, Annex A).

[27] In addition, a Healthcare Services ISAC is currently being formed.

[28] The ISAC provides its members with "a wide range of information on threats and vulnerabilities (physical, cyber-security, and interdependencies); early notification of physical and cyber-threats; possible responses to those threats (e.g., information technology solutions and patches, and physical and information security tips); alert conditions; best practices [guidelines]; and a forum for members to communicate in a secure environment" (ISAC 2004a).

made with caution; the available public information is insufficient to accurately assess the success of each ISAC, and, further, it is not clear that all ISACs pursue the information-sharing goal that was envisioned by PDD 63.[29] To the extent that ISACs were formed to enforce norms of information sharing and other norms that enhance the security and reliability of the networks that the ISAC members share, it seems that some ISACs are dissatisfied with the results.

The Electricity ISAC seems to send such signals. The North American Electric Reliability Council, which operates the ISAC, has recently stated,

> The changes taking place in the electric industry are altering many of the tradi-
> tional mechanisms, incentives and responsibilities to the point that our voluntary
> system of compliance with reliability standards is no longer adequate. In response
> to these changes, NERC (2004) is promoting the development of a new manda-
> tory system of reliability standards and compliance, backstopped in the United
> States by the Federal Energy Regulatory Commission.

This statement does not refer specifically to the ISAC or to norms regarding information sharing, but it openly admits the PLS's failure to enforce compliance with reliability standards and calls for assistance from the public legal system. This pattern of a private legal system conceding norm enforcement to the public legal system is not unlike the one observed in the late nineteenth century, when railroad companies that formerly opposed government regulation shifted to support such regulation, possibly because the market structure did not allow them to enforce norms amongst themselves privately (Aviram 2003).[30] Other ISACs, however, do not broadcast the same signals of distress.

Explanations for ISAC members' reluctance to share information freely include (1) fear of increased liability due to the disclosure of information on vulnerabilities and specific incidents of attack, (2) risk of antitrust violations resulting from the information exchange, and (3) loss of proprietary information, primarily through use of the Freedom of Information Act to access information disclosed to the ISAC and through it to the government

---

[29] For example, it is possible that some ISACs may have been formed to appease regulators or to better coordinate lobbying and communications with the government. Or it is possible that some ISACs were formed or are maintained because of the public subsidies described in Section II.C (e.g., in order to have access to information that the government provides the ISAC).

[30] "Indeed, the railroads, not the farmers and shippers, were the most important single advocates of federal regulation from 1877 to 1916. Even when they frequently disagreed with the details of specific legislation, they always supported the principle of federal regulation as such" (Kolko 1965, 3).

(Frye 2002). Some have viewed these concerns as not substantial enough to explain the limited information exchange that takes place.[31]

This article suggests a theory as to why some ISACs succeed in enforcing information sharing and other network security norms whereas others fail. From a public policy perspective, by understanding which ISACs (or other PLSs) are more likely to succeed in effectively enforcing network security norms, we can direct public subsidies to those PLSs while denying less effective PLSs subsidies that may be artificially maintaining them. I conclude this section with a brief look at the public subsidies available to private network security associations before turning to the theory of PLS formation and applying it to such associations.

C. Public Subsidies of Private Network Security Associations

An attack on (or failure of) the network of a critical infrastructure obviously harms the network's members. It also harms many others who are not network members. For example, an attack or accident that shuts down the electric power grid would impose large losses on the utility companies themselves but would result in losses of greater magnitude to the end users of the electricity. The August 14, 2003, blackout that affected portions of the U.S. Midwest and Northeast as well as Ontario, Canada, imposed costs estimated at $4 billion to $10 billion in the United States alone. The same incident drove Canadian gross domestic product down 0.7% in August (U.S.-Canada Power System Outage Task Force 2003).

Thus, enhancing network security to reduce the likelihood or magnitude of attacks on or failures of the network creates significant positive externalities for nonmembers. If network security is enhanced by a PLS, the PLS members bear the costs. As with positive externalities in general, the PLS members have an incentive to underinvest in network security (compared with the socially optimal amount of investment) since they do not reap all the benefits of the enhanced security.[32] Given the large number of people who are indirectly

---

[31] Frye (2002) argues that fear of increased liability is unfounded if all firms provide information; Frye (2003) argues that antitrust liability is unlikely in most circumstances and that a better explanation for the limited information-sharing is lack of trust among ISAC members.

[32] "In fact, subsidies can be a socially beneficial means of encouraging an optimal level of production. When a good confers a positive externality on society, a firm in a free market will underproduce that good (unless, of course, the good also produces an equal or greater negative externality). Because consumers will, by definition, be unwilling to pay for this positive externality, the firm will not reap all the social benefits of that good. By compensating firms for the positive externalities they confer on society, subsidies can function as efficient tools for states to encourage the optimal level of production" ("Note, Functional Analysis" 1997, 1547–8).

affected by network security, the network members are unlikely to be able to internalize the externalities. Many critical infrastructure industries charge their end users for their services and could attempt to recoup a portion of the cost of the increased security through a surcharge.[33] However, even if regulators allowed this surcharge (which may be an attractive platform for "gold plating"),[34] this can only internalize benefits to end users, not to all people who would be affected by a failure of the critical infrastructure. This would leave a significant portion of the benefits of network security uninternalized and thus unaccounted for in the PLS's decisions on investing in network security.

For this reason, public subsidy of network security may be appropriate in some cases. Government may be able to internalize the benefits of network security to people indirectly affected by the network's failure better than network members could. A subsidy that is both appropriate in its amount and in its recipients may assist in approaching a socially optimal investment in network security.

Subsidies can take the form of pecuniary payments, government purchases at favorable prices, tax breaks, and other pecuniary forms. Nonpecuniary subsidies are also possible, and some such subsidies are being used to benefit ISACs. One form of subsidy is the provision of government information to ISACs. PDD 63 envisioned ISACs as facilitating the exchange of information not only among private parties but also between private parties and government.[35] Membership in an ISAC gives preferential access to information supplied by government (or puts a member on equal footing with other members in terms of access to the information). Thus, a member of an ineffective ISAC may remain in the ISAC in order not to be disadvantaged in its access to information supplied by government.[36]

---

[33] An example (though not from a critical infrastructure industry) is the imposition of security charges by Israeli restaurants. Waves of suicide bombings of Israeli restaurants caused most restaurants to hire security guards. Some restaurants have added a security charge to patrons' bills to recoup the cost of the guards (Thorne 2002).

[34] "Gold plating" (or "cost padding") is a technique used by businesses whose prices are subject to rate-of-return regulation, in order to increase their profits. "When a carrier's profits are limited to a certain percentage return on its investment, it will increase its investments to increase its earnings – when investment goes up, profits go up – regardless of whether the additional investment is necessary or efficient" (Griboff 1992, 445).

[35] "The center could also gather, analyze and disseminate information from [the government's National Infrastructure Protection Center] for further distribution to the private sector" (White House 1998, Annex A).

[36] This does not mean that the subsidy is inappropriate but merely that it dulls private incentives that discipline ISACs to be efficient. Using ISACs to disseminate information may be a cost-effective way for government to convey information to most members of the relevant industry.

Another subsidy to ISACs takes the form of an exemption from laws that may apply to them. Under Section 214 of the Critical Infrastructure Information Act of 2002,[37] information that is voluntarily submitted to a covered federal agency regarding critical infrastructure benefits from several privileges. First, it is exempt from disclosure under the Freedom of Information Act,[38] and limitations are placed on its disclosure under state and local laws.[39] Second, it is not subject to agency rules or judicial doctrine regarding *ex parte* communications with a decision-making official.[40] Third, it is not to be used by the agency, by any federal, state, or local authority, or by any third party in any civil action arising under federal or state law.[41] Fourth, significant limitations are imposed on the disclosure of such information by federal, state, and local governments.[42] Fifth, providing the information does not constitute a waiver of any protection of privilege under law.[43]

Additional subsidies to ISACs are currently contemplated. Representatives Thomas Davis and Jim Moran introduced in Congress a bill to enact the Cyber Security Information Act,[44] Section 5 of which would provide that antitrust laws shall not apply to conduct engaged in for the purpose of facilitating the correction of a cybersecurity-related problem or the communication and disclosure of information to help correct or avoid a cybersecurity problem.[45]

At present, antitrust laws apply to collaborations among firms to form and operate ISACs.[46] Antitrust enforcement agencies have generally taken a friendly stance toward such collaborations. To provide the potential members of a proposed ISAC with some degree of certainty as to the ISAC's compliance with antitrust laws, the antitrust enforcement agencies have been willing to review the proposed ISAC and issue "business review letters" stating that the agencies have no intention of challenging the ISAC if it is formed and operated

---

[37] Enacted as §§ 211–24 of the Homeland Security Act of 2002, Pub. L. 107–296.

[38] 5 U.S.C. § 552.

[39] Homeland Security Act of 2002, §§ 214(a)(1)(A), (E)(i).

[40] Homeland Security Act of 2002, § 214(a)(1)(B).

[41] Homeland Security Act of 2002, § 214(a)(1)(C).

[42] Homeland Security Act of 2002, §§ 214(a)(1)(D), (E)(ii), (iii).

[43] Homeland Security Act of 2002, § 214(a)(1)(F).

[44] Cyber Security Information Act, H.R. 2435, 107th Cong. (2001). The bill was first introduced as H.R. 4246, 106th Cong. (2000). On the bill, see Lichtenbaum and Schneck (2002).

[45] Section 5(b) of the bill states an exception to the exemption: conduct will not be exempt if it involves or results in an agreement to boycott any person, to allocate a market, or to fix prices or output. If this exception was understood to limit the exemption to agreements that do not have anticompetitive effects, then the entire section would be superfluous, because agreements not falling into the exception would also not run afoul of antitrust laws. Thus, the exception must be narrower, leaving an exemption for agreements that would, absent this bill, be seen as anticompetitive under antitrust laws.

[46] On the antitrust analysis of ISAC, see Abbott (2003).

in accordance with the information provided to them by the ISAC founders (U.S. Department of Justice 2000). The business review letter approach allows a case-by-case assessment of the effectiveness and anticompetitive concerns of each proposed ISAC.[47] An antitrust exemption, as proposed in the Cyber Security Information Act, will replace the case-by-case assessment with a broader exemption of ISAC activities (unless those are mere cover for collusion). This shift risks providing a public subsidy (i.e., an exemption from antitrust laws) to inefficient PLSs, biasing private incentives and potentially maintaining PLSs that otherwise would have been purged by the invisible hand of the market.

To be effective, a case-by-case analysis requires tools to assess in advance whether a PLS has the potential to effectively enforce norms that enhance network security (such as a norm of disclosing information on attacks aimed at a member's portion of the network or on vulnerabilities discovered by a member). In the next section, I will suggest such tools.

III. A THEORY OF THE EVOLUTION OF PRIVATE LEGAL SYSTEMS

A. Enforcement of Norms by Networks and Hierarchies

Though PLSs can (and do) take many different forms, most PLSs that govern large numbers of people are facilitated by networks. Networks are collections of facilities and rules that facilitate contact between users of a good or service ("network members") and thus enable the realization of network effects. Network effects (or network benefits) are demand-side economies of scale. That is, network effects are the phenomena that occur when the utility[48] of a good or service to an individual user increases as additional people use it.

Networks benefit their members by enforcing norms that facilitate a variety of activities, such as social interaction, spiritual support, the opportunity to exchange goods, etc. The Pax Dei movement is a vivid example of regulation through use of network effects. The movement formed around a religious, mystical social network that centered on the belief that the peace oaths were covenants with God. Each individual member of the group enjoyed social interaction, a sense of identity, and spiritual support by being a part of the

---

[47] For arguments that the business review letter process is not suitable for reviewing ISAC formation, see Miller (2002).

[48] The "utility" of and "benefit" from an action measure the satisfaction of an individual's (or a group's) preferences as a result of the action. Satisfaction is affected by receiving goods, services, or experiences (e.g., money, other material benefits, spiritual elation, a sense of being loved, etc.). Utility can also be negative, when an action results in dissatisfaction (e.g., loss or devaluation of material possessions, a sense of rejection, exploitation, etc.).

group. An increase in the membership of the group enlarged the pool of people with whom one could socialize, turn to for support, etc.[49] An individual who would split from the group would lose those group benefits (the network effects), because no individual (nor even a small group of individuals) could provide the same benefits that the larger group could.

Being part of the group, each individual member adhered to the group norms. Many of the group's norms were perceived by the individual as being part of her identity, and thus the individual would comply with them even absent repercussions for failing to do so. But even when the individual did not want to comply with one of the group's norms, failure to do so could result in expulsion from the group and loss of the benefits it provided the individual. Thus, she would have been inclined to comply even with those group norms that were not appealing to her absent the group's sanction. Thus, the group's power to enforce norms turned on its ability to manipulate its network effects and deny them to those who violated the group's norms.

Indeed, this seems to explain religion's power to enforce the peace oaths of the Pax Dei movement. The Christian social network in western Europe of that era provided its members with significant spiritual benefits, including a sense of belonging to a community and a sense of security derived from belief in divine oversight. Any person reneging on what was perceived to be a covenant with God would be excommunicated, losing the benefits religion and social interaction provided. The ability to threaten exclusion from the religious group thus facilitated cooperation among even those members of the group who personally believed that breaking the peace oaths would not invite divine wrath (provided those members anticipated that the group would have excluded them for breaking the oaths).

Enforcement of norms is not always based on networks. It can also be based on hierarchy. A powerful individual can coerce others not through denying network externalities but through threatening to use force. An individual who is not powerful may coerce others if he can make a credible claim that a powerful person or entity will use force on his behalf. Thus, a judge has the ability to enforce norms by hierarchy not because he personally can use force against an

---

[49] At some point an increase in group size adds very little to the benefits a group confers on a member. For example, an increase in the size of a group from one million to two million people may not increase by much the average benefits of a member. Since no individual could maintain social ties with a million people, the addition of another million members to the group expands an already sufficient membership. On the other hand, the expansion of the group may increase divergence within the group, weakening individuals' identification with the group as well as the group's ability to agree on its norms and values. Thus, at some point a social group ceases to have positive network externalities. It is still a network, because up to that point it does have network externalities.

offender, but because government law enforcement institutions will back the judge's decree with the use of force, if necessary. Similarly, a party to a contract may be able to enforce the norms set in the contract through the threat of suing the breaching party in court and receiving government backing.

This is not to say that it is only the threat of (public) legal sanction that causes individuals to adhere to contractual obligations. Norms may be enforced by several legal systems at once: some public and others private; some based on hierarchy and others based on network effects. In some cases, personal morality suffices to ensure performance.[50] In other cases, community norms force the would-be breaching party to abide by the contract.[51] In that case, the norm is enforced through use of network effects. But in some cases, neither personal morality nor community norms suffice, yet an individual abides by the contract for fear of being sued.[52] This latter situation is an example of a norm enforced by hierarchy rather than by network.

That a network enforces a norm does not automatically mean that the norm is enforced through network effects. Networks, like other entities, may enforce norms by hierarchy as well as by network effects. For example, soon after the formation of the American Bankers Association, it created a "standing Protective Committee" to increase the security of banks by deterring bank robberies (American Bankers Association 2004). The committee offered rewards for the conviction and prosecution of bank robbers and hired a detective agency to track them. The association seems to have been quite successful in enforcing an anti-bank-robbery norm: in 1896–7, for example, there was only one successful robbery of a member of the association.[53] This success resulted in a surge

---

[50] Ellickson (1991) discusses "first-party regulation" governed by personal morality and compares it with four other modes of regulation.

[51] Macaulay (1963) observes that few contractual disputes are litigated and that most are settled without resorting to government-enforced laws.

[52] In this latter group we find the hypothetical "bad man," which law must incentivize, according to Justice Oliver Wendell Holmes (1897). "You can see very plainly that a bad man has as much reason as a good one for wishing to avoid an encounter with the public force, and therefore you can see the practical importance of the distinction between morality and law. A man who cares nothing for an ethical rule which is believed and practised by his neighbors is likely nevertheless to care a good deal to avoid being made to pay money, and will want to keep out of jail if he can" (p. 992). In reality, people do not fall neatly into one or another of these categories. A person may abide by some norms due to personal morality, by others in order to avoid nonlegal sanctions such as social ostracism, and by yet other norms only because of fear of civil or criminal sanction.

[53] Even this robbery can be explained away, for although the robbed bank displayed the small metal sign saying "Member American Bankers Association" under the ledge of the teller's window, it was not seen by the criminals when they surveyed the lobby (American Bankers Association 2004).

in the association's membership.[54] Both the bounty offer and hiring a detective agency are actions based on hierarchy, not network effects. An individual bank could have hired the detective agency or offered the bounty, deterring the bank robbers (i.e., enforcing a "no robbery" norm on them) with the same effectiveness.[55] As for enforcing the bounty promise and overseeing the detective agency, the former is likely to be enforced through a contractual lawsuit (public enforcement based on hierarchy), while the latter would be enforced by the supervision of the detective agency by the association's employees (private enforcement based on hierarchy) or, if the detective agency ignored the instructions of the association, by contractual lawsuit.

Contrast this with another norm enforcement activity undertaken by the American Bankers Association – the creation of a standard for magnetic ink character recognition, which serves "as a common machine language for check handling" (American Bankers Association 2004). Standards exhibit network effects: the more banks use the same standard of magnetic ink, the more checks can be exchanged and processed uniformly. A standard used only by a single small bank is not as useful as a standard followed by many banks. If sufficiently significant, these network effects may ensure compliance with the standard even without the threat of an additional sanction.

The economic theory of the firm long ago made a distinction between activities that are governed by hierarchy and those governed by network effects (in the terminology of that literature, markets).[56] In 1937, Nobel laureate Ronald Coase pioneered the theory of the firm, explaining why some business activities were done within firms while others were done using arm's-length market transactions (Coase 1937). The answer, noted Coase, lies in transaction costs incurred in the business activity. An activity would be done in the form (either

---

[54] "Between 1894 and 1898 membership in the association almost doubled to 3,350 as banks joined to be under the protection of the ABA" (American Bankers Association 2004).

[55] There may be some ways in which the actions taken by the association differ from a situation in which the same actions were taken by an individual bank. If the antirobbery measures reduced overall bank robbery (i.e., diverted bank robbers to other activities), then there would be a collective action problem, for each bank would hope other banks would bears the cost of these measures and reduce crime affecting all banks. In that case, the association could solve the collective action problem of financing the bounty and detective agency, since it could apportion the costs among its members. On the other hand, if the antirobbery measures merely diverted bank robbers to rob other banks, each bank that took measures to deter crime against it would impose a negative externality on its rivals by diverting criminals to them. The association eliminates those negative externalities among its members.

[56] Markets are networks and exhibit strong network effects. The more sellers attend the market, the greater the utility of the market to the buyers and the more buyers will attend. And the more buyers attend the market, the greater the utility of the market to the sellers and the more sellers will attend. Aviram (2003) explains why Internet marketplaces such as eBay are networks.

within a firm or in the market) that minimizes transaction costs. In other words, "a firm will tend to expand until the costs of organizing an extra transaction [by command and control] within the firm become equal to the costs of carrying out the same transaction by means of an exchange on the open market" (p. 386).

This distinction between hierarchies and markets, now central to the economic analysis of corporate law, is not emphasized in the private ordering literature. The literature rarely emphasizes the role network effects play in facilitating private ordering and even more rarely makes the distinction between norm enforcement through network effects and norm enforcement through hierarchy.

Many PLSs are networks because individuals migrate to the most efficient (i.e., least costly) regulator, and networks are often the most efficient regulators. The first point may not be intuitive – why would individuals care about the social efficiency of their regulator? For obvious reasons, parties seek regulation that is least costly *to them*. Ultimately, however, costs of regulation that are imposed on other parties will also be internalized. For example, if two parties to a transaction adopt a form of second-party regulation to prevent opportunistic default – such as having a bank guarantee a payment – the payer may pay the bank's fee, but ultimately the transaction price would be modified to share that expense. Therefore, in most cases all parties will prefer to adopt regulation that is least costly *to the regulated group as a whole*.

As for the second point, networks are often efficient regulators because network effects galvanize four mechanisms that are frequently more effective at enforcing norms than governments or bilateral arrangements (Aviram 2003).[57] The first of these mechanisms is the information mechanism: collecting and disseminating among the members information on the credibility of member firms. This mechanism facilitates the development of reputation capital by providing the information that allows others to judge the desirability of transacting with an individual based on that individual's reputation. While the information mechanism is used by some nonnetwork institutions, it is particularly powerful when used by a network, for several reasons. First, networks usually incur lower costs than other institutions in monitoring their members' behavior within the network. Second, networks enjoy credibility when providing negative information on their members (since they generally have an incentive to promote their members). Finally, by monitoring all of their members, networks can exploit economies of scale in gathering and verifying information. The private ordering literature frequently discusses manifestations of the information

---

[57] The following paragraphs summarize some of the arguments made in that paper.

mechanism, which is commonly employed by networks (e.g., reputation-conveying mechanisms in merchant coalitions are described in Greif 1993 and Clay 1997, gossip among neighbors is described in Ellickson 1986 and 1991, etc.).

The second mechanism is the switching mechanism; that is, replacing a defaulted transaction with a successful alternate transaction, resulting in minimal loss of transaction-specific investment. Typical bilateral examples are a buyer covering for a contract breached by the seller or a seller reselling goods sold under a contract breached by the buyer; both remedies are provided by the Uniform Commercial Code.[58] In this way, a party injured by a breach of contract enters another contract, with someone else, that closely resembles the breached contract. This minimizes the injured party's harm from the breach and sometimes deters a party from breaching. An example of this sort of deterrence was provided in a paper by Thomas Palay (1984). His article describes how railroads and shippers contract to reduce the risk of opportunism resulting from the need to make a transaction-specific investment to ship certain goods by rail.[59] Palay (1984) examined those elements of a transaction that insure the vulnerable party against the risk of renegotiation. He found that one of the important elements was the potentially opportunistic party's knowledge that the other party could contract with someone else without losing much of its transaction-specific investment.

While Palay describes a bilateral switching mechanism (one bilateral transaction is negotiated in lieu of another bilateral transaction that has been breached), the switching mechanism is usually more effective when it benefits from network effects. Transacting within networks tends to mimic perfect competition better than bilateral contracting, and therefore the market that serves as an alternative to the defaulted transaction is more liquid. Also, investments used to transact within a network tend to be less transaction specific. Thus, the investments can be salvaged from the defaulted deal and used in an alternate transaction. For example, a good reputation may be required for certain transactions. In a world of bilateral contracting, it takes time and effort to establish a good reputation. If Jill had established a good reputation with only one transacting partner (Jack), she may acquiesce to Jack's opportunistic

---

[58] U.C.C. § 2-706 (2003) (seller's right to resell); U.C.C. § 2-712 (2003) (buyer's right to cover).

[59] The risk of opportunism is due to the fact that specially fitted rail cars are needed to safely transport certain goods. This exposes one of the parties to opportunistic renegotiation of the contract by the other party: once one of the parties – a railroad or a shipper – invests in the rail cars, the other party is in a position to renegotiate the terms of the contracts in its favor, knowing that its partner stands to lose its transaction-specific investment if it refuses to renegotiate.

renegotiation of the transaction knowing that if she refused to renegotiate and the transaction was abandoned, she would have to expend a lot of time and effort to establish a good reputation with another person. If Jack and Jill transacted through a network (e.g., eBay), however, then Jill's reputation would be established networkwide. If Jack threatened to discontinue transacting unless his new demands were met, Jill could transact almost costlessly with someone else. This fact would deter Jack from demanding to renegotiate in the first place.[60]

The third mechanism that networks employ to regulate is the control mechanism. In some networks, all transactions are processed through centralized facilities. For example, the electric grid is managed centrally and can facilitate transactions between many power generators and power consumers. Similarly, transactions in an electronic marketplace are often facilitated centrally through the marketplace's server, which records the terms of the transactions. A centralized transacting facility can often reduce the cost of monitoring transactions to detect prohibited behavior and may block or deter harmful (e.g., fraudulent or illegal) transactions. For example, eBay can prevent unlawful ticket scalping by removing offers that violate state antiscalping laws (prevention) or by reporting such transactions *ex post* to the relevant attorney general (detection, which leads to deterrence) (Wolverton 2002).[61] Alternatively, the central facility may be kept transparent, allowing individuals to observe and detect norm violations.[62] As with the other mechanisms, the control mechanism may exist in nonnetworked environments. However, economies of scale often make centralized transacting facilities more feasible in networks than in bilateral transactions, since in the former both total transaction volume and transaction complexity tend to be higher.

Finally, the fourth mechanism used by networks to enforce norms is the exclusion mechanism: denying a firm the network benefits of transacting with the other network members by excluding the rogue firm from the network either temporarily (suspension) or permanently (expulsion). This mechanism might be seen as a combination of the information mechanism with an additional element: coordination of the network members' responses to the information

---

[60] Unlike the other three mechanisms, the switching mechanism does not require the implementation of any rules in order to have an effect. The very existence of a network produces both the harm mitigation and the deterrent effects. Nonetheless, this mechanism is no different from the other three in differentiating the abilities of networks to regulate behavior.

[61] It should be noted, however, that ticket scalping specifically proves to be a field in which it is more difficult for networks to combat fraud because of the great discrepancy among state laws and the large number of cross-jurisdictional transactions, which raise ambiguity as to the applicable law (Courtney 2001; "Will the Net End Ticket Scalping?" 1999).

[62] For example, some sport teams monitor eBay auctions to detect ticket scalping (Drury 2002).

provided. This combination ensures that the entire network's transacting power and network effects are withheld from the party that violates the norm.

The remainder of this section concerns "network responses" to network threats – that is, PLSs that enforce norms through network effects rather than through hierarchy. In particular, it explains the pattern by which such PLSs form and evolve.

B. The Paradox of Spontaneous Formation

Ronald Coase (1960) anticipated a significant role for PLSs. In a world with no transaction costs, according to one form of the Coase theorem, parties would renegotiate inefficient entitlements granted by law to achieve an optimally efficient allocation. For example, suppose that tort law imposes liability on a rancher whose cattle trespass onto a farmer's land. This rule may be inefficient in regions with many ranchers and very few farmers, because it would be cheaper to fence in the few farms and have the cattle roam freely in the pasture than to fence in the cattle.[63] If transaction costs were negligible, having this inefficient rule would not result in an inefficient outcome. Instead, the ranchers would agree to pay the farmers to fence themselves in, and the ranchers would let the cattle roam freely. This outcome would be feasible, since the cost for the ranchers to comply with the rule and fence their cattle in would be greater than the cost of fencing the farms in (which is why the rule was inefficient). As a result, the ranchers would be willing to bear the lesser cost of fencing in the farmers, plus a small premium to obtain the farmers' consent. The farmers, on the other hand, would agree to opt into the private regime in return for this small consent premium, since the private regime would not increase their exposure to trespass risk. Under the public (legal) regime, they would be compensated through tort law for the trespass; under the private regime the cattle would be fenced out, preventing the trespass from occurring.

In other words, in a world with no transaction costs, PLSs would form spontaneously, through ad hoc contracting. Of course, no such world exists. There are costs to identifying an efficient regime and negotiating its terms among its stakeholders. When there are many ranchers and many farmers, there might be free-riding, holdout problems, or other forms of strategic (or irrational) behavior that could prevent an efficient bargain from being reached. And, of course, there are enforcement costs incurred to ensure that the parties abide by the agreed terms. Enforcement costs become significant when parties perform their parts of the bargain nonsimultaneously. They may also be significant if the

---

[63] Private ordering of liability for cattle trespass is a central issue in Ellickson (1986, 1991).

public regime (i.e., the law) does not defer to the private regime (and instead allows parties to the private regime to opt out opportunistically by suing and receiving their entitlements under law at any time, even if they purported to contract those away).

Scholars recognized long ago that institutions form to reduce these transaction costs. One way institutions solve collective action problems is by appointing an agent (e.g., a trade association) to act on behalf of the collective (thus coordinating their actions) (Greif 1989)[64] and by ensuring the enforceability of the private regime (e.g., through mandatory arbitration).[65]

No institution reduces transaction costs to zero. However, the lower the transaction costs, the closer the parties get to the efficient allocation of entitlements. Since transaction costs impede parties from reaching bargains that they would otherwise want to reach, such parties are likely to adopt the institutions that most reduce transaction costs. Therefore, prevalent institutions are likely to be ones that most reduce transaction costs.

As mentioned,[66] the efficient use of four enforcement mechanisms that employ network effects makes networks, in many cases, the least-cost regulator. However, these mechanisms are usually ineffective when they form spontaneously (i.e., are imposed for the first time unassisted by existent enforcement mechanisms) due to a "chicken and egg" paradox:[67] they are very effective in enforcing behavior once they are perceived as able to enforce that behavior, but they cannot enforce behavior effectively as long as the network members do not perceive them as able to do so. Therefore, it would be difficult for these enforcement mechanisms to form spontaneously. Absent existing enforcement power, they would not be as effective as other methods of regulation (e.g., government regulation, bilateral self-regulation).

Consider, for example, the exclusion mechanism. To enforce a norm, the network threatens its members with ostracism if they fail to conform. The significance of this threat to a member depends on what this ostracism would deny it – what benefits it currently derives from the network. An established network already provides benefits to the members; even a network doing nothing but preventing opportunistic behavior will provide its members with a more amicable transacting environment once it is effective. But until the network has undertaken enforcement for a while and has assured members of its ability to function, its members significantly discount (or do not consider at all) any

---

[64] For an expanded discussion of institutions facilitating collective actions, see Ostrom (1990).
[65] Bernstein (1992) discusses the use of arbitration among diamond dealers to enforce their PLS.
[66] See Section III.A.
[67] The term "chicken and egg paradox" alludes to the jesting question, Which came first, the chicken or the egg? If the chicken came first, what did it hatch from? If the egg – who laid it?

benefits of membership and will not be deterred by the threat of exclusion. This becomes a self-fulfilling prophecy as the more skeptical members ignore the threat of exclusion and act opportunistically, dissipating the network's benefits and persuading those members who initially had faith in the network that the benefit of the network, and hence the cost of exclusion, is negligible.

The same pattern occurs with the other enforcement mechanisms. The switching mechanism, for example, can only deter opportunism if the would-be opportunistic party anticipates that its victim would find a viable alternative transaction. Until the network is active and has proven its ability to offer feasible alternative transactions, would-be opportunists lack a deterrent to renegotiating the transaction. As a result, honest parties, who experience a high incidence of opportunistic renegotiation, will avoid this network and seek either a more effective network or an alternative regulator (bilateral contracting or government intervention). The abandonment of the network by honest members will exacerbate the problem of finding a feasible alternative transaction, further weakening the switching mechanism.

This paradox need not conclude with the desertion of all members. Not all network members react identically to the perceived effectiveness of the network. Some find it almost costless to follow the norms and do so regardless of the perceived effectiveness of the enforcement mechanisms. Other network members benefit so much from a network (as opposed to the next best alternative available to them) that they find it feasible to remain in the network even when compliance with the norm is low (and thus are sufficiently deterred by the exclusion mechanism). However, this significantly affects only inframarginal firms; that is, the firms that benefit most from the network or find it least costly to follow the norms. Most other firms find the spontaneous network regulator ineffective, as I explain below. These firms seek the least costly alternative regulator. In some cases, the least costly alternative would be a nonnetwork regulator, such as government regulation or bilateral contracts. But in many circumstances, networks are the most efficient regulators. Thus, most firms will seek another network that avoids the paradox of spontaneous formation.

At the heart of the paradox that impedes spontaneous formation is a problem of assurance – if most network members were assured of the network's ability to enforce a norm, they would follow that norm and in so doing enable the network to enforce the norm on the few strays that violate it. Frequently the public legal system supplies this assurance, through contract law and the ability to sue a PLS member who reneged on a promise to abide by the norms, through criminal law, etc. But using the public legal system to solve the assurance problem may be of questionable benefit: if the network is not as good a regulator as the public legal system, it might seem preferable to do away with the network and have the law regulate directly rather than support a less efficient regulator (the network). And if the network is more efficient than the public legal system, the use of the public legal system to support the network would likely introduce the costs and inefficiencies of the public legal system, which the network had avoided.

PLSs also attempt to provide assurance to transacting parties. A common way of doing so is through posting "bonds" (Williamson 1983). Bonds are interests of the assuring party[68] that are placed at the mercy of the assured party. Upon receiving a bond, the assured party may confiscate or destroy it at will, causing harm to the assuring party. Knowing that the assured party will use this power if the assuring party reneges on an obligation, the assuring party will not renege. This provides the assured party with peace of mind. Indeed, the use of bonds by PLSs – in particular, reputation bonds – is well documented.[69]

Reputation bonds, however, are not a very useful tool for newly formed PLSs that do not rely on preexisting counterparts. For these networks, as for the warlords in the earlier discussion of Pax Dei,[70] one failed episode would lead to elimination, and hence network members discount future interactions with the network (and its members). As discussed in the next subsection, reputation might still be an effective bond if the network members interact with each other outside the network (e.g., are members of the same social circle), or if the network already enforces other norms that will survive its failure to regulate the new norm. But absent either of these, members will not value establishing a good reputation in a network that is expected to fail.

Bonding, whether using tangible or intangible collateral, is an expensive assurance system, and usually a crude one. Nonreciprocal bonding (providing a bond without receiving one) leaves the party offering the bond vulnerable to the other party's ability to confiscate the bond without cause. Reciprocal bonding is subject to reciprocal confiscation, which may leave both parties worse off but not by enough to deter an opportunist.[71]

---

[68] Such as property, rights, reputation, or other matter the destruction or confiscation of which affects the assuring party's utility.

[69] Bernstein (1992) discusses the development and function of reputation bonds among diamond traders. Clay (1997) describes the effect of reputation bonds within merchant coalitions in Mexican California. Greif (1993) describes reputation bonds among Maghribi trades. Ellickson (1986) examines the impact of reputation bonds on reducing disputes among neighbors over cattle trespass incidents.

[70] See Section II.A.

[71] Some bonds do not offset each other because they harm one party without providing the other party with any utility (e.g., killing a hostage). But even with such collateral, there is a risk of insufficient deterrence. First, it might be done to create deterrence (R. A. Posner 1998b discusses the rationality of revenge as a deterrence-creating mechanism in the absence of law enforcement). The excessive sensitivity that creates deterrence also undoes collateral

Thus, bilateral bonds are an expensive and often inefficient assurance mechanism. Indeed, Greif, Milgrom, and Weingast offer a formal game-theoretic model that proves that bilateral bonds (such as bilateral reputation mechanisms) do not deter opportunistic behavior when transactions are at what would be the efficient level absent the threat of opportunism (Greif 1993).[72] Their model predicts that when coordination among merchants can be enforced, the merchants may be able to deter a city's opportunistic behavior, because the income lost from harming a marginal merchant comprises not only profits the city could have made from that merchant's future dealings but also from future dealings with all coordinated merchants (Greif 1993).

Applying this to our inquiry, it is possible that coordinated (centralized) bonding can assure members of a PLS to a degree sufficient to escape the paradox of spontaneous formation. But if the PLS has just begun to regulate behavior of its enforcement ability, a reputation bond is likely to be ineffective (as explained earlier). Pecuniary bonds (e.g., membership fees that are confiscated if a member is expelled for violating norms) are possible but entail significant administrative costs. A lower-cost alternative is the sanction of expulsion from preexisting functionalities of the PLS.

Since parties seek the least-cost regulator,[73] it is expected that in situations in which network-based regulation is more efficient than other forms of regulation, networks will evolve in a manner that ultimately overcomes the paradox of spontaneous formation by developing from preexisting coordinated bonding

mechanisms by triggering them before a breach is committed. Second, even when exaggerated sensitivity can be avoided, the value of the collateral is often hard to determine. There is a cost to providing collateral (both the inability to enjoy the collateral that was given and the risk of unjustified confiscation). This cost creates an incentive to reduce the size of the collateral as much as possible. On the other hand, collateral only deters opportunistic action that is no more profitable than the collateral's value. Since gains from opportunistic behavior vary widely, it is hard to anticipate the optimal value of the collateral, and almost any value of collateral would fail to deter some extremely profitable opportunistic behavior. Agreeing on the value of the collateral is further complicated if the parties differ in the degree to which each is vulnerable to the other party's opportunism and in the loss of utility they suffer in providing the bond.

[72] The model assumes a city that may or may not protect the property and safety of merchants doing business in it. Failing to provide the necessary protection saves the city the cost of providing it and garners the city a gain from property confiscated from the merchants. The merchants in this model consider their past experience with the city and may boycott it and do their business elsewhere if the city has failed to protect them in the past. They are not able, however, to coordinate their responses. The model predicts that when trade is at an optimal level, the future stream of income to the city from the individual marginal merchant is almost zero and therefore less than the value of the goods confiscated or the cost of the protection services that are sometimes withheld. Absent coordination between the merchants, bonding would be insufficient to deter opportunism when the transacting level is optimal.

[73] See Section III.A.

mechanisms. This quest for the least-cost regulator, in the face of the paradox that plagues spontaneously formed PLSs, results in a pattern of nonspontaneous evolution – the assumption of responsibility for enforcing a norm by networks that already facilitate other, low–enforcement cost norms. I now elaborate on what nonspontaneous evolution of PLSs entails.

C. The Evolution of Private Legal Systems

Centralized bonding mechanisms are almost invariably network based. By having the ability to coordinate a response to a party's opportunism (and by thus deterring opportunism), the centralized coordinator provides a benefit to its members. This benefit is characterized by network effects – the more individuals' responses are coordinated, the greater the deterrence of would-be opportunists. Thus, the addition of another member to the centralized bonding mechanism increases the utility of each existing member – precisely the definition of a network effect.[74]

The evolutionary process that results in a PLS has two stages. First, a network creating a centralized bonding mechanism develops, most likely not as an end in itself but as a side effect of regulating a low–enforcement cost norm (i.e., a norm to which members adhere without coercion). Then, at stage 2, the network undertakes to regulate a higher–enforcement cost norm using its ability to deny members the benefit of the low–enforcement cost norm to coerce members to abide by the higher–enforcement cost norm. The most ubiquitous example of a network that facilitates centralized bonding is a social network. Social networks use reputation bonds. I argued earlier that reputation bonds are ineffective when individuals expect the network to fail. Many social networks, however, continue to exist over long periods of time – one's neighbors, for example, will continue to affect one's social life indefinitely.[75] By gossiping about each other within the social network, and by reacting to the gossip according to common norms, the social network can align most members' responses to a member's deviant behavior. When members of the same social circle are also part of another network that attempts to regulate behavior, they will work to preserve their reputations. While the regulating network cannot in itself harm members of the circle, the negative reputation they build will spread throughout the social network, and there the centralized bonding mechanism will punish them. There is no need for two separate networks, however – one to regulate

---

[74] The investment each member makes in a network is in itself a bond that expulsion from the network will confiscate (Kranton 1996).

[75] This section explains why social networks may spontaneously form whereas regulating networks tend to fail if they form spontaneously.

and the other to punish deviance. If there is demand for certain regulation and networks are the efficient providers, existing networks that enable centralized bonding – such as social networks, religious groups, etc. – will evolve to provide the required regulation.

Looking again at the Pax Dei movement, we may now better understand what made the warlords abide by the imposed constraints on warfare. The religious network provided each member, including the warlords, with the fulfillment of spiritual needs and a sense of security and well-being derived from membership in a community. Coordination was achieved both through formal means (religious leaders such as bishops) and informal means (norms and beliefs deeply rooted in the members of the community). Then, when a need to restrict warfare arose, the religious network was the least-cost regulator and quickly evolved to accommodate this need. The community was driven to act in uniform hostility to breaches of the peace because their formal coordinators – bishops and keepers of saints' relics – told them to do so (directly or indirectly). Thus, norms of regarding certain forms of violence as "unchristian" could easily take shape. Once the religious network evolved to undertake not just spiritual salvation but also regulation of warfare, the warlords were threatened by the religious network with ostracism (which would deny them the spiritual and social benefits provided by the religious network) and faced the possibility of a coordinated violent response from the members of the religious network. This enforcement power, which existed before the network undertook the regulation of warfare, was effective, for a time, in restricting the warlords' belligerence.

Of course, such social or religious networks must themselves overcome the paradox of spontaneous formation to create a centralized bonding mechanism. The reason they can succeed, while other norms (e.g., those restricting warfare) may fail to evolve spontaneously, is because the original norms usually have lower enforcement costs. People migrate to the lowest-cost regulator (holding regulation quality constant). Thus, less costly enforcement mechanisms are likely to survive, while more costly counterparts are likely to fail, even if the high-cost mechanism's benefits outweigh the enforcement costs (because the same benefits would be achieved by using the less costly mechanism).

High–enforcement cost norms do not remain unregulated for long, however, because low–enforcement cost networks expand to encompass them.[76] Once a network regulates a norm that has low enforcement costs, the (less costly)

---

[76] This is true only if enforcement costs do not outweigh the benefits of enforcement. But as was demonstrated in Section III.B, because of the spontaneous formation paradox, spontaneously formed networks will fail to enforce norms with high enforcement costs even when those costs are lower than the benefits internalized by all members together. This is where other, preexisting networks may evolve to enforce the high-cost yet welfare-enhancing norm.

enforcement mechanisms the network has developed are able to enforce more costly norms, resolving the spontaneous formation paradox.[77] Thus, the network evolves to accommodate the new norm.[78]

For example, because of its low enforcement costs, a social or religious network is likely to survive and continue to provide its members with a sense of community, social interaction, and spiritual guidance. This, in turn, will strengthen its enforcement mechanisms (e.g., by increasing the harm it can inflict on a member by excluding her from the network). In contrast, a spontaneously formed network attempting to restrict warfare is likely to fail owing to the difficulty its fledgling enforcement mechanisms will have in overcoming the high enforcement costs. This failure – due to the paradox of spontaneous formation – will occur even if the benefits of restricting warfare outweigh the costs of enforcement. The reason for the failure is not necessarily the infeasibility of enforcing restrictions on warfare but the low likelihood that an effective enforcement mechanism could overcome the collective action problem and form spontaneously.

Since the barrier to regulating warfare lies not in the infeasibility of doing so but in an absence of a spontaneously formed enforcement mechanism, a social or religious network can utilize its enforcement mechanisms to regulate warfare. Initially, it can threaten to withhold from noncomplying members the benefits they would otherwise receive from the religious and social functions facilitated by the network. Then, after this threat causes members to comply and peace ensues, the network's enforcement mechanisms become even stronger: expulsion from the network now results not only in a loss of social and spiritual benefits but in exclusion from the benefits of the restraints on warfare (since members are not restricted when waging war on the excluded party). The expanded network, wielding more powerful enforcement mechanisms, may then evolve to encompass even more costly (and beneficial) norms.

---

[77] A network can expand to enforce another norm only if its existing enforcement mechanisms are effective against the individuals who need to be disciplined in order to enforce the new norm. For example, a social network in a certain town can perhaps assume a new norm of enforcing peace among the inhabitants of that town. But it cannot enforce peace among inhabitants of other towns, since the enforcement mechanisms of the network can be employed only against network members, and enforcing peace in other towns requires influencing nonmembers (the inhabitants of the other towns).

[78] Since it is the least costly enforcer that will likely become the regulator, two additional conditions must be satisfied in order for a network enforcing a certain norm to eventually enforce a more costly norm: (1) the network is the lowest-cost regulator of this norm (as opposed to government intervention or bilateral contracting, for example), and (2) the network has lower costs of enforcement than any other network governing the same group of members.

To recap, the conditions that a network needs to satisfy in order to expand to regulate another, higher-cost norm are as follows: (1) the norms originally enforced by the network have sufficiently low enforcement costs to form spontaneously and survive (i.e., succeed in enforcing the low-cost norm); (2) the benefits to be internalized by network members from the newly assumed norm outweigh the costs of enforcing the norm; (3) enforcement of the new, higher-cost norm is possible through control of the existing members of the network; (4) the network has lower costs of enforcement than any other network satisfying the previous three conditions; (5) the network is the lowest-cost regulator (e.g., as opposed to government intervention or bilateral contracting) of the newly assumed norm.

I later suggest guidelines for assessing the enforcement costs of norms.[79] As explained, differences in a norm's enforcement costs affect the evolution of the institutions facilitating it, because they affect the likelihood that a network enforcing the norm can survive spontaneous formation (the lower the enforcement costs, the higher the likelihood of spontaneous formation). These networks may, in time, evolve to enforce norms requiring high enforcement costs. A reverse direction of evolution, from facilitating norms that require high enforcement costs to facilitating norms that require low enforcement costs, is much less likely.

D. A Note on Game Types

A game type is an abstraction of the incentives of people involved in a given interaction (in the context of this article, a norm administered by a network).[80] The abstraction is made by determining the "payoff" to each player (i.e., the benefit conferred on the player) based on both what that player did and what those interacting with that player do. The payoff is measured in "utils," a generic scale measuring benefits of any kind conferred on a player (e.g., money, other material benefits, spiritual elation, a sense of being loved, etc.). A player might receive a different payoff for each combination of her and others' actions; mirroring real life, the choice a player makes affects her welfare, but so do the choices others make.

---

[79] See Section III.E.

[80] On game theory generally, see, for example, Eatwell et al. (1987) and Baird et al. (1994). Even games that correctly portray incentives may be mere parts of a larger game with different incentive structures. "One must also guard against looking at interactions between players in isolation. A problem that may look like a prisoner's dilemma or some other simple two-by-two game may be part of a much larger game. One cannot assume that, once embedded in a larger game, the play of the smaller game will be the same" (Baird et al. 1994: 45).

The real-life situations that games mimic are often intricate, but games are structured in a simple, abstracted form in order to allow easy logical (or mathematical) analysis. To reduce complication, several abstractions will be made in the games examined in this article. First, there are two players in each game – a network member and the other network members (or a network member and the network governance institution). Second, each player is limited to a choice between two actions. These actions change from game to game depending on the illustrative story of the game but are usually called "Cooperate" and "Default."[81]

To assess the likely outcome of a game, one needs to determine whether the game has one or more Nash equilibria. A Nash equilibrium is a state of affairs in which each player, knowing what the other player's actions will be, cannot improve her own situation by changing her actions.[82] This means that if the game repeats itself several times, and at a given iteration of the game the players reach a Nash equilibrium, each is likely to repeat her actions in following games as long as she expects the other player to repeat his actions as well. Therefore, the Nash equilibrium indicates the likely status quo in an iteration of a game (if a game has more than one Nash equilibrium, the status quo is likely to be the first Nash equilibrium that the players reach). A Nash equilibrium is not necessarily the efficient outcome of a game[83] but merely a likely outcome of that game.

Generic game types commonly applied include Harmony, Meeting Place, Battle of the Sexes, Stag Hunt, Chicken, Deadlock, and Prisoner's Dilemma.[84]

---

[81] Often, the more socially beneficial of the two actions is called "cooperating," and the other, less virtuous action is called "defaulting." But this is not always the case. There does not have to be anything morally or socially better in an action called "cooperating" as compared to an action called "defaulting." In some games the two options would be equivalent morally and from a welfare-maximizing perspective. For example, in the Battle of the Sexes game (Aviram 2004), the "cooperating" action is going to see a baseball game, while the "defaulting" action is going to see a movie. The two tags are used merely to make this game comparable to other games discussed in this section and not to suggest either action is positive or negative.

[82] A more formal definition of a Nash equilibrium is a set of actions (one for each player) under which a player knowing what the other players' actions are could not improve her utility by changing her action. On Nash equilibrium, see Nash (1950, 1951) and Kreps (1987).

[83] Unless explicitly stated otherwise, whether the outcome of a game is "efficient" (or "optimal") depends on all players' utility considered jointly (not the utility for any individual player). Externalities on nonplayers need not be considered, since (for abstraction purposes) it is assumed that only the players of a game are affected by the game's outcome. However, when the chapter refers to an "efficient" (or "optimal") outcome outside the context of a game, the perspective of all of society's members is included (including those who are not "players," because even though their actions have no impact on the outcome, the outcome affects them).

[84] For a description of these games, see Aviram (2004).

E. Assessing Enforcement Costs of Regulated Norms

PLSs form by regulating low–enforcement cost norms and then expand to regulate norms that are more expensive to enforce. A rough idea of the enforcement costs of the relevant norms is needed to evaluate PLSs in the lens of this theory.

Several factors affect enforcement costs. For example, it is easier for a regulator to enforce a norm when the costs and benefits of its enforcement are roughly equal for each of the members. The greater the divergence in the interests of individuals, the more expensive it is to secure adherence to the norms (or even to formulate them).[85] The reasons for this can perhaps best be shown through an example. Assume a society of people of equal health but widely differing wealth. In such a society, it would be relatively easy to enforce a norm mandating that people infected with dangerous contagious diseases should be quarantined. The probability and severity of harm from the imposition of this norm is distributed in a roughly equal manner. Each person, whether rich or poor, is (roughly) equally vulnerable to diseases, and thus everyone benefits equally from the norm. Each person is also subject to a (roughly) equal probability of being infected by the dangerous disease and thus bearing the cost of the norm – isolation until recovery.

Contrast this with the formation of a norm regarding tax structure (e.g., progressive or regressive taxation, estate taxes, etc.). In this scenario, benefits from the tax would presumably be distributed equally, but its burdens would shift significantly depending on the tax structure. If the tax is progressive, people with higher income will pay a larger percentage of their income than poorer people; similarly, estate taxes place widely varying burdens depending on accumulated wealth. Disagreement, along with enforcement costs, would be expected to be greater for the latter norm (taxes) than the former norm (medical quarantine).

Not only does the variance of costs and benefits of a norm affect enforcement costs, so does the average net benefit. A network's use of the exclusion, information, or control mechanisms is more effective the more a member benefits from the network. Thus, the enforcement ability of a religious network is likely to be less powerful among a group of secular people than among devoutly religious people, since the latter derive more utility from the spiritual benefits they receive.

Market structure (both that of the various networks in the same market and that of the various individuals within each network) is yet another factor affecting enforcement costs. A network that provides significantly more utility

---

[85] "While diversity makes gains from cooperation larger, it also makes cooperation harder to achieve" (Galbi 2002).

to its members than its rivals do is likely to have lower enforcement costs than a network that has to compete with rival networks that can offer members as much (or more) utility. Competition among networks depends not only on the number of competing networks but on the costs of switching between networks and on the number of networks that provide comparable benefits.[86] The effects of internetwork competition have been discussed thoroughly in the antitrust literature (Cohen 1996; Kolasky 1999; Lemley and McGowan 1998; Piraino 1995) and in the corporation law literature[87] and to a lesser degree in the private ordering literature.

To illustrate the relationship between competition and enforcement costs, consider a sparsely populated rural area that has a single social circle (or several circles that form a single network). A more densely populated urban area, in contrast, might accommodate several different social networks, with little contact among them. Enforcement mechanisms would be more effective in the single rural network than in any of the urban networks, which a rogue member can abandon in favor of another social network at a low cost.[88]

Intranetwork competition also affects enforcement costs: the lower the market power of the network's members, the lower the enforcement costs. Network members with significant market power are more likely to degrade connectivity within the network (e.g., by not following the rules, transacting outside of the network, etc.) (Aviram 2003). For example, Lisa Bernstein (1992) notes

---

[86] Networks provide comparable benefits to members when they have a similar transacting volume or a similar number of members, provided that most of the utility derived from the network is due to network effects rather than due to the intrinsic value of the facilities that form the network. For example, a telephone has very little intrinsic value; it may serve as a piece of furniture, but most of its utility is derived from the network effects that result from connecting the telephone to a network with many other phones. On the differentiation between the intrinsic value of a network good and the network value of the same good, see Ahdieh (2003).

[87] Bebchuk and Roe (1999) argue that network effects may induce persistence of preexisting corporate structures. Klausner (1995) discusses the presence and effects of network externalities in corporate contracts. Ribstein and Kobayashi (2001) present empirical evidence that the choice of incorporation form (e.g., partnership, LLP, LLC, corporation) is driven not by network lock-in effects but by relative business advantages of a given form over the other forms.

[88] This is not to say that less competition among networks is net welfare enhancing. While a reduction in competition increases the network's ability to regulate (which is welfare enhancing), it also decreases the network's incentive to regulate efficiently, as the network may regulate in a manner that enhances or maintains its market power rather than in a manner that reduces opportunism. Whether the increased ability to regulate outweighs the reduced incentive to regulate or vice versa depends on particular circumstances. On differentiating between networks' ability to regulate and networks' incentive to regulate, see Aviram (2003).

that larger diamond dealers (presumably having more market power than their smaller rivals) often trade outside of the diamond exchange.[89]

This list of factors affecting enforcement costs is not exhaustive. A reader familiar with antitrust scholarship may notice the similarity between these criteria and the criteria that facilitate collusion among firms (Dick 1996; Stigler 1964). This is no coincidence, as cartels exhibit one form of behavior regulation. A cartel will discipline firms to maintain their prices and outputs at a level maximizing the its profits.[90] It will fail if it is unable to enforce its mandates – the same enforcement problem that socially beneficial PLSs face.

An important factor in cartel stability that carries less importance for many PLSs is the number of participants. In a cartel, enforcement costs increase vastly, and therefore stability plummets, when the norm is enforced on a larger number of firms. Thus, the stability of a two-member cartel is vastly greater than that of an eight-member cartel, all else equal. The number of people on whom a norm is enforced affects enforcement costs for noncartel norms as well. However, many PLSs enforce norms on a very large number of members. The marginal cost of enforcing a norm on an additional individual is initially very high but decreases rapidly. Thus, enforcing a norm on 200 people is less expensive than enforcing the same norm on 800 people, but not by much. Indeed, cartels of thirty firms are almost unheard of because of their enforcement costs, while many PLSs number thirty members, or many, many more.

The cartel stability literature places more emphasis on the group size criterion than would be relevant to the typical PLS, but it fails to address another criterion of much relevance to the typical PLS – the game type of the norm.[91] It is easier to get people to interact socially with their neighbors than to get them to keep their contractual obligations to the same neighbors. Social interaction benefits most people more than isolation, and most people would rather interact with some people even if others in the same group snub them. So there are few costs involved in getting people to cooperate in agreeing to interrelate. On the other hand, if some network members break their promises, this will encourage other members to do the same so that they are not taken advantage of by the first

---

[89] "Most large and important dealers are members of the club, but they do not usually conduct their business in the club's trading hall ... large scale transactions tend to be consummated in private offices" (Bernstein 1992, 120). On the strategy of degradation, see Cremer et al. (2000) and Aviram (2003).

[90] Of course, this level is typically not optimal from the perspective of a single firm, assuming that other firms abide by the cartel rules. It is also not optimal from the perspective of all of society (consumers and producers together), since the utility loss by consumers is greater than the utility gain by all producers.

[91] For a discussion of the relative enforcement costs of various game types, see Aviram (2004).

group. In some cases, a member will not commit to a promise, even when he knows that everyone else is committing, in the hope of taking advantage of the others. In either of these cases, some enforcement costs are necessary to secure members' commitment to the promises they have made.

Game types are convenient packages of sometimes complex incentive structures. They frequently include the other factors mentioned earlier as influencing the enforcement cost of norms. Variance of benefits is often reflected in game types.[92] Intranetwork competition also often affects the game type of the norm,[93] and other structural issues affect the game type as well.[94]

The failure of the cartel stability literature to consider game types is not due to shortsightedness on the part of the scholars in this area but rather due to a common trait of cartels: the cartel norm (i.e., to abide by the cartel-mandated price or quantity) is nearly always of the Prisoner's Dilemma game type. A cartel member would rank her preferences in abiding by cartel rules as follows: (1) she does not abide by cartel rules but other members do (she increases her profits above the cartel level by undercutting the cartel); (2) she abides by cartel rules and so do the other members (she gains cartel-level profits); (3) she does not abide the cartel rules and neither do the other members (she receives competitive market profits); and finally (4) she abides by cartel rules but other

---

[92] For example, Battle of the Sexes is a Meeting Place game with the added feature of variance in the benefits from mutual behavior (i.e., both players prefer {Cooperate, Cooperate} and {Default, Default} over the other outcomes, but one player prefers {Cooperate, Cooperate} over {Default, Default}, while the other prefers {Default, Default}).

[93] For example, a Chicken game is more likely to be played in oligopolistic market structures in which there are few players, each possessing significant and approximately equal market power (e.g., a social network in a small, rural community), rather than among many players each of whom possesses little market power or among a few unequally powerful players. In contrast, a Bully game is more likely to characterize payoffs when the market contains one player who is markedly more powerful than the others. It is this power (and hence lesser vulnerability) that enables that player to credibly threaten to play Deadlock rather than Chicken; weaker players would like to bluff and masquerade as Deadlock players, but without market power they cannot credibly persuade their rivals that they will default even when the more powerful players threaten to default as well (e.g., that they will engage in a price war even if their more powerful rivals posture to do the same).

[94] For example, the choice between a Meeting Place game and a Battle of the Sexes game could depend on whether this is the first time the norm in question is set or whether there are competing norms to choose from. If there are competing norms, most likely each network member has some costs associated with switching to the other norm. As a result, each member will have a preference for the incumbent norm, even if she would, as second preference, follow another norm rather than be the only one using the incumbent norm while all others used the other one. This is a Battle of the Sexes payoff structure. In contrast, if no member has adopted an existing norm, the members may be indifferent toward all norm alternatives, as long as one norm is agreed upon and adopted universally. This is a Meeting Place payoff structure.

members do not (she receives zero profits, since everyone undercuts her higher, cartel-level price).

The same set of preferences holds for each member of the cartel. This set of preferences is characteristic of the Prisoner's Dilemma game. Since (almost) all cartels are Prisoner's Dilemma games, the literature examining cartel stability is not concerned with the underlying game type.

This explains why cartels tend to be small while other PLSs often have many more members. The cartel norm – a Prisoner's Dilemma norm – is of a game type that is expensive to enforce. When considering the broader range of norms that a network can enforce, however, one finds a richer variety of game types. The difference in game types matters, because different game types require different costs to enforce an outcome optimal for the players – a Prisoner's Dilemma game requires more costly enforcement than, say, a Meeting Place game. Because some of those game types incur significantly lower enforcement costs, PLSs enforcing them can apply to larger groups than can cartels before enforcement costs limit the PLSs' growth.

IV. APPLYING THE THEORY TO PRIVATE NETWORK SECURITY ASSOCIATIONS

A. Network Security Norms as Noncooperative Game Types

Having explained a theory of the evolution of PLSs' enforcement mechanisms, I now apply it in the context of private network security associations, in particular ISACs. ISACs exist to facilitate the exchange of information between their members. The idea behind forming ISACs is that the security of a network can be enhanced by real-time exchange of information between firms regarding attacks on the network, identified vulnerabilities, etc. An ISAC serves two roles in facilitating the information exchange. First, it provides the physical means to exchange information (e.g., a hotline, Internet website, central computer, or other facility that members contact to convey information or receive it). Second, it enforces the norm that certain agreed-upon information be supplied by the members (e.g., it can threaten to expel a member who refuses to contribute information to the ISAC).

These two functions are not completely distinct from each other. As Larry Lessig (1999) pointed out, architecture (such as the structure of the information-sharing facilities) can manipulate behavior and enforce norms just as a legal system does. Therefore, structuring an ISAC in a certain way can increase the willingness of members to share information even if no further sanction is imposed. One such possibility suggested by Lior Strahilevitz

(2003a) is structuring the ISAC so that it overemphasizes the members that share information and underemphasizes those who shirk, giving members a sense that compliance with the information-sharing norm is very high. The sense that everyone else is complying with the information-sharing norm may increase a member's compliance.

Even when architecture, rather than the threat of exclusion, is used as the norm enforcement mechanism, its effectiveness depends on the network effects of the PLS. Architecture that induces compliance to a certain norm is of no use if an individual who does not wish to comply with the norm can simply avoid it at little cost to herself. An individual's ability to avoid using the PLS depends on the benefits conferred on her by the PLS. The same parameter indicates the effectiveness of the PLSs' exclusion mechanism.

Therefore, the effectiveness of ISACs and other network security PLSs depends on the benefits they confer on their members. As explained,[95] if a norm has high enforcement costs, a PLS is unlikely to succeed in enforcing it unless the PLS confers significant benefits through a preexisting functionality (typically, through successfully enforcing other norms on the same individuals who need to comply with the network security norm).[96]

Network security norms are frequently very costly to enforce. Network security is often as strong as its "weakest link." Suppose that several firms are connected to a network and that an attacker who manages to bypass the safeguards of one firm can then attack any of the firms on the network. In that situation, if a firm cannot disassociate itself from the network, it would invest no more than the amount it believes is invested by the least-protected firm. To invest more would be wasteful, as an attacker would simply target the least-protected firm and reach the more-protected firms. This incentive structure is a Stag Hunt game – each firm would prefer that all firms invest the optimal amount in protecting the network, but if each firm believes that any of the other firms invests less that the optimal amount, it too will underinvest.

Stag Hunt norms are moderately expensive to enforce. Some network security norms are of even less cooperative game types. When the norm involves information sharing, for example, a party assured that the other parties will comply with the norm may refuse to comply nonetheless. Gathering helpful

---

[95] See Section III.B.

[96] It is crucial that the benefits of the preexisting functionality apply to most or all of the individuals who need to comply with the new norm. For example, if a PLS currently enforces Norm A on Alan, Betty, and Charlie, and it now attempts to enforce Norm B on Betty, Charlie, and David, enforcing Norm A would not suffice to overcome the paradox of spontaneous formation unless both Betty and Charlie find it worthwhile to comply with Norm B even if they expect David not to comply with it.

information (e.g., discovering a vulnerability in the network) requires expending resources. Once collected, the information may benefit equally all who are privy to it, whether they gathered it themselves or received it from another. If the value of the information to each individual network member is greater than the cost of gathering the information, a Chicken game results. Each member would shirk from gathering information if she thinks other members would gather the information and share it with her. But if she believes that the other network members will not gather the information, she will gather it herself.

The norm is even more expensive to enforce if the cost of gathering the information is greater than the value of the information to each individual member (though lower than the value to all network members together). In that case, each network member will face a Prisoner's Dilemma game: if the others are providing her with information, she would be better off receiving the information but expending no resources in reciprocating. If others, making the same calculation, fail to share information with her, she would still be better off not sharing information with the others. Thus, all parties shirk, and no information is shared.

Although the enforcement costs are high, a PLS can align private incentives with the group's joint welfare by requiring each member to compensate the member who gathered the information or be excluded from receiving the information if she refuses to pay.[97] When the information exchange is to be made between competitors, another Prisoner's Dilemma game forms. Since withholding information from a rival gives the ISAC member an edge in competing with this rival, there is a significant hidden cost in sharing the information: tougher competition from the now more knowledgeable (and thus more effective) rival.[98] The information (e.g., a report of an attack that harmed a company's computer network) may also be leaked to the media by rivals, damaging the reporting company's reputation. Unlike the one previously mentioned, this noncooperative game cannot be averted by the threat of exclusion from the PLS, because exclusion is precisely what the nondisclosing member wants. The value of receiving information from a rival is lower for that member than the benefit of withholding information from the rival.

---

[97] This sanction is viable only if members can by excluded from the network. So, if physical disconnection is impossible, or if some members may disobey the PLS's order to exclude a member, then members will shirk, knowing that the PLS's threats of exclusion are not credible. Further, if a network is only as strong as its weakest link, excluding a member from receiving information without excluding her from the network may make her more vulnerable to attacks, reducing network security for all network members.

[98] For a more thorough analysis of this impediment to information sharing, see Aviram and Tor (2004).

Thus, network security norms tend to belong to noncooperative (and thus expensive to enforce) game types. Other criteria that affect the enforcement cost of norms often increase the cost of enforcing network security norms.[99] For example, often the number of firms that share a network (in the sense that the network security of each of them depends on precautions taken by another firm) is larger than the number of firms that can form a stable cartel in the same industry. Network security, while important, is often not the most important consideration for firms (taking second place to, e.g., competing against the other network members). Thus, the *average utility* to a network member from enforcing network security norms may not be as high as the value of other actions that contradict compliance with the network security norms. Finally, there is often a large *variance in the utility* to each network member from complying with the network security norms. Some firms depend more on the security of the network than others.

Thus, many network security norms are costly to enforce. The theory discussed in this article would therefore suggest that PLSs enforcing such norms are unlikely to form without a preexisting basis that applies to the same network members. A PLS that lacks such a preexisting basis is therefore unlikely to efficiently enforce the network security norms. On the other hand, we expect successful ISACs to form around a preexisting functionality. I examine next an example of an ISAC that seems to have formed in such a way.

B. Reliance on Existing Functionality in the Chemical Sector ISAC

The Chemical Sector ISAC is "a key centralized resource that gathers, analyzes and disseminates threat information that is specific to the Chemical Sector community. The Chemical Sector ISAC will enable fast and cost-effective access to sensitive information about cyber, physical and contamination issues."[100] The ISAC was formed and is operated by the Chemical Transportation Emergency Center (CHEMTREC).

CHEMTREC offers a cost-effective way for shippers of hazardous materials to comply with regulations promulgated by the U.S. Department of Transportation, which require shippers to provide a twenty-four–hour emergency telephone number on shipping documents that can be accessed in the event of an emergency involving the hazardous material that was shipped.[101] CHEMTREC provides this twenty-four–hour emergency service to shippers of hazardous

---

[99] In some situations, however, these same criteria may make the network security norm less costly to enforce than the game type would indicate (e.g., if the relevant group is very small).

[100] Chemical Sector ISAC web page, at http://chemicalisac.chemtrec.com/.

[101] 49 CFR § 172.604.

materials for an annual fee.[102] Manufacturers and shippers that register with CHEMTREC are required to provide safety information on the hazardous material they manufacture or ship, as well as emergency and administrative contacts for their companies that allow CHEMTREC to acquire more information when necessary.

CHEMTREC offers a preexisting functionality to the shippers that use its services. The norm it enforces is ensuring that members provide full and accurate information on their products. It also provides its members with a cost-effective method of complying with the hazardous material regulations' hotline requirement. Hotlines, like many emergency services, maintain significant excess capacity that is idle much of the time but is able to be put into action immediately when an emergency occurs. Maintaining this excess capacity is costly to any individual shipper. It is sensible for many shippers to reduce their costs by sharing a hotline. This is precisely the service CHEMTREC offers. The norm of providing safety information is likely very inexpensive to enforce. The information is required in order for CHEMTREC to act as the shipper's agent and respond to an emergency. By not providing the information, a shipper is harming CHEMTREC's ability to respond to its emergencies, not those of other members. Thus, members are likely to provide the information to CHEMTREC even if they suspect other members will not do so. As a result, we should not be surprised to see a spontaneous formation of CHEMTREC.

CHEMTREC first expanded into enforcing another norm when it formed CHEMNET. CHEMNET is a mutual aid network that utilizes one member's response team (or a for-hire response team) to respond to an accident that occurred to a shipment of another member. CHEMNET provides companies that have limited or no emergency response resources with nationwide emergency response coverage.[103] The benefits of this program are obvious. As a shipper's vehicles roam across the country, an accident may occur almost anywhere. Maintaining a response team in every locale is very expensive, and sending a response team far away to respond to an emergency may take too long. CHEMNET's facilitation of response teams allows shippers to economize, yet again, on the costs of their emergency services. The norm enforced by CHEMNET is the commitment to engage one's response team in the service of another shipper. This norm is somewhat more expensive to enforce. There is a cost associated with allowing the use of one's team for another's benefit. This cost should be offset by the benefit of being able to use other members' response

[102] About CHEMTREC, at http://www.chemtrec.com/chemtrec/chemtrec.nsf/content/Overview.
[103] CHEMNET and Mutual Aid Networks, at http://www.chemtrec.com/chemtrec/chemtrec.nsf/content/CHEMNET.

teams if they comply with the norm themselves. If a member expects the other members not to comply, it too will not comply. This is similar to a Stag Hunt game, though less costly to enforce than that game because a member may still find it beneficial to comply with the norm even if it suspects that some of the other members will not comply, as long as most members will.

In rare cases, degradation might be a feasible strategy, and thus the norm would have a Prisoner's Dilemma game type. This would happen when Acme's vehicle has an accident in Ajax's territory, and Ajax believes that if it does not respond, exacerbating the harm from Acme's accident, Acme would suffer repercussions that would make it a less effective competitor and increase Ajax's market position and profits. This is an unlikely scenario. First, the large number of shippers and the surmountable barriers to entry make the elimination of a single competitor unlikely to increase significantly the profitability of another shipper. Second, public response to a severe accident involving hazardous material may affect all shippers, and so allowing Acme's accident to deteriorate may harm Ajax (e.g., by triggering more restrictive regulation).

The CHEMNET norm is, therefore, of moderate enforcement cost. It developed over the core of CHEMTREC's activities. Only CHEMTERC members may become CHEMNET members. Whether or not the moderate enforcement costs of the CHEMNET norm would have prevented the formation of CHEMNET without reliance on a preexisting functionality, the existence of CHEMTREC reduced the enforcement costs of the CHEMNET norms, as exclusion from CHEMNET entailed not only the loss of potential sharing of response teams (a dubious benefit, because even if only some members default, CHEMNET loses much of its value) but also the loss of the certain and significant benefits of CHEMTREC.

On this already expanded foundation formed the ISAC. The ISAC's norm of information sharing varies from the moderately expensive Chicken game type to the very expensive Prisoner's Dilemma game type. If the ISAC formed spontaneously, our theory would predict that it would fail. The preexisting foundation, however, threatens a violator of the ISAC norm with ostracism from the group that provides the violator with the certain benefits of a joint hotline and mutual aid network. This significantly reduces the cost of ensuring compliance with the ISAC norm and thus increases the ISAC's likelihood of success.

The Chemical Sector ISAC divulges limited information on its functioning and effectiveness, and therefore it is not possible to evaluate if this ISAC is successful in facilitating information sharing. In fact, it is not even clear if the goal of the ISAC members, and thus the norm enforced by the ISAC, is to facilitate information sharing amongst the members. The ISAC may be used to enforce different norms. Absent this information, this description of the Chemical Sector ISAC serves not as proof of the correctness of the theory discussed earlier but as an illustration of the nonspontaneous development of PLSs.

C. Implications on the Public Subsidy of ISACs

This article suggested that when a PLS attempts to enforce a high–enforcement cost norm, the PLS is unlikely to form unless it relies on a preexisting basis. On the other hand, such a norm is far more likely to be successfully enforced by the PLS if the PSL has a significant existing functionality applying to those whose behavior the new norm is intended to affect. Criteria were given to assess the cost of norms.

Since it seems that network security norms tend to incur high enforcement costs, a PLS enforcing them is unlikely to form spontaneously. It may form over a preexisting functionality.

Positive externalities from maintaining the network security of critical infrastructure possibly justify public subsidies to network security PLSs. Any subsidy carries a social cost that may be offset by a redeeming benefit – in this case, the enhanced security of critical infrastructure networks. But for this trade-off to be socially beneficial, a protected ISAC must achieve this redeeming benefit; that is, it must be able to effectively facilitate information sharing. Furthermore, subsidizing ineffective PLSs may cause these PLSs to be maintained despite their inefficiencies (so that the PLS members can benefit from the subsidies). This may not only waste the subsidies but potentially preclude more efficient PLSs from forming.

Since we now have criteria to assess the likelihood of a PLS's success in enforcing a norm (depending on the enforcement cost of the norm and the existence and substance of a preexisting functionality), blanket subsidies that exempt every PLS (rather than apply on a case-by-case basis) may be inappropriate. This calls into question the wisdom of the broad antitrust exemption in Section 5 of the Cyber Security Information Act.

The case-by-case analysis, whether regarding the antitrust laws or other subsidies, should examine whether the relevant network security norm is expensive to enforce and whether the PLS requesting the exemption has a preexisting functionality that provides sufficient benefit to the same individuals that the network security norm applies to.

The suitable type of preexisting network is highly dependent on case-specific details. This article can only give guidelines as to the characteristics of an effective network. It shifts the focus from looking only at the likelihood of potential abuse of the subsidy[104] to identifying an effective preexisting social or commercial network that may serve as an enforcer of efficient information sharing. The more the ISAC membership resembles the membership of this preexisting network, the lower the barriers will be to efficient information sharing.

Currently, ISACs are delineated by industry. The industry categories are very broadly defined, which may result in overinclusion (i.e., including firms that are in the same industry but do not transact much with most other members and do not share membership in a low–enforcement cost regulator) as well as underinclusion (i.e., omitting firms that are not within the same industry but transact frequently with ISAC members and are members of the same low–enforcement cost regulator).[105]

A sectorwide membership criterion may also not be optimal from the perspective of the information exchange that is facilitated. It is possible that to protect critical infrastructure, information need not be shared with all firms within an industry but only with a smaller group of firms whose facilities are dependent on each other for security. This group may even include firms that are not within the same industry (e.g., suppliers, customers) but not include some rivals with which the member firms have little interaction.

The key to delineating the correct membership in an ISAC is to identify a group of firms that are dependent on each other for the security of their facilities[106] and also belong to a preexisting network that provides its members

---

[104] For example, in an antitrust scrutiny, current analysis mainly addresses the risk of abusing the ISAC to facilitate collusion. It is noteworthy that sometimes the same networks that are effective enforcers of beneficial norms are also effective enforcers of socially harmful norms (such as cartels). From the perspective of maximizing social welfare, it may be sensible to allow some PLSs that may have anticompetitive effects but are also effective facilitators of beneficial norms that would otherwise not be enforced effectively.

[105] For example, even if there is a single trade association encompassing all firms in a sector such as "the food industry" or "the information technology industry," these sectors involve so many differently situated firms that smaller commercial and social networks are likely to be more significant in individual firms' transactions and in the lives of these firms' managers. At the same time, these preexisting networks might encompass others that are not in the industry but have frequent transactions with the industry firms and would benefit from sharing information with them. By adding these out-of-sector firms into the ISACs and splitting current ISACs into groups that share tight social or commercial networks, ISACs should be able to increase information sharing. Information sharing between these smaller ISACs is possible even if they are not within the same network by having a secondary network of networks in which a member from each ISAC, acting as a hub of information, share information with its counterparts from other ISACs. Of course, to be effective, these hubs need to be members of a low–enforcement cost regulator themselves, and the selection of the firm that should serve as the hub in each ISAC should take that into account.

[106] That is, breaching the security of one firm would reduce the security of the other firm.

with some significant benefits.[107] Correct assessment of these factors would allow private parties to form more effective PLSs and would allow government to allocate public subsidies to the PLSs that most deserve to benefit from them.

V. CONCLUSION

The economic theory of the firm has long ago distinguished between activities that are governed by hierarchy and those that are governed by networks (in that literature's terminology, markets). Private legal systems are similarly distinguishable. Some enforce norms through hierarchy while others (perhaps the majority of private legal systems) enforce norms through network effects. As indicated by the theory of the firm, each method incurs different transaction (enforcement) costs. Institutions employing each method also form and evolve differently and may require separate analysis.

This article examined network responses to network threats: "Network responses" in the sense of private norm enforcement utilizing network effects as opposed to public or private norm enforcement that utilizes hierarchy. The term "network threats" suggests a particular context of norms, focusing the discussion on the security of networks (in particular, critical infrastructures that are network industries, such as critical computer networks, telecommunications networks, electricity grids, etc.).

To enhance network security (i.e., combat the network threats), appropriate norms must be devised and then enforced on the network members. This article addressed only the enforcement aspect, assuming that the appropriate norms have been identified. Voluntary private legal systems of network members may form to enforce those norms by taking advantage of network effects, and in some instances such enforcement may be more effective than government enforcement.

However, PLSs formed by network members are likely to have incentives to underinvest in network security (compared to the socially optimal level) owing to the significant positive externalities that network security confers on nonmembers. Public subsidies may realign incentives so that the investment in network security is closer to being socially optimal. On the other hand, subsidizing an inefficient PLS may sustain it despite its inefficiency. To allocate

---

[107] This network could be a social network, but it is unlikely that any social network would predominantly consist of the interdependent firms. More likely, an appropriate preexisting network would be a business network (e.g., companies that frequently buy or sell from each other). The close and repeated business connections may serve as a preexisting foundation that would prompt each firm to be more forthcoming in its compliance with the network security norms.

subsidies wisely, one needs tools to assess whether a given PLS is likely to be an effective norm enforcer. This article suggests such tools.

There is a pattern to the evolution of PLSs. A PLS starts by enforcing norms that are not costly to enforce (i.e., norms that members would adhere to without coercion). Once this core is formed, the PLS can undertake the enforcement of norms that are more costly to enforce and require coercion by using the sanction of expulsion from the core group if the new norm is not followed. Successful enforcement of this new norm increases further the benefit the PLS confers on its members and thus increases the magnitude of the sanction of exclusion from the PLS. Armed with a more powerful sanction, the PLS can undertake to enforce yet another norm, which in turn increases its ability to enforce additional norms, and so forth. Thus, PLSs evolve in a gradual expansion of scope, following a progression in the effectiveness of the network's enforcement mechanisms.

In assessing a PLS's ability to enforce a network security norm on network members, we can expect its likelihood of success to increase if it already enforces another norm (or, better yet, several other norms of significant benefits) on the same group of network members. On the other hand, a PLS that has no preexisting functionality (i.e., that has formed ad hoc to enforce the network security norm and does not rely on preexisting relations between the network members) is likely to fail. Public subsidies (appropriate in their amount and type)[108] to the former PLS may result in a socially efficient amount of investment in network security. Public subsidies to the latter PLS may result in network members maintaining an ineffective PLS merely because of the benefit of the subsidies, not only wasting the cost of the subsidies but also obstructing the creation of a more effective PLS.

REFERENCES

Abbott, Alden F. 2003. Remarks before George Mason University Law School Tech Center. Critical Infrastructure Protection Conference on Antitrust and the Exchange of Cyberthreat Information (Arlington, VA, Jan. 30, 2003).
Ahdieh, Robert. 2003. Making Markets: Network Effects and the Role of Law in the Creation and Restructuring of Securities Markets. *Southern California Law Review* 76:277.
American Bankers Association. 2004. 125th Anniversary Timeline 1890–1899. http://www.aba.com/aba/125/timeline1890-1899.htm.
Aviram, Amitai. 2003. Regulation by Networks. *Brigham Young University Law Review* 2003:1179.

[108] This article limits itself to the issue of identifying suitable beneficiaries of network security subsidies. The appropriate amount and types of subsidies are outside its scope.

————. 2004. A Paradox of Spontaneous Formation: The Evolution of Private Legal Systems. *Yale Law and Policy Review* 22:1.

————. 2005. In Defense of Imperfect Compliance Programs. *Florida State University Law Review* 32:397.

Aviram, Amitai, and Avishalom Tor. 2004. Overcoming Impediments to Information Sharing. *Alabama Law Review* 55:231.

Baird, Douglas G., et al. 1994. *Game Theory and the Law*. Cambridge, MA: Harvard University Press.

Bebchuk, Lucian A., and Mark J. Roe. 1999. A Theory of Path Dependence in Corporate Ownership and Governance. *Stanford Law Review* 52:127.

Benson, Bruce L. 1989. The Spontaneous Evolution of Commercial Law. *Southern Economic Journal* 55:644.

Bernstein, Lisa. 1992. Opting out of the Legal System: Extralegal Contractual Relations in the Diamond Industry. *Journal of Legal Studies* 21:115.

Brooks, Robin A. 1998. Deterring the Spread of Viruses Online: Can Tort Law Tighten the Net? *Review of Litigation* 17:343.

Church, Jeffrey, and Ian King. 1993. Bilingualism and Network Externalities. *Canadian Journal of Economics* 26:337.

Clay, Karen. 1997. Trade without Law: Private-Order Institutions in Mexican California. *Journal of Law, Economics, and Organization* 13:202.

Coase, Ronald H. 1937. The Nature of the Firm. *Economica* 4:386. Reprinted in Ronald H. Coase, *The Firm, The Market, and the Law* (Chicago: University of Chicago Press, 1988).

————. 1960. The Problem of Social Cost. *Journal of Law and Economics* 3:1.

Cohen, William E. 1996. Competition and Foreclosure in the Context of Installed Base and Compatibility Effects. *Antitrust Law Journal* 64:535.

Cooter, Robert D. 1996. Decentralized Law for a Complex Economy: The Structural Approach to Adjudicating the New Law Merchant. *University of Pennsylvania Law Review* 144:1643.

Courtney, Will. 2001. Are Online Auctions Guilty of E-Scalping? *Eagle Tribune*. http://www.eagletribune.com/news/stories/20010304/FP_004.htm.

Cremer, Jacques, et al. 2000. Connectivity in the Commercial Internet. *Journal of Industrial Economics* 48:433.

Cunningham, Lawrence A. 2004. The Appeal and Limits of Internal Controls to Fight Fraud, Terrorism, Other Ills. *Journal of Corporate Law* 29:267.

DHS, SEC Talking about Requirements to Disclose Information about Cybersecurity. 2003. *Law Week* 72:2234.

Dick, Andrew R. 1996. When Are Cartels Stable Contracts? *Journal of Law and Economics* 39:241.

Drury, Allan. 2002. When It Comes to Ticket Scalping, the Net's the Wild West. *USA Today*. http://www.usatoday.com/tech/webguide/internetlife/2002-10-07-e-scalping_x.htm.

Eatwell, John, et al., eds. 1987. *Game Theory*. New York: Norton.

Eisenberg, Melvin A. 1999. Corporate Law and Social Norms. *Columbia Law Review* 99:1253.

Ellickson, Robert C., 1986. Of Coase and Cattle: Dispute Resolution among Neighbors in Shasta County. *Stanford Law Review* 38:623.

————. 1989. A Hypothesis of Wealth-Maximizing Norms: Evidence from the Whaling Industry. *Journal of Law, Economics, and Organization* 5:83.

_____. 1991. *Order without Law: How Neighbors Settle Disputes.* Cambridge, MA: Harvard University Press.

Ellickson, Robert C., and Charles D. Thorland. 1995. Ancient Land Law: Mesoportamia, Egypt, Israel. *Chicago Kent Law Review* 71:321.

Frye, Emily. 2002. The Tragedy of the Cybercommons: Overcoming Fundamental Vulnerabilities to Critical Infrastructures in a Networked World. *Business Law* 58:349.

_____. 2003. Information-Sharing Hangups: Is Antitrust Just a Cover? *CIP Report* 1:6.

Galbi, Douglas A. 2002. Revolutionary Ideas for Radio Regulation. http://papers.ssrn.com/sol3/papers.cfm?abstract_id-316380.

Gentile, Carmen J. 2000. Israeli Hackers Vow to Defend. *Wired News,* November 15. http://www.wired.com/news/politics/ 0,1283,40187,00.html.

Glaber, Ralph. 2004. Miracles de Saint-Benoit. http://www.fordham.edu/halsall/source/glaber-1000.html.

Goodman, Marc D., and Susan W. Brenner. 2002. The Emerging Consensus on Criminal Conduct in Cyberspace. *University of California Los Angeles Journal of Law and Technology* 2002:4.

Greif, Avner. 1989. Reputation and Coalitions in Medieval Trade: Evidence on the Maghribi Traders. *Journal of Economic History* 49:857.

_____. 1993. Contract Enforceability and Economic Institutions in Early Trade: The Maghribi Traders' Coalition. *American Economic Review* 83:525.

Greif, Avner, et al. 1994. Coordination, Commitment, and Enforcement: The Case of the Merchant Guild. *Journal of Political Economy* 102:745.

Griboff, Howard. 1992. New Freedom for AT&T in the Competitive Long Distance Market. *Federal Commercial Law Journal* 44:435.

Grow, Brian. 2004. Nothing's Foolproof, but Early Warning Antivirus Systems Are Getting Better Jumps on Mischief Makers. *Business Week,* June 21. P. 84.

Hayek, Friedrich A. 1978. *Law, Legislation and Liberty.* Chicago: University of Chicago Press.

Head, Thomas, and Richard Landes, eds. 1992. *The Peace of God: Social Violence and Religious Response in France around the Year 1000.* Ithaca, NY: Cornell University Press.

Holmes, Oliver Wendell. 1897. The Path of the Law. *Harvard Law Review* 10:457. Reprinted in *Harvard Law Review* 110 (1997):991.

ISAC. 2004a. Frequently Asked Questions. http://www.energyisac.com/faq.dfm.

_____.2004b. Energy ISAC Subscriber Agreement. http://www.energyisac.com/docs/local/subscriberagreement.pdf.

Islamic Hackers Step up Attacks. 2002. *BBC News,* October 29. http://news.bbc.co.uk/1/hi/technology/2372209.stm.

Israel under Hack Attack. 2002. *BBC News,* April 16. http://news.bbc.co.uk/1/hi/sci/tech/1932750.stm.

Katyal, Neal K. 2001. Criminal Law in Cyberspace. *University of Pennsylvania Law Review* 149:1003.

Klausner, Michael. 1995. Corporations, Corporate Law and Networks of Contracts. *Virginia Law Review* 81:757.

Kolasky, William J. 1999. Network Effects: A Contrarian View. *George Mason Law Review* 7:577.

Kolko, Gabriel. 1965. *Railroads and Regulation.* New York: Norton.

Kranton, Rachel E. 1996. The Formation of Cooperative Relationships. *Journal of Law, Economics, and Organization* 12:214.

Krawiec, Kimberly D. 2005. Organizational Misconduct: Beyond the Principal-Agent Model. *Florida State University Law Review* 32:263.

Kreps, David M. 1987. Nash Equilibrium. In *Game Theory*, ed. John Eatwell et al., 167. New York: Norton.

Lemley, Mark A., and David McGowan. 1998. Legal Implications of Network Economic Effects. *California Law Review* 86:479.

Lessig, Lawrence. 1999. *Code and Other Laws of Cyberspace*. New York: Basic Books.

Lichtenbaum, Peter, and Melanie Schneck. 2002. The Response to Cyberattacks: Balancing Security and Cost. *International Law* 36:39.

Macaulay, Stewart. 1963. Non-Contractual Relations in Business: A Preliminary Study. *American Sociological Review* 28:55.

Malone, Robert J., and Reuven R. Levary. 1994. Computer Viruses: Legal Aspects. *University of Miami Business Law Journal* 4:125.

McAdams, Richard H. 1997. The Origin, Development, and Regulation of Norms. *Michigan Law Review* 96:228.

McCarthy, John. 2003. Focus on Information Sharing. *CIP Report* 1:4.

Milhaupt, Curtis J., and Mark D. West. 2000. The Dark Side of Private Ordering: An Institutional and Empirical Analysis of Organized Crime. *University of Chicago Law Review* 67:41.

Miller, Harris N. 2002. Testimony Presented to United States Senate Committee on Governmental Affairs. http://www.itaa.org/infosec/050802testimony.pdf.

Nash, John F. 1950. Equilibrium Points in *n*-Person Games. *Proceedings of the National Academy of Sciences* 36:48.

———. 1951. Non-Cooperative Games. *Annals of Mathematics* 54:286.

NERC. 2004. About NERC. http:/www.nerc.com/about.

Note, Functional Analysis, Subsidies, and the Dormant Commerce Clause. 1997. *Harvard Law Review* 110:1537.

Oedel, David G. 1993. Private Interbank Discipline. *Harvard Journal of Law and Public Policy* 16:327.

Olsen, Erik. 2001. Hacking for the Cause. *ABC News*, October 15. http://abcnews.go.com/sections/scitech/DailyNews/strikes_hacker_yihat)011015.html.

Ostrom, Elinor. 1990. *Governing the Commons: The Evolution of Institutions for Collective Action*. Cambridge: Cambridge University Press.

Palay, Thomas M. 1984. Comparative Institutional Economics: The Governance of Rail Freight Contracting. *Journal of Law and Economics* 13:265.

Piraino, Thomas A., Jr. 1995. The Antitrust Analysis of Network Joint Ventures. *Hastings Law Journal* 47:5.

Posner, Eric A. 1996. Law, Economics, and Inefficient Norms. *University of Pennsylvania Law Review* 144:1697.

Posner, Richard A. 1998a. *Economic Analysis of the Law*. 5th ed. Gaithersburg, MD: Aspen Publishers.

———. 1998b. *Law and Literature*. Cambridge, MA: Harvard University Press.

Ribstein, Larry E., and Bruce H. Kobayashi. 2001. Choice of Firm and Network Externalities. *William and Mary Law Review* 43:79.

Smith, Adam. 1776. *An Inquiry into the Nature and Causes of the Wealth of Nations*. Ed. E. Cannan. New York: Bantam Classics.

Stigler, George J. 1964. A Theory of Oligopoly. *Journal of Political Economics* 72:44.

Strahilevitz, Lior. 2003a. Charismatic Code, Social Norms, and the Emergence of Cooperation on the File-Swapping Networks. *Virginia Law Review* 89:505.

————. 2003b. Social Norms from Close-Knit Groups to Loose-Knit Groups. *University of Chicago Law Review* 70:359.

Sunstein, Cass R. 1996. Social Norms and Social Roles. *Columbia Law Review* 96:903.

Thorne, Susan. 2002. Premiums Least of Owners' Worries in Israel. *Shopping Centers Today.* http://www.icsc.org/srch/sct/sct0902/page85.html.

U.S.-Canada Power System Outage Task Force. 2003. Final Report on the August 14, 2003 Blackout in the United States and Canada: Causes and Recommendations. http://www.nerc.com/pub/sys/all_updl/docs/blackout/ch1-3.pdf.

U.S. Department of Justice. 2000. Business Review Letter to Electric Power ISAC. http://www.usdoj.gov/atr/public/busreview/6614.htm.

White House. 1998. Presidential Decision Directive/NSC-63. http://www.fas.org/irp/offdocs/pdd/pdd-63.htm.

Will the Net End Ticket Scalping? 1999. *MSNBC.com.* http://zdnet.com.com/2100-11501311.html.

Williamson, Oliver E. 1983. Credible Commitments: Using Hostages to Support Exchange. *American Economic Review* 73:519.

Wolverton, Troy. 2002. Online Ticket Market Pressures Scalpers. *CNET News.com.* http://msn.com.com/2100-1106-918772.html.

Zywicki, Todd J. 2003. The Rise and Fall of Efficiency in the Common Law: A Supply Side Analysis. *Northwestern University Law Review* 97:1551.

SIX

THE DARK SIDE OF PRIVATE ORDERING: THE NETWORK/ COMMUNITY HARM OF CRIME

Neal K. Katyal*

The common conception of crime, as an act that harms an individual victim, needs rethinking. Instead of examining the impact of crime on the individual victim, this chapter argues that the harm of a criminal act must also be understood with reference to its effect on the community. Once crime is understood in those terms, the dominant conception of criminal policy changes, sometimes in drastic ways. In particular, it will cast some doubt on the desirability of solutions rooted in private ordering and demonstrate the primacy of public enforcement against cybercrime.

Cyberspace presents the easiest vantage point from which to view the community harm of crime. For example, it is commonly argued that many computer crimes, including those that target critical infrastructure, are ones of "curiosity" and result in "no real harm" and that the government should stay out of cyberspace. But even when there is no harm to an individual, acts of cybercrime can undermine the formation and development of networks. For example, the quintessential privacy-violating hacker, who does nothing more than peer into the records of a corporation's server, does not directly damage the corporation's profits. Instead, the upshot of the hacker's activity is more subtle, and likely to take the form of stifling that corporation's network connections in the future. The Internet is the paradigmatic sphere in which the positive advantage of "network effects" is central – that the greater the size of the network, the greater the benefits.[1] The stifling of network connections thus can have dramatic negative consequences. In cyberspace, therefore, we

---

[1] A network effect occurs when the utility of a good increases with the number of other agents who are consuming the same good (Katz and Shapiro 1985). "Because the value of membership [in a network] to one user is positively affected when another user joins and enlarges the network, such markets are said to exhibit 'network effects,' or 'network externalities'" (Katz and Shapiro 1994, 94). See also Liebowitz and Margolis (1994).

*John Carroll Research Professor, Georgetown University Law Center.

may punish crime even when there is no direct harm to an individual victim because of the harm in trust to the network. Vigorous enforcement of computer crime prohibitions can help ensure that the network's potential is realized.

But punishment is appropriate not only because of the potential loss of network effects and trust from the criminal act. After all, there may be, in this technological age, architectural "fixes" to the computer trespasser that may prevent intrusion without much damage to connectivity. But these electronic intrusion detection systems are likely to be adopted disproportionately, and with severe distributional consequences to boot. If law enforcement did not police cybercrime, so that the burden of fending off attacks was left to individual victims, only the better off may be able to thwart the attacks, leaving the rest of the computer-using population vulnerable. Effective government protection against cybercrime is essential, not only to thwart instances of computer crime, but also to encourage users to let more of their lives and work unfold on the Net. Oftentimes, we have more to fear from the reaction to crime than from the crime itself.

Over the past two centuries, analysts have circled around the community/network harm of crime. Émile Durkheim (1956) claimed famously that punishment "serves to sustain the common consciousness itself" and produces solidarity. Following Durkheim's lead, much research in twentieth-century criminology concerned itself with how community social organization is crucial to reducing crime (Shaw and MacKay 1942). Yet the central focus of that scholarship, and of criminal law more generally, revolves around punishment and control. The relevant questions concern why and how we punish, not what the harms are from crime itself. And so it is not surprising to find modern analysis of criminal law still focused on the three variables identified by Shaw and MacKay's influential work as causes of crime (economic status, ethnic heterogeneity, and residential mobility) and not trained on the impact of crime on the community (see, e.g., Sampson and Groves 1989; Sampson et al. 1997).

Once we see the community impact as central, it will reorient criminal law and policy. For example, it will explain why governments must invest more to protect against crime, and why strategies like the White House's Plan to Secure Cyberspace are likely to be exceptionally ineffective at controlling the threat to vibrant networks. It will shed new light on the role of the government in modern-day real-space policing and reveal new justifications for laws such as hate crime prohibitions and gang-loitering ordinances. These laws target crimes that fragment networks, and when crimes are aimed at disrupting the well of public trust, special sanctions are appropriate. And, perhaps most controversially, community impact will explain why some instances of the exact same crime are deserving of greater sanction than are others.

I. THE NETWORK HARMS FROM COMPUTER CRIME

Consider two stories. In the first, a young teenager is prosecuted for breaking into computer networks although he did nothing more than prove he could get into them. He doesn't steal any secret information, his aim was simply to showcase his cyberprowess. His name is unimportant, for so many hackers do exactly this – break into networks not to steal but to prove their skills and satiate their curiosity. The defense here, as one hacker put it, is that the act "is just harmless exploration. It's not a violent act or a destructive act. It's nothing."[2] Elements of this story appear in most of the famous hacker accounts – those of Mitnick, Poulsen, Lamo, and the like.[3] The young man in the story contests the prosecution, claiming that he did no harm.

A dominant way of thinking about this action among today's cyberspace mavens is to agree with the teenager. The strong arm of the criminal law has no business when the only harm to a victim is remote and intangible. The hacker is guilty of being overly curious but of not much else.

The fallacy with this reasoning lies in its stunted conception of the damage wrought by a criminal act. Instead of having the propriety of criminal sanction turn solely on the harm to an individual victim, the community effect of crime should enter into the calculus. The upshot of a computer intrusion like that described in the paragraph above is to raise the fear of using computers for sensitive transactions – whether it be making credit card purchases, sending love letters, or transmitting sensitive business information. The teenager is punished not for what he did to the individual victim as much as what he did to deplete the reservoir of trust among computer users.

In the second example, a woman parks her car on a city street, eats at a restaurant, and emerges to find that her car has been stolen. The police, due to budget constraints, tell the woman that they don't investigate such crimes, and they even decide to announce a policy to that effect. In addition to conserving scarce enforcement resources for more serious crimes, the police reason, not without some justification, that the announcement of a policy that they will not investigate auto theft will actually *decrease* the amount of automobile theft. If the police don't protect against the crime, they reason, the numbers of people who own automobiles and drive will be fewer. And those that do drive will take

---

[2] Interview with Anonymous Juvenile Hacker who Pled Guilty to Breaking into NASA. http://www.pbs.org/wgbh/pages/frontline/shows/hackers/interviews/anon.html. The identity of this person was later revealed to be Jonathan James (Chron 2000).

[3] Lamo broke into databases at the New York Times, Worldcom, Microsoft, and other corporations. In his defense, it was argued that he "never tried to profit from his hacking" and that he was a "security researcher" (Poulson 2004).

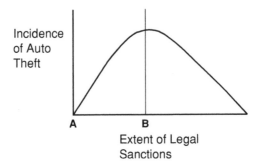

Figure 6.1. Relationship between legal sanction and auto theft.

special precautions to guard against theft – from locking their doors to buying fancy electronic antitheft systems.

As the second example underscores, legal sanctions against crime are not driven exclusively by the harm of the criminals acts. Indeed, the incidence of auto theft may *increase* with legal protection because the absence of law enforcement means that very few will own cars and that those who do will self-protect against theft.

In Figure 6.1, space between points A and B represent the hidden problem of criminal sanctions – the space in which increasing the legal sanction on auto theft has the somewhat perverse effect of increasing it. Some might be tempted to reason that, as a result, the government should stay out of the business of policing auto theft altogether. To get the incidence of auto theft back down, it would take a massive amount of criminal sanctions. Instead, the argument goes, let individuals be responsible for their property. This argument can be made with most types of crime. Do you fear credit card theft on the Internet? If so, then abandon enforcement of laws against theft and fraud on the Net. If government did not enforce these laws, then no one would use their credit cards, and the theft would disappear.

But governments, of course, do not think that way. Indeed, they consistently risk the creation of the space between points A and B. The reason why governments act in this seemingly counterintuitive way has everything to do with the costs of private precaution. If auto theft is reduced via reducing the numbers of cars on the road, it will have all sorts of costs exogenous to crime rates – costs incurred because the automobile has become a fixture of life for many. If, by contrast, auto theft is reduced, not by reducing the number of cars, but by expenditures for better security systems (car alarms, The Club, and the like), then it will raise severe distributional concerns. (Notably, these concerns do not disappear even if private ordering is more efficient.) If only the more wealthy can afford the private protection strategies, then they will be able to drive whereas the poor will not. As we will see, each of these costs has an analogy in cyberspace.

A. Network Harms

There are two ways of understanding the harm of computer crimes. One way is the teenager's above: he never used the information for profit, revenge, or anything else, he simply looked at the data. In this way, his crime was a combination of curiosity and bravado. But it created no direct harm to the victim. On this view, serious government enforcement of the computer crime statute makes little sense, for the victims suffer no tangible harm. The harm here is even less than the oft-maligned "pain and suffering" damages in tort – for without destruction or misuse of the data, there is no financial harm and little emotional harm suffered by a corporation.

But consider, instead, the harm to the universe of computer users. The crime has ramifications for everyone because it erodes the basis of trust on the network. The fact that someone deliberately accessed the data will lead users not to trust the network. Already, a great many fear buying products on the Net due to credit card fraud. With additional instances of intrusion, that fear will increase.

The harm here is not simply commercial – for if hackers start to target individual users' personal files, people will reduce their connections to the Internet. One of the great transformations in computing today is the emergence of "always on" networks at home and in the office.[4] These networks are a promising means of increasing communication and connectivity between users, and can facilitate the instantaneous transfer and use of data.[5] But as the incidence of computer intrusion mounts, individuals will fear that their "always on"

---

[4] Approximately 50% of homes in the United States with Internet connections are expected to be using broadband very shortly. There has been a 60% growth rate in U.S. broadband use during the past year, with half of that growth taking place since November 2003 ("Broadband Finally Dominates" 2004). Worldwide broadband installations number 100.8 million as of December 2003, a rise of 62.8% from the previous year ("DSL Dominates" 2004).

[5] For a discussion of broadband's societal benefits, see U.S. Department of Commerce (2002): "Broadband is an incredible *enabling* technology. It allows businesses that are willing to embrace Internet business solutions to transform business processes and realize significant returns on investment. It offers consumers new opportunities to work or learn more productively (at their desks or from home), publish multimedia, switch from viewers of entertainment to participants, and – most importantly – dramatically expand their communication possibilities."

connection will increase the chance of an intruder reaching into their system. The occurrence of crime will induce users to structure their computer use in ways to minimize the harm, and one way to minimize the harm is to turn the computer off.

Put differently, the individual user contributes to a public good when her computer is on and she makes some of her data accessible via the Net. One reason for the startling number of such contributions has to do with the low costs of being public minded – there are very few additional costs involved when someone uses her computer to publish items on the Web. It is not simply publishing material – but even the raw processing power a computer has – that constitutes a public good. As Yochai Benkler (2002) has shown, thousands of individuals are making their computers accessible to take advantage of their distributed computing power to solve complicated tasks – such as finding the next prime number. Large numbers of people today can and do publish information as well as donate their computers' processing power at little expense to themselves. But as the risks of privacy crime increase, the low costs suddenly balloon. Now the individual has to fear the consequences for her other, private data once the computer is connected to the outside world. In this way, a privacy crime can have effects that ripple far beyond the initial victim, striking fear in the universe of users more generally.

It is always tempting to think that technology, in greater and more sophisticated amounts, will solve these problems. If only encryption, firewalls, remote servers, intrusion-detection systems, and other forms of technology were pervasive, the tempting argument goes, the community harms from crime would cease to exist. It is worth pointing out at the outset that, even if adopted, these technological countermeasures amount to a deadweight loss, a consequence of the crime that supposedly caused "no real harm." But it is a deep mistake to think that all of this technology will save us. After all, some forms of computer crime are not amenable to technical solutions. Not only does the march of technology work to benefit criminals as well as noncriminals, thereby conferring ever greater intrusion prowess, it is often impossible to build systems fully secure against intrusion. Encryption may work between two users, but it cannot stop keystroke loggers and intrusion methods that capture screen images. Electronic detection systems are always susceptible to a criminal masquerading as an authorized user. It is foolish to expect too much from technology, just as it is foolish to think that architecture in real space will eliminate crime altogether.

There are of course crimes that can be forestalled through better technology, but that technology often comes at considerable cost. It is here where the distributional consequences become pervasive.

B. Distributional Harms

The criminal law exists, in part, as a subsidy to poorer elements in a community. If everyone had to fend for themselves to prevent crime, the richer in society would be able to externalize some of the crime onto their poorer neighbors. The case for crime control, then, is not simply predicated on the fraying of community. It is also based on the fact that private precautions cost money and that to expect those with less wealth to bear a greater share of crime offends notions of distributional justice.

Forcing individuals to bear the cost of computer crime will promote sales of anti-virus software, intrusion systems, and the like. Yet the ability to afford, and the knowledge to use, such technologies will not be distributed equally. Those with less resources will not be able to adopt them in the same way that richer individuals and institutions can. Further, because these technologies are often complicated, there will be some who have the resources to purchase them but lack the skills necessary to use them effectively.

The distributional consequences of this drift toward private precautions can be devastating. Already, users of America Online, a group that tends toward less technical sophistication, are being inundated with spam in ways that other users are not. As the technical capacities of computer criminals grow, unacceptable danger lurks to less sophisticated and poorer users. The result will be a less private, more vulnerable Internet experience for these groups, and this may drive some off the Net altogether, and leave others afraid to have as public a presence on the Net.

It is tempting to think that technology can solve this problem, too. After all, many of the devices that protect against computer crime are simply pieces of software – antivirus programs, some firewalls, and the like. Because additional software units can be manufactured at low marginal cost, the argument goes, the distributional divide will not occur; richer users will pay for a product's research and development and in turn such payments will subsidize use by the relatively poorer. While undoubtedly software product manufacturers, like purveyors of most products, will attempt to recoup their research and development costs from larger commercial sales, there is little reason to think that this will lead to effective cybersecurity for everyone else. For one thing, it is unlikely that the manufacturers of these products would cut their costs enough to make their more sophisticated systems cheaply available. (Anyone who doubts this should take a look at the pharmaceutical industry.) And even if they did, the upshot could be to diminish cybersecurity overall. If the great majority of computer users adopted the same firewall and the same antivirus system, danger of a different kind would lurk: the lack of diversity. Just as biodiversity can ward off the spread of disease in realspace (the Irish potato blight spread through Ireland and caused the famine because Ireland had little diversity in its potato stock),[6] so too does software diversity contain the spread of computer epidemics. A virus may attack Windows users but not Mac user, Linux users but not Windows user, Microsoft Outlook users instead of Netscape Navigator users, and so on. Multiple systems can reduce the harm once a computer virus is unleashed. Indeed, it may be that richer computer users have interests that are adverse to those of poorer ones – they do not want the protection software they use to be widely implemented – for if it were, their security may suffer. Greater prevalence may make their program not only a more prominent, but also a more inviting, target.

None of this is to ignore the power of the open-source movement and the accompanying possibility that some major anti-crime precautions might be available to users at nominal cost or no cost at all. Just as a computer trespasser may not be motivated by profit, a computer programmer might simply want to make the digital world a more secure place. But whatever the motivations of the programmer, the adoption of such security technologies will have distributional consequences of its own. The problems that occur will be most acute in the transition to widespread implementation of the program. In the early stages of a security program's life, there are likely to be bugs, errors, and vulnerabilities. Those problems exist for high-priced commercial variants as well, but paid testers at least ferret out some of them. In the case of a low-priced program, the testers are the users themselves, leading some to avoid the program altogether and leaving others stranded with a poor security protocol.

Some open-source devotees have responded with the claim that their programs are inherently more secure than closed-source ones by dint of the number of eyeballs testing the code.[7] This argument is almost always overstated, even

---

[6] The Irish potato famine of the 1840s proved so deadly both because of the lack of genetic diversity in Ireland's potato crop and because of Irish peasants' overreliance on potatoes. O'Grada (1999) explains that one reason that the potato blight hit Ireland harder than its neighbors was because the potato was a more central staple of the Irish diet. The potatoes that predominated in Europe originate from two similar South American potato lines, creating a lack of biodiversity (Adams 2001). This genetically similar potato stock proved susceptible to *Phytophthora infestans*, the late blight fungus, which struck Europe in 1845 (Adams 2001). Even more unfortunately, the Irish poor had increasingly shifted their agriculture and diet to the "Lumper" potato, a watery and tasteless variety that was more reliable and flexible (O'Grada 1999, 20). This overreliance on the Lumper was tragic, as the Lumper was especially susceptible to *Phytophthora infestans* (p. 20). Consequently, when the blight arrived in Ireland, it destroyed three out of four seasons of potato crops. Since the Irish relied so heavily on the potato, this fungus caused the death and dislocation of over a million poor peasants (Crawford 1995).

[7] The Open Source Initiative (2004) argues that closed sources "create a false sense of security"; Warfield (2003) notes, "The closed source camp likes to point out every open

when one disregards the distributional concerns. For certain forms of software that are highly specialized, it is not realistic to think that there will be citizen-activist eyeballs monitoring the code for flaws. Rather, openness in the code might reveal – more than would happen with closed code – security flaws that can be exploited.[8] With these highly specialized systems, then, the case for closure may be stronger than that for openness.

These specialized systems stand in contrast to ubiquitous programs like computer operating systems. Here, the multitude of users makes it more likely that the envisioned citizen-activists will examine the code and reveal its flaws. It therefore follows that open-source platforms and some open-source applications may prove effective at containing viruses and other invaders by producing strength through numbers. But the transitional problems are immense before such software becomes useful, and the distributional consequences can loom large.

II. SOME IMPLICATIONS OF A COMMUNITY HARM APPROACH

Cybercriminals like Kevin Mitnick have analogized their crime to walking into an open door of a house and looking around without doing any damage. This is clever rhetoric, for it suggests that when there is no damage to the victim, government should stay out, particularly when the victim was careless. But we should think seriously about whether such claims make sense in realspace itself. For reasons that are precisely the same as the ones in cyberspace, the answer is no.

source security advisory as evidence that open source is insecure. In doing so, they conveniently ignore the counter examples in their own advisories. They also conveniently overlook the fact that open source problems are often found and fixed before they're widely exploited, while some closed source problem go unaddressed for months, or longer." See also Raymond (1999) and Hatch et al. (2001). "If having the source code makes it easy to spot weaknesses, the best way to find and plug security holes is to make the source code as widely available as possible and solicit the input of those who use it" (Petreley 2000).

While empirical data are limited, Microsoft's closed source web server, IIS, was the most frequently targeted web server for hacking attacks in 2001, despite the fact that there are a larger number of open source Apache systems in use (Wheeler 2003). Indeed, some firms are switching to Apache to avoid the viruses that attack Microsoft server software. Yasin (2001) explains that after the Code Red virus, the law firm Fenwick & West switched to Apache. TruSecure (2001) discusses how a patch to remove a major security vulnerability, the so-called Ping of Death, whereby a remote user could flood a computer and cause it to crash, was posted on Linux within hours of the problem's discovery, yet it took far longer for Microsoft to patch it. Warfield (2003) discusses how an open source model quickly solved a problem with the PGP2.6 encryption program.

[8] Brown (2002) argues that opening the code teaches hackers how to attack it. Schreiner (2003) argues that open source models are inherently less secure.

Walking into someone's house without doing harm is a classic example of a criminal act, the act of trespass.[9] The law is typically justified because of the fear of the victim,[10] yet, as with cyberspace, there is a community-centered aspect to the problem. The idea of public crime control is not to bust people for trespass after it has been committed; rather it is to encourage people to keep their doors relatively open in the first place. Of course, there may be some locking mechanisms on the door, but nothing like what we see in other countries where policing is dismal. The prosecution of trespass makes it possible for people to avoid the draconian step of putting bars on every window and deadbolts on every door.

If the government did not enforce laws against physical trespass, more potential victims would probably buy locks for their doors. But the upshot of that system can be profoundly regressive. Those who could afford the best locks, doors, and security systems would have the lowest crime rates; the poorer would suffer more crime than they did before. Moreover, such private precautions cost money and would incur deadweight loss, and to the extent that expenditures are necessary, economies of scale might favor greater public enforcement. Finally, because only the state can invoke the coercive apparatus of the criminal law, it might be best situated to shape attitudes and beliefs in ways that make crime less likely (Katyal 1997).

Consider a final cost of private ordering in realspace: It turns out that private precautions might actually *increase* crime instead of reducing it. When cheap wire fences are placed around crime-ridden areas, iron bars on windows become pervasive, and "the Club" is ubiquitous, serious negative externalities can emerge, particularly the crippling of interconnectivity and the destruction of reciprocity (Katyal 2002). A private precaution may help the individual user, but it expresses fear and reflects the attitude that lawlessness has become pervasive. Bars on windows and other target hardening scare people away, fragmenting the community and the development of an ethos that promotes order. Thus, instead of decreasing crime, these acts of self-help can actually increase it (Katyal 2002). Viewed this way, gated communities are a byproduct of public disregard of architecture, not a sustainable solution to crime.[11]

---

[9] See, for example, N.J.S. §2C: 18–3 (1997): "A person commits [criminal trespass] if, knowing that he is not licensed or privileged to do so, he enters or surreptitiously remains in any . . . structure."

[10] See, for example, *State v. Von Loh*, 458 N.W.2d 556, 559 (Wis. App. 1990): "As applied to the offense of criminal trespass to a dwelling, the required breach of the peace need only be such as to put the victim in fear of bodily harm or otherwise disturb or disrupt the peace and sanctity of the home."

[11] Gated communities generally apply only one architectural precept, to reduce access. They tend to have minimal natural surveillance and poor opportunities for social interaction, thereby

In all of these cases, the public expression of fear cues additional crime. It suggests that norms of reciprocity have broken down and that one cannot trust one's neighbor. Not only does this weaken the public norm against crime in the area, it also means that those who have a greater propensity to follow the law will move out of such a neighborhood (or never move there in the first place) (see, e.g., Wilson 1975).

Weak public approaches to crime, whether through law enforcement or other means, stimulate these pernicious methods of self-help. A central goal of public enforcement is to provide a backdrop of security so that individuals do not have to resort to their own clumsy patches to the system.

The case for law enforcement, then, is not one centered solely, or even predominantly, on the harm to the individual victim. Of course, that harm is important as well, but we use the massive coercive power of criminal law not to make the victim feel whole again (for no prosecution can accomplish that) but to foment attitudes of trust within the society. After all, there are any number of other ways to spend money to alleviate greater suffering of individuals. The billions of dollars could be put toward food and shelter for the poor, for example. If helping the poor is believed to squander resources on those who are not deserving (on the view that being poor or homeless is the fault of the individual), then the money could be put toward helping those who suffer calamities in regard to which they are faultless (leukemia patients, natural disaster victims, and the like). Of course, as with crime control, the dollars given to such faultless individuals will have diminishing returns, and so it might be that at some point the government might do more good by giving some money to

creating a false sense of security (Katyal 2002). Wilson-Doenges (2000) summarizes an empirical study showing that the sense of community in gated communities is lower.

"[W]alls, street patterns and barricades that separate people from one another reduce the potential for people to understand one another and commit themselves to any common or collective purpose...." (Blakely and Snyder 1987).

"Gated enclaves tend to be nothing more than an assemblage of individuals lacking any communal spirit.... [S]tudies conducted by police departments have failed to indicate a decline in property crime due to such elaborate and expensive measures" (Greinacher 1987).

In addition, the social meaning of a gated community is one of fear – one that reinforces a view of crime as prevalent rather than controlled. "[G]ated areas ... represen[t] a concrete metaphor for the closing of the gates against immigrants and minorities and the poverty, crime, and social instabilities in society at large." (Blakely and Snyder 1997). Indeed, gated communities can attract criminals instead of repel them. Allman et al. (2001) quote police detective Mike Reed as saying that "some criminals think if it's a gated community, there must be something in there worth getting." As a result of these factors, empirical studies have found that gated communities do not decrease crime. Allman et al. (2001) include a study of fourteen gated and fourteen nongated communities. (See also Wilson-Doenges 2000; Ellin 1987; Carlton 1989.)

victims of crime. But the point here is that in no way can our current spending mix be justified on the basis of helping the individual victims of crime.

Rather, we punish crime because it frays the bonds of trust within our society. The pain of an individual victim, of course, is intrinsically part of the reason we punish, but that pain is also relevant because crimes that put victims into great pain tend to be those that have greater community harms. Nevertheless, some crimes inflict more harm on the community than others, and harm to the victim can be a weak proxy for a crime's community-centered impact.

A. The Case for Unlike Punishments for Like Crimes

The trope in criminal law is that like punishment should exist for like crimes – that it, is "unfair" to punish two murderers or two thieves differently. This principle, formulated against the backdrop of centuries of unequal punishments on the basis of skin color, contains an important core truth: that punishment should not be imposed in different ways on the basis of characteristics that are exogenous to the crime. Calibrating punishments on the basis of community impact, however, is an altogether different matter. Two murders, or two instances of theft, can result in different harms to a community. To consider them the "same" is to obscure relevant differences.

To take the most obvious example, compare two apartment burglaries in which an item worth $1,000 is stolen. In the first, the victim tells no one besides a police officer about the burglary and tells the police officer only on the condition that secrecy about the episode be maintained. In the second, the police sirens surround the apartment after the burglary, the burglary is televised, reporters are on the scene, and a series of public notices about the burglary ensue. In this second example, the crime's impact on the community is far more pronounced than it is in the first. Private precautions may increase, fear of crime may be exacerbated, and trust in the neighborhood is likely to be frayed. It is impossible to conceive of these crimes as having the same impact.

The open secret about computer crime is that many of its occurrences mirror the first scenario above. That is, the victims, most particularly financial and corporate institutions, prefer to keep the crime secret because they don't want to scare their customers away.[12] And so they often do not report the crime at all,

---

[12] William J. Cook, who authored the U.S. Department of Justice's computer prosecution manual, states that "[o]rganizations often swallow losses quietly rather than notifying the authorities and advertising their vulnerability to shareholders and clients" (Lee et al. 1999). See also Economic Cyber Threats: Hearing before the Joint Economic Comm., 106th Cong., 2000 WL 11068387 (2000), which included the following statement of Vinton G. Cerf, Senior Vice President of Internal Architecture and Technology, MCI Worldcom: "Companies are concerned that revealing and admitting past mistakes, shortcomings, negative experiences or

or if they do report it, they insist on disclosure conditions like those mentioned above. In these settings, it is worth considering whether high expected sanctions make sense, for the prosecution itself may contribute to the perception of lawlessness and heightened danger on the Net.

Here we come to discover a problem with another economic trope, that the probability of detection is interchangeable with the extent of the sanction. Economists who hold this view – who essentially argue that a 10% chance of a one-year sentence is equivalent to a 50% chance of a two-month sentence (Becker 1968) – fail to consider the way in which prosecution can send signals to a community about the extent of crime. If cybercrime prosecutions make public enough information to scare people from using the Net, it is worth considering whether the prosecutions will be counterproductive. Instead, it might be better to maximize deterrence by increasing the extent of the sanction but reducing its actual enforcement – so as to minimize the number of public prosecutions.

This strategy, in effect, reverses so-called "broken windows" policing. The key insight of broken windows is the idea that low-level offenses reveal disorder in a community and cue additional crimes and that enforcement of such crimes should therefore be stepped up. And it is worth noting that, by moving the conception of a crime out of the paradigm of the individual victim, the proponents of "broken windows" policing have performed a mighty social service.[13] The tendency of instances of crime to foster additional crime, however, is itself only one example of a larger phenomenon: the impact of a crime on a community is often different from its impact on an individual victim. Further, by ramping up enforcement at every turn, it is possible that such enforcement techniques wind up fraying the bonds of trust in a community, making crime appear more rampant than it really is and eventually exacerbating crime instead of controlling it.

B. Crimes against Networks

Traditional criminal law focuses on crimes against individuals or property. This is an atomized way of understanding crime. Instead, some forms of crime target the human network, and these are, in some ways, worse than those that

---

incidents can open them up for [public] criticism [or potential legal liability]. . . . [C]ompanies are [also] loath to share proprietary or privileged corporate information. Additionally, firms run the risk of eroding consumer, customer, partner and investor confidence."

[13] Their analysis of what actually reduces crime, however, has severe problems. In particular, they overplayed the role of law enforcement and neglected the role of architecture in the program they studied (Katyal 2002).

do not. This is true in realspace as well as in cyberspace, but the language of cyberspace – which focuses on networks and connectivity – allows us to see the point.

Being human means, in part, being interconnected.[14] Cybercrimes such as the creation of worms – which clog network connections – are obvious examples of crimes against networks. These crimes are designed precisely to make it more difficult for people to communicate with each other. Because both visibility and tangibility are missing in cyberspace, individuals have even more of a need to trust what they are seeing on their screens. When crimes damage that trust, the result can be to prevent people from coming onto the Net and to prevent those that do from sharing information. As one researcher put it:

> During the Internet worm attack I experienced problems in my research collabo-
> ration with U.S. colleagues when they suddenly stopped answering my messages.
> The only way to have a truly international research community is for network
> communication to be reliable. If it is not, then scientists will tend to stick to
> cooperating with people in their local community even more than they do now.
> (Nielsen 1990, 524–5)

A network, after all, is more than the sum of its individual parts. Economic theory predicts that cooperation will yield collective payoffs that are much greater than those derived when individuals only pursue self-interest. A computer network like the Internet is nothing more than a structure for this cooperation. Each user derives benefits that exceed those she would otherwise receive, provided that everyone else is similarly cooperating. The trouble with cooperation in practice is that it is very difficult to achieve because the individual gains from defection exceed those derived from cooperation, which is a standard collective action problem (Axelrod 1984). The Internet, for example, could not have been built privately because every entity would have waited for another entity to build it first, hoping to free-ride off of the other's hard work. It took the government's sponsorship for the network to emerge.

Now that this network exists, some forms of computer crime can be understood simply as defections from its cooperative protocols. Computer worms, for example, undermine the positive externalities of the network by making it more difficult for individuals to receive benefits from cooperation. While the payoffs to the criminal may be large (e.g., if she own a virus-protection software firm or has some interest in preventing communication), the collectivity suffers. The enforcement of computer crime statutes, then, is a way to prevent this harm to the collective network and an attempt to preserve the network's cooperative protocols.

---

[14] Aristotle (1958) described humans as *zoon politikon* ("social animals").

Crimes that target the network, therefore, should be treated differently because they impose a special harm. This harm is not victim centered but community centered, and it is the reason that victims alone should not be able to make decisions about whom to prosecute. We punish not simply because of the harm to the individual victim but because the crime fragments trust in the community, thereby reducing social cohesion and creating atomization. (A similar point may be made in regard to rape and hate crimes.) Just as the law must worry about private self-help measures that impede interconnectivity, so too it must worry about private actors who try to sabotage interconnectivity for their own nefarious reasons. Again, while this concept is not one unique to cyberspace, thinking in computer terms, such as network effects, helps us understand it.

C. The Third-Party Liability Debate

The community perspective on crime also helps underscore what is to be feared about third-party liability. In an earlier article, I argued that placing liability on third parties like ISPs has the potential to be counterproductive because of asymmetric incentives (Katyal 2001). The problem turns out to be a further example of how a breakdown in networks can be engendered by private solutions to the cybercrime problem. Now along comes an excellent contribution to this volume by professors Lichtman and Posner (Chapter 7) that takes issue with that article. Casting my article as raising a "primary objection" to ISP liability, they respond by arguing that (1) the problem identified with liability has to do with positive externalities, (2) the same problem arises not only with respect to ISPs but in other industries, and (3) the correct solution is to use subsidy-based arrangements:

> The problem with respect to Internet access is not that the ISPs do not capture the full value of the sale but that *subscribers* create positive externalities enjoyed by advertisers, information providers, merchants, friends, and acquaintances, and thus subscriber willingness to pay understates the social value created when a new subscriber comes online. Reframed this way, it becomes clear that this is a standard problem – in many markets there are substantial positive externalities – and that the right response is not a reduction in the incentive to take care. Restaurants create positive externalities by drawing crowds that in turn patronize neighboring businesses and stimulate the local economy, yet no one suggests that in response local authorities should stop enforcing the health code. The right response to a substantial positive externality is a tax break or other subsidy that encourages marginal subscribers to stay online even as the costs of service rise. (Chapter 7, p. 225)

Lichtman and Posner then go on to highlight the benefits of ISP liability. Alas, in regard to these benefits, there is very little that the article they are critiquing does not agree with. Of course, a key claim for ISP liability is that the primary actors are "Beyond the Law's Reach" (Chapter 7, p. 233); that is why the article opened its section on ISP liability by explaining how the international nature of the problem, cryptography, and a variety of characteristics of cybercrime make it hard to use first-party strategies and why third-party strategies are promising:

> In cyberspace, there are many reasons to think ISPs may prevent crime at a cheaper cost than the government. In part, this is because the speed of criminal activity in cyberspace suggests legal sanctions will be less effective than cost-deterrence and architectural strategies. The internet gives a criminal the resources to start up a criminal enterprise very quickly, access to millions of potential targets, the technology to reach those targets within moments, and the ability to terminate the enterprise instantaneously. Complicating law enforcement even further is the fact that the criminal may weave his crime through computers in several countries, making investigation even more difficult. While multilateral cooperation among governments sounds nice in theory, it is very difficult to achieve in practice. As a result, it may be more efficient for third parties to stop cybercrime from happening rather than to rely on prosecution after a crime takes place. (Katyal 2001, 1095–16)

My article goes on to explain that, on Kraakman-like "gatekeeper liability" analysis, ISPs can perform the roles of chaperoning conduct, bouncing offenders, and whistle-blowing, as well as other roles that will reduce incidents of cybercrime (p. 1096). The point is that Posner and Lichtman are boxing with a shadow that I did not create.

This shadow looms even larger when they discuss the asymmetric incentives point, for it is not the case that by reframing the question in the way that they do that something new is illuminated or that analogies to realspace bloom. After all, I have always understood that the asymmetric incentive problem is a problem throughout the law, offline as well as online, and the article is explicit in deriving the problem from realspace. Indeed, the very way the article formulates the asymmetric incentive problem captures precisely the positive externalities that Lichtman and Posner appear to suggest are missing:

> We shall call this the asymmetric incentives problem, and it is another general quandary in law. The problem arises when the law places burdens on actors that are accommodated by forgoing a benefit with large *positive externalities*. Here are two examples drawn from realspace. A very robust "hostile environment" test for employment discrimination could lead businesses to terminate any questionable employees, as the benefit from one questionable employee is dwarfed by the liability of a potential lawsuit. A standard of care that imposes drastic liability

on employers for torts committed by their employees may lead employers not to hire anyone with even the slightest blemish on their records. (Katyal 2001, 1092–3)

A central theme of the article is precisely that these positive externalities are generated by subscribers and not fully captured by the ISP.[15]

There is a way, however, in which Lichtman and Posner, by using realspace liability as their touchstone, miss an important aspect of cybercrime: scale. Indeed, many instances of cybercrime are quite different from Lichtman and Posner's restaurant because a single bad apple can create much higher amounts of liability for an ISP. In a world in which a fifteen-year-old boy can do a billion dollars' worth of damage (Banham 2000), an ISP will find itself in a very different situation than will a restaurant, whose maximum liability is far more circumscribed. For this reasons, if ISP solutions turned out to be necessary because other methods of controlling cybercrime were impractical or otherwise inefficient, I advocated a far smaller amount of liability than that which might be typical in realspace (Katyal 2001).

Lichtman and Posner (Chapter 7) claim, however, that the asymmetric incentive concern is overdrawn because subscribers will often reflect the positive externalities in their choices.[16] The example chosen is itself revealing:

Lichtman certainly benefits from the fact that his mother is regularly online and hence available for easy email correspondence, but that is not an externality because Lichtman and his mom have a rich relationship through which he can indicate to her how much he values her presence and, if necessary, contribute in cash or kind toward the monthly costs of her subscription. (Chapter 7, p. 240)[17]

---

[15] "The internet's value lies, at least in part, in exploiting these network effects. As more people come online, the value of the internet increases. E-mail, for example, is more valuable to me this year than it was last year because my mother has now learned how to use e-mail" (Katyal 2001, 1085). In Chapter 7, Lichtman and Posner, perhaps unconsciously, use a very similar example. Katyal (2001) also describes the asymmetric incentive problem as potentially leading ISPs to purge users because benefit gained from the marginal customer is outweighed by the legal risks.

[16] "Many of what at first sound like positive externalities turn out to be influences that are well accounted for in a subscriber's decision whether to subscribe" (Chapter 7, p. 240).

[17] This example is a very similar to that considered in note 15. The authors also provide a second example of Amazon.com giving rewards to a mom as an incentive to stay online. Again, this one-to-one example is unlikely to work in practice as well as the authors suppose. If individuals are kicked off of ISPs because they are perceived to be risky, and even if some ISP emerges that specializes in taking on risky customers (just as with car insurance markets), it is quite hard to understand how Amazon.com (or other companies like them) would find subsidizing risky users' subscriptions with the high-paying ISP a profitable investment. The problem is that the benefit to Amazon from any particular subscriber is likely to be too undifferentiated.

This paradigm, while it might work in realspace, misses the rupture of the one-to-one paradigm created by the Net.[18] A chief advantage of cyberspace is its "one-to-many" nature, which facilitates contact with people with whom one cannot cheaply contract (a point Lichtman and Posner appear to appreciate elsewhere in their article). The point about asymmetric incentives, and about the network harm of crime more generally, is that those contracts or paying relationships can be less likely to flower under certain circumstances. One such circumstance is when an ISP fears a huge amount of liability for taking on a customer that it believes is risky.

Lichtman and Posner go on to argue that without ISP liability, fewer people will be on the Net due to fear about viruses and worms, and that ISP liability is therefore appropriate. This is, however, a false choice: No one seriously thinks that the choice is between ISP liability or nothing at all. Of course, they are correct in arguing that viruses and worms can stifle the growth of the network (that is one of the arguments of this chapter), but the question is, how to best contain these crimes against networks? While there are brief mentions in passing of liability imposed on victims,[19] on software manufacturers,[20] and for architectural methods,[21] far more work is necessary before ISP liability should be embraced.[22] It may be that such strategies, or a combination of them, may reduce the incidence of viruses and worms without generating as much deleterious network harm. At the very least, it seems inappropriate to advocate for ISP liability without fully considering those options.

Nonetheless, Lichtman and Posner postulate a dreamy scenario of subsidies for ISP usage or perhaps ISP fees for the transmission of messages. I have no doubt that increasing amounts of money can solve the asymmetric incentive problem (and most others in life); the question is whether that is the right use of social resources that might be spent elsewhere. And the only way to answer that question is to know which strategy (first-, second-, or third-party liability, or a combination of them) is the best for controlling instances of cybercrime.

---

[18] "Of course, in realspace, pay telephones, cell phones, and regular mail offer users some degree of anonymity, but these methods provide mostly point-to-point communications between sender and recipient. On the internet, however, one person can reach millions with a single message" (Katyal 2001, 1048).

[19] Compare Lichtman and Posner (Chapter 7) discussing self-help with Katyal (2001) analyzing second-party strategies of liability.

[20] Compare, e.g., Lichtman and Posner (Chapter 7) discussing suing Microsoft with Katyal (2001) analyzing hardware and software manufacturer liability.

[21] Compare Lichtman and Posner (Chapter 7) mentioning an architectural solution with Katyal (2003) describing advantages of architectural solutions.

[22] As is evident, I do not believe that second-party strategies are generally appropriate because of the harm to networks, but I am not sure that Lichtman and Posner are as sanguine about them as I.

And now we circle back to the initial claim of my old article, which was complicated for precisely these reasons:

> Should law require ISPs to use these five [Kraakman-like] strategies? Not always, because following the strategies may incur deadweight losses that outweigh their utility.... If ISPs were liable for pirated material on their networks, they might more vigilantly police subscribers to the point where privacy would be eroded. And the perception, often unwarranted, that the government has broad surveillance powers may exacerbate the public's fears of loss of privacy. This is one example of the asymmetric incentive problem as applied to ISPs. If ISPs are liable for the sins of their users, they will purge anyone about whom they have the slightest suspicion of committing criminal wrongdoing. When AOL suspects that Smith spread a virus, even unintentionally, it will eliminate Smith because the benefit to AOL of one additional customer will be outweighed by the risk of harboring a virus-spreader.
>
> The point of these quick examples is not to suggest that third-party deterrence is always inappropriate, but simply to caution that there are tough calculations to work out. Because government is usually unlikely to have information about optimal third-party precaution, it should not use sanctions to force ISPs to engage in particular forms of prevention.... The government is likely to over- or under-estimate the costs and benefits of prevention, and this runs the risk of either prompting actors to forgo utility-producing activity or inducing them to take wasteful precautions.
>
> Government thus should recognize that it lacks information about proper third-party crime prevention. Yet ISPs may at times be the cheapest cost avoiders, and forgoing their assistance risks inefficiencies and a loss in deterrence.... The difficulty lies in writing legal rules that recognize this efficiency.
>
> ... [A]ny use of the tort system must account for the asymmetric incentive problem. Placing burdens on ISPs risks balkanizing the net and inducing ISPs to purge risky users. Again, these results might be worth the cost; the point is simply that this can become part of the price tag. It is therefore necessary that assessments of ISP liability incorporate the full social cost of prevention before they are employed. A formula that simply compares an ISP's cost of prevention against the harm of the crime would ignore these other important costs. Lowering the amount of damages, say to a fraction of the ultimate harm, may be one way to maintain security incentives without incurring suboptimal preventative costs. (Katyal 2001, 1098–1100)

To summarize, the claim then (and now) is not that ISP liability is inappropriate but rather that the case one way or another cannot be definitively made without comparing it to other regimes (thus eschewing the red herring of ISP liability or nothing at all) and acknowledging the looming asymmetric incentives problem that ISP liability would engender. Nothing in Lichtman and Posner's excellent analysis refutes these fundamental points.

D. The Problem with Current Law Enforcement and White House Cyberstrategy

Law alone will not solve the cybercrime problem, for police officers can't be everywhere. Instead, society relies on citizens to prevent the bulk of crime. But as we have seen, some private action will be ineffective and perhaps even harmful. One underappreciated function of public law enforcement, which might be called a liberal argument for crime control, is to cultivate and protect public networks. In cyberspace, the network concerns are omnipresent: For example, a virus will scare computer users into restricting their computer connections (particularly their e-mail and p2p networking), fear of interception leads many to fear using e-mail, and the possibility of credit card theft prompts many not to make online purchases ("Many Worry," 2002). Assurances about security are necessary to promote the Internet's growth, just as they are necessary in realspace for vibrant and dynamic cities.

Without a strong public law enforcement presence on the Net, the Net risks balkanization into a series of separate systems. When people fear computer crime, they may connect only with other "trusted" computers, stifling one of the greatest communication innovations in our lifetime – a network that gives us the ability to connect directly with and learn from people with whom we lack any prior experience.[23] Some today are even proposing a division of the Internet into two networks to bolster its security (Hundley et al. 2001).[24] In other words, we should fear one potential response to cybercrime – the implementation of private architectures of control – nearly as much as cybercrime itself. Because computer crime will become easier to perpetrate as a result of increasing automation, bandwidth, and skills, private developers will have reason to put these architectures in place, with grave consequences for the network and freedom.

---

[23] For example, at the time when the U.S. Supreme Court was hearing its first major Internet case, a constitutional challenge to an act of Congress that regulated online pornography, the entire Court had only two computers with Internet access due to security fears. Woodall (1997) quotes the Supreme Court's public information officer as saying at the time that "[f]or security reasons . . . the computers in the court are part of an internal network that prevents the justices from surfing the Web or exchanging e-mail with outsiders," that "the court has two stand-alone computers with Internet access," and that it is doubtful whether "any of the nine Supreme Court justices had an Internet account at home."

[24] Apart from preventing balkanization, assurances about trust are necessary to exploit positive network effects. Consider a search engine, which requires two levels of trust: the trust between the engine and the sites it indexes and the trust between the individual user and the particular target websites identified by the engine. Both of these levels can be compromised by fears about computer security. Owners of sites may not give search engines sufficient access to their content to adequately index it, and they may forbid unknown users from entering the sites at all.

The social costs of private precautions are not typically given much weight in legal discourse. Consider the famous Learned Hand test in torts, that negligence depends on whether the expense of private precautions exceeds the probability of an accident multiplied by the harm of the resulting injury. In the case that gave rise to the test, a ship had broken away from its tow and smashed into a tanker. The ship owner sued the towing company, but the towing company said that the ship owner was contributorily negligent for not having an attendant on board. Hand sided with the towing company, reasoning that the ship owner could have avoided the accident with an attendant.[25] Hand, however, focused only on the cost of precautions to the ship owner. While perhaps appropriate in this particular case, this formula treats all forms of prevention as equal and unfortunately fails to consider the negative externalities of private precautions.

It is from this vantage point, that a key cost of crime lies in the private reactions of potential victims, that one should assess the effectiveness of any computer security plan. Take, for example, the new cybersecurity initiative by the White House (2003). Far from being a breakthrough document, the *National Strategy to Secure Cyberspace* is a hodgepodge of concepts and consulting talk, devoid of a serious agenda.[26] Both simple and complicated solutions to cybercrime were obscured by an antiregulatory, antigovernment bias that infected the strategy's outlook and thinking from the start. In its single-minded focus on computer security, moreover, the White House did not pause to think about what values the Net serves. These failures are yoked together: The White House wants private industry to do the work of securing cyberspace, but the most

---

[25] *United States v. Carroll Towing Co.*, 159 F.2d 169, 173 (2d Cir. 1947).

[26] The White House (2002) released a draft of its proposal that received much criticism along these lines. The report stated that the White House draft proposes "voluntary, tactical responses to an inherently strategic problem of national importance" and "largely failed to exercise any of its powers besides persuasion" and that there "are essentially little or no consequences for Federal government agencies and officials who do not take prudent steps to improve cyber security." Mark D. Rasch (2002) writes, "If security is in the national interest, the government must, through the purse and the sword, force itself and the private sector into compliance" and that the White House strategy "specifies no sanctions" for the failure to adhere to any of the government's recommendations for minimizing the risk of cyberattacks. A *Capital Times* ("Critics" 2002) article quotes a computer security expert as stating that the "voluntary security plan" is analogous to "asking ordinary citizens to erect a nuclear shield when it's obviously the government's job to organize those things." Marcus J. Ranum (2002) makes a similar criticism. James Lewis, Director, CSIS Council on Technology and Public Policy, stated, "Companies will only change their behavior when there are both market forces and legislation that cover security failures. Until the U.S. has more than just voluntary solutions, we'll continue to see slow progress in improving cybersecurity" (CSIS 2002). It is worth noting, however, that the final draft of the *National Strategy* did propose a few significant changes that may augment cybersecurity, such as a national response system and some use of procurement power (White House 2003).

obvious private sector response is to diminish connectivity. And if, as some have suggested, the burden for crime prevention is placed on the ISPs, so that they are responsible for the criminal acts of their subscribers, the result will be harm to the Net and its users if ISPs purge their subscriber base of customers who arouse the faintest whiff of suspicion. There is a different path, one that situates the government as an active protector of the Net and its users, just as government protects city streets and their users.

The *National Strategy* announces that "[t]he federal government should . . . not intrude into homes and small businesses, into universities, or state and local agencies and departments to create secure computer networks" (White House 2003, 11). While government intrusion is not typically something to be preferred, a careful discussion must examine the costs of failing to intrude. Yet all the *National Strategy* gives us is some weak guidance in this regard,[27] coupled with proclamations about the power of the market such as "federal regulation will not become a primary means of securing cyberspace" and "the market itself is expected to provide the major impetus to improve cybersecurity" (White House 2003, 15).[28] But throughout its sixty-page report, the White House never really stopped to consider the harm caused by private ordering to prevent computer crime. This isn't merely an oversight.[29] The "market itself" can help minimize cybercrime, but often at a cost that is too high to bear.

---

[27] "The federal role in these and other cases is only justified when the benefits of intervention outweigh the associated costs" (White House 2003, ix).

[28] "The federal government alone cannot sufficiently defend America's cyberspace. Our traditions of federalism and limited government require that organizations outside the federal government take the lead in many of these efforts" (White House 2003: xiii). Jennifer Lee (2003) explains how the *National Strategy* backs away from government regulation in favor of market approaches; Jonathan Krim (2003) describes similar findings. Even the draft released in September was criticized for its belief in the market. Brian Krebs (2002) states that "intense lobbying from the high-tech industry has pulled nearly all the teeth from the plan when it comes to steps the technology industry should take," and he quotes Bruce Schneier as stating that the plan will have "absolutely zero effect." Paul Magnusson (2002) writes, "Thanks to heavy lobbying by the tech sector, The National Strategy to Secure Cyberspace Report, released Sept. 18 by the White House, substitutes weak suggestions for tough directives. Gone from previous versions: a special government-and-industry-fed fund to be used to upgrade network security; requirements for Internet service providers to boost customer protection; and mandatory moves to enhance wireless-network security. Cybersecurity 'is an area that cries out for government regulation, but the response has been "Yawn, ho hum." ' . . . That, many experts fear, could set the stage for future security lapses" (quoting Russ Cooper, TrueSecure Corporation).

[29] In a few places, the White House (2003) does mention law enforcement. Far from containing a single new idea, the *National Strategy* does not even explain what the need for law enforcement is, let alone provide a blueprint for how to achieve it. Again, this flaw is attributable to the document's not being tethered to an understanding of cybercrime's harm. The White House knows that cybercrime can cause billions of dollars in damage. But the key is not to focus on the harm of cybercrime; it is to zero in on the social cost of the precautions private actors, left to their own devices, will take to avoid being victims.

The reconceptualization of the harm of crime allows us to see how weak the White House cyberstrategy really is. If crimes were isolated incidents that struck individuals living alone on islands, with few ramifications beyond those for the individual victims, one would expect to go about cybersecurity in the way that the White House has proposed. But precisely because cybercrimes have the potential to erode support for the Net, a more vibrant public presence is needed. This paper aims not to outline what that public presence should look like; rather it is content to leave the details of that presence to further discussion. But that discussion will not take place unless we are forthright about what the case for public enforcement really is.

III. CONCLUSION

Crime hurts not only victims but communities. The modern conception of crime, however, slights all of this by exalting only the individual victim. This is unfortunate, and not only because of its incompleteness. By focusing on only one set of harms, the modern view stunts the case for effective crime control and does not yield answers to why we punish in the way that we do. A focus on the community, by contrast, helps to explain the practice and theory of modern punishment.

If the greatest dangers from crime include the private precautions people take to try to prevent crime *ex ante*, we need to change the way we think about the control of crime online and offline. Governments write laws against computer crime, and enforce them, not only because crime would otherwise spiral, but also because they fear the way in which private actors would structure their interactions without the government backbone of security. The model here may suggest that the trend toward victim impact statements may be misguided because it obscures a set of central harms to the community. It may also shed light on why prosecutors have the power to prosecute cases even when the victims do not seek punishment.

REFERENCES

Adams, Robert P. 2001. DNA Analysis of Genetic Diversity of Vetiver and Future Selections for Use in Erosion Control. http://www.vetiver.com/PRVN_IVC2_06.PDF.

Allman, John, et al. 2001. Sense of Security Can Be an Illusion. *Sun-Sentinel*, February 25, p. A1.

Aristotle. 1958. *The Politics*. Bk. 1. Trans. E. Barker. Oxford: Oxford University Press.

Axelrod, Robert M. 1984. *The Evolution of Cooperation*. New York: Basic Books.

Banham, Russ. 2000. Hacking It. *CFO Mag*, August 1. http://www.cfo.com/printarticle/1,1883,0/1/AD/874,00.html.

Becker, Gary S. 1968. Crime and Punishment: An Economic Approach. *Journal of Political Economy* 76:169.

Benkler, Yochai, 2002. Coase's Penguin, or Linux and the Nature of the Firm. 2002. *Yale Law Journal* 112:369.

Blakely, Edward J., and Mary Gail Snyder. 1987. Divided We Fall: Gated and Walled Communities in the United States. In *Architecture of Fear*, ed. Nan Ellin, 85. Princeton: Princeton Architectural Press.

———.1997. *Fortress America.* Washington, D.C.: Brookings Institution.

Broadband Finally Dominates the United States. 2004. *Broadband Business Forecast*, May 4.

Brown, Kenneth. 2002. Opening the Open Source Debate. White paper.

Carlton, Jim. 1989. Behind the Gate. *L.A. Times*, October 8, p. 3.

Chron, Augusta. 2000. Teen Gets a Six-Month Jail Term for Hacking. *Augusta Chronicle*, September 23. http://www.augustachronicle.com/stories/092300/tec_LA0666-2.001.shtml.

Crawford, E. Margaret. 1995. Food and Famine. In *The Great Irish Famine*, ed. C. Poirteir, 60. Chester Springs, PA: Dufour Editions.

Critics: National Cybersecurity Plan Too Weak. 2002. *Capital Times*, September 19, p. 4E.

CSIS. 2002. Cybersecurity: Current Challenges Larger Than National Strategy Response. CSIS press release, September 18.

DSL Dominates as World Broadband Hits the 100-Million Mark. 2004. *Broadband Business Forecast*, April 6.

Durkheim, Émile. 1956. *The Division of Labor in Society*. New York: The Free Press.

Ellin, Nan. 1987. Shelter from the Storm or Form Follows Fear and Vice Versa. In *Architecture of Fear*, ed. Nan Ellin, 13. Princeton, NJ: Princeton Architectural Press.

Greinacher, Udo. 1987. Fear and Dreaming in the American City. In *Architecture of Fear*, ed. Nan Ellin, 288. Princeton, NJ: Princeton Architectural Press.

Hatch, Brian, et al. 2001. *Hacking Linux Exposed: Linux Security Secrets and Solutions.* Emeryville, CA: Osborne/McGraw-Hill.

Hundley, Richard O., et al. 2001. *The Future of the Information Revolution in Europe.* Rand National Defense Researc Institute. http://www.rand.org/publicationsCF/CF172.

Katyal, Neal. 1997. Deterrence's Difficulty. *Michigan Law Review* 95:2385.

———. 2001. Criminal Law in Cyberspace. *University of Pennsylvania Law Review* 149:1003.

———. 2002. Architecture as Crime Control. *Yale Law Journal* 101:1039.

Katz, Michael L., and Carl Shapiro. 1985. Network Externalities, Competition, and Compatability. *American Economic Review* 75:424.

———.1994. Systems Competition and Network Effects. *Journal of Economic Perspective* Spring 1994:93.

Krebs, Brian. 2002. Cybersecurity Draft Plan Soft on Business Observers Say. *Washingtonpost.com*, September 19. http://washingtonpost.com/ac2/wp-dyn/A35812-2002Sep18?.

Krim, Jonathan. 2003. Cybersecurity Strategy Depends on Power of Suggestion. *Washington Post*, February 15, p. E1.

Lee, Jennifer. 2003. White House Scales Back Cyberspace Plan. *New York Times*, February 25, p. A14.

Lee, Michael, et al. 1999. A Regulatory Proposal. *Berkeley Technical Law Journal* 14:839.

Liebowitz, S. J., and Margolis, Stephen E. 1994. Network Externality: An Uncommon Tragedy. *Journal of Economic Perspective*, Spring, p. 133.

Magnusson, Paul. 2002. Commentary: Is Business Cheaping out on Homeland Security? *Business Week.com*, September 30. http://www.businessweek.com/magazine/content/02_39/b3801063.htm.

Many Worry Net Is Not Safe, Study Finds. 2002. *CNN.com*, October 16. http://www.cnn. com/2002/TECH/internet/10/16/internet.report/index.html.

Nielsen, Jakob. 1990. Disrupting Communities. In *Computers under Attack*, ed. P. Denning. 524. Boston: Addison-Wesley.

O'Grada, Cormac. 1999. Black '47 and Beyond. Princeton, NJ: Princeton University Press.

Open Source Initiative. 2004. *Open Source FAQ*, February 3. http://www.opensource.org/ advocacy/faq.php.

Petreley, Nicholas. 2000. Microsoft's Road to Consumer Trust Is Open Source Windows. *Infoword*, November 13. http://www.infoworld.com/articles/op/xml/00/11/13/ 001113oppetreley.xml.

Poulson, Kevin. 2004. Lamo's Adventures in Worldcom. *Securityfocus.com*. http://www. securityfocus.com/news/296.

Ranum, Marcus J. 2002. Federal Cybersecurity: Get a Backbone. *TISC Insight*, September 24. http://www.csis.org.press/pr02_43.htm.

Rasch, Mark D. 2002. What about Our Cyber-Security? *Washington Post*, September 26, p. A32.

Raymond, Eric S. 1999. *The Cathedral and the Bazaar*. Sebastopol, CA: O'Reilly.

Sampson, Robert J., and Byron Groves. 1989. Community Structure and Crime: Testing Social Disorganization Theory. *American Journal of Sociology* 94:774.

Sampson, Robert J., et al. 1997. Neighborhoods and Violent Crime: A Multilevel Study of Collective Efficacy. *Science* 277:918.

Schreiner, Rudolf. 2003. Open Source Software Security. *Objectsecurity.com*, January 9. http://www.objectsecurity.com/whitepapers/open_source/open_ source_security.html.

Shaw, Clifford, and MacKay, Henry. 1942. *Juvenile Delinquency and Urban Areas*. Chicago: University of Chicago Press.

TruSecure. 2001. Open Source Security: A Look at the Security Benefits of Source Code Access. http://www.trusecure.com/cgi-bin/refer.pdf?wp = open_source_security5.pdf.

U.S. Department of Commerce. 2002. *Understanding Broadband Demand: A Review of Critical Issues*. Washington, DC: U.S. Department of Commerce, Office of Technology Policy.

Warfield, Michael H. 2003. Musings on Open Source Security Models. *Linuxworld.com*, February. 27. http://www.linuxworld.com/linuxworld/lw-1998-11/1e-11-ramparts.html.

Wheeler, David A. 2003. Why Open Source Software/Free Software (OSS/FS)? Look at the Numbers! www.dwheeler.com/oss_fs_why.html.

White House. 2002. Fourth Annual Report to the President and the Congress on the Advisory Panel to Assess Domestic Response Capabilities for Terrorism Involving Weapons of Mass Destruction. http://www.rand.org/nsrd/terrpanel/.

———.2003. *The National Strategy to Secure Cyberspace*. http://www.whitehouse.gov/ pcipbcyberspace_strategy.pdf.

Wilson-Doenges, Georjeanna. 2000. An Exploration of Sense of Community and Fear of Crime in Gated Communities. *Environment and Behavior* 32:597.

Wilson, James Q. 1975. *Thinking about Crime*. New York: Basic Books.

Woodall, Martha. 1997. First Computerized Brief Filed with Supreme Court. *Philadelphia Inquirer*, February 21, p. A1.

Yasin, Rutrell. 2001. So Many Patches, So Little Time. *InternetWeek*, October 4. http://www. internetweek.com/newslead01/lead100401.htm.

Regulation and Jurisdiction for
Global Cybersecurity

SEVEN

HOLDING INTERNET SERVICE PROVIDERS ACCOUNTABLE

Doug Lichtman and Eric P. Posner*

ABSTRACT

Internet service providers are today largely immune from liability for their role in the creation and propagation of worms, viruses, and other forms of malicious computer code. In this essay, we question that state of affairs. Our purpose is not to weigh in on the details – for example, whether liability should sound in negligence or strict liability, or whether liability is in this instance best implemented by statute or via gradual common law development. Rather, our aim is to challenge the recent trend in the courts and Congress away from liability and toward complete immunity for Internet service providers. In our view, such immunity is difficult to defend on policy grounds and sharply inconsistent with conventional tort law principles. Internet service providers control the gateway through which Internet pests enter and reenter the public network. Service providers should therefore bear some responsibility not only for stopping malicious code but also for helping to identify those individuals who originate it.

Computer viruses and related strains of Internet contagion impose a significant cost on the many individuals and entities that rely on Internet access for commerce, research, and communication. The U.S. government has responded to this problem with efforts to identify and deter those who create and propagate Internet pests. Thus, for example, both the Federal Bureau of Investigation

*Professor of Law, and Kirkland and Ellis Professor of Law, respectively, both at the University of Chicago Law School. This paper was prepared for The Law and Economics of Cyber Security, a conference held on June 10, 2004, at George Mason University School of Law. It ultimately formed the basis for an amicus brief filed at the Supreme Court as part of the *Grokster* litigation. See *Brief of Kenneth J. Arrow et al.*, MGM Studios, Inc. v. Grokster Ltd., No. 04-480 (2005). For helpful comments, we thank conference participants, especially Amitai Aviram, Emily Frye, Neal Katyal, and Peter Swire, as well as readers Laura Heymann, Wayne Hsiung, Orin Kerr, Jacques Lawarree, Saul Levmore, Ira Rubinstein, Lior Strahilevitz, and Alan Sykes. Lastly, for financial support, Posner thanks the Russell Baker Scholars Fund, and Lichtman thanks the John M. Olin Program in Law and Economics at The University of Chicago Law School.

and the Department of Homeland Security allocate substantial resources to the battle against cybercrime, and Congress has passed a number of criminal statutes designed to target the troublemakers who create Internet viruses and other forms of malicious computer code.[1] Government efforts along these lines have been augmented by the actions of private parties as well. Microsoft, for example, has offered cash rewards for any information leading to the arrest and conviction of those responsible for particularly disruptive Internet attacks, and many computer hobbyists volunteer to help trace the sources of Internet mischief.

These tactics obviously have the potential to reduce the total amount of harm caused by cyberinsecurity; however, we doubt that direct intervention aimed at perpetrators of Internet mischief can be a sufficient response. Our concern is that the perpetrators of cybercrime are too often beyond the effective reach of law, both because these individuals are almost impossible to track and because, even when identified, these individuals usually lack the resources necessary to pay for the damage they cause. Thus, in this essay, we join a growing chorus of legal commentators in arguing that attempts at direct intervention must be supplemented by a legal rule that brings Internet service providers (ISPs) into the chain of responsibility. Specifically, ISPs should to some degree be held accountable when their subscribers originate malicious Internet code, and ISPs should also to some degree be held accountable when their subscribers propagate malicious code by, for example, forwarding a virus over e-mail or adopting lax security precautions that in turn allow a computer to be co-opted by a malevolent user.

This might sound harsh. But rules that hold one party liable for wrongs committed by another are the standard legal response in situations where, as here, liability will be predictably ineffective if directly applied to a class of bad actors and yet there exists a class of related parties capable of either controlling those bad actors or mitigating the damage they cause. Phrased another way, while indirect liability comes in a wide variety of flavors and forms – strict liability and negligence, explicit statutory provisions and also more flexible common law standards, and so on – it is the norm, and we do not see any reason why legal rules associated with cybersecurity should be an exception to the pattern of rules that govern structurally identical interactions throughout the offline world.

---

[1] See, for example, the Electronic Communications Privacy Act, Pub. L. No. 99-508, 100 Stat. 1848 (1986) (codified as amended in scattered sections of 18 U.S.C), and the Computer Fraud and Abuse Act, Pub. L. No. 98-473, 98 Stat. 1837, 2190 (Oct. 12, 1984) (codified as amended at 18 U.S.C. § 1030 (2002)).

Our position admittedly runs counter to recent legal trends. In Section 230 of the Communications Decency Act of 1996, for example, Congress announced that a provider of "interactive computer service" is not to be treated as "the publisher or speaker of any information provided by another information content provider,"[2] in many ways immunizing Internet service providers from liability for defamatory content that is provided by business partners or customers but disseminated by the ISP itself. Similarly, the Digital Millennium Copyright Act of 1998 sharply limits service provider liability for copyright infringement in cases where the service provider merely acts as a conduit for the incriminating material,[3] and that statute more broadly limits liability in instances where the service provider did not know about the infringing activity, was not aware of facts or circumstances from which the activity is apparent, did not receive a direct financial benefit from the infringement, and acts in accordance with statutory guidelines to expeditiously disable access to the material in question.[4] Courts interpreting these provisions have reinforced this apparent trend away from ISP liability by, among other things, interpreting these statutes to preempt state laws that would otherwise have encouraged ISPs to take due care.[5]

Then again, maybe these trends are not as one-sided as they at first appear. Our argument in favor of service provider liability is primarily based on the notion that ISPs are in a good position to reduce the number and severity of bad acts online; and that intuition finds support even within the aforementioned immunity and safe harbor statutes.[6] So, for example, while the Communications Decency Act does remove the specter of indirect liability for the transmission of indecent or defamatory content, the act also encourages ISPs to address inappropriate content through voluntary private action. To that

---

[2] 47 U.S.C. § 230(c)(1).
[3] 17 U.S.C. § 512(a).
[4] 17 U.S.C. § 512(c)–(d).
[5] We discuss and criticize several of these cases in Section III.
[6] The Communications Decency Act is an immunity provision in that it waives off liability for a certain class of actions without explicitly making that immunity contingent on particular precautions. The Digital Millennium Copyright Act, by contrast, is a safe harbor provision in that it creates immunity for entities that take specific precautionary steps (but only such entities). Interestingly, some commentators have suggested that the Communications Decency Act should be read as a safe harbor provision, with its immunity applying only where the relevant service provider has attempted to block indecent or otherwise inappropriate communications. (See, e.g., Schruers 2002, 217 n. 61.) No court has yet adopted that view, although it is attractive on policy grounds and seems consistent with both the language of the act and its structure. See *Doe v. GTE Corp*, 347 F.3d 655, 660 (7th Cir. 2003) (discussing interpretations of Section 230 immunity that would nevertheless encourage filtering by ISPs).

end, one provision immunizes service providers from liability for "any action voluntarily taken in good faith to restrict access to or availability of material that the provider or user considers to be obscene, lewd, lascivious, filthy, excessively violent, harassing, or otherwise objectionable, whether or not such material is constitutionally protected."[7] On this same theme, not only is much of the immunity available under the Digital Millennium Copyright Act contingent on a service provider's efforts to quickly remove content plausibly associated with infringement, but also, like the Communications Decency Act, the Digital Millennium Copyright Act protects service providers from "any claim based on the service provider's good faith disabling of access to, or removal of, material or activity claimed to be infringing or based on facts or circumstances from which infringing activity is apparent, regardless of whether the material or activity is ultimately determined to be infringing."[8]

In any event, ours is not an argument about the state of the positive law, nor an attempt to divine Congressional intent. Our point is simply that, faced with the growing problem of cyberinsecurity, ISPs should be called into the service of the law. Much as the threat of liability puts pressure on the owners of bars and restaurants to watch for any copyright infringement that might take place within their establishments;[9] and the common law principle of vicarious liability obligates employers to monitor, train, and otherwise exercise control over the behavior of their employees;[10] common law tort liability or more carefully tailored federal statutes should be used to encourage ISPs to do their part in responding to Internet worms, viruses, denial-of-service attacks, and the like. Service providers control the gateway through which Internet pests enter and reenter the system. As such, service providers can help to stop these pests before they spread and to identify the individuals who originate malicious code in the first place. ISPs should be required by law to engage in these precautions.

We anticipate two primary objections. The first – and a concern that is repeated throughout the literature – is that liability will cause ISPs to overreact. As Neal Katyal (2001) puts the point, "Because an ISP derives little utility from providing access to a risky subscriber, a legal regime that places liability on an ISP for the acts of its subscribers will quickly lead the ISP to purge risky ones from its system" (pp. 1007–8).[11] Assaf Hamdani (2002) similarly worries

---

[7] 47 U.S.C. § 230(c)(2)(A).

[8] 17 U.S.C. § 512(g)(1).

[9] See, for example, *Herbert v. Shanley Co.*, 242 U.S. 591 (1917) (hotel owner can be held liable when copyrighted work is performed at the hotel without permission).

[10] See Restatement (Second) of Agency, § 216.

[11] Katyal (2001, p. 1098) does not in the end oppose liability for Internet service providers. As he writes later in his article, his point "is not to suggest that third-party deterrence is always inappropriate, but simply to caution that there are tough calculations to work out."

that ISPs will inefficiently exclude some users because "ISPs do not capture the full value of the conduct they are entrusted with policing" (p. 918).[12] These arguments are in our view misstated, as in every market where goods are sold at or near marginal cost, the relevant seller "derives little utility" from the sale; and in every market where the market price is less than the customer's willingness to pay, the relevant seller "does not capture the full value" of the buyer's purchase. The problem with respect to Internet access is not that the ISPs do not capture the full value of the sale but that *subscribers* create positive externalities enjoyed by advertisers, information providers, merchants, friends, and acquaintances, and thus subscriber willingness to pay understates the social value created when a new subscriber comes online.[13] Reframed this way, it becomes clear that this is a standard problem – in many markets there are substantial positive externalities – and that the right response is not a reduction in the incentive to take care. Restaurants, after all, create positive externalities by drawing crowds that in turn patronize neighboring businesses and stimulate the local economy, yet no one suggests that in response local authorities should stop enforcing the health code; that response would just drive customers away. For similar reasons, a reduction in ISP liability is unattractive. As we will explain more fully below, the right response is a tax break or other subsidy that encourages marginal subscribers to stay online even as the costs of service rise.

The second objection is echoed in the preamble to Section 230 of the Communications Decency Act, where Congress notes that immunizing ISPs from liability will have the indirect effect of encouraging "the development of technologies which maximize user control over what information is received"[14] and also "the development and utilization of blocking and filtering

---

[12] Other scholars, and indeed some courts, have raised similar concerns. "ISPs do not fully share the benefits its subscribers derive from placing material, whether infringing or non-infringing, on the network. As a result, imposing liability on ISPs for subscribers' infringing material induces ISPs to overdeter, purging any material that a copyright holder claims is infringing" (Netanel 2003, 13 n. 30). See *Zeran v. America Online*, 129 F.3d 327, 333 (4th Cir. 1997). ("Because service providers would be subject to liability only for the publication of information, and not for its removal, they would have a natural incentive simply to remove messages upon [accusation], whether the contents were defamatory or not.")

[13] We are not just splitting hairs. For example, because of the way he phrases the problem, Hamdani (2002, 918–20) wrongly concludes that there is no problem with overzealous enforcement in cases where the subscriber uses in-house equipment rather than purchasing access in the competitive market. In such a case, subscriber benefits are fully internalized by the ISP (which satisfies Hamdani), and yet the mismatch between private and social benefits remains. More generally, by framing the problem as they do, Katyal and Hamdani leave their arguments open to a simple response: ISPs should raise prices and in that way capture a larger share of subscriber utility. This is surely not what Katyal and Hamdani have in mind, and the reason is that they, like us, are actually worried about the problem of positive externalities.

[14] 47 U.S.C. § 230(b)(3).

techniques"[15] that similarly might empower Internet subscribers to bar un-wanted messages. The objection is that allowing ISPs to shirk will increase the incentive for subscribers to engage in self-defense and, through that, the incentive for independent firms to step in and offer technological solutions along the lines of virus protection software and firewalls. That is all true, but, as we will argue, the logical implication is not complete immunity for ISPs. Instead, liability should be tailored in light of this possibility, the goal being to encourage service providers to adopt the precautions that they can provide most efficiently while leaving any remaining precautions to other market actors. This is again a standard scenario. Pedestrians can exercise care in crossing the street. They can also stay at home rather than venturing near the roads, and they can wear unfashionably bright attire so as to increase the odds of being seen at night or during inclement weather. Yet no one suggests that, because pedestrians can engage in their own forms of precaution, automobile drivers should be immune from tort liability. The same intuitions apply here. The fact that multiple parties can take precautions against malicious computer code might argue for some form of a balanced liability regime that leaves both subscribers and ISPs with some incentive to take care, but that fact does not in any way argue for complete immunity for ISPs. There are precautions in which ISPs can and should engage, and shifting the full costs of cybersecurity to Internet subscribers would inefficiently reduce each ISP's incentive to take them.

Now a word on our terminology. We do not need a formal definition for the term "Internet service provider" in order to capture the basic idea that these are the entities that provide individual and institutional subscribers with access to the Internet. The precise features associated with that access are not of concern. Some ISPs offer e-mail services, news, storage space, and even games to their subscribers. Others simply receive data, convert that data into a form consistent with the TCP/IP protocol, and forward the results to independent computers that then provide richer services and interactions. All of these entities, however, are for our purposes considered "Internet service providers" in that each controls the point at which information residing on a privately owned computer network first comes in contact with the public network. Thus – and perhaps these will quickly sound to readers like historical references, given the pace of change in the industry – SBC is an Internet service provider in our vernacular, as is America Online, Road Runner, and RCN.

We similarly see no need to adopt technical definitions for concepts like the computer worm, the computer virus, the denial-of-service attack, or even the software Trojan horse. For us, these serve as placeholders for any category of

[15] 47 U.S.C. § 230(b)(4).

malicious computer code that is propagated on the Internet, using or interfering with privately owned computer equipment, and done in a way such that the relevant private party has not given informed consent for that use or interference. Details beyond that – while certainly relevant to an understanding of the specific steps that might be available to combat pests – have no impact on the legal argument we present.

Our discussion proceeds in five sections. Section I summarizes the conventional economic account of indirect liability and applies those teachings to the specific case of ISPs. Section II considers in more detail the two primary objections sketched above, namely, (1) that liable ISPs will be overly cautious and thus inefficiently exclude marginal subscribers and (2) that liability will reduce user incentives to engage in efficient self-help. Section III questions several recent court decisions that seem unnecessarily reluctant to hold ISPs accountable for the bad acts of their subscribers. Finally, Section IV concludes with some remarks on the limitations of our analysis and how our discussion differs from what might otherwise be a comparable discussion of ISP liability in the context of online copyright infringement.

I. THE THEORY OF INDIRECT LIABILITY

A. The Standard Model

Indirect liability is said to attach in instances where the law holds one party liable for a wrong committed by another.[16] A familiar setting is the employment relationship, where an employer can be held liable for torts committed on the job by his employees. But other examples abound. Bars are sometimes held liable when bartenders serve alcoholic beverages to patrons who later harm others while driving under the influence.[17] A motor vehicle owner can be held

---

[16] The terminology used for this concept varies considerably in the literature. Economists seem to prefer the phrase "vicarious liability" even though, in copyright law at least, vicarious liability is merely one specific type of indirect liability, namely, liability that attaches because the third party has control over the direct bad actor and also benefits from the bad acts in question. Other commentators use phrases like "secondary liability" or "third-party liability" to capture the intuition that this is liability that attaches not to the bad actor directly but to some other related party. We use the term "indirect liability" as our generic phrase.

[17] North Dakota's dram shop statute, for example, provides that any person "injured by any obviously intoxicated person has a claim for relief... against any person who knowingly disposes, sells, barters, or gives away alcoholic beverages to a person under twenty-one years of age, an incompetent, or an obviously intoxicated person." D. Cent. Code 5-01-06.1. Arizona law, by contrast, immunizes from liability parties who merely furnish or serve "spirituous liquor to a person of the legal drinking age." Ariz. Rev. Stat. Ann. 4-301, 4-311 to -312 (West 1995).

to account if a driver to whom he loans his car ends up causing an accident.[18] Landlords are sometimes on the hook if they take inadequate precautions against criminal activity that in turn harms tenants.[19] Mall owners can be responsible if merchants use mall premises to sell counterfeit or gray-market goods.[20] Even product liability law has this same basic structure: A buyer might use a dangerous product in a negligent manner and cause injury to a third party; if the victim can show that the accident would not have occurred had the manufacturer employed a better design, the victim may be able to recover from the manufacturer instead of (or in addition to) the buyer.[21]

Conventional economic analysis suggests that an explicit rule imposing indirect liability is not necessary when two conditions are simultaneously met: First, the relevant direct actors are subject to the effective reach of the law, by which we mean that the employees, drivers, and merchants discussed in our previous examples are easy to identify and have assets that are sufficient to pay for any harm caused. Second, transaction costs are such that those direct actors can use contract law to shift responsibility to any party that might otherwise be an attractive target for indirect liability.[22] The intuition is that, when these conditions are satisfied, the various parties can create indirect liability by contract, and – albeit subject to some second-order constraints[23] – they will do so where that would be efficient.[24]

To see this, consider the employment setting in more detail. If the driver of a delivery van is himself easy to identify, and, further, the driver has adequate resources to pay for whatever harm he might cause in the event of an accident, then there is no strong argument for imposing liability on the associated retailer. No matter what the legal rule, the driver and the retailer will efficiently allocate liability through their employment contract. Thus, if the optimal rule would

---

[18] This is usually done as a matter of statute; see Dobbs (2000, 934).

[19] See, for example, *Sharp v. W. H. Moore, Inc.*, 796 P.2d 506 (Idaho 1990).

[20] See, for example, *Fonovisa v. Cherry Auction*, 76 F.3d 259 (9th Cir. 1996).

[21] See Restatement (Third) of Products Liability, § 402A. We could go on with a variety of other examples. Perhaps most eerily similar to our current topic: a physician can be held liable for failing to warn a patient's spouse that the patient has a real-world ailment like Rocky Mountain spotted fever and thus might expose the spouse to it. See *Bradshaw v. Daniel*, 854 S.W.2d 865 (Tenn. 1993) (physician had, and failed to fulfill, a duty to warn patient's wife of one such health risk).

[22] For a general introduction, see Alan Sykes (1998).

[23] Among these constraints are (1) the costs a victim would incur to identify and then sue the liable parties and (2) cognitive limitations that might lead to incorrect predictions regarding the likelihood or extent of any expected accidents.

[24] We assume that the indirectly liable parties are subject to the effective reach of the law, which is to say that they can be identified and they have sufficient assets to pay for any harms they might cause. While that is typically true, it is not always true, especially in instances where the harm in question is catastrophic.

impose on the retailer the obligation to inspect every delivery van each morning, or to test employees randomly for drug and alcohol abuse, the driver and retailer will agree by contract to those desired monitoring activities. Similarly, to the extent that driving the truck poses an unavoidable risk of injury to others, the driver will either shift that risk to the employer through an indemnity clause or assume that risk himself and demand higher wages in compensation. The legal rule in this situation is just a default; where transaction costs are low and employees have adequate resources, contracts allow private parties to shift and divide legal responsibility efficiently.

Things change when either of the conditions identified above fails to hold. For instance, where contracts are easily negotiated between the driver and the retailer, but the driver himself lacks the resources necessary to pay for the harm he might cause, the absence of indirect liability would tempt the retailer to leave tort liability on the shoulders of the driver, in essence using the driver's financial limitations as a cap on legal liability. Similarly, where contracts are possible but a negligent employee's identity cannot be ascertained – for example, witnesses report that a Federal Express van hit the pedestrian but no one saw the driver – again the absence of indirect liability would act as a *de facto* cap on tort liability, putting the driver in a position where he would not be fully liable for his accidents and thus leading the retailer and driver together to take suboptimal care. Where the driver has adequate resources but the parties cannot contract effectively, the legal rule clearly matters as well, this time because the inability to contract would make it impossible for the parties to shift responsibility to the cheaper cost avoider.

Thus the interesting cases are those where either the relevant bad actors are beyond the reach of the law, or transaction costs make reallocation by contract implausible. For these cases, economic analysis identifies two additional considerations: First, indirect liability might be attractive in cases where one party is in a good position to detect or deter another's bad act. Second, indirect liability might be attractive in cases where liability would serve to encourage a party to internalize some significant negative externality unavoidably associated with its activities.[25]

Start with the first consideration: that indirect liability might be particularly attractive where the potentially liable party is in a good position to detect and deter bad acts. This is, for example, one of the main reasons why employers are responsible for the torts committed by their employees. An employer can control his employees. He can monitor their behavior, screen them before

---

[25] Our discussion follows the analysis in Shavell (1987), Sykes (1981, 1984, 1988), and Kraakman (1986). Two helpful overviews are Sykes (1998) and Kraakman (1998).

entrusting them with dangerous equipment, develop compensation schemes that encourage them to exercise due care, and otherwise beneficially influence their on-the-job decisions. The prospect of indirect liability pressures employers to make use of these mechanisms and, in that way, to minimize the expected cost of accidents. Now admittedly, employer liability is typically strict, which is to say that – despite what we just said – liability does not turn on a specific court finding that the relevant employer should have taken additional precautions given the particular accident at issue. However, the logic is likely that the more detailed inquiry would prove too cumbersome, and thus the law errs on the side of holding employers accountable. In essence, strict liability in this application presumes that there was something that the employer should have done differently, and that presumption is made irrebuttable for reasons of administrative convenience. In many other settings, by contrast, some form of a negligence standard is used, and that maps well to the intuition that the liable party had the ability to control the erstwhile bad actor and inefficiently failed to do so.[26]

Turn now to the second consideration: that even in situations where the indirectly liable party cannot meaningfully detect or deter bad acts, indirect liability might still be attractive as a way to force that party to account for significant negative externalities unavoidably associated with its activities. Again, the employment setting is instructive. Even where a retailer can do nothing more to ensure that the drivers of its delivery vans take appropriate care, it is likely efficient to have the retailer pay at least some fraction of the costs of any delivery accidents. The reason is that this forces the retailer to account for the costs of accidents when deciding the price and frequency of deliveries. If accidents are unavoidable, liability means that price will rise and quantity will fall, which is exactly what should happen given this unavoidable harm. This is referred to in the literature as an effect on "activity level," the vocabulary there designed to emphasize that the purpose of liability here is not to encourage precautions but instead to influence how often the harmful activity in question takes place. Importantly, note that where activity level is the concern, strict liability is often appropriate, in that the logic of liability is not at all tied to any negligent failure on the part of the indirectly liable party to take some cost-justified precaution.

These factors – call them "control" and "activity level" – help to identify cases where liability might be attractive. The actual question of whether liability should be imposed, however, typically turns on other, often setting-specific considerations. Thus, while the telephone company surely has the ability to

---

[26] See, for example, *Sharp v. W. H. Moore, Inc.*, 796 P.2d 506 (Idaho 1990); *Fonovisa v. Cherry Auction*, 76 F.3d 259 (9th Cir. 1996).

deter crank phone calls by more carefully monitoring calling patterns, it is unlikely that telephone company liability would be attractive, both because of obvious privacy concerns and because of worries that, in its attempts to address the problem of crank calls, the telephone company would inadvertently interfere with substantial legitimate telephone activity. To reject indirect liability in this situation is to announce that the costs of crank telephone calls are not sufficiently high as compared to the costs of indirect prevention. Similarly, the mere fact that an airport provides a venue from which airlines generate pollution and noise does not itself justify imposing liability for those harms. After all, private parties who own property near the airport themselves make decisions that increase and decrease the importance of airport externalities; in a world where the airport absorbed the costs in full, neighbors might inefficiently decide to use their properties to raise livestock or care for the elderly, two uses so sensitive to noise and pollution that they likely should be disfavored given the proximity of the airport.

That said, control and activity-level considerations do helpfully sketch the contours of efficient indirect liability rules. For instance, these factors make clear why employers should not typically be held accountable for torts committed by their employees in instances where the employees are acting outside the scope of employment. The employer has no special advantage when it comes to stopping his employees from abusing their spouses or picking fights at bars.[27] Moreover, neither activity is rightly understood as a consequence of the employer engaging in his core business; whether the employer is in his current line of business or another, the employee is probably just as likely to commit those bad acts. Thus, except in exceptional circumstances, neither the control nor the activity-level rationale fits, and liability for torts committed outside the scope of employment is therefore inappropriate.[28]

To take another example, an efficient indirect liability regime should be reluctant to wave off liability in cases where the potentially liable party asserts,

---

[27] The right question to ask is whether the employer can influence the relevant behavior more effectively than can the state. Thus, while an employer can fine an employee for bad acts committed on the employee's own time, and while such a system could be used to discourage bar fights and spousal abuse, the government can implement such a system of fines just as easily, and the government might even better suited to do so because, for example, the government has the ability to incarcerate bad actors for whom the fine turns out to be an insufficient disincentive.

[28] See Sykes (1998) (discussing employee torts outside the scope of employment). Note that there might be more of a link here than we indicate above. An employer who places enormous stress on his employee, for example, surely increases the likelihood that that employee will abuse his spouse or become involved in barroom brawls. Thus there might be at least a small activity-level effect to consider, and certain types of employers should perhaps bear liability for employee behavior that takes place after hours.

as a defense, that he lacked control over the alleged bad actor due to a contractual provision, an affirmative technology choice, or some detail related to corporate structure. The idea behind the control rationale is to encourage private parties to develop mechanisms and adopt organizational structures that effectively allow for the control of possible bad actors. Allowing parties to hide from this obligation through some voluntary limitation threatens to undermine that logic, in essence encouraging a potentially liable party to knowingly and intentionally stick his head in the sand. Sadly, courts accept these sorts of excuses all too often – this is exactly the ruse at play in situations where taxi cab companies structure their affairs such that each taxi is, in the eyes of the law, a separate corporate entity[29] – but the basic economics of indirect liability remind us that courts should instead direct a skeptical eye toward any party's self-imposed inability to detect or deter.[30]

In sum, the conventional economic account makes clear that private parties cannot create the optimal liability regime on their own in instances where the party directly responsible for the bad act is beyond the effective reach of the law, and private parties also cannot create the optimal liability regime on their own in instances where transaction costs make contract negotiations implausible. The conventional account further stresses that liability should be considered in instances where one party has the ability to deter or detect the bad acts of another, and also where liability can serve to encourage a party to internalize some significant negative externality associated with his activities. As we will argue in the next section, violations of cybersecurity take place in a setting where these conditions all seem likely to hold.

B. Applied to Internet Service Providers

There are strong arguments for imposing liability on ISPs for violations of cybersecurity, and they track the four core intuitions outlined in the previous section. Consider each in turn.

---

[29] For a discussion, see *Goldberg v. Lee Express Cab Corp.*, 634 N.Y.S.2d 337 (1995).

[30] This is similarly a good reason for the Ninth Circuit to look askance at Grokster, the entity that intentionally designed its peer-to-peer music trading system such that, once activated, the technology (arguably) cannot effectively monitor for copyright infringement. See *MGM Studios, Inc. v. Grokster, Ltd.*, 259 F. Supp. 2d 1029 (C. D. Cal. 2003), appeal pending. On the general theme of intentional ignorance in the context of indirect liability, see *In re Aimster Copyright Litigation*, 334 F.3d 643, 650–51 (7th Cir. 2003) ("a service provider that would otherwise be a contributory infringer does not obtain immunity by using encryption to shield itself from actual knowledge of the unlawful purposes for which the service is being used").

1. **Beyond the Law's Reach.** Individuals who originate malicious computer code are typically far beyond the reach of conventional law. For one thing, they are hard to identify. Sophisticated saboteurs use the Internet's topology to conceal their tracks by routing messages through a convoluted path that is difficult for authorities to uncover. Moreover, by the time a computer virus or worm is detected, the trail often is cold. Internet pests like worms and viruses are routinely programmed to sit idle for a period of time before triggering, which primarily allows mischief-makers to time their attacks to coincide with important world moments – the start of the new millennium, for example – but also creates a period of time during which the mischief-makers can effectively disappear. The fact that many hackers reside overseas only exacerbates the problem, introducing issues of jurisdiction and the need for international cooperation.

Even if caught, individuals who create malicious computer code rarely have sufficient assets to pay for the losses they impose. Some estimates put the costs of prominent Internet worms and viruses in the billions of dollars, and those estimates might undercount the harm as they measure only commercial productivity losses and disruptions to commerce, thus ignoring the costs of countermeasures like antivirus software as well as less quantifiable harms such as missed opportunities for communication and the frustration experienced by computer users who are victimized. Obviously, hackers will rarely have resources sufficient to pay up. Criminal liability could, in theory, substitute as a deterrent; however, where the risk of apprehension is sufficiently small and the magnitude of the loss is sufficiently large, criminal punishments often cannot be made high enough to deter adequately. Juries, after all, are reluctant to impose too large a sentence for nonviolent crime, and, besides, long-term incarceration is expensive to the state.[31]

Interestingly, concerns about bad actors being beyond the reach of the law do not apply to the individuals and entities who, instead of creating an Internet pest, inadvertently propagate one. An example might be a firm whose server is run in such a way that an outside party can easily take it over, or an unsophisticated user who installs a malicious program when prompted to do so by an anonymous e-mail solicitation. There is no reason to believe that careless

---

[31] There are second-order concerns as well, such as the fact that defendants will invest more resources resisting long sentences than they will short ones. There are also equitable concerns, as it might seem inappropriate to establish a legal system where, by design, only a small fraction of the culpable parties are punished, but those that are punished suffer extraordinarily large penalties. Lastly, it is often important to keep penalties low enough that there is a plausible threat of an additional penalty if the relevant bad actor further misbehaves. Otherwise, after crossing the relevant threshold, bad actors have no incentive to mitigate the harm they cause.

firms and users lack the resources necessary to pay for whatever share of the harm they cause. Moreover, careless firms and users would typically not be that hard to track down. Computer users who fail to exercise appropriate caution when opening e-mail attachments, for instance, are hardly sophisticated enough to cover their tracks in the event of a problem. The only sense in which these bad actors are beyond the reach of law is the practical concern about the costs of identifying and suing them as compared to the fraction of the damages for which they might be held legally responsible. Beyond that, parties who propagate but do not create malicious code are not beyond the reach of the law, although, as will become clear below, there are other reasons why indirect liability might be warranted even in these sorts of cases.

2. **Contracts and Transaction Costs.** A second consideration raised in our baseline analysis concerned the ability of the relevant parties to allocate liability by contract. We are not here referring to the contract that a given subscriber might sign with his chosen ISP; obviously, such contracts exist, and through their various terms of service those contracts do in fact allocate liability between each ISP and its subscribers. Our focus is instead on contracts that would obligate an ISP to protect other ISPs from any harm caused by the first ISP's subscribers. Our point is that ISPs in theory can use contract law to create this sort of systemwide liability. That immediately raises the question of why those obligations are not in place, and whether the law should respond by imposing them.

An intuitive answer is that there are today so many ISPs that the transaction costs of negotiating the necessary web of contracts would be prohibitive. But that explanation is only marginally satisfying, in that ISPs are already all part of a complicated and fully inclusive network of contracts, specifically "peering" and "transit" agreements under which the various private owners of the Internet backbone agree to carry traffic one to another.[32] A more satisfying explanation is that any network of contracts focusing on issues of cybersecurity would be perpetually out of date, and updating such a complicated network of interdependent security obligations would be all but impossible given the number of parties involved and the complicated questions any update would raise regarding appropriate adjustments to the flow of payments.[33]

---

[32] For an introduction to these interconnection issues, see Benjamin, Lichtman, and Shelanski (2001).

[33] Bounded rationality might be an additional limitation on the ability of Internet subscribers to efficiently create the optimal indirect liability regime through private contracts. The many users who today are still clicking to download e-mail attachments from strangers are as a practical matter unlikely to be sufficiently rational contract negotiators. Their blind spots undermine any argument that private parties will, if left to their own devices, be able to efficiently shift and allocate responsibility for online security.

Still, there are puzzles lurking. Microsoft has licensing agreements with a huge percentage of home computer users, and thus the firm seems to be in the perfect position to ensure that users take sensible precautions like updating their virus software and downloading system patches. Microsoft could even make those obligations self-executing by blocking Internet access for any computer whose software is (say) more than 10 days out of date. Instead, Microsoft merely offers updates to its customers and allows each customer to decide whether the private benefits of a given update warrant the private costs in terms of time and inconvenience. The result might very well be a classic case of externalities leading to suboptimal behavior: Microsoft's customers as a group would be better off were each to update regularly, but, without coordination, each customer opts to update less frequently. This suggests that there must be a bigger problem with contractual solutions – public relations? privacy concerns? security?[34] – although in truth the explanation might simply be that Microsoft is at the moment in too precarious a position vis-à-vis worldwide antitrust authorities to do anything that might be perceived as the use of its market power to foist additional software on unwilling consumers.

3. Control. As we noted in the more general discussion, indirect liability is primarily attractive in cases where the indirectly liable party can detect, deter, or otherwise influence the bad acts in question. ISPs seem to be a natural choice under this criterion. Consider, for example, an ISP through which a troublemaking user obtains access to the Internet. Such an ISP can detect criminal behavior by analyzing patterns of use, much as a bank can detect credit card theft by monitoring each customer's pattern of purchases. Easiest to catch would be patterns that are intrinsically suspicious, such as a continuous stream of communications from a home user or the repeated appearance of identical computer code attached to a large number of outgoing e-mail messages. But an ISP could also detect patterns that are suspicious because they represent a radical departure from the user's ordinary behavior. The ISP would need only maintain a profile that captures in broad strokes each subscriber's rough practices and then evaluate recent activity against that historical backdrop. Again, credit card companies actually do this, and ISPs could do it too.

Another option might be to record a subscriber's data stream and store that information, ideally in encrypted form, for a period of time. Many offenders could be traced if ISPs were to record traffic in this manner. But ISPs do not

---

[34] An automatic update system like the one we propose would become an attractive target for hackers because it could conceivably be used to corrupt a large number of computers simultaneously. Then again, the current voluntary system suffers the same flaw, albeit on a slightly smaller scale.

routinely record traffic today, both because of privacy worries and because of the enormous volume of communications. Legal rules, however, could ease those concerns. For instance, the law could require that ISPs store the information securely and release it only to law enforcement officials, thus lessening the worry that stored information would leak out by accident or be used for impermissible purposes. The law could also require that ISPs record information about the data communication – size, duration, timing, and so on – but not its substance, thus protecting privacy and reducing volume. The law could even require ISPs to record information only when particular triggers raise suspicion, or perhaps only in response to specific government requests.[35] The amount of time that information would need to be stored could also be tweaked to address concerns about storage costs, assuming those concerns are valid and not a pretext advanced by ISPs to avoid regulation.

We have focused thus far on bad acts engaged in by a subscriber or accomplished using a subscriber's account, but turn now to the role ISPs might play in detecting criminal behavior that originates on a rival firm's network. When an ISP receives a packet or message from another ISP, it might be able to detect aspects of the packet that indicate a likelihood of criminal activity. For example, an ISP might alone, or in cooperation with other ISPs, notice an unusual spike in demand, indicating a denial-of-service attack or a rapidly multiplying virus or worm. ISPs might even be able to develop efficient protocols for pooling information about changes in traffic patterns and in that way alert one another, and also customers, of suspicious behavior in time to trace it back to its source or at least to shut it down before it can cause substantial harm.

We could go on for some time with examples along these lines. However, our goal for now is not to determine the precise precautions that ISPs should or will take in response to liability – quite the opposite, we are painfully aware of our outsider status when it comes to technology design – but instead to make clear that ISPs are in a good position to influence the number and severity of cyberattacks. Indirect liability would pressure service providers to take this

---

[35] The right approach might be to empower government officials to require ISPs to store information without any particular showing or court order, but then to permit government officials to access that information only with a court order in hand. This would free the government to act quickly in terms of preserving evidence, but it would still respect privacy interests until the government could make a sufficient case. This approach has many virtues: For instance, it preserves evidence during that gap between when the government first becomes suspicious and when the government can corroborate its suspicions, a gap during which evidence today is often lost; and it allows for narrow searches of stored information to be followed up with broader searches in cases where later events suggest that there is more to be learned from the stored data. Computer scientist Carl Gunther has been working on various technologies along these lines and was helpful in explaining these technologies to us.

task seriously, ensuring that those who have the proper technical expertise will themselves work to identify and then implement whatever turn out to be the most effective precautions.

4. Activity Level. In theory, indirect liability can be attractive independent of its role in encouraging detection and deterrence because liability encourages a party to account for any negative externalities unavoidably associated with its product or service. In practice, however, we doubt that we would favor ISP liability on this argument alone. Our hesitation does not derive from any doubts over whether ISPs impose negative externalities as they enroll new customers and offer new services; of course they do, given that any new subscriber can turn out to be a careless user and that any new service can quickly devolve into a portal for Internet contagion. Our hesitation instead derives from the fact that there are drawbacks to imposing liability solely because of negative externalities, and those drawbacks are significant in this particular application.

One drawback associated with the activity-level rationale is that it might distort behavior by forcing parties to internalize negative externalities even though they often cannot internalize equally sizable positive externalities. As applied here, the negative externality is the aforementioned concern that each new subscriber could materially reduce cybersecurity by engaging in unsafe practices or intentionally introducing an Internet pest.[36] The comparable positive externality is that each subscriber can just as plausibly turn out to be a homemaker who makes significant purchases online or a college student who posts to newsgroups and contributes to the development of open source software. Liability that encourages ISPs to take precautions is one thing, but a legal rule that relentlessly brings home negative externalities while completely failing to account for positive externalities cannot claim to be creating optimal incentives. Thus, a rule that imposes liability based on negative externalities might do more harm than good – although the actual analysis turns on the relative size of any ignored positive externalities and the difficulty of accounting for those externalities through other means. We will say more about that later.

A second drawback to the activity-level rationale – and on this, too, we will say much more later – is the concern that imposing liability on one party almost inevitably discourages another party from taking adequate precautions. Applied here, the worry is that imposing liability on ISPs might inefficiently reduce subscriber incentives to install virus protection software and to maintain adequate firewalls and backups. This is a concern associated with indirect liability no matter what the rationale, but the concern resonates with particular

---

[36] See discussion in Section II.B.1.

force in cases where indirect liability is being used solely as a means by which to influence the liable party's activity level. The reason: these are cases where by assumption the liable party cannot take additional cost-justified precautions; reductions in the level of care taken by other parties therefore warrant considerable weight.

A third argument against imposing strict liability solely because of activity-level concerns is that activity levels in this setting are already significantly suppressed. Worms, viruses, and the like reduce the allure of Internet access and thus discourage Internet use no matter what the liability rule. This is a natural reduction in activity levels, and, while there is no reason to believe that it leads to efficient levels of activity,[37] the existence of this natural disincentive does combine with the concerns discussed earlier to make any additional reduction seem not only less important but also more difficult to calibrate.

All that said, activity-level concerns can be important, and hence we do harbor some uncertainty over where to draw this line. Consider again Microsoft. Even if Microsoft cannot take additional precautions against Internet contagion, the price increase that would likely result from an increase in liability would itself have social benefits in that the resulting price would better reflect the relative value of the Windows operating system as compared to alternatives like Apple Computer's operating system, Mac OS. Many computer enthusiasts believe that Mac OS is more stable and secure than Windows. If so, this benefit is not today adequately captured in the products' relative prices. By increasing liability and hence disproportionately increasing the price of Windows software, however, an indirect liability rule could help to solve that problem, ultimately driving business toward the more secure and efficient alternative.

More generally, in situations where several competing products are each capable of generating a comparable positive externality, it might be attractive to use indirect liability as a way of pressuring firms to select prices that accurately reflect each product's unique negative externalities. Suppose, for example, that ISP access provided over the telephone lines using DSL technology is worse, from a cybersecurity standpoint, than ISP access provided using the cable infrastructure. If true, and even if providers of those technologies cannot take any additional cost-justified precautions, liability might be attractive. All else

---

[37] The disincentive discussed above perfectly calibrates activity levels in situations where externalities are sufficiently symmetric. Imagine a simple such case: a world with three subscribers where each imposes on each of the other two a negative externality of two dollars. The first subscriber in this setting imposes four dollars worth of harm, namely, two dollars imposed on each of two peers, but also suffers a total of four dollars worth of harm, again two dollars from each of two peers. To the extent that similar sorts of symmetry might be created in the ISP setting – for example, by forcing each ISP to serve a similar population – activity levels could be calibrated without the introduction of legal liability.

held equal, the technology that imposes the greater security risks would under a liability regime cost more, and the resulting price difference would drive customers to the socially preferred technology.[38]

II. OBJECTIONS

Our argument thus far is that indirect liability is attractive primarily because ISPs are in a good position to deter the various bad acts associated with cyber-insecurity, and perhaps secondarily because liability would force ISPs to internalize some of the negative externalities they impose. Further, we have argued that any indirect liability regime needs to be created by law rather than by contract, both because many of the relevant direct bad actors are beyond the reach of law and because transactions costs are a serious obstacle to contractual solutions in any event. We turn now to what we anticipate to be the primary objections to our analysis: first, that liability will cause ISPs to overreact and thus exclude subscribers who should be online, and, second, that liability will inefficiently interfere with subscriber efforts at self-help.

A. Overzealous ISPs

The most common objection to ISP liability is that it will deter ISPs from offering service to innocent but risky users. Phrased in the more formal language of economics, the concern is that a positive externality is created every time a new user subscribes to Internet service, and thus, if Internet access is priced at marginal cost, some subscribers will not purchase Internet access even in situations where the social benefits of access exceed the social costs.[39] More intuitively, indirect liability will inevitably raise the price of service because of the added costs and legal exposure, and, while that higher price might better represent the real costs associated with Internet access, it will also drive some marginal subscribers out of the market despite the fact that advertisers, information providers, merchants, friends, and various other subscribers might in the aggregate prefer that these marginal customers remain. The problem is just an externality – a mismatch between the private incentive to subscribe to Internet service and the social benefits made possible by that same subscription.

---

[38] The details turn out to be slightly more complicated, as DSL prices are distorted by the unbundling rules of the Telecommunications Act of 1996, which require existing local telephone companies to rent their infrastructure – arguably including DSL capability – to rivals at regulated rates. For an introduction to the issues, see Benjamin et al. (2001, 715–55).

[39] If the social costs exceed the social benefits, by contrast, there is no problem, because under this condition the subscriber should not be online.

Our first response is that this concern, while plausible, seems overdrawn. Many of what at first sound like externalities turn out to be influences that are already accounted for in a subscriber's decision whether to subscribe. For instance, Lichtman certainly benefits from the fact that his mother is regularly online and hence available for easy e-mail correspondence, but that is not an externality because Lichtman and his mom have a rich relationship through which he can indicate to her how much he values her presence and, if necessary, contribute in cash or kind toward the monthly costs of her subscription. So, too, the online bookseller Amazon.com benefits from his mom's Internet access, but Amazon also has ways of helping her to internalize that effect, for instance by rewarding her with free shipping on her purchases. This is obviously not to say that all externalities are internalized, but only to suggest that the problem is not as stark as it might at first seem, and not all that different from a million other markets where incidental positive externalities slip through the decision-making cracks.[40]

Second, even if there are nontrivial positive externalities at play, note that it would be counterproductive to respond to the problem by reducing ISP liability from its otherwise optimal level. Simply put, if the concern here is that higher prices will force marginal subscribers to leave the market, the reality is that an increase in worm and virus activity will also drive away marginal subscribers. That is, cyberinsecurity, like an increase in price, is a cost associated with online access; it, too, will make Internet access less attractive to private parties, and thus it too threatens to inefficiently drive away customers whose private benefits fall short.

Now the choice between these evils is itself an interesting question. One might at first suspect that indirect liability produces the better form of exclusion because ISPs will channel that exclusion such that it affects more significantly those users who are perceived to pose the greatest likelihood of harm. Thus, a user whose actions online reveal him to be a risky user will be charged a higher

---

[40] One way to think about this economic problem is to note that connecting to the Internet is a prerequisite to shopping online, talking with friends, receiving advertisements, and so on, and that this is an expensive prerequisite both in terms of the price charged and in terms of the frustration experienced by users who are not quite computer literate. Knowing this, parties that benefit from having a marginal subscriber online will attempt to compensate that subscriber by, for example, offering sale prices. But there are two limitations to that approach. One is that some parties have no clear mechanism by which to reward the marginal consumer. The other is that there will be some free-riding, which is to say that some parties with the ability to reward the marginal consumer will choose not to, hoping that other parties will sacrifice sufficiently to induce the subscription. This latter problem is actually a generic problem that plagues any market where there is some form of a prerequisite, as Lichtman (2000) explains more fully.

price by his ISP, whereas a user who credibly signals safety will be charged a correspondingly lower fee. The economic effect is that indirect liability should disproportionately exclude those subscribers who are in fact the least desirable subscribers. The exclusion caused by worms and viruses, by contrast, lacks such nuance. A denial-of-service attack can slow even the most responsible user's machine to a crawl, and viruses that interfere with the delivery of e-mail messages likewise disrupt communication for every user. Then again, Internet pests impose greater costs on careless users than they do on careful ones; a user who regularly updates his virus software and backs up his files has less to fear from Internet contagion, because his computer will more likely be resistant. But this argument does not apply to malicious users who intentionally contaminate the network, and because of them it seems likely that the targeted exclusion caused by indirect liability is more appealing than the less focused exclusions caused by worms and viruses.

Regardless, there is no reason to choose from among these second-best alternatives, as quickly becomes apparent when one switches attention away from Internet access and toward more conventional legal settings. Inventors produce devices that stimulate further innovation. In response, society rewards them by granting them valuable property rights called patents. Does anyone really believe that society should instead shield inventors from liability if their inventions cause harm? Similarly, restaurants draw crowds that patronize neighboring businesses and stimulate the local economy. Local authorities therefore sometimes offer tax breaks to restaurants that are willing to locate in depressed neighborhoods. Would it be desirable to instead entice entry by offering to stop inspecting for violations of the health code? People who generate positive externalities are not typically compensated by legal immunity. Quite the opposite, even an entity that produces positive externalities should still take due care while engaged in its beneficial activities. There is nothing special in this respect about the Internet. Immunizing ISPs from liability is not the correct mechanism for encouraging them to provide positive externalities.

We see two better approaches. One is to subsidize the provision of Internet access, for example by offering tax incentives to ISPs based on the size of their subscriber base. The government today already subsidizes Internet access by providing a great deal of the equipment that makes up the Internet backbone, and also by forbidding states from collecting sales tax on large categories of otherwise taxable Internet transactions.[41] Those existing subsidies alone might

---

[41] Internet Tax Freedom Act, Pub. L. No. 105-277, 112 Stat. 2681, 2719 (1998) (included as Title XI of the Omnibus Consolidated and Emergency Supplemental Appropriations Act of 1999).

be sufficient;[42] but, if necessary, the government can do more. For instance, in the context of the regular voice telephone system, the federal government subsidizes the purchase of local telephone service both through specific programs designed to assist poor and rural subscribers and through more general pricing policies that favor residential users over commercial ones.[43] The logic there is similar to the logic under consideration here; the telephone system is just another network out of which individuals might inefficiently opt but for the appropriate governmental subsidy.

A second approach would have the government work with ISPs to redesign Internet protocols so that ISPs could more precisely charge one another for transferring information.[44] Under the current system, when a new user joins the network, neither that user nor his ISP captures the full benefits associated with the new subscription. However, if ISPs could charge one another for relaying messages back and forth and then in turn pass those costs and payments along to their customers, each ISP would internalize the benefits of adding a new user and thus each would better weigh the benefits as well as the costs every time it confronted the question of what price to charge for access.

B. Subscriber Self-Help

It is true that, by imposing liability on ISPs, our approach would reduce subscriber incentives to practice safe computing, install firewalls and virus protection software, and similarly engage in prudent self-help. This is troubling because subscribers are often in a better position than their ISP to determine that their computers have been hacked, and, relatedly, users are often themselves in a good position to take simple, inexpensive, but effective precautions like using appropriate passwords in order to prevent unauthorized use in the first place. Furthermore, when subscribers are looking to protect their computers from cybermischief, the competitive market responds with third-party software and technology; that market might not be as active in a world where subscribers are uninterested and thus the only buyers are regulated telephone companies and other entities that provide Internet infrastructure.[45]

---

[42] These subsidies were originally put in place when the Internet was in its infancy and the market for Internet service was therefore subject to rapid and unpredictable change. Now that the market has matured, any justification along these lines seems less valid, but the issues identified in the text suggest that the subsidies perhaps should remain.

[43] Again, for more information, consult Benjamin et al. (2001, 614–23, 712–14, 768–91).

[44] Telephone companies do this, exchanging cash when one company originates a call that another company terminates. (For discussion, see Benjamin et al. 2001, 749–55, 927–45.)

[45] Then again, changing the identity of the buyers might have beneficial effects, as ISPs are surely more educated consumers. The only obvious concerns would be these: (1) the worry that ISPs

It is important, however, not to overstate these tensions. ISPs have a direct contractual relationship with their subscribers, and so surely a liable ISP will require that each of its subscribers adopt rudimentary precautions along the lines sketched above. Better still, those contract terms can be enforced by technology, which is to say that an ISP can block any subscriber whose virus definitions are horribly out of date or whose firewall is malfunctioning. Even outside of any contractual obligations, it is typically in a subscriber's own interest to protect his computer, at least to the extent that precautions are not too cumbersome. In fact, one suspects that the real obstacle to self-protection at the moment is merely a lack of information. Were ISPs to better explain to users exactly how to minimize their exposure, many users would happily cooperate, wanting to protect their personal documents, digital music, and family photos from contamination and irreversible loss.

All that to one side, our main response to this concern about reduced incentives to engage in self-help is that, even at its strongest, this effect does not argue against indirect liability writ large but instead simply suggests a need for a tailored threshold of liability that would pressure subscribers to take adequate care. This is just like the airline example where the conventional wisdom argues against holding airports strictly liable for pollution and noise externalities, the fear being that neighbors would then ignore those factors when deciding how best to use nearby properties. The fact that multiple parties can take precautions against malicious computer code does not in any way argue for complete immunity for ISPs. There are precautions in which ISPs can and should engage, and shifting the full costs of accidents to Internet subscribers would inefficiently reduce each ISP's incentive to do so.

On this same theme, note that nothing that we say about indirect liability for ISPs is meant to suggest that Internet subscribers should themselves be immunized from liability. Many users have deep pockets – businesses and universities, for example – and making them liable for cybermischief will create additional incentives to take precautions. Liability would also create a beneficial cascade in which these businesses and universities would then work to prevent employees, students, and the like from similarly engaging in intentional bad acts or adopting inadequate security precautions. The general insight, then, is that neither users nor ISPs should be given a complete pass when it comes

might enjoy sufficient market power such that they can arrogate to themselves more of the benefits created by innovative third-party security options, thereby depressing other firms' incentives to create those new options in the first place, and (2) the worry that regulations applicable to ISPs might somehow interfere with their ability to purchase security assistance through normal market interactions.

to cybersecurity. Each has a role to play, and each should therefore be held accountable at least in part.

C. Other Objections

While the previous sections consider the two primary objections to ISP liability, there are of course other issues to address. We survey a few of those here.

One problem with ISP liability is that often the harm will be spread so thin that no victim in isolation will have a sufficient incentive to bring suit. An example might be a situation where a user launches a worm that slows down the Internet somewhat, resulting in some delays and loss of business, but does not harm any individual or business very much. This is a classic case of diffuse harm, similar to pollution that bothers many people but not enough to motivate litigation. There are two standard solutions to this problem. First, entrepreneurial lawyers might combine all the victims into a single class and sue on behalf of the class. Attorney fees give the lawyers an incentive to launch the lawsuit. Second, the government – through assistant attorneys general or an appropriate agency such as the Federal Trade Commission – could bring the lawsuit. There are advantages and disadvantages to these approaches, but those arguments are well known and hence we will not repeat them. (Shavell 1987, 277–85, contains an excellent discussion.)

A related problem concerns allocation of liability across ISPs. A communication that originates a virus, for example, might pass through dozens or hundreds or thousands of ISPs before claiming its first victim. Suppose any one of them could have detected the virus; should liability be allocated such that each ISP pays only its pro rata share? Certainly one good answer here is joint and several liability, which allows victims to sue any of the liable ISPs for the entire harm. The chosen ISP could then pass along some of the expense to its culpable peers. In this way joint and several liability lowers the barrier to litigation as faced by the injured party. Rather than having to identify and sue all the relevant ISPs, the victim can sue the easiest target and leave any division up to litigation between, and perhaps contracts among, the various ISPs.

An additional worry related to ISP liability is the possibility that imposing liability will have perverse effects, for example, encouraging ISPs to store less information and in that way make effective legal intervention more difficult.[46] These sorts of concerns can be addressed either by the procedures for proving liability or its substance. Thinking first about the standard, if the

---

[46] For a discussion of these concerns in other contexts, see Arlen (1994) and Chu and Qian (1995).

burden of proof is placed on the ISP to prove adequate precautions, these sorts of strategic responses become less attractive from the ISP's perspective. With respect to the substance, meanwhile, the decision not to keep adequate information could itself be deemed actionable, thus more explicitly encouraging ISPs not to strategically destroy information. All this is fully consistent with our earlier remarks concerning employer/employee liability; as we pointed out there, employers are typically held strictly liable for the torts of their employees, in part because the more careful inquiry into exactly what precautions were and should have been taken is also subject to these sorts of informational games.[47]

A final objection to ISP liability is the familiar concern that any domestic legal regime will have only a limited effect because of the problem of foreign ISPs. Suppose that the United States adopts the optimal ISP liability regime, with one result being that any major cybercrime originating with an American ISP can be traced back to its source. According to this argument, American Internet users would nevertheless remain vulnerable to foreign criminals who launch attacks from computers in countries with weaker Internet regulation and to American criminals who are able to hide their identities by routing incriminating packets through those same foreign ISPs. Imposing liability might therefore seem to be an empty gesture, merely shifting criminal behavior from one ISP to another.

The problem is acute because of the "weakest-link" nature of the Internet. There are roughly 200 states; suppose that 199 of them have the optimal Internet security system. The other state – call it Estonia – has no regulation. The ISPs there keep no records, so law enforcement authorities cannot trace cybercrimes to particular users. Not only can criminals in our hypothetical Estonia therefore launch untraceable attacks on users anywhere in the world, criminals in the 199 other countries can launch untraceable attacks on users anywhere in the world by routing their messages through Estonian ISPs. Worse, authorities in, say, Canada cannot solve this problem by refusing to allow packets that pass through Estonia to cross Canadian borders because (absent a massive change to the architecture of the Internet) there is no way for a Canadian ISP to determine whether a packet it receives ever passed through an ISP located in Estonia unless it receives that packet directly from an Estonian ISP rather than an ISP in a third country. Thus, as long as there is one state with bad regulations – and currently there are dozens of states with bad regulations – cybercrime, including purely domestic cybercrime routed through foreign ISPs, will be difficult to trace and stop.

[47] See note 26 and accompanying text.

However, even in a world where foreign rules offer little assistance and it is relatively easy for cybercriminals to take advantage of the weakest state's rules – and one might wonder whether those statements are true, given how often cybercriminals are being arrested abroad[48] – domestic regulations can still reduce the likelihood that any given pest will propagate. Indeed, as we have pointed out before, domestic ISPs can detect disturbing patterns in the packets they receive from other sources, they can pressure subscribers to adopt appropriate security precautions, and they can themselves adopt policies that mitigate the harm caused by worms, viruses, and the like. Weak foreign regimes therefore might interfere with some of the deterrence effect that would otherwise be achieved by the optimal ISP regime, but it certainly does not fully eliminate an ISP's ability to adopt effective precautionary techniques.

Moreover, one country's rules can and certainly do influence the rules adopted by economic and political partners. Thus, if the United States were to adopt a more stringent set of ISP regulations, it could pressure allies and trading partners to adopt a similarly forceful regime. It might do so using the normal tools of international diplomacy – adjusting terms of trade, offering an economic or political quid pro quo, and so on – or it might do so by adjusting the rules that govern the flow of Internet traffic.[49] For instance, suppose that the United States and a few other core states such as Japan, the European Union nations, and Canada were enter into an agreement requiring each state to exclude Internet packets from (1) all states that have bad Internet regulation and (2) all states with good Internet regulation that do not exclude packets from states with bad Internet regulation. With a core group signed onto such an agreement, a state like China would face the choice between adopting the required Internet policies and enjoying free communication with its main trading partners or persisting with a less secure regime but no longer being able to communicate over the Internet with member countries. China, we suspect, would choose the former option, and that would in turn put more pressure on the next outlier nation to capitulate as well. As more states made this decision

---

[48] See, for example, "High School Student Admits Creating 'Sasser' Internet Worm," *Chicago Tribune*, May 10, 2004, p. A-11 (creator of worm arrested in Germany).

[49] In theory, a state involved in some cooperative enterprise with other states can always sanction a free-rider by bombing them, cutting off trade, and so on, but in practice states almost never do this within particular treaty regimes. For example, when France failed to allow a certain kind of Pan Am jet to land in Paris – an apparent violation of the Civil Aviation Convention – the United States retaliated not by banning trade in some important commodity, but instead by refusing to allow Air France to land flights in Los Angeles. See *Case Concerning the Air Services Agreement between France and the United States*, 18 U.N.R.I.A.A. 417 (1978). It is an interesting question why states usually retaliate "in kind" rather than via substitutes, but whatever the reasons, the pattern seems relatively robust.

and entered the secure bubble, the opportunity cost of remaining outside the bubble would increase, and eventually a healthy percentage of the world's states would be working within a more secure Internet architecture.

III. RECENT CASES

We have argued thus far that Internet service providers should be held liable for a variety of cybersecurity harms; yet recent trends in the law have pressed in the opposite direction. The trend in the legislature we mentioned at the outset: the Communications Decency Act of 1996 and the Digital Millennium Copyright Act of 1998 both immunize ISPs from liability that common law principles would otherwise impose. The trend in the courts looks no better. One recent decision, for example, reads the Communications Decency Act to provide immunity even in settings where the "communication" at issue is not a defamatory statement but rather a snippet of malicious computer code. Another questions ISP liability more broadly, asking whether ISPs should ever be held liable for harms imposed on "strangers" – that is, Internet users who connect using an ISP other than the one accused of failing to take adequate care. These and related decisions are troubling from our perspective, as they stand as an obstacle to the legal rules we think appropriate.

In this final section of the essay, we therefore set out to consider several of these decisions in fuller detail. We should make clear before doing so that we do not have strong prior convictions as to whether ISP liability should be imposed via federal statute or, instead, through the more gradual mechanism of common law development. There are advantages and disadvantages to both approaches, and in the end much turns on which approach better gathers, communicates, and updates information about ISP capabilities. Our purpose, then, is not to weigh in on that particular trade-off but instead to address some of the stumbling blocks that have unnecessarily and prematurely derailed that worthwhile inquiry. Our position is that one should not read the Communications Decency Act to sweepingly preempt state and common law liability for ISPs and that likewise one should not interpret the common law to excuse ISPs from a duty to exercise care in the first place. Beyond that, we understand that reasonable minds might disagree about the precise mechanisms for and contours of ISP liability, and we simply urge that some form of liability be brought to bear.

A. The Communications Decency Act

In cases involving business disparagement, defamation, and related state and common law wrongs, the standard legal approach has been to hold speakers and publishers liable for the communications they put forward but to immunize booksellers, libraries, and similar "distributors" so long as they neither knew, nor had reason to know, of the underlying bad act.[50] Thus, if an article in *Time* magazine is found to impermissibly besmirch an individual's reputation, the writer might be held accountable for defamation, and the publisher might be required to pay damages, but, barring exceptional circumstances, shops that sell the magazine and libraries that lend it face no legal exposure.

Before the Communications Decency Act was enacted, courts endeavored to apply this liability framework to ISPs. Thus, in *Cubby v. Compuserve*,[51] the court refused to hold an early ISP accountable for defamatory statements communicated through its equipment, primarily because the relevant ISP was, in the court's view, a passive distributor of that information rather than its active publisher. "A computerized database is the functional equivalent of a more traditional news vendor, and the inconsistent application of a lower standard of liability to an electronic news distributor than that applied to a public library, book store, or newsstand would impose an undue burden on the free flow of information."[52] Soon after came *Stratton Oakmont v. Prodigy Services*,[53] where on similar facts a different court determined that the relevant ISP was more appropriately characterized as a publisher. "By actively utilizing technology and manpower to delete notes from its computer bulletin boards ... [this ISP] is clearly making decisions as to content, and such decisions constitute editorial control."[54] Other courts similarly worked to select the appropriate analogy based on the facts of the dispute at hand, with the result in each case being heavily influenced by the accused ISP's own choices with respect to its usage policies, its enforcement practices, and its technologies.

This gradual development of touchstones and distinctions might have continued for some time but for a simple and predictable problem: the liability rules were discouraging ISPs from attempting to filter problematic communications.

---

[50] This history is recounted in virtually all of the cases involving ISP liability for defamation, and it is also echoed in nearly all of the scholarly commentary that was written in response. See, for example, *Cubby, Inc. v. Compuserve, Inc.*, 776 F. Supp. 135, 139–40 (S.D. N.Y. 1991), and Ku (2001). Interestingly, most of these sources neglect to mention that there exists a third common law category consisting of telephone companies, mail carriers, and similar conduits and that these entities typically enjoy complete immunity because they lack the practical ability to filter or otherwise discriminate based on content. On conduits, see *Lunney v. Prodigy Servs.*, 94 N.Y.2d 242, 249 (1999).

[51] *Cubby v. Compuserve*, 776 F. Supp. 135 (S.D. N.Y. 1991).

[52] Id. at 140.

[53] *Stratton Oakmont v. Prodigy Services*, 23 Media L. Rep. (BNA) 1794 (N.Y. Sup. Ct. 1995).

[54] Id. at 10 (internal citations omitted).

After all, an ISP that refused to self-regulate was likely to fall under the *Cubby* analysis and be characterized as passive and, hence, virtually immune. An ISP that endeavored to filter, by contrast, was vulnerable to the *Stratton Oakmont* line of reasoning and its associated legal risks. The result was that, because ISPs were so flexible in terms of the precise role they could play in online communication, the standard liability framework created a perverse incentive to sit idly by without even attempting to detect and deter bad acts.[55] That strange state of affairs led Congress to revamp the ISP liability regime by enacting the Communications Decency Act of 1996.

For our purposes, the key provision is Section 230, which states that an ISP will not be "treated as the publisher or speaker of any information" provided by a subscriber or other information source.[56] Debates over the proper interpretation of this clause rage, and along two distinct dimensions. First, does the provision fully immunize ISPs from liability for defamation and related wrongs, or does it leave open the possibility that an ISP can be held liable as a "distributor" even if not liable as a "publisher" or "speaker" per se? Second, does the word "information" include only communications that would otherwise be regulated under defamation and similar tort theories – legal rules that obviously implicate serious First Amendment concerns – or does it expand to include any data transmitted by an ISP, including the various forms of malicious computer code of interest here? Courts have answered these questions so as to preempt all forms of ISP liability and, further, to apply that immunity to all forms of information; but those readings are flawed, in our view, in that they interpret the statute far too broadly.

On the first question, the leading case is *Zeran v. America Online*,[57] where a panel on the Fourth Circuit held that Section 230 "creates a federal immunity to any cause of action that would make service providers liable for information originating with a third-party user of the service," irrespective of whether the ISP in forwarding that information acted as publisher, distributor, or both.[58] Speaking to the distinction between publishers and distributors, the court held that by its express terms Section 230 immunizes both types of disseminator, because, according to the court, distributors are just a type of publisher anyway. As the court put it, distributor liability is "merely a subset, or a species, of publisher liability, and is therefore also foreclosed by § 230."[59]

---

[55] This echoes the concerns we expressed earlier regarding strategic ignorance. See note 30 and accompanying text.

[56] 47 U.S.C. § 230(c)(1).

[57] *Zeran v. America Online*, 129 F.3d 327 (4th Cir. 1997).

[58] Id. at 330.

[59] Id. at 332.

The court bolstered its analysis with policy arguments regarding an issue that we addressed earlier, namely the concern that distributor liability would lead ISPs to be overzealous in their filtering of online communications.

> If computer service providers were subject to distributor liability, they would face potential liability each time they receive notice of a potentially defamatory statement – from any party, concerning any message. Each notification would require a careful yet rapid investigation of the circumstances surrounding the posted information, a legal judgment concerning the information's defamatory character, and an on-the-spot editorial decision whether to risk liability by allowing the continued publication of that information. Although this might be feasible for the traditional print publisher, the sheer number of postings on interactive computer services would create an impossible burden in the Internet context. Because service providers would be subject to liability only for the publication of information, and not for its removal, they would have a natural incentive simply to remove messages upon notification, whether the contents were defamatory or not. Thus, like [publisher] liability, [distributor liability] has a chilling effect on the freedom of Internet speech.[60]

We will not here address issues of statutory construction and legislative history; those issues are important to the *Zeran* decision, to be sure, but they have been analyzed in great depth by others,[61] and they are as of this writing under active review in the courts.[62] We therefore want to focus instead on the policy argument excerpted above and point out that it, too, is suspect. As a general matter, we have already discussed the limitations associated with arguments about overzealous ISPs. Our points were that market forces will largely discipline this sort of behavior and that, to the extent that any significant externalities remain, tort immunity is not an efficient response. But note that

---

[60] Id. at 333–4. The court also worried that "notice-based liability would deter service providers from regulating the dissemination of offensive material over their own services" because "efforts by a service provider to investigate and screen material posted on its service would only lead to notice of potentially defamatory material more frequently and thereby create a stronger basis for liability" (Id. at 333). That strikes us as a fear that can be easily addressed, specifically by applying some form of a "knew or should have known" standard. That is, an ISP should not be allowed to shield itself from liability simply by choosing not to investigate. Whether an ISP investigates or not, if it should have known about a particular statement, it should be held accountable. Again, this is the concern about parties hiding their heads in the sand, first mentioned in note 30 and accompanying text. Standards that use the "knew or should have known" structure avoid this problem – under such a standard, there is no incentive to remain ignorant – whereas standards that turn on actual knowledge do not.

[61] See, for example, Sheridan (1997), and Lidsky (2000).

[62] See *Barrett v. Rosenthal*, 12 Cal. Rptr. 3d 48 (Cal. 2004) (pending appeal from lower court findings with respect to statutory construction and legislative history of Section 230); *Grace v. eBay, Inc.*, 2004 WL 2376664 (Cal. 2004) (similar appeal also pending).

the *Zeran* court makes an additional mistake when it assumes that a mere accusation would be sufficient to trigger ISP liability. In a more familiar setting, that sounds absurd. Would a court really hold a large bookseller accountable for defamation solely because a random patron informed the cashier that a particular title contained an unlawful communication? Of course not. Tort law requires only that a distributor take reasonable precautions. As applied to ISPs, that likely means that an ISP would not be required to do anything in cases where the only warning was an isolated accusation; a serious response would be required only upon a greater showing, such as the sort of detailed showing that the Digital Millennium Copyright Act requires before the protections and obligations of that statute are triggered.[63]

On the second looming interpretive question – whether the word "information" as used in Section 230 includes only those communications that would otherwise be regulated under defamation and similar expressive tort theories or instead expands to include the various forms of malicious computer code of interest to us – we have found only one case. In *Green v. America Online*,[64] a subscriber (a man named John Green) claimed that another user sent him a malicious program through a chat room. In the words of the court,

> Green alleges that John Doe 1 "sent a punter through [Green's ISP, America Online (AOL)], which caused Green's computer to lock up and Green had to restart his computer." Green's complaint describes a "punter" as a computer program created by a hacker whose purpose is to halt and disrupt another computer. . . . Green alleges that he lost five hours of work restarting his computer, causing him damages of approximately $400.[65]

Green apparently asked AOL to take action against the unidentified hacker, but AOL refused to do so. Green sued AOL for negligently failing to "police its services."[66]

The court held that Green's tort claim was barred. First, citing *Zeran*, the court neglected the distinction between publisher-style strict liability and distributor-style negligence liability, announcing simply that holding AOL liable for negligence would impermissibly treat AOL as a speaker or publisher.

---

[63] See 17 U.S.C. § 512(c)(3)(A) (requiring that a complainant submit, among other things, a statement under penalty of perjury certifying that the complainant is providing accurate information regarding the alleged infringement and that the complainant is either the owner of the copyright in question or an authorized agent representing that owner).

[64] *Green v. America Online*, 318 F.3d 465 (3d Cir. 2003).

[65] Id. at 469. John Doe 1 and another user also allegedly posted defamatory statements about Green.

[66] Id.

Then the court applied this expanded immunity to the facts at hand, reasoning that John Doe 1 is an information content provider, and AOL must therefore be immune from any form of liability thanks to Section 230. Green had argued that John Doe 1 is not an information content provider because Doe sent a malicious computer program rather than any intelligible "information." But the court rejected that argument, noting that the dictionary definition of "information" includes any "signal," and a computer program sent through the Internet is just a collection of encoded signals.[67] In short, the court concluded that malicious code is "information," John Doe I is an "information content provider," Section 230 applies to all tort claims involving third-party information, and thus AOL is not liable.

This reasoning is dubious. In terms of the statute, the word "information" is ambiguous: it could include any set of signals that is not random noise, or it could be limited to signals that are used to communicate with humans. More importantly, the concern that motivated Section 230 was the worry that, as a practical matter, ISPs cannot control or police defamatory content without violating the privacy of their users and chilling legitimate discussion. But that concern does not extend to situations like the one presented here. Judgments about defamation are unavoidably subjective and context-specific, a reality that makes it all but impossible for ISPs to detect and hence deter that bad act. A computer program that shuts down a target computer, by contrast, can be more readily and less intrusively identified. Besides, the social costs of a system where a few innocent programs are accidentally delayed by an overly cautious ISP seem much less onerous than the social costs associated with an equivalently imperfect filter that might interfere with socially important free speech.

Given all this, we urge courts to reject the analysis of *Green v. America Online* and instead to interpret Section 230 such that its immunity extends to "information" that is intelligible to human beings – either in the raw or as translated by communication devices such as telephones or computers – but not to mere signals that interfere with Internet communication by shutting down computers or clogging bandwidth.[68] That would link Section 230 to the tort claims it was designed to regulate; it is fully consistent with the language, history, and policies associated with the Communications Decency Act; and it would free courts to consider the proper contours for ISP liability with respect to issues of cybersecurity.

---

[67] Id. at 471.

[68] Consistent with our remarks at the start of this section, we would be equally happy to see Congress amend the Communications Decency Act in this manner.

B. Common Law Principles

Not only have courts been expanding the scope of the immunity offered by the Communications Decency Act, they also have been questioning whether common law liability ought to extend to ISPs in the first place. The best discussion we have found of this issue is in *Doe v. GTE Corporation*.[69] The case involved a suit by various athletes who were secretly filmed while undressing in locker rooms. The athletes sued the producers and sellers of the videotapes – Franco Productions and other entities – but, because they correctly anticipated that these defendants would disappear without a trace, the athletes also sued the several ISPs that had hosted Franco's websites. Judge Easterbrook wrote for the panel, and, after resolving some interpretive questions regarding a federal privacy statute and offering some ideas about the various ways to read Section 230 of the Communications Decency Act, he held that plaintiffs had failed to assert a state common law claim. His analysis on this point is why the case is of interest to us.

Easterbrook makes several observations that will be familiar from our discussion. He notes that landlords are not held liable for dangerous activities that occur on their premises, carriers such as Federal Express are not held liable for failing to prevent shipments of dangerous objects, telephone companies are not liable for allowing customers to use phone lines maliciously, and so forth. Easterbrook then suggests that ISPs should be no different:

> That [one of the defendant ISPs] supplied some inputs . . . into Franco's business does not distinguish it from the lessor of Franco's office space or the shipper of the tapes to its customers. Landlord, phone company, delivery service, and web host all *could* learn, at some cost, what Franco was doing with the services and who was potentially injured as a result; but state law does not require those providers to learn, or to act as good Samaritans if they do. The common law rarely requires people to protect strangers, or for that matter acquaintances or employees.[70]

Easterbrook is right that the common law rarely requires anyone to be a Good Samaritan. Where Easterbrook errs, however, is in assuming that ISP liability is best understood as a Good Samaritan rule rather than as a traditional tort. The distinction is important because, while the common law rarely creates Good Samaritan obligations, it routinely uses tort law to accomplish similar goals. Thus it is tort law, rather than any Good Samaritan obligation, that pressures drivers to watch out for stranger-pedestrians, and it is again tort law that encourages firms to think twice before polluting a stranger-neighbor's

---

[69] *Doe v. GTE Corporation*, 347 F.3d 655 (7th Cir. 2003).
[70] Id. at 661 (emphasis in original).

land. Easterbrook never explains why he dismisses ISP liability as if it is some unusual obligation to do nice things for strangers rather than a conventional application of familiar tort law principles.[71]

We are sympathetic if Easterbrook was simply trying to reach the right outcome in the case at hand. It is difficult and perhaps even impossible for ISPs to monitor websites for the sale of illegal videotapes because such tapes cannot easily be distinguished from perfectly legitimate video content. Given those difficulties, we agree that the ISPs sued in this particular case should not have been held accountable for their role in transmitting the tapes. We resist Easterbrook's analysis, however, because in other settings ISPs may be able to do more. Just as a delivery service might be held liable for delivering a package that obviously contains a bomb, or a landlord might be held liable for permitting a use of his premises that is overtly illegal,[72] ISPs might rightly be held liable for permitting malicious behaviors that they could have detected or deterred at reasonable cost. Easterbrook's opinion gives the impression that ISPs ought never be held liable for harms done to third parties. That judgment is overbroad and premature.

IV. CONCLUSION

Controversies over indirect liability have been prominent in recent years, sparked in no small measure by questions over who, if anyone, should be held liable for the rampant copyright infringement that as of this writing continues to be a significant feature of life online. With that in mind, we conclude with some remarks about how our comments on cybersecurity relate to that other debate, along the way clarifying the outer limits of our position and also suggesting areas for further research.

At the outset, it must be noted that, on its own terms, indirect liability knows few bounds, and thus there is almost always an argument to bring yet another entity into the chain of liability. In the copyright wars, for example, the first round of litigation was against the websites that facilitate infringement by offering services that directly or indirectly match would-be music uploaders with would-be music downloaders.[73] The battle soon expanded to ensnare the

---

[71] For some insight into where to draw the line, see *Stockberger v. United States*, 332 F.3d 479, 481 (7th Cir. 2003) (Posner, J.) (suggesting reasons not to compel rescues and other magnanimous behaviors).

[72] See, for example, *Fonovisa v. Cherry Auction*, 76 F.3d 259 (9th Cir. 1996).

[73] See *A&M Records, Inc. v. Napster, Inc.*, 239 F.3d 1004 (9th Cir. 2001); *In re Aimster Copyright Litigation*, 334 F.3d 643, 650–1 (7th Cir. 2003); *MGM Studios, Inc. v. Grokster, Ltd.*, 259 F. Supp. 2d 1029 (C. D. Cal. 2003).

venture capital firms that fund those entities[74] and even the ISPs that provide the infrastructure over which music piracy takes place.[75] In our setting, one could quite similarly talk about imposing liability on Microsoft, the theory being that the vulnerabilities in the Windows operating system are akin to the design defects actionable in products liability law, or Dell, for the role its nearly ubiquitous computer systems play in the struggle for cybersecurity.

Extending liability in this way would not necessarily be unwise. Microsoft, for example, surely can design its initial software to be less vulnerable to Internet misbehavior. This is simply a matter of investing more resources in product design as well as testing. Microsoft could also redesign its software such that customers would be required to download patches when necessary, perhaps under the threat that the software will stop working if the latest patch is not downloaded within a specified period. This would be a minimally intrusive way to ensure that users keep their antivirus precautions up to date – a bit like mandatory vaccinations for school children. Further, even if Microsoft cannot take additional precautions, we pointed out earlier that the price increase that would result from an increase in liability would itself have some policy allure in that the resulting price would better reflect the relative value of the Windows operating system as compared to competing alternatives like Mac OS.

All that said, however, as a practical matter the chain of liability cannot extend forever, and thus in the end choices must be made as to which entities are best positioned to support enforcement of the law. The right thought experiment is to imagine that all the relevant entities and all the victims and all the bad actors can efficiently contract one to another and then to ask how the parties would in that situation allocate responsibility for detecting and deterring bad acts. Our firm suspicion in the cybersecurity arena is that ISPs would in that negotiation end up with significant responsibilities for policing Internet activity; but that might not be true in the copyright setting, and it is certainly a conclusion that might change if there are radical changes in the abilities of other entities to prevent and deter bad acts.

Another distinction between the literature on copyright infringement and our own inquiry regarding cybersecurity comes in understanding the direction of the externality imposed. The possibility of copyright infringement increases the average subscriber's willingness to pay for broadband Internet service. Indeed, music piracy is in many ways the "killer app" that is today driving

---

[74] The venture capital firm of Hummer Winblad, e.g., was sued for its role in funding Napster (Lemley and Reese 2004, 1347 n. 11).

[75] See *RIAA v. Verizon Internet Servs.*, 351 F.3d 1229 (D.C. Cir. 2003) (dispute over the conditions under which an ISP must identify subscribers who are accused of being involved in online infringement).

the deployment of broadband Internet service to the home. As such, there is a silver lining to the bad act of copyright infringement. The opposite is true, however, for worms and viruses, each of which imposes a cost on the average user and thus reduces the incentive to subscribe. This leads to two conflicting implications. One is that policymakers should on this theory be marginally more interested in imposing liability for cyberinsecurity than they are in imposing liability for music piracy; in essence, the former is a barrier to broadband deployment whereas the latter is a camouflaged subsidy. The other implication is that legal rules might at the same time be less necessary, because ISPs already have a strong incentive to improve cybersecurity (subscribers favor it) whereas ISPs have no similar incentive when it comes to fighting copyright infringement.

Yet another important distinction is that the copyright dispute is in many ways a dispute about the propriety of the underlying property right rather than a dispute about the proper contours of indirect liability per se. Many of those who oppose liability in the copyright setting also question, in a more fundamental way, the scope and duration of federal copyright grants. That radically alters the nature of the debate as compared to our setting, where there is widespread agreement that worms, viruses, and denial-of-service attacks are rightly deemed illegal and the real question comes only in determining how best to discourage these counterproductive behaviors.

Finally, the copyright dispute is one where there are a variety of plausible legal responses, and thus policymakers must tread carefully as they try to determine which approach offers the best balance in terms of costs and effectiveness. Is the best approach to facilitate lawsuits against the specific individuals who upload and download music?[76] Would it be better to recognize indirect liability as a supplement to direct liability or even a substitute for it?[77] What about the idea of rejecting legal responses entirely and encouraging instead self-help techniques like more effective encryption of digital content?[78] These are plausible

---

[76] Some commentators believe so and argue that copyright law should reject indirect liability and instead focus on procedural reforms that would make direct lawsuits less costly. Lemley and Reese (2004), for example, take this position. The challenge for these commentators comes in squaring their argument with the real-world empirical data: thousands of lawsuits have been filed, and yet illegal file swapping continues, largely undeterred.

[77] For discussion, see Lichtman and Landes (2003).

[78] For one effort along these lines, see Implementation of Section 304 of the Telecommunications Act of 1996, 18 FCC Rcd. 20885 (2003) (requiring hardware manufacturers to cooperate with efforts to encrypt digital content distributed via cable and broadcast television). Interestingly, the possibility of self-help has posed a significant challenge to the federal government's efforts to control the online distribution of offensive material that is inappropriate for minors. The problem? The Supreme Court seems to think that filters installed by home users can be so effective that they render more heavy-handed restrictions on speech – like the Child Online Protection Act – unconstitutional. See *Ashcroft v. ACLU*, 124 S. Ct. 2783 (2004).

questions in the copyright setting; parallel questions in the context of cybersecurity, however, ring hollow. That is, as we have already emphasized, holding individuals directly responsible for worms and viruses is all but impossible given that individual bad actors are so difficult to track and, even when identified, usually lack the resources necessary to pay for the damage they cause. And as we have also pointed out, while self-help techniques like firewalls and antivirus software do have a role to play in improving cybersecurity, it is hard to imagine that these sorts of precautions can be a sufficient response to the problem, let alone a response that is so attractive as to justify blanket immunity for ISPs. The viability of alternative legal strategies is thus a final important distinction to draw between these two settings. The existence of such strategies should give pause to advocates and critics alike in the copyright debates, but they seem significantly less salient when it comes to the question of whether ISPs should be liable for their role in creating and propagating malicious Internet code.

REFERENCES

Arlen, Jennifer. 1994. The Potentially Perverse Effects of Corporate Criminal Liability. *Journal of Legal Studies* 23:833.

Benjamin, Stuart M., Douglas G. Lichtman, and Howard A. Shelanski. 2001. *Telecommunications Law and Policy.* Durham, NC: Carolina Academic Press.

Chu, C. Y. Cyrus, and Yingyi Qian. 1995. Vicarious Liability under a Negligence Rule. *International Review of Law and Economics* 15:205.

Dobbs, Dan B. 2000. *The Law of Torts.* Eagan, MN: West.

Hamdani, Assaf. 2002. Who's Liable for Cyberwrongs? *Cornell Law Review* 87:901.

Katyal, Neal Kumar. 2001. Criminal Law in Cyberspace. *University of Pennsylvania Law Review* 149:1003.

Kraakman, Reinier. 1986. Gatekeepers: The Anatomy of a Third-Party Enforcement Strategy. *Journal of Law and Economics* 2:53.

———. 1998. Third Party Liability. In *The New Palgrave Dictionary of Economics and the Law,* ed. Peter Newman, 583. New York: Palgrave Macmillan.

Ku, Ray. 2001. Irreconcilable Differences? Congressional Treatment of Internet Service Providers as Speakers. *Vanderbilt Journal of Entertainment Law and Practice* 3:70.

Lemley, Mark A., and R. Anthony Reese. 2004. Reducing Digital Copyright Infringement without Reducing Innovation. *Stanford Law Review* 56:1345.

Lichtman, Douglas. 2000. Property Rights in Emerging Platform Technologies. *Journal of Legal Studies* 29:615.

Lichtman, Douglas, and William Landes. 2003. Indirect Liability in Copyright: An Economic Perspective. *Harvard Journal of Law and Technology* 16:395.

Lidsky, Lyrissa. 2000. Silencing John Doe: Defamation and Discourse in Cyberspace. *Duke Law Journal* 49:855.

McManus, Brian. 2001. Rethinking Defamation Liability for Internet Service Providers. *Suffolk University Law Review* 35:647.

Netanel, Neil. 2003. Impose a Noncommercial Use Levy to Allow Free Peer-to-Peer File Sharing. *Harvard Journal of Law and Technology* 17:1.

Schruers, Matthews. 2002. The History and Economics of ISP Liability for Third Party Content. *Virginia Law Review* 88:206.

Shavell, Steven. 1987. *Economic Analysis of Accident Law.* Cambridge, MA: Harvard University Press.

Sheridan, David. 1997. Zeran v. AOL and the Effect of Section 230 of the Communications Decency Act upon Liability for Defamation on the Internet. *Albany Law Review* 61:147.

Sykes, Alan. 1981. An Efficiency Analysis of Vicarious Liability under the Law of Agency. *Yale Law Journal* 91:168.

———. 1984. The Economics of Vicarious Liability. *Yale Law Journal* 93:1231.

———. 1988. The Boundaries of Vicarious Liability: An Economic Analysis of the Scope of Employment Rule and Related Legal Doctrines. *Harvard Law Review* 101:563.

———. 1998. Vicarious Liability. In *The New Palgrave Dictionary of Economics and the Law,* ed. Peter Newman, 673. New York: Palgrave Macmillan.

EIGHT

GLOBAL CYBERTERRORISM, JURISDICTION, AND INTERNATIONAL ORGANIZATION

Joel P. Trachtman*

I. INTRODUCTION

The rise of cyberspace has greatly facilitated all kinds of activity, including commercial, social, and governmental interaction. There is no doubt that cyberspace today constitutes valuable real estate indeed. We have also routed our control of many real-world processes through cyberspace. Because of this increased value, the security of cyberspace has grown in importance.

The rise of cyberspace and the rise of terrorism may be understood as antagonists in a modernist drama. Both have evolved from state sponsorship into relatively independent and decentralized phenomena. Both exist outside the state. Both use network forms of organization alongside other forms of organization. Cyberspace is both a tool and a target of terrorists. It could also be a tool against terrorists. Most critically, cyberspace is a tool of human interaction and commerce, while terrorism is the nemesis of human interaction and commerce. So, these forces, although similar in structure, are natural opponents.

The rise of terrorism, as one type of asymmetric and distributed warfare, has threatened not only the gains derived from cyberspace but the activities that now come to depend on communication through cyberspace infrastructure. Individuals and governments wish to ensure that they will continue to reap the benefits of cyberspace and that cyberspace controls will not be turned against them. Their enemies see cyberspace as a high-value target. And indeed, during Al Qaeda's reign in Afghanistan, it developed an academy of cyberterrorism,

*Professor of International Law, The Fletcher School of Law and Diplomacy, Tufts University. This paper was prepared in connection with the Conference on the Law and Economics of Cybersecurity, George Mason University School of Law, June 11, 2004. Thanks to participants of that conference for helpful comments as well as to Carolyn Gideon, William Martell, Viktor Mayer-Schoenberger, and Jonathan Zittrain for comments. Thanks also to Christine Makori for able research assistance. Any errors are mine.

seeking means to attack the cyberspace infrastructure of the West (Gellman 2002).

This chapter is concerned with a narrow component of the cybersecurity policy analysis that the United States and similar countries must perform. It analyzes the jurisdictional and organizational facets of international security against cyberterrorism. In order to do so, it first posits a set of terrorist threats to cyberspace and a set of social goals in response to these threats. This is a "nested," iterative, and recursive analysis, which requires assessment or assumptions regarding goals at one level in order to move on to the next level. Once we reach an understanding of what is possible at the next vertical level, it may be necessary to go back and modify our assessment at an earlier level. Part of the complexity, of course, arises from the fact that different states will experience these threats differently, with a resulting asymmetry of concern.

In order to examine the need for and potential structure of international cooperation to combat cyberterrorism, it is necessary first to examine several subsidiary questions. First, to what extent, and in what contexts, is government regulation appropriate to combat cyberterrorism? This is the first level of the subsidiarity analysis: is government action necessary? Second, to what extent, and in what contexts, is domestic government, while possibly necessary, insufficient to combat cyberterrorism? This is a second level of subsidiarity analysis: is local regulation sufficient or is international cooperation necessary?[1] Third, what form shall international cooperation take: should it be in the form of ad hoc or nonlegal and nonorganizational relationships among states, or should it be in the form of more formal law or organization? Fourth, what should be the content or responsibilities of this more formal law or organization? This chapter cannot answer these questions, but it suggests an analytical framework that may be used to address these questions in a broader research project.

As suggested, where regulation is called for, the next question is a choice of levels of regulation: subnational, national, regional, international law, or international organization. This paper provides a brief analysis of the problem of allocation of authority – of jurisdiction – over different components of cyberspace, both horizontally and vertically. This analysis is dependent on the particular facts of cyberspace and threats to cybersecurity. This analysis uses tools from property rights theory, regulatory competition theory, and game theory. Next, this paper examines some potential sources of analogy with the international problem of security against cyberterrorism.

---

[1] While I state these concerns in rather stark terms of necessity and sufficiency, the more correct analysis speaks in more nuanced terms of relative efficiency.

These sources of analogy include arrangements to control cybercrime, arrangements to control financing of terrorism, and security arrangements for ocean transport.

II. CATEGORIZING CYBERTERRORISM SECURITY THREATS

It is not possible to eliminate global threats to cybersecurity completely, except by an extreme and highly damaging form of autarky. By "global threats," I mean threats that originate outside the target state's borders or that originate within the target state's borders but are initiated by foreign persons or agents of foreign persons. However, there are different types of threats to different types of targets, and it is important to differentiate. Differentiation may allow a selective response that would be less damaging than autarky but would provide sufficient protection.

A. Terms and Parameters

It is also worth noting that cyberterrorism from a domestic source is no less dangerous than cyberterrorism from abroad. While domestic cyberterrorism may be more amenable to surveillance, identification, and response, at least in legal terms, neither domestic nor foreign cyberterrorism is wholly preventable.

Before we can consider appropriate government responses to international cyberterrorism, it is necessary to define some terms and parameters for analysis. Important terms are "cyberspace," "cybersecurity," "cybercrime," and "cyberterrorism."

In this paper, by "cyberspace," I mean simply the Internet, a network of networks to handle communications between computers. The main activities in cyberspace are accessing web pages and communicating through e-mail. "Cybersecurity" is a broad term for security against disruption and misuse of Internet facilities. "Cybercrime" includes a full range of traditional crime effected using the Internet as well as "new" crimes involving criminalized disruption and misuse of the Internet. "Cyberterrorism" is a type of cybercrime that is categorized as terrorism.[2] This paper examines the issue of security against cyberterrorism without addressing the difficulties involved in distinguishing terrorists from freedom fighters.

Thus, cybersecurity includes more than defense against cyberterrorism. Cybersecurity includes protection against all forms of cybercrime, including fraud, theft of information, and theft of goods or services through

---

[2] On the difficulty of defining "cyberterrorism," see Goodman (2003).

cybermanipulation; destruction in real space through cybermanipulation; cybervandalism; destruction or impairment of networks; and other hacking. Given its link to cybercrime, cyberterrorism is, to begin with, an issue of surveillance, interdiction, and punishment, often through law enforcement rather than military action. It is in this sense that the border between cybercrime and cyberterrorism may be unclear.

One possible feature of terrorism is uncertainty about the author of the act of terrorism. This feature is often available in real-space terrorism, and it seems also available in cyberterrorism. Obviously, uncertainty regarding the author makes response and deterrence difficult.

While the border between cybercrime and cyberterrorism may be unclear in some contexts, smaller scale cybercrime may be more satisfactorily addressed through conventional methods of detection, deterrence, law enforcement, and evolution of networks than cyberterrorism or cyberwarfare. The magnitude and the efficacy of *ex post* responses, often incorporating lessons learned from the attack, matter. The magnitude of the risk presented by cyberterrorism or cyberwarfare may be such that we cannot afford to absorb a certain level of risk: it is not acceptable to absorb the risk of a first attack and allow networks to evolve in response. It is in this sense that one cyber–Pearl Harbor or cyber-9/11 is said to be unacceptable (Clarke 1999). It is also worth noting that the motivations of cyberterrorism are different from those of ordinary cybercrime. This difference in motivation may indicate the need for a different response, as ordinary law enforcement techniques may not be able to deter a perpetrator motivated by political or religious zeal.

B. Analytical Framework

As we attempt to describe some of the parameters of cyberterrorism, it is useful to establish an analytical framework for discussion. There are two main categories: (1) the value, vulnerability, and protection available with respect to the target ("risk variables"), and (2) control over the target and control over the potential attacker ("control variables"). Control variables will determine the response to risk variables and can be used to reduce or increase the aggregate risk. The risk variable profile will affect the importance of control variables. So, the first analytical question is, how big is the existing risk, to whom does it accrue, and how can it be modified? The second analytical question is, who controls the target and the attacker and do they have appropriate incentives and capability to respond to – to modify – the risk profile presented by the risk variables? The controlling person could be a private person, one or more governments, and/or an international organization. The choices of private persons may be constrained through legal rules, while the choices of governments may be constrained through international law.

Theory would suggest that states should seek an optimal level of congruence, which will be less than full congruence, between control and risk. This is no different from saying that in domestic property rights analysis policymakers seek to achieve an optimal level of internalization of externalities.

C. Factors Relating to the Value, Vulnerability, and Protection of the Target

Thus, our first analytical question regards the risk-adjusted value of a particular target and the degree to which the risk may be reduced through a variety of protective actions.

1. **Type of Network and Value as a Target.** There is no such thing as a completely secure network. As noted, advanced societies have come to depend more and more on electronic communications and information-processing networks in order to communicate, coordinate production, and transmit all manner of information. Advanced societies are thus more vulnerable to cyberterrorism than less industrialized societies. This is one way in which cyberterrorism may be understood as a form of asymmetric warfare: the cost of disruption of cyberspace is greater to advanced societies. This asymmetry may make international cooperation more difficult.

Not all networks are, or must be, attached to the Internet, and all networks are not alike in susceptibility to attack or attractiveness as a target. It is important to distinguish the different types of networks that may be subjected to attack.

- First are military and civilian defense networks. These networks must be hardened against the most aggressive attack, whether in real space or cyberspace. On the other hand, these networks are eligible for seclusion or quarantine in a way that may make them far less susceptible to attack.
- Second are other government networks, including networks for emergency response, police, fire, health, and traffic control and other critical government service networks. These networks may utilize the public Internet or separate facilities, but they also may be separated from the public Internet.
- Third are privately or publicly owned networks used to control public utilities and other systems for providing infrastructural services or goods. These include networks that control provision of electricity, oil and gas, water, food, financial services, communication services, and medical services.

- Fourth are public networks used by individual consumers and businesses for communication, education, shopping, and other less directly critical activities.

The more protection concentrated in the highest-value targets, the greater the threat to the lower-value targets. This is a paradox of terrorism generally: when military targets are hardened, civilian targets become more attractive; when airlines have impenetrable security, terrorists attack trains. So it is difficult to rely on distinctions among targets in terms of their relative attractiveness. This paradox also means that increasing target-specific protection creates increasing the need for protection, as additional targets become relevant.

Nevertheless, different types of networks will vary in terms of their attractiveness as targets; the costs, including opportunity costs, of protecting them; and the ease with which they may be attacked.

2. Type of Attack. This paper is not a technical treatment of the risks of cyberterrorism, but for expositional purposes, it is useful to briefly list the types of cyberattacks available to the cyberterrorist. Cyberterrorists may disrupt networks through malevolent software ("malware") known as worms, viruses, Trojan horses, etc. Attacks using such software affect individual computers. Cyberterrorists can target particular sites through denial-of-service (DOS) attacks, which seek to overload sites.[3] Cyberterrorists can also attack the very infrastructure of the Internet itself, such as nodes, routers and other parts of the physical backbone, disrupting the Internet more centrally. The Internet's logical backbone might also come under attack, such as domain name servers and search engines.

In addition to disrupting networks, cyberterrorists may engage in breach-of-security attacks for espionage or other purposes. They may steal information valuable to national security in the real world. They may replace true information with false information. They may attack real-space assets by taking command of networks used to control infrastructure assets and causing havoc with those assets. By co-opting these assets, they may cause damage or disrupt the ability of these assets to perform their tasks. These assets could include public utilities such as communications, transportation, power, and water or could include public services such as police, fire, and health services. Importantly, they could include private sector assets critical to the economy, including banking, communications, and even retail industry assets.

---

[3] As this paper was being prepared, the British Government disclosed a significant flaw in TCP protocols, allowing disruption of the capacity of routers by sending false reset signals. See http://www.uniras.gov.uk/vuls/2004/236929/index.htm.

All of these activities may have substantial effects in real space and, in particular, in the real economy. As then U.S. National Security Advisor Condoleeza Rice said, at least for the United States, the cybereconomy is the economy (Verton 2002).

3. Types of Response Available. Threats vary, networks vary, contexts vary, and tools available to different private sector actors and to different governments vary. Therefore, there is no universal best response, at the private sector or government level, to the risk of cyberterrorism. There are several important tools. These include (1) limitation of terrorist access to networks, (2) *ex ante* surveillance of networks in order to interdict or repair injury, (3) *ex post* identification and punishment of attackers, and (4) establishment of more robust networks that can survive attack. For purposes of our analysis of jurisdictional and international cooperation issues, we assume that governments will wish to operate in each of these categories of response.

a. Access Limits. Cyberterrorism may be prevented by limiting access to networks. This can be achieved through ingress and egress filtering in the relevant routers, or firewalls. There are three main ways to implement access limitations: (1) by reference to location of origin, (2) by reference to the person of origin, and (3) by reference to content. However, the U.S. Central Intelligence Agency opined in April 2001 as follows:

- The growing connectivity among secure and insecure networks creates new opportunities for unauthorized intrusions into sensitive or proprietary computer systems within critical U.S. infrastructures, such as the nation's telephone system.
- The complexity of computer networks is growing faster than the ability to understand and protect them by identifying critical nodes, verifying security, and monitoring activity. The prospects for a cascade of failures across U.S. infrastructures are largely known and understood (Gannon 2001).

It is very difficult to limit access reliably by reference to location or person of origin, as it is fairly easy to establish relay or alias arrangements that will mask these characteristics or to use satellite or telephone access that will evade filters (Froomkin 1997). Moreover, location and personality limitations may not provide sufficient security, as persons from permissible locations, and permissible persons, may commit acts of cyberterrorism.

Reliable digital passports or digital fingerprints or a unique biometric identification that would reliably identify the sender might reduce the possibility of cyberterrorism, or of cyberterrorism without the ability to identify the author. However, if terrorists are willing to be suicide bombers in the real world, they presumably will be willing to identify themselves in cyberspace. It is entirely possible for a terrorist to satisfy the requirements of trust simply in order to obtain sufficient access to perform the planned act of terrorism.

Content filtering is more reliable, but comes at significant cost in terms of speed of connection and loss of benign content. It is also possible to monitor and limit messages associated with DOS attacks. Other prophylaxis measures may be possible.

b. Ex ante Surveillance, Detection, and Interdiction. Surveillance is related to both identification and content monitoring. It would also examine flows and groups of data packets in order to identify trends that suggest threats. Once attacks are detected, specific avenues of attack may be closed or particular damage may be repaired. In addition, if these packets can be traced back to their origin, it may be possible to respond with either cyberspace or real-space measures. Surveillance, detection, and interdiction raise jurisdictional issues discussed in the next subsection.

c. Identification of Author, Response, Deterrence, and Punishment. What is the purpose of identifying the authors of a cyberterrorist attack? As noted, the likelihood of identification and punishment may not result in deterrence. However, identification of the author may deter some terrorists and may deter state-sponsored cyberterrorism or even state toleration or hosting of cyberterrorism. No state will wish to be identified as the electronic Afghanistan vis-à-vis an electronic Al Qaeda.

Furthermore, either cyberspace or real-space response, whether interdiction or punishment, may raise important jurisdictional issues. Does the target state have jurisdiction to take action against citizens or residents of the home state, either virtual action or physical action? These questions of jurisdiction to adjudicate and enforce raise significant legal issues. These issues are raised in connection with law enforcement. However, to the extent that state toleration or sponsorship is at play, they may be converted to issues of *casus belli*: whether the attacked state has a basis for military response under international law (U.S. Department of Defense 1999) and in public opinion. Of course, *casus belli* will only matter where the attacked state poses a real military threat to the sponsor state.

From the standpoint of international cooperation, the important point here is that it may be difficult to identify the source of cyberterrorism, and therefore it may be difficult to identify defection by any government. This would place emphasis on monitoring the quality of the measures taken by foreign governments to prevent cyberterrorism by persons subject to their jurisdiction.

d. Robust Networks. The Internet itself was designed to achieve a certain measure of robustness inherent in decentralization. However, these features do not necessarily result in diversity or in complete invulnerability. Of course, even if there was such a thing as a perfectly secure network, it would be prohibitively costly and constrained. But could networks be made in such a way that they have characteristics of decentralization, diversity, robustness, and redundancy that allow them to survive any plausible attack? Would networks evolve this way without government intervention, or is government intervention needed to provide appropriate incentives for this evolution? Collective production could produce more robust technology (Benkler 2002).

One benefit of decentralization, as regards both hardware and software, is the development of diversity, with the evolutionary benefits of a diverse stock of technological DNA.[4] Under these circumstances, networks would evolve in Darwinian terms and would withstand shocks. However, the shocks of Darwinian evolution might be more disruptive than we wish to endure, and there is no assurance that the entire network might not become extinct.

D. Factors Relating to the Control and Jurisdiction over the Network and the Attacker

Once the nature of the network and the threat against it are understood, it becomes important to evaluate issues of control: do those responsible for making decisions regarding protection have appropriate incentives to take efficient protective action?

1. Whose Network? Cyberterrorism may involve threats to either government networks or private networks. The point is that cyberterrorism is not by any means limited to attacks on government. In fact, with critical infrastructure largely in the hands of private actors, cyberterrorism attacks on critical infrastructure will largely involve attacks on private networks. Therefore, protection against cyberterrorism will require protection of private networks, raising the question of whether private actors have sufficient capability and incentives to take appropriate precautions or whether government intervention is required.

---

[4] But see Chapter 4 in this book.

2. Which Government? In Section V, I assess from a theoretical standpoint the question of allocation of authority over cyberspace activities, with reference to cyberterrorism. In this section, I describe some of the factual aspects of control.

Cyberspace is a global network. It involves many linked computers located around the world. Its hardware and software structures are relevant to the question of how different states or international organizations may exercise power – in legal terms, jurisdiction – over cyberspace.

The original root file of top-level domains – the list of domain names and their translation to numerical IP addresses that is consensually accepted as definitive – is physically located in the United States on a server controlled by ICANN (Internet Corporation for Assigned Names and Numbers). It is ultimately under the control of the U.S. government. This is a source of power over other governments that depend on the root file for their national domain names. It is also a source of power over some of the most significant domains, like .com, .net, and .org.

In other respects, the Internet is not subject to centralized power. Rather, it is a "network of networks" by which packets of data are transferred from one computer on one network to another computer on the same network or on another network. The critical power points are "backbone providers" (Kende 2000) and Internet service providers and the routers they operate (Mueller 2004). The backbone, which is the means of transmission from one network to another, is provided by backbone providers to Internet service providers. The backbones and local loops that form the physical conduits through which packets flow on the Internet are subject to the jurisdiction of the state in which they physically exist. Therefore, they are distributed among a number of jurisdictions – each country has control over the backbones and local loops physically located in its territory (Mueller 2004). This does not necessarily mean that any particular country can block all Internet access in its territory; access through satellite or difficult-to-block international telephone connections do not flow through local backbones and local loops.

The United States has substantial power vis-à-vis other governments and legitimate businesses in Internet society because of its size and the value of its market, which would allow it to impose a change in standards for the United States that would be difficult for foreign persons to reject. In this sense, the United States is capable of unilateral action to regulate the Internet but is also capable of providing incentives for other states to accept multilateral agreement along the lines of the U.S. standard: "uni-multilateralism."

3. Type of Attacker. There are two main types of terrorists: those willing to be caught and punished, so long as they carry out their mission, and those who will carry out their mission only if they have a plausible plan of escape. The first type of terrorist cannot reasonably be deterred, while the second can be deterred by effective means of identification, apprehension, and punishment. Because of the widespread fear of the first type after September 11, 2001, systems of *ex post* identification, apprehension, and punishment can offer only limited security.

Terrorists may be wholly independent, sponsored by a state, or directed by a state. Sponsorship or direction by a state, if identifiable, may provide a useful means of deterrent. On the other hand, the very purpose of state sponsorship of terrorism, instead of direct attack, is covert action and plausible deniability. The fact that cyberterrorism may be state sponsored, or part of a cyberwarfare campaign (Brenner and Goodman 2002), means that any framework for cooperation could break down just when it is most crucial to security.[5] Therefore, in order to cooperate effectively, states that are potential enemies will need to be able to provide one another with powerful assurances that they will not violate their commitments. These assurances may be similar to those needed in arms control agreements, but the problem may be that cyberwarfare agreements may be even less verifiable than real-space arms control agreements. Thus, the relationship between states that are potential enemies will differ from that between states that see themselves as long-term allies.

4. Location and Nationality of Attacker. Of course, the location and nationality of the attacker determines much about amenability to jurisdiction and the possibility of physical, as well as virtual, interdiction. Here, of course, attackers may be mobile in terms of their location and nationality, raising important questions about the utility of subuniversal arrangements for control of cyberterrorism.

III. PRIVATE SECTOR RESPONSES

Importantly, private action and private order may transcend national boundaries. Therefore, international "cooperation" through private initiatives does not face the same array of jurisdictional barriers that government initiatives face. If private action or private order can respond efficiently to the threat of cyberterrorism, then there is no need for government intervention or intergovernmental coordination. In fact, a subsidiarity perspective, congruent with a perspective based on normative individualism, would call for government action only to the extent that government action can achieve individual goals

---

[5] Many states appear to be developing cyberwarfare capabilities (Serabian 2000).

more efficiently. It is not possible to provide a complete analysis of comparative efficiency of private order compared with public regulation, even within the limited context addressed here. However, in this subsection, we try to provide a suggestive analysis of the relative benefits of private versus public order in the cyberterrorism context.

Security against cyberterrorism, even more than security against cybercrime, may be understood as a public good. Many types of security against cyberterrorism would appear to be nonrivalous in the sense that consumption by one user of this type of security would not diminish the availability of security to others. Security against cyberterrorism appears generally nonexcludible in the same sense as national security more broadly: it is impractical, and ethically suspect, to exclude some from its umbrella. There are ways in which security against cyberterrorism may be made excludible. For example, to the extent that the security is derived from software or hardware resident on the end user's computer or can be provided by an Internet service provider through its servers and made available only to that provider's customers, it is excludible. To the extent that security is excludible, it is a "club good" (Buchanan 1965; Cornes and Sandler 1996). Of course, to the extent that the Internet itself – in particular, its breadth of inclusion – provides network externalities (Economides 1996), damage to others' ability to access the Internet reduces its value even to those who retain access.

There may also be significant externalities in connection with the threat of cyberterrorism. A particular state or private sector entity may have relatively little at stake with respect to its network, but it may be that its failure to take care imposes risks on other states or other private sector actors.

Will individuals overcome the transaction cost issues to develop mechanisms to provide this public good or internalize relevant externalities without government intervention, or is government intervention necessary? It is true that the Internet has substantial transaction cost advantages that allow it to facilitate coordination.

Which group of individuals are we talking about: end users, the backbone providers and Internet service providers, or both? The number of backbone providers and Internet service providers is relatively small, which also facilitates coordination. Moreover, it may be that backbone providers and Internet service providers have appropriate incentives based on their desire to maintain the value of their networks to service consumers. Business end users that depend on the Internet for business-to-business communication and business-to-consumer selling will also have high-powered incentives to ensure the security of the Internet. These incentives are likely to be highest in connection with wealthier countries.

It is possible that even endusers would have appropriate incentives with respect to the protection of their ability to access the Internet. However, here the collective action problem is significant, and we would expect underprovision of this public good, given the difficulties in coordinating (but see Benkler 2002; see also Johnson, Crawford, and Palfrey 2004). On the other hand, as was noted, software or hardware prophylaxis may be excludible and therefore may not be a public good. In that case, we would have greater reason to expect efficient provision of security.

Do private sector actors have the tools to deliver security against cyber-terrorism? Will private sector responses result in an accentuated digital divide or other adverse social effects?[6] It is possible that private ordering might focus on solutions to the cyberterrorism problem that will not be socially optimal.

IV. GOVERNMENT INTERVENTION

It appears that some kinds of cyberterrorism security issues may be amenable to private ordering solutions. These might include issues involving spam, viruses, worms, and other methods of attacking individual computers at the end-user level. Under circumstances of sufficient diversity, decentralization, resiliency, and redundancy, society could afford to accept the risk of this type of cyberattack. Computer scientists and others skilled in assessing risk would be required to evaluate the extent to which this type of response would suffice: the extent to which conditions of diversity, decentralization, resiliency, and redundancy are sufficiently satisfied to reduce risk to a socially acceptable level.

We must compare the risk-adjusted magnitude of damage (D) with the cost of taking care (C). This is simple cost-benefit analysis where the magnitude of damage avoided constitutes the benefit. So, the subsidiarity question in this context is whether $D_p - C_p > D_g - C_g$, where D_p is the risk-adjusted magnitude of damage under private ordering, C_p is the cost of private ordering measures to take care, D_g is the risk-adjusted magnitude of damage under government regulation, and C_g is the cost of government regulation to take care. Of course, the more nuanced, and likely, comparison will examine different public-private partnerships: multiple combinations of private ordering and regulation.[7]

---

[6] On the potential dangers of exclusion generally, see Katyal (2003).

[7] There is a higher level of subsidiarity analysis that is addressed later: whether it is better to take action at an international level. Here the question is whether $D_g - C_g > D_i - C_i$, where D_i is the risk-adjusted magnitude of damage under international cooperation and C_i is the cost of international measures to take care. Again, we are likely to have hybrid measures utilizing action at all levels.

It is possible that private ordering could under some circumstances provide sufficient protection, but it is also possible that it would be efficient under some circumstances for its protection to be enhanced by public order, for example, in the form of law enforcement–type action.

It appears that other kinds of cyberterrorism security issues, those relating to essential infrastructures where risk is unacceptable, including military command and control networks, will benefit from isolation and redundancy designs. In quantitative terms, the risk of loss is preemptive and swamps the costs of taking care under any conceivable calculation. These networks must be made secure against terrorism – both cyberterrorism and real-space attack – and need not be integrated with other networks. Alternatively, firewall technology may be sufficient to isolate these networks from attack while permitting partial integration with other networks.

Therefore, it is a middle group of cyberterrorism security issues – where private ordering does not provide sufficient security, or could be assisted by supplementation, and where isolation is not acceptable or is not technologically feasible – that will require public order. These include protection of infrastructures that must remain attached to the network and for which firewalls cannot provide sufficient protection. Examples include Internet backbone networks; Internet service provider networks; banking and other financial services; telecommunication services; transportation services; health services; and fire, police, emergency, and other public services. How to protect the networks and end-user systems in these areas? Stronger firewalls, filters, and protected access to critical components seem worthy of consideration. It would be possible to establish a variety of levels of protection, dependent on the level of risk of attack and the magnitude of loss expected to be incurred from a successful attack.

Would there be sufficient incentives for any one of these sectors, or for particular entities within these sectors, to develop appropriate protection and to implement the protection? While some types of protection may best be implemented on a decentralized basis, there may be types of protection, including surveillance and interdiction, that are best implemented collectively. Is this area characterized by a collective action problem?

While not all public goods problems or collective action problems are suitable for government intervention, under some transaction costs and in some strategic circumstances government intervention will be the preferred solution.

A. The Role of Law in Different Societies

As was noted, variations in contexts, threats, and potential responses indicate that we are likely to see variations in the determination by each state of its unilateral optimal response to the threat of global cyberterrorism. Some states may determine to do nothing. They may determine that the threat is to the private sector, that there are no potential externalities or information asymmetries that would justify regulation, and that it is up to the private sector to act.

Other states may determine that a regulatory response is merited. In some circumstances, an effective regulatory response may require international coordination or cooperation. In this section, we examine the possible effectiveness of private ordering, the possible areas in which public regulation may be required, and the possible areas in which international coordination of public regulation may be required.

The degree to which public intervention is preferred in a particular state will depend on the preferences of persons in that state as well as on the available governance structures and transaction cost structures within that state. It is clear that law plays different roles in different societies, and the private-public balance is likely to be achieved in different ways in different societies. These differences produce a type of path dependency in which subsequent institutional choices are constrained.

B. Public Goods and Collective Action Problems

Not all public goods need to be provided by government, and not all collective action problems need to be solved by government. However, in some transaction cost and strategic circumstances, government may be the optimal provider of public goods and may resolve collective action problems. We have noted that some types of cyberspace security will have public goods characteristics and therefore may be underprovided without intervention of some kind. This will be an argument for government intervention. Interestingly, it will often (but not always) also be an argument for international cooperation, as the existence of public goods or collective action characteristics that call for government intervention at the domestic level may call for government intervention at the global level. This is not to say that all arguments for regulation are arguments for global regulation. There are likely to be subglobal "optimal regulatory areas" (Esty 1999; Fox 2003).

C. Externalities

Public goods problems and collective action problems are actually types of externalities where the decision of one person has effects, beneficial or detrimental, on another and where those effects are not necessarily incorporated in decision making. There are many possibilities for externalities in connection with security against cyberterrorism. Most importantly, one person's insecure network may be used to mount an attack against another person's network. Second, because of the benefits of cyberspace network externalities, the failure of one person to protect his own network may have adverse effects on others.

D. Costs of Regulation

One of the major arguments made by those who argue against all cyberspace regulation is that it is prohibitively costly, if technically possible, to regulate the "borderless" Internet. It is true that the Internet makes avoidance of national regulation by relocation easier. However, this argument militates against national regulation and makes a case for international regulation.

V. CHOICE OF HORIZONTAL PUBLIC ORDER: A TRANSACTION COST ANALYSIS OF PRESCRIPTIVE JURISDICTION IN CYBERSECURITY

Once we accept that states will have different preferences and different ways of articulating those preferences, it becomes apparent that there will be some variety in the way states approach the problem of security against cyberterrorism. Clashes of values and clashes of methods will be significant. States may have sharply divergent goals, and there may be substantial externalities. If we think of cyberterrorism as a type of cyberwarfare, some states will take the view that they benefit from the insecurity of other states.[8]

In the legal system, states initially contend over power in the form of jurisdiction. We conventionally divide jurisdiction into three components: jurisdiction to make law applicable (prescriptive jurisdiction), jurisdiction to adjudicate, and jurisdiction to enforce.[9] Without prescriptive jurisdiction and jurisdiction to adjudicate, there will be no jurisdiction to enforce within the legal system. Without jurisdiction to enforce, prescriptive jurisdiction and jurisdiction to adjudicate result only in a judgment without a means to enforce the judgment.

A. Territoriality and Aterritoriality

Just as possession is nine-tenths of the law of property, territoriality is nine-tenths of the law of jurisdiction. Of course, we must initially divide territoriality

---

[8] Contrast the network externality perspective, which suggests that each state may benefit from the security experienced by others. For a general discussion of cyberwarfare, see the Congressional Research Service (2001).

[9] The American Law Institute (1987) distinguishes prescriptive jurisdiction from judicial or enforcement jurisdiction.

into categories of conduct and effects: territorial conduct and territorial effects. Few states question the basic rule that each state has prescriptive, adjudicative, and enforcement jurisdiction over territorial conduct. In real space but even more so in cyberspace, it may sometimes be difficult to distinguish conduct from effects. For example, where firms establish a cartel to fix prices outside a state's territory and implement the price-fixing agreement by virtue of the prices that they charge inside the state's territory, is it conduct within the target state's territory?[10] Even if it is not, few states would abjure the right to respond in legal terms to actions outside their territory that cause bad effects inside their territory.

The novelty of cyberspace from a legal perspective stems from the fact that the cost of splitting conduct among multiple jurisdictions, or of locating conduct in a jurisdiction of choice, is much reduced (Trachtman 1998).

This paper adopts the fundamental analytical perspective that prescriptive jurisdiction – the right to make a state's law applicable to a particular matter – is analogous to property in a private context (Trachtman 2001). That is, jurisdiction is the right of a state to control physical assets and the activities of individuals, while "property" is the right of individuals to control physical assets. The analogy becomes more evident when we recognize that both of these rights (jurisdiction and property) involve legally constructed packages of control over things of value. The fundamental unit of analysis in both cases is the transaction: the transaction in property and the transaction in prescriptive jurisdiction. It is worth recognizing at the outset that an initial institution-building transaction creates property rights, while subsequent transactions transfer property rights. Similarly, in prescriptive jurisdiction, an initial transaction creates the initial allocation of jurisdiction, while subsequent transactions transfer it.

States act to maximize state preferences.[11] States will seek jurisdiction over matters as necessary to allow them to achieve their preferences. This is analogous to individuals seeking ownership of property that will allow them to achieve their preferences. In a primitive context, states encounter one another and may find it appropriate to engage in a particular immediate transaction. This transaction is similar to a "spot" market transaction in domestic markets. The international legal system is engaged at two moments. First, the international legal system is engaged to assign initial jurisdiction rights to the actors. Second, when these exchanges take place over time, when they are not "spot"

---

[10] In the well-known *Wood Pulp* decision, the European Court of Justice held that this was conduct within the European Communities. See Joined Cases 89, 104, 114, 116, 117 and 125-29/85, *A. Åhlstrom Oaskeyhtio v. Commission*, 1988 E. C. R. 5193, 4 Common Mkt. Rep. (CCH) ¶ 14,491 (1988); Friedberg (1991).

[11] In the context of this paper, we may elide the public choice critique of this statement.

transactions but longer-term transactions requiring the security of treaty or other law, the international legal system is engaged to facilitate these transactions, through the law of treaty and other international law.

While the international legal system contains some rules for allocation of prescriptive jurisdiction, these rules are unclear and incomplete. They are often unclear insofar as a rule, for example, of territoriality does not distinguish between territorial conduct and territorial effects: does not distinguish between what is conduct and what are effects. Furthermore, conduct may occur in multiple territories, as may effects. More importantly perhaps, rules for allocation of prescriptive jurisdiction are incomplete because they do not necessarily tell us the limits of a state's behavior in relation to its jurisdiction. For example, while states have jurisdiction over their citizens, international human rights law limits the scope of state exercise of this jurisdiction.

The international legal problem of jurisdiction over activities that may relate to or prevent cyberterrorism may be understood as a problem of incompleteness of rules allocating jurisdiction: to what extent may the United States use its territorial sovereignty over top-level domain names or other parts of the Internet as a basis to demand changes in the way that Mongolia regulates Internet service providers who locate their servers in Mongolia? Of course, rules allocating jurisdiction may be efficiently incomplete. In circumstances of low value, one would not expect property rights to arise: one would expect a *res nullius* regime. In a *res nullius* regime, as the property becomes more valuable, a common pool resource problem, or tragedy of the commons, may develop and may provide incentives to develop property rights. Similarly, as the importance, or value, to states of regulatory jurisdiction rises with the rise of the regulatory state and with enhanced transportation and communications, it is not difficult to imagine that there may be incentives to clarify rules of jurisdiction heretofore left unclear (Anderson and Hill 1975; Ault and Rutman 1979; Demsetz 1967; Field 1989; Hartman 1982; Merrill 1985; Umbeck 1977).

This can be said to be the case in connection with security against cyberterrorism. With the rise in value of the Internet and the rise in risk from terrorism, jurisdiction to address this risk has become more valuable, and it is likely that states will move from what is in effect a *res nullius* regime (at least as it addresses jurisdiction to regulate prior to an act of terrorism) to a system of property rights. Alternatively, we might say that the likely move will be from a system of jurisdiction based on territorial conduct or nationality to one that more accurately reflects the risks to the jurisdiction of territorial effects.

In circumstances where a relatively clear rule like territorial conduct would minimize the transaction costs of reallocation, as when the conduct occurs in only one location, theory predicts that such clear rules would be chosen (Trachtman 2001).

This position assumes that it would be more costly to get the initial allocation right (to align allocation with states' preferences) than to establish a system that would allow states through their autonomous actions to get the reallocation right (to engage in subsequent transactions in order to align allocation with states' preferences). Territoriality is the leading jurisdictional principle today, but it might be argued that territoriality is under pressure from two sources. First, technology like cyberspace makes territoriality less clear, as conduct relating to a particular matter may more easily occur in multiple territories. Second, territorial conduct-based jurisdiction is increasingly inconsistent with territorial effects, giving rise to greater externalities. In these circumstances, territoriality as a default rule seems less stable.

On the other hand, where it is not costly to determine which state should initially be allocated jurisdiction in order to maximize aggregate wealth, states should agree on these allocations in order to avoid the potential transaction costs of reallocation to reach these positions. Thus, where one state is affected substantially more than other involved states and the costs of reallocation are positive, it might be best to initially allocate jurisdiction to the state that is more affected. In these transaction cost circumstances, allocation of jurisdiction in accordance with effects might be selected. This would argue for allocation of authority necessary to prevent cyberspace terrorism to the United States, which (1) has the most to lose of any state, (2) is a likely target, and (3) has substantial expertise to address these problems. Alternatively, authority might be shared among the states with the most to lose. This would suggest an OECD-based regime or an ostensibly multilateral regime driven by U.S. and European interests: uni-multilateralism.

In high–transaction cost circumstances, one possibly appropriate strategy would be to establish an organization to "hold" and reallocate jurisdiction. Thus, it might be useful – it might be efficient in terms of maximizing overall welfare – to share jurisdiction over these types of problems in an organization. So horizontal jurisdiction problems may manifest themselves as subsidiarity problems: should the state retain jurisdiction or should jurisdiction be delegated to an international organization? Of course, when we ask this question, we must also ask about the governance structure of the proposed international organization.

More specifically, states would establish organizations where the transaction costs occasioned by allocation through the organization are less than those occasioned by allocation through ad hoc transactions, all other things being equal. High transaction costs of ad hoc transactions characterize circumstances in which it is difficult to make an initial allocation based on effects, combined with high transaction costs in the formal reallocation of prescriptive jurisdiction.

Furthermore, where effects are dispersed, and "holdout" problems are likely in trying to negotiate a particular "transaction" in prescriptive jurisdiction, it may be useful to states to step behind a partial veil of ignorance by establishing an organization that has some measure of "transnational" power to address the relevant issue. By "transnational," I mean that the organization's decisions are subject not to the control of each individual member but to some shared governance. A historical example of this type of conduct is the agreement of the Single European Act in 1987, in which member states of the European Community decided to accept broader use of qualified majority voting. No state could predict the circumstances in which it would be in the minority (hence, the partial veil of ignorance), but each state (presumably) estimated that it would benefit on a net basis from this modification.

Note that any assignment that differs from the status quo would have adverse distributive effects on the states ceding jurisdiction. Of course, where there is no net gain from transacting, we would expect states to refrain from transactions. Where there is a potential net gain, some type of compensation may be required in order to induce states to cede jurisdiction. These distributive consequences would implicate strategic concerns along the lines discussed below.

B. Regulatory Competition and Regulatory Cartelization

We have seen, in international taxation and in other contexts, the possibility that one state will attract market entrants, or the businesses in one state will find it efficient to export and will compete effectively against other states, because of lax regulation. Although there is still scholarly contention over empirical support for the pollution haven hypothesis, the theoretical basis for the hypothesis is unimpeachable. One of the factors that may make regulatory competition attractive – one of the assumptions in Tiebout's model – is costless mobility. The Internet provides something very close to costless mobility. And indeed, the Principality of Sealand, with hosting services administered by Havenco, is but one example of the possibility for states, or quasi-states, to position themselves at or near the bottom in terms of quantity of regulation (Gilmour 2002).[12]

Regulatory competition is thought to occur under certain conditions, suggested by the work of Tiebout. These conditions include, *inter alia*, mobility of citizens, knowledge of variations in regulatory regimes, and absence of

---

[12] It is interesting that Sealand has avoided reaching the very bottom, in terms, for example, of permitting child pornography, demonstrating that territorial jurisdiction over real assets and over people in places the people wish to live may still assert some discipline.

spillovers. Where these conditions are met, Tiebout theorized, regulatory competition could lead to pressure on governments to improve regulation. However, if the regulatory competition is predicated upon regulatory arbitrage by private actors that results in the regulating state failing to bear the costs of its lax (or inefficiently strict) regulation, leading to spillovers, regulatory competition can demean national regulation.

What has this to do with allocation of regulatory jurisdiction over the Internet? The rules for allocation of jurisdiction will determine the extent to which the regulating state will bear the costs (or experience the benefits) associated with its regulation. For example, a strict rule of territorial conduct will leave the regulating state unaccountable for extraterritorial adverse effects. Thus, the possibility of regulatory competition provides an additional source of enhanced welfare derivable from transactions in jurisdiction. Furthermore, under circumstances where externalities could cause unstable regulatory competition – races to the bottom – the availability of contingent intervention by a centralized authority, such as an international organization, can act to provide a stable equilibrium (Trachtman 2000). This latter insight provides an additional reason for states to form an organization to "share" jurisdiction in certain circumstances.

VI. STRATEGIC CONSIDERATIONS AND INTERNATIONAL LEGAL AND ORGANIZATIONAL RESPONSES

The discussions in Sections III, IV, and V suggest some of the costs and benefits, including transaction costs, of international cooperation against cyberterrorism. The transaction costs perspective outlined above assumes nonstrategic action to maximize aggregate welfare. However, an additional analytical perspective examines the strategic context of cooperation to enhance security against cyberterrorism. The payoff structure that forms this strategic context will be affected by transaction costs and by considerations of regulatory competition. Most importantly, as noted above, different states will have different, even inconsistent, preferences regarding security against cyberterrorism. One reason is that cybersecurity will be less valuable to states that use cyberspace less. Furthermore, some states will view cyberterrorism or cyberwarfare as a strategic option in the event of war and will view other states' security against cyberwarfare negatively.

Moreover, different phases or components of the cyberterrorism security issue will have different payoff structures and so will best be analyzed by analogy to different games. Some games will contain an efficient dominant strategy that will benefit each individual state and therefore will have an efficient Nash equilibrium. Other games will be characterized best as coordination or assurance games, similar to the "stag hunt" parable. Still other games will be cooperation games, more like the "prisoner's dilemma."[13]

Of course, there is also the possibility that cooperation is inefficient, resulting in a "deadlock" game in which at least one player's dominant, and efficient, strategy is to defect (Abbott 1989). Furthermore, it is likely that cyberspace security will involve asymmetric games, as cooperation will be more valuable to some players than to others.

It would be possible to generate a large number of individual games within the cyberterrorism security field. There are bilateral games and multilateral games, along with a wide array of payoff structures, including some that are symmetric and some that are asymmetric. The problem of global cyberterrorism has a payoff structure that cannot be assessed without substantial empirical analysis. These game models are simply names for particular payoff structures. As we will see later, at least under some of these games, it may be possible for states to overcome coordination problems or cooperation problems in order to reach implicit or explicit agreements. We would expect these agreements to occur, if at all, only in circumstances where the benefits to states as a group exceed the costs: where the agreements are Kaldor-Hicks efficient. Side payments may be necessary in order to reach Kaldor-Hicks efficient transactions. Side payments are by definition "outside" the initial game but may be understood as part of a broader strategic context.

In this paper, it is necessary to limit the scope of our analysis. Therefore, we will focus on three potential contexts and a possible game model for each. These analyses assume that, in at least a significant number of cases, private initiatives are not sufficient, and government intervention is necessary but not sufficient to provide an efficient level of security. The three contexts are the following:

The Cybersecurity Public Goods Game
The Coordination Problem: The Global Cyberspace Stag Hunt
The State Sponsorship of Cyberterrorism Game under Symmetric and Asymmetric Preferences

We review each of these in turn.

A. The Cybersecurity Public Goods Game

To a certain extent, the same characteristics that make some aspects of security against cyberterrorism a public good within a domestic society may also

---

[13] For an analysis of these games in the arms control context, see Abbott (1993).

Table 8.1. *A prisoner's dilemma game*

		State *B*	
		Contribute	Free-ride
State *A*	Contribute	2, 2	0, 3
	Free-ride	3, 0	0, 0

make it a "global public good." That is, given the global nature of the Internet and the global dimension of the nonrivalrous and nonexcludible nature of security against cyberterrorism discussed above, there are certain aspects of global security against cyberterrorism that would seem to have the characteristics of a public good. Therefore, states may attempt to free-ride on security measures taken by other states, resulting in underprovision of this public good. Of course, to the extent that it is possible not to share new technologies that prevent cyberterrorism, these may be understood as club goods rather than public goods. However, there will be strong incentives to share these technologies once they are produced, including marginal cost pricing and the network externalities that derive from cyberspace.

The existence of a public good often gives rise to a collective action problem: while the aggregate benefits of cooperating to produce the public good exceed the costs, each state expects the others to contribute and fails to contribute itself. Some collective action problems have payoff structures that make them prisoner's dilemmas: coordination to contribute is the optimal collective strategy, but the individual dominant solution is to decline to contribute. States may choose to contribute to the production of the public good or attempt to "free-ride." Thus, the payoff structure might be as shown in Table 8.1.

How can this problem of cooperation be resolved? As a matter of fact, in many circumstances, including some relating to the global environment, states are able to reach implicit (customary) or explicit (treaty) agreements to cooperate and are able to enforce these agreements (Barrett 2003; Norman and Trachtman forthcoming). They are able to do so among relatively patient states, in circumstances of frequently repeated, or linked, interaction, over a long duration, where information about the compliance or failure of compliance of others is readily available.[14] This problem is analogous to other global public goods problems, which are most closely analyzed in connection with environmental protection.

---

[14] For an extended analysis, see Norman and Trachtman (forthcoming).

It may well be, also, that this component of the problem of global security against cyberterrorism has characteristics of a network, in which the more states that take action to contribute, the greater the value to each state: payoffs increase with the number of states that participate. In these circumstances, it may be easier to sustain cooperation among large numbers of states (Norman and Trachtman forthcoming).

Finally, it is worth noting that a number of arms control contexts may also have the characteristics of a prisoner's dilemma, with similar responsive dynamics (Downs, Rocke, and Siverson 1985). While there may come a time when attempts are made to subject cyberwarfare to arms control, any efforts along these lines will encounter substantial problems of verification.

B. Coordination Problem: The Global Cyberspace Stag Hunt

In other areas, there is a different type of collective action problem. It may be possible for each state to choose whether to protect its own networks in a less effective way or to join together to protect global cyberspace. However, the effectiveness of the latter approach may be dependent on the extent to which other states make a similar decision. In the stag hunt, which is a type of "assurance" game, each state may obtain smaller payoffs – a lower level of protection – by seeking to protect only its networks, but if states are able to coordinate to forego settling for a lesser level of local protection or other local benefits in favor of global protection, they will each achieve a higher level of security. Cooperation may break down if players are uncertain about the preferences and strategy of others.

The stag hunt game is derived from a Rousseauian fable of cooperation among hunters (Abbott 1987). Unless all hunters are committed to catching the stag, it will escape. Each individual hunter may be tempted by a passing rabbit. Each hunter prefers a share of stag to an individual portion of rabbit but is uncertain about whether other hunters are sufficiently committed to capturing a stag. The analogy to cybersecurity is as follows: each state prefers its share of global security against cyberterrorism (stag) but may be distracted by the opportunity to provide local security (rabbit), especially if it is unsure of the commitment of other states (Table 8.2).

In international organization terms, a stag hunt context requires a lesser level of international legal inducements to compliance than a prisoner's dilemma context. Sufficient clarity regarding the definition of the cooperative behavior, monitoring to ensure compliance, and modest penalties should be sufficient. Note that we are assuming symmetry of preferences: no player actually prefers rabbit.

Table 8.2. *A stag hunt game*

		B	
		Hunt stag/global protection	Chase rabbit/local protection
A	Hunt stag/global protection	4, 4	1, 3
	Chase rabbit/local protection	3, 1	2, 2

Source: Adapted from Abbott (1989).

C. State Sponsorship of Cyberterrorism: A Game of "Chicken" or of "Bully"?

As noted above, public goods and collective action problems often involve externalities. In connection with security against cyberterrorism, we have a more direct international externality problem. It may be beneficial to state A to permit, encourage, or perpetrate cyberterrorism against state B. Even where state A does not benefit from harm to state B, it may be that acts under the jurisdictional control of state A confer harm on state B without being taken into account by state A. The potential function of international law in this context is to internalize these externalities, where it is worthwhile to do so in substantive and transaction cost terms.

In the cyberwarfare context, we may understand this as a deterrence game. In this "chicken" game, neither player has a dominant strategy (Table 8.3). In this particular case, there is no unique efficient equilibrium. Each player has two Nash equilibria: attack when the other plays peace, and play peace when the other attacks. However, both players wish to avoid the circumstance where they each play "attack," and the even split in the northwest quadrant of Table 8.3 seems intuitively attractive, although it is unstable. In order to achieve it, the players should each commit to playing "cyberpeace." International law

Table 8.3. *A chicken game*

		B	
		Cyberpeace	Attack
A	Cyberpeace	3, 3	2, 4
	Attack	4, 2	1, 1

Source: Adapted from Brams and Kilgour (1998).

Table 8.4. *A bully game involving asymmetric payoffs*

		B (deadlock player)	
		Cyberpeace	Attack
A (chicken player)	Cyberpeace	2, 1	1, 3
	Attack	3, 0	0, 2

or organization can be used to implement this commitment, by ensuring that the payoffs to defection are reduced to 3 or below through a penalty of 1 or more. It should be noted that, as with any deterrence threat, this strategy may suffer from lack of credibility: after the other party has attacked, the victim may not have incentives to retaliate (Brams and Kilgour 1988).

Each of the other models presented here assumes symmetrical preferences among states. This is obviously counterfactual. It is important to note the asymmetry among states in terms of the relative value to each state of security against cyberterrorism, on the one hand, and the relative value of cyberterrorism, on the other hand. Poor states are unlikely to be adversely affected in a significant and direct way by cyberterrorism, unless the impairment of developing country economies would have an adverse effect on them. On the other hand, cyberterrorism is a weapon that may be more available to the poor than other weapons, and so restrictions on cyberterrorism – like restrictions on sleeping under bridges – may be less attractive to the poor.

In the bully game (Table 8.4), B's dominant strategy is to attack. A does not have a dominant strategy, but if A understands B's dominant strategy to attack, it can increase its payoff from 0 to 1 by playing "cyberpeace" while B attacks. If B understand's A's dilemma, it will simply attack. If B does not understand A's dilemma, A may be able to convince B to compensate A for playing "cyberpeace," as doing so increases B's payoff from 2 to 3. This game may illustrate an asymmetric circumstance in which a global network breakdown would not harm the deadlock player much relative to the chicken player.

D. Relative and Absolute Gains

Where enmity overcomes all other values, we might understand states as engaging in a game where winning relative to other states is more important than absolute gains from interaction.[15] This can be understood in standard

---

[15] There is disagreement between institutionalists and "realists," who claim that states' interests in international relations are characterized by a search for relative gains rather than absolute gains. These realists reject the possibility of cooperation where it results in relative gains to a competitor (Busch and Reinhardt 1993; Snidal 1991).

rationalist absolute gains terms by considering that the losses associated with falling behind – with losing – are unacceptably great (Powell 1991). This is a distinction between ordinary cybercrime and cataclysmic cyberterrorism. The United States can afford to accept the risk of a few billion dollars loss due to a particularly effective virus. It cannot afford to accept the risk of sabotage of its missile control system or of destruction of its financial system.

E. Information Problems

In any real world context, there will be serious information problems that will impede both the ability of particular states to determine an appropriate strategy and the ability of states to join together in a cooperative arrangement. First, it will be difficult for one state to know another's preferences. Second, it will be difficult for one state to know another's strategy if there are multiple available strategies. This presents a problem of coordination, even where cooperation is otherwise feasible. Law may be used to help to resolve this coordination problem. Finally, as mentioned above, it could be difficult to identify the true author of any attack, making real-space or cyberspace retaliation difficult.

VII. VERTICAL CHOICE 2: INTERNATIONAL INTERVENTION

The discussions in Sections IV, V, and VI illustrate some of the reasons that states may determine to cooperate with one another to address cyberterrorism. This section discusses some possible international legal and international organizational tools available to effect cooperation, drawing from examples in cybercrime, terrorism financing, and maritime security.

A. Use of Analogs and Precedents

This paper explores analogies to other areas of international cooperation. However, there has been a debate among academics as to whether the Internet is exceptional or unexceptional in terms of its susceptibility to regulation. This debate challenges the possibility of analogical reasoning applied to cyberspace. While this debate is of some interest, there is no reason to choose between the exceptionalists and unexceptionalists in connection with cyberterrorism. There is both continuity and change in the adoption of new technologies; our question is how continuing concerns carry over into new contexts and how existing policies and mechanisms address those concerns. While there is no need to reinvent the wheel, we must be sensitive to new concerns and the need for new policies.

From their first days in law school, budding lawyers learn to analogize and to distinguish. And it is true that the law of the Internet, like the law of the horse (Easterbrook 1996; Lessig 1999b), may be understood as simply an amalgam of law that is generally, or functionally, applicable: the tax law of the horse or the Internet, the property law of the horse or the Internet, etc.

There is no doubt that much in the cybersecurity problem is analogous, both substantively and doctrinally, to preexisting problems (Trachtman 1998). And those preexisting problems have preexisting solutions. It would be foolish to argue that we can learn nothing from analogs. However, it would be equally foolish to argue that there is nothing different about cyberspace and cybersecurity or that existing solutions are presumptively sufficient. The differences may be characterized at least partially as differences of degree: of velocity and volume and of human behavior induced by these initial differences. At what point do differences of degree become differences of quality? This is not a well-posed question – the aptly posed question is, when do these differences merit a different response? And it is important to note a degree of comparative law path dependence. Not every society will require the same response, nor will every society require a response at the same time. This is a source of asymmetry even among states with the same fundamental goals.

Furthermore, it is a mistake to say that code is law (Boyle 1997; Lessig 1996a), just as it is a mistake to say that physics, biology, architecture, or automobile design is law. Yes, the physical or engineering limits on automobile design limit or otherwise affect the role of law: we do not have to regulate the interaction between automobiles and airliners in flight because automobiles do not yet fly. So, in this sense we might say that the limits of practical automobile design "take the place" of law. We might say the same about code: to the extent that code prevents activity that might otherwise raise concerns that could be addressed through law, it takes the place of law. Furthermore, it is entirely possible for law to regulate code, just as law can regulate automobile design. In this regard, code is a tool of law (Shah and Kesan 2003) and may be shaped by law, but it is not a replacement for law.

Finally on this point, another way of understanding the relationship between code and law is to understand code as an autonomous activity by at least some group of people with some set of incentives. Some have argued that through decentralized production of autonomous governance, individual actors will produce satisfactory governance.[16] To the extent that this group has incentives

---

[16] For a recent argument, see Johnson, Crawford, and Palfrey (2004).

to write code so that what would otherwise be legal concerns are addressed, then this autonomous "social norm" type of code may take the place of law. But we know that social norms do not preempt every type of law (Basu 1998). Rather, there are circumstances in which law is a more efficient solution to the problem of cooperation.

Law can also guide the development of social norms toward selected equilibria. In fact, the line between autonomous norms and law is not as clear as sometimes assumed. We might say that the state and its powers developed and are constantly changing through autonomous action, including governance mechanisms that we now bundle together as "the state." Yet, in appropriate historical and anthropological perspective, this is only different in degree from what we label "social norms."

B. Cybercrime and Cyberterrorism: The Council of Europe Cybercrime Model

On November 23, 2001, thirty states, including the United States, Canada, Japan, and South Africa, signed the Council of Europe's Cybercrime Convention.[17] This convention addresses cybercrime broadly and deals with a number of legal issues, including harmonization of substantive law, harmonization of certain procedural aspects of investigations, and facilitation of mutual legal assistance.

Under the Cybercrime Convention, states are required to establish a number of defined offenses, including crimes against the confidentiality, integrity, and availability of computer systems; their processing capacity; and their data content (Articles 2–6). These provisions require states to prohibit most types of cyberterrorism.

Under the Cybercrime Convention, each member state is required to establish laws that will enable it to intercept, preserve, search, and seize data on its networks. These include real-time monitoring of traffic data (Article 20) and interception of content data (Article 21).

Article 22 of the Cybercrime Convention provides that each party shall extend its jurisdiction over offences committed in its territory or by its nationals (where the offence is criminal under the law of the territory where it was committed or if it was committed outside any state's territory).

Perhaps the most important and interesting parts of the Cybercrime Convention for our purposes are the provisions dealing with international cooperation,

---

[17] Convention on Cybercrime, opened for signature November 23, 2001, Europ. T.S. No. 185 [hereinafter Cybercrime Convention], available at http://conventions.coe.int/Treaty/en/ Treaties/Html/185.htm. For analyses, see Kaspersen (2003) and Keyser (2003).

including extradition and mutual assistance (Articles 23–35). A broad range of cybercrimes are made extraditable offenses, and signatories are required to provide mutual assistance to the greatest extent possible in connection with the preservation and collection of requested data.

Much of the Cybercrime Convention is oriented toward law enforcement after the commission of a crime rather than interdiction of crime or cyberterrorism. Article 31 deals with mutual assistance regarding access to stored computer data, Article 33 deals with mutual assistance with respect to real-time collection of traffic data, and Article 34 deals with mutual assistance with respect to interception of content data. Thus, it can be said that, in the sense used herein, the Cybercrime Convention is a cybercrime law enforcement convention, not a cyberterrorism convention. While it would be expected to have some incremental benefits against cyberterrorism, it could not be expected to substantially reduce the risk of cyberterrorism by the most dedicated actors.

C. Data Flows and Funds Flows: Finance for Terrorism and the Financial Action Task Force Model

There is only a rough analogy between financing for terrorism, which plays an infrastructural role in terrorism, and cyberterrorism, in which cyberspace can be both the tool and the target of terrorism. The analogy is further challenged because money is a creation (at least in the final analysis) of governments. Furthermore, the less direct creators of money tend to be large financial institutions, which, although they may be co-opted for terrorism, are subject to greater scrutiny and safeguards. However, we might analogize large banks to ISPs or backbone providers. We might also understand the financial system as analogous insofar as its destruction would have substantial effects in the real economy and insofar as money can be a tool of real-world terrorism, just as cyberspace can be a tool of real-world terrorism. It is therefore worthwhile to review in general terms the structure that has developed thus far to address the problem of international financing for terrorism.

The problem of financing for terrorism may be seen as a lower-stakes version of some aspects of the cyberterrorism problem. That is, a failure of the system would not directly result in a "Pearl Harbor." Yet, wide international participation is necessary to prevent particular states emerging as terrorist financing havens. And the Financial Action Task Force (FATF)[18] mechanism is

---

[18] The FATF describes itself as "an inter-governmental body whose purpose is the development and promotion of policies, both at national and international levels, to combat money laundering and terrorist financing. The Task Force is therefore a 'policy-making body' which works to generate the necessary political will to bring about national legislative and regulatory

built around information-sharing and surveillance (FATF 2003). This operates at two levels. First, each country is required to obtain information from and perform surveillance in connection with its private sector actors, including financial institutions and their customers. Second, it provides for countries' systems to be monitored and evaluated with respect to compliance with international standards. The latter is achieved through mutual evaluations performed by regional bodies as well as IMF and World Bank assessments of compliance.

It is not appropriate in this paper to describe the entire FATF mechanism, but the following highlights are salient to the problem of cyberterrorism.

Interestingly, the FATF recommendations suggest that financial institutions be "deputized" to perform certain surveillance on their customers. For example, financial institutions should "undertake customer due diligence measures, including identifying and verifying the identity of their customers. . . ." (R. 5). Would it be possible and useful to require the same of ISPs? Financial institutions should gather information regarding foreign correspondent financial institutions, including information regarding their terrorist-financing controls (R. 7). Again, consider similar requirements for ISPs or backbone providers. Financial institutions should maintain records of transactions for at least five years (R. 10). Financial institutions "should pay special attention to all complex, unusual large transactions, and all unusual patterns of transactions, which have no apparent economic or visible lawful purpose" (R. 11). This also has direct analogs for ISPs and backbone providers. Furthermore, financial institutions should be required to report any suspicious activity (R. 14). Finally, as a measure to extend the scope of application of the recommendations and to provide incentives for compliance, financial institutions "should give special attention" to transactions with persons from countries that do not comply with the FATF recommendations (R. 21).

The FATF recommendations also impose important requirements on countries. Countries "should ensure that financial institutions are subject to adequate regulation and supervision and are effectively implementing the FATF Recommendations" (R. 23) They should establish a national center to receive, request, analyze, and disseminate suspicious transaction reports and other information regarding terrorist financing (R. 26). Several recommendations deal with the powers and responsibilities of law enforcement officers and other competent authorities, including access to information, resources, and

reforms in these areas." http://www1.oecd.org/fatf/AboutFATF_en.htm#What%20is. As of February 2, 2004, the FATF had 33 members, but its standards are endorsed by more than 130 countries. The FATF is housed at the offices of the OECD in Paris but is an independent organization.

international cooperation. These provisions seem to exceed those contained in the Cybercrime Convention. Recommendation 40 concludes by stating, "Countries should ensure that their competent authorities provide the widest possible range of international cooperation to their foreign counterparts."

In addition to the Forty Recommendations, there are eight "Special Recommendations on Terrorist Financing" promulgated by FATF.[19] These include adherence to and implementation of the 1999 United Nations International Convention for the Suppression of the Financing of Terrorism as well as implementation of relevant U.N. resolutions. In general, these eight special recommendations do not substantially add to the Forty Recommendations.

Finally, a group of countries has been designated as noncooperative. The following list of noncooperative countries and territories is current as of February 18, 2005: Myanmar, Nauru, and Nigeria.[20] Countermeasures may be applied against these designated countries. These countermeasures could include conditioning or restricting financial transactions with persons from these countries.[21]

D. Data Packets and Shipping Containers: The Maritime Security Model

Another type of analogy, involving slow transport instead of near instantaneous communications but otherwise exhibiting some significant parallels, is protection against marine cargo that may be used as terrorist weapons. Marine cargo could contain nuclear, biological, chemical, or other types of dangerous cargo or weapons, including terrorists (OECD Directorate for Science and Technology 2003; van de Voort and O'Brien 1993).[22] The analogy here is that dangerous things can travel either by sea or by electronic impulse. Furthermore, marine cargo could contain a weapon that might wreak destruction of the magnitude of a Pearl Harbor. Like the Internet, much of the ocean shipping infrastructure, including vessels and port facilities, is privately owned. One parallel is the sheer volume of ocean traffic, involving approximately 46,000 ships and 3,000 ports (Weiner 2004). There are also obvious differences in terms of velocity, frequency, tangibility, visibility, etc. Clearly, while it may be feasible to require human beings to inspect every container, it is not feasible to inspect every information packet.

---

[19] See http://www1.oecd.org/fatf/AboutFATF_en.htm#Eight%20Special%20Recommendations.
[20] For an update, see http://www1.oecd.org/fatf/NCCT_en.htm.
[21] See http://www1.oecd.org/fatf/pdf/NCCT_en.pdf.
[22] "A recent exercise by consultants and business researchers estimated that a terrorist attack involving dirty bombs in several U.S. ports – creating a cargo backlog taking months to clear – would cost the country almost [$60 billion]" (Murray 2003).

The United States has taken unilateral action, as well as international action, in order to enhance security against terrorism via cargo shipments. The international action has included both bilateral and multilateral initiatives.

Unilateral action has included passage of the Maritime Transportation Security Act of 2002.[23] This statute called for development of an automatic vessel identification system, a long-range vessel-tracking system, risk assessments, and security plans. One critical part of this statute requires foreign port assessments in order to evaluate security arrangements in foreign ports. If a vessel or any of the last ten ports that it has visited has not been certified, it can be excluded from U.S. ports.

Under the International Maritime Organization's International Ship and Port Facility Security Code,[24] which went into effect on July 1, 2004, each vessel's flag state is responsible for reviewing and certifying its security plan. The mandatory portion of this code requires certain actions by contracting governments, shipowners, and ports. Governments are required (1) to determine and communicate to their ships "security levels" in order to sensitize them to threats and (2) to ensure completion of port security assessments and compliance by shipowners and ports with other portions of the code. The code requires shipowners to implement ship identification and security alert systems as well as security assessments and organizational changes to improve security. It requires ports also to implement security assessments and security plans.

E. Results of Analogical Assessment

The examples discussed above, combined with the game models discussed previously, exhibit several potential tools that may be used to address the problem of cyberterrorism (see Table 8.5).

The United States often seems to combine unilateral action with multilateral action: uni-multilateralism. Individual action by the United States, whose power allows it to take effective individual action, has limits and is supplemented by unilateral requirements for cooperation or negotiation in international organizations for agreements requiring the same or similar activity.

Furthermore, it is clear that much action (and cost) is delegated to private actors or gatekeepers.

The law enforcement model found in the Cybercrime Convention is limited in its ability to preempt terrorism. The gatekeeper-certification model used in

[23] Pub. L. No. 107–295, 116 Stat. 2064 (2002).
[24] See http://www.imo.org/home.asp.

Table 8.5. *Tools for addressing cyberterrorism*

	Stag hunt	Prisoner's dilemma	Chicken	Deadlock
Legal strategy suggested by game	Information sharing; assurances	Punishment for defection to provide incentives for cooperation	Punishment for defection to provide incentives for cooperation	Domestic risk-reducing strategies to change game
Cybercrime	Information sharing; international legal assistance	Presumably, capacity for reciprocal punishment	Presumably, capacity for reciprocal punishment	Exclusion from treaty arrangements; disengagement
Financing for terrorism	Information sharing; conditional access	Punishment through exclusion; rogue state designation	Punishment through exclusion; rogue state designation	Rogue state designation; disengagement
Maritime security	Information sharing; conditional access	Punishment through exclusion	Punishment through exclusion	Rogue state designation; disengagement

connection with money laundering and maritime security has an important limitation in terms of its adaptability to cyberterrorism. The character of cargo does not change rapidly, and money itself does no direct damage. Therefore, reliance on gatekeepers or certification may not provide complete security against the subversion of an initially benign computer or node. As noted above, even biometric identification or digital passports may not provide complete security. However, these methods may be of significant value.

The surveillance model found in the money-laundering context, which requires financial institutions to look for and notify suspicious anomalies, may work as a model for the regulation of ISPs or backbone providers.

VIII. CONCLUSION

It is clear that cyberterrorism poses a threat. The threat is probably greater than that posed by terrorist financing or cybercrime and may also be greater than that posed by marine-borne terrorism. There would seem to be important reasons for international cooperation in this area, although it is possible that international cooperation would not be as efficient a route to security as hardening domestic targets. More research is needed on this point. Thus far, there seems to be little formal international activity comparable to that observed in other areas. Once the need for international cooperation is determined, it would be appropriate to consider mechanisms similar to those discussed above, *mutatis mutandis*. For example, it would at least be worth considering a global certification scheme for ISPs and backbone providers along the lines observed in the maritime and financing contexts. The utility of a certification scheme would depend on the degree to which actions taken at this level could prevent or ameliorate the consequences of cyberterrorism.

This paper cannot do more than identify a number of areas for further inquiry and suggest how information might be assessed in determining a course of action. An appropriate next step in this inquiry is to combine institutional knowledge with technical knowledge in order to determine the utility and feasibility of further action. The legal/institutional inquiry must be integrated in a recursive deliberative process with the technological inquiry. Code is not law and law is not code, but in order for law to be effective in achieving the desired goals, it must deal with the real world as it is and as it will be.

REFERENCES

Abbott, Kenneth W. 1987. Collective Goods, Mobile Resources, and Extraterritorial Trade Controls. *Law and Contemporary Problems* 50:117.

———. 1989. Modern International Relations Theory: A Prospectus for International Lawyers. *Yale International Law Journal* 14:335.

———. 1993. Trust but Verify: The Production of Information in Arms Control Treaties and Other International Agreements. *Cornell International Law Journal* 26:1.

American Law Institute. 1987. *Restatement (Third) of Foreign Relations Law*. Philadelphia: American Law Institute.

Anderson, Terry, and Peter Hill. 1975. The Evolution of Property Rights: A Study of the American West. *Journal of Law and Economics* 18:163.

Ault, David, and Gilbert Rutman. 1979. The Development of Independent Rights to Property in Tribal Africa. *Journal of Law and Economics* 22:183.

Barrett, Scott. 2003. *Environment and Statecraft: Strategies of Environmental Treaty-Making*. Oxford: Oxford University Press.

Basu, Kaushik. 1998. Social Norms and the Law. In *The New Palgrave Dictionary of Economics and the Law*, ed. Peter Newman, 476. New York: Palgrave Macmillan.

Benkler, Yochai. 2002. Coase's Penguin, or, Linux and the Nature of the Firm. *Yale Law Journal* 112:369.

Boyle, James. 1997. Foucault in Cyberspace: Surveillance, Sovereignty, and Hardwired Censors. *University of Cincinnati Law Review* 66:177.

Brams, Steven J., and D. Marc Kilgour. 1988. *Game Theory and National Security*. Oxford: Basil Blackwell.

Brenner, Susan W., and Marc D. Goodman. 2002. In Defense of Cyberterrorism: An Argument for Anticipating Cyber-Attacks. *Illinois Journal of Law, Technology, and Policy* 2002:1.

Buchanan, James M. 1965. An Economic Theory of Clubs. *Economica* 32:1.

Busch, Marc, and Eric Reinhardt. 1993. Nice Strategies in a World of Relative Gains: The Problem of Cooperation under Anarchy. *Journal of Conflict Resolution* 37:427.

Clarke, Richard. 1999. Keynote Address: Threats to U.S. National Security: Proposed Partnership Initiatives toward Preventing Cyber Terrorist Attacks. *DePaul Business Law Journal* 12:33.

Congressional Research Service. 2001. Cyberwarfare. June 19. http://usinfo.state.gov/usa/infousa/tech/gii/rl30735.pdf.

Cornes, Richard, and Todd Sandler. 1996. *The Theory of Externalities, Public Goods and Club Goods.* 2nd ed. Cambridge: Cambridge University Press.

Demsetz, Harold. 1967. Toward a Theory of Property Rights. *American Economic Review Papers and Proceedings* 57:347.

Downs, George, David Rocke, and Randolph Siverson. 1985. Arms Races and Cooperation. *World Politics* 38:118.

Easterbrook, Frank. H. 1996. Cyberspace and the Law of the Horse. *University of Chicago Legal Forum* 1996:207.

Economides, Nicholas. 1996. The Economics of Networks. *International Journal of Independent Organizations* 14:2.

Esty, Daniel. 1999. Toward Optimal Environmental Governance. *New York University Law Review* 74:1495.

Field, B. C. 1989. The Evolution of Property Rights. *Kyklos* 42:319.

Financial Action Task Force on Money Laundering ("FATFML"). 2003. The Forty Recommendations. June. http://www1.oecd.org/fatf/40Recs_en.htm.

Fox, Merritt. 2003. Optimal Regulatory Areas for Securities Disclosure. *Washington University Law Quarterly* 81:1017.

Friedberg, James J. 1991. The Convergence of Law in an Era of Political Integration: The Wood Pulp Case and the Alcoa Effects Doctrine. *University of Pittsburgh Law Review* 52:289.

Froomkin, A. Michael. 1997. The Internet as a Source of Regulatory Arbitrage. In *Borders in Cyberspace*, ed. B. Kahin, and C. Nesson, 129. Cambridge, MA: MIT Press.

Gannon, John C. 2001. Speech to the National Security Telecommunications and Information Systems Security Committee. April 3. http://www.odci.gov/nic/speeches_telecommunications.html.

Gellman, Barton. 2002. Cyber-Attacks by Al Qaeda Feared: Terrorists at Threshold of Using Internet as Tool of Bloodshed, Experts Say. *Washington Post*, June 27, p. A01.

Gilmour, Kim. 2002. Wish You Were Here? The Principality of Sealand Is a Self-Proclaimed Sovereign State in the North Sea. It's Also the Place to Host Your Site If You Want to Escape Draconian Internet Privacy Law. *Internet Magazine*, December 1.

Goodman, Seymour E. 2003. Toward a Treaty-based International Regime on Cyber Crime and Terrorism. In *Cyber Security: Turning National Solutions into International Cooperation*, ed. James Lewis, 65. Washington, DC: Center for Strategic and International Studies.

Hartman, R. S. 1982. A Note on Externalities and Placement of Property Rights: An Alternative Formulation to the Standard Pigouvian Results. *International Review of Law and Economics* 2:111.

Johnson, David R., Susan P. Crawford, and John G. Palfrey. 2004. The Accountable Net: Peer Production of Internet Governance. Draft. http://cyber.law.harvard.edu/ The%20Accountable%20Net%20032504.pdf.

Kaspersen, Henrik. 2003. A Gate Must Either Be Open or Shut: The Council of Europe Cyber-crime Convention Model. In *Cyber Security: Turning National Solutions into International Cooperation*, ed. J. Lewis, 1. Washington, DC: Center for Strategic and International Studies.

Katyal, Neal Kumar. 2003. Digital Architecture as Crime Control. *Yale Law Journal* 112:2261.

Kende, Michael. 2000. The Digital Handshake: Connecting Internet Backbones. FCC Office of Public Policy Working Paper No. 32. http://www.fcc.gov/Bureaus/OPP/working_papers/oppwp32.pdf.

Keyser, Mike, 2003. The Council of Europe Convention on Cybercrime. *Journal of Transnational Law and Policy* 12:287.

Lessig, Lawrence. 1999a. *Code, and Other Laws of Cyberspace.* Boulder, CO: Perseus Books Group.

———. 1999b. The Law of the Horse: What Cyberlaw Might Teach. *Harvard Law Review* 113:501.

Merrill, Thomas. 1985. Trespass, Nuisance, and the Costs of Determining Property Rights. *Journal of Legal Studies* 14:13.

Mitchell. William. 1996. *City of Bits.* Cambridge, MA: MIT Press.

Mueller, Markus. 2004. Who Owns the Internet? Ownership as a Legal Basis for American Control of the Internet. Working paper. http://papers.ssrn.com/paper.taf?abstract_id=520682.

Murray, Sarah. 2003. Monitoring Cargo Becomes a High Global Priority. *Financial Times*, December 3, p. 4.

Norman, George, and Joel Trachtman. Forthcoming. The Customary International Law Game.

OECD Directorate for Science and Technology. 2003. Security in Maritime Transport: Risk Factors and Economic Impact. July. http://www.oecd.org/dataoecd/63/13/4375896.pdf.

Powell, Robert. 1991. Absolute and Relative Gains in International Relations Theory. *American Political Science Review* 85:1303.

Serabian, John A. 2000. Statement for the Record before the Joint Economic Committee on Cyber Threats and the U.S. Economy. February 23. http://www.odci.gov/cia/public_affairs/speecs/2000/cyberthreats_022300.html.

Shah, Rajiv C., and Jay P. Kesan. 2003. *Manipulating the Governance Characteristics of Code.* Illinois Public Law Research Paper No. 03–18. http://papers.ssrn.com/sol3/papers.cfm?abstract_id=475682.

Snidal, Duncan. 1991. Relative Gains and the Pattern of International Cooperation. *American Political Science Review* 85:701.

Trachtman, Joel P. 1998. Cyberspace, Sovereignty, Jurisdiction and Modernism. *Indiana Journal of Global Legal Studies* 5:561.

———. 2000. Regulatory Competition and Regulatory Jurisdiction. *Journal of International Economic Law* 3:331.

———. 2001. Economic Analysis of Perspective Jurisdiction and Choice of Law. *Virginia Journal of International Law* 42:1.

Umbeck, John. 1977. A Theory of Contract Choice and the California Gold Rush. *Journal of Law and Economics* 20:163.

————. 1981. Might Makes Rights: A Theory of the Formation and Initial Distribution of Property Rights. *Economic Inquiry* 19:38.

U.S. Department of Defense. 1999. An Assessment of International Legal Issues in Information Operations. U.S. Department of Defense, Office of General Counsel. http://downloads.securityfocus.com/library/infowar/reports/dodio.pdf.

Van de Voort, Maarten, and Kevin A. O'Brien. 1993. Seacurity: Improving the Security of the Global Sea Container Shipping System. Leiden, Netherlands: RAND Europe.

Vatis, Michael. 2003. International Cyber-Security Cooperation: Informal Bilateral Models. In *Cyber Security: Turning National Solutions into International Cooperation*, ed. J. Lewis, 1. Washington, DC: Center for Strategic and International Studies.

Verton, Dan. 2002. Corporate America Now on Front Lines of the War on Terrorism. *Computerworld*, September 9.

Weiner, Tim. 2004. U.S. Law Puts World Ports on Notice. *New York Times*, March 24, p. A6.

INDEX

Lightning Source UK Ltd.
Milton Keynes UK
UKHW012313271119
354378UK00009B/127/P